Object-Oriented
Software Composition

THE OBJECT-ORIENTED SERIES

D. COLEMAN, P. ARNOLD, S. BODOFF,
C. DOLLIN, H. GILCHRIST, F. HAYES
AND P. JEREMAES
*Object-Oriented Development:
The Fusion Method*

S. COOK AND J. DANIELS
Designing Object Systems

B. HENDERSON-SELLERS
A Book of Object-Oriented Knowledge

B. HENDERSON-SELLERS AND J. EDWARDS
*Book Two Object-Oriented Knowledge:
The Working Object*

H. KILOV AND J. ROSS
Information Modelling: An Object-Oriented Approach

P. KRIEF
Prototyping with Objects

K. LANO AND H. HAUGHTON
Object-Oriented Specification Case Studies

J. LINDSKOV KNUDSEN, M. LÖFGREN,
O. LEHRMANN MADSEN AND B. MAGNUSSON
*Object-Oriented Environments:
The Mjølner Approach*

M. LORENZ
*Object-Oriented Software Development:
A Practical Guide*

M. LORENZ AND J. KIDD
Object-Oriented Software Metrics

B. MEYER
*An Object-Oriented Environment:
Principles and Applications*

B. MEYER
Eiffel: The Language

B. MEYER
*Reusable Software:
The Base Object-Oriented Component Libraries*

B. MEYER
*Object Success:
A Manager's Guide to Object Orientation,
its Impact on the Corporation,
and its Use for Reengineering the Software Process*

B. MEYER AND J.-M. NERSON (eds)
Object-Oriented Applications

D. MANDRIOLI AND B. MEYER (eds)
Advances in Object-Oriented Software Engineering

O. NIERSTRASZ AND D. TSICHRITZIS
Object-Oriented Software Composition

G. POMBERGER AND P. BLASCHEK
*An Object-Oriented Approach to
Software Engineering*

R. RIST AND R. TERWILLIGER
Object-Oriented Programming in Eiffel

P. J. ROBINSON
Hierarchical Object-Oriented Design

R. SWITZER
Eiffel: An Introduction

K. WALDÉN AND J.-M. NERSON
*Seamless Object-Oriented Software Architecture:
Analysis and Design of Reliable Systems*

R. WIENER
*Software Development Using Eiffel:
There Can Be Life Other Than C++*

(Various editors)
*Proceedings of TOOLS Conferences, 4 to 16:
Technology of Object-Oriented Languages and Systems*

Object-Oriented Software Composition

Edited by

Oscar Nierstrasz
University of Berne

and

Dennis Tsichritzis
University of Geneva

Prentice Hall
London   New York   Toronto   Sydney   Tokyo   Singapore
Madrid   Mexico City   Munich

First published 1995 by
Prentice Hall International (UK) Ltd
Campus 400, Maylands Avenue
Hemel Hempstead
Hertfordshire, HP2 7EZ

A division of
Simon & Schuster International Group

© Prentice Hall 1995

All rights reserved. No part of this publication may be reproduced,
stored in a retrieval system, or transmitted, in any form, or by any
means, electronic, mechanical, photocopying, recording or otherwise,
without prior permission, in writing, from the publisher.
For permission within the United States of America
contact Prentice Hall Inc., Englewood Cliffs, NJ 07632

Printed and bound in Great Britain by
T.J. Press (Padstow) Ltd, Padstow, Cornwall.

Library of Congress Cataloging-in-Publication Data

Object-oriented software composition / edited by Oscar Nierstrasz and
Dennis Tsichritzis.
    p.   cm.—(The Object-oriented series)
Includes bibliographical references and index.
ISBN 0-13-220674-9
    1. Object-oriented programming (Computer science)   I. Nierstrasz
Oscar Marius, 1957–   . II. Tsichritzis, Dionysios C. III. Series:
Prentice-Hall object-oriented series.
QA76.64.O277   1995
005.1'1—dc20   95–7616
                                                                   CIP

British Library Cataloguing in Publication Data

A catalogue record for this book is available from
the British Library
ISBN: 0-13-220674-9

---

1 2 3 4 5   99 98 97 96 95

Contents

Contributors ix

Foreword xi
Akinori Yonezawa

Preface xiii
Oscar Nierstrasz and Dennis Tsichritzis

PART I Introduction 1

1 Component-Oriented Software Technology 3
Oscar Nierstrasz and Laurent Dami
    1.1   Introduction   3
    1.2   Objects vs. Components   7
    1.3   Technical Support for Components   9
    1.4   Component Engineering   20
    1.5   Conclusions   24

PART II Concurrency and Distribution 29

2 Concurrency in Object-Oriented Programming Languages 31
Michael Papathomas
    2.1   Introduction   31
    2.2   Design Space   33
    2.3   Criteria for Evaluating Language Design Choices   43
    2.4   Exploring the Language Design Space   49
    2.5   Conclusion   63

3 Interoperation of Object-Oriented Applications 69
Dimitri Konstantas
- 3.1 Reusing Objects from Different Environments 69
- 3.2 Procedure-Oriented Interoperability 71
- 3.3 Object-Oriented Interoperability 73
- 3.4 Comparison of Interoperability Support Approaches 75
- 3.5 Interface Bridging — Object-Oriented Interoperability 76
- 3.6 Interface Adaption 81
- 3.7 Object Mapping 87
- 3.8 Conclusions and Research Directions 90

PART III Specification and Composition 97

4 Regular Types for Active Objects 99
Oscar Nierstrasz
- 4.1 Introduction 99
- 4.2 Types, Substitutability and Active Objects 101
- 4.3 Intersecting Service Types 103
- 4.4 Request Substitutability 105
- 4.5 Viewing Objects as Regular Processes 108
- 4.6 Subtyping Regular Types 110
- 4.7 Request Satisfiability 113
- 4.8 Open Problems 117
- 4.9 Concluding Remarks 119

5 A Temporal Perspective of Composite Objects 123
Constantin Arapis
- 5.1 Introduction 123
- 5.2 Propositional Temporal Logic 126
- 5.3 The Specification of Temporal Properties 132
- 5.4 Verification 144
- 5.5 Concluding Remarks 150

6	**Functions, Records and Compatibility in the λN Calculus**		**153**
	Laurent Dami		
	6.1	Introduction	153
	6.2	A Lambda Calculus with Named Parameters	156
	6.3	The Calculus at Work	162
	6.4	Compatibility Relationship	167
	6.5	Conclusion	172

PART IV Software Information Management		**175**

7	**Component Classification in the Software Information Base**		**177**
	Panos Constantopoulos and Martin Dörr		
	7.1	Introduction	177
	7.2	The Software Information Base	179
	7.3	Information Retrieval and User Interface	183
	7.4	The Classification Scheme	186
	7.5	Streamlining the Classification Process	191
	7.6	Experiences	192
	7.7	Conclusion	197
8	**Managing Class Evolution in Object-Oriented Systems**		**201**
	Eduardo Casais		
	8.1	Object Design and Redesign	201
	8.2	Class Tailoring	203
	8.3	Class Surgery	206
	8.4	Class Versioning	212
	8.5	Class Reorganization	218
	8.6	Change Avoidance	230
	8.7	Conversion	233
	8.8	Filtering	236
	8.9	Conclusion	240
9	**The Affinity Browser**		**245**
	Xavier Pintado		
	9.1	Introduction	245
	9.2	Browsing Requirements	251
	9.3	The Affinity Browser	252
	9.4	The Affinity Browser by Example	259
	9.5	Conclusion	270

PART V Frameworks and Applications   273

10 Visual Composition of Software Applications   275
Vicki de Mey
- 10.1 Introduction   275
- 10.2 Related Work   276
- 10.3 A Framework for Visual Composition   278
- 10.4 Vista — A Prototype Visual Composition Tool   287
- 10.5 Sample Applications   290
- 10.6 Discussion   297
- 10.7 Conclusion   300

11 Multimedia Component Frameworks   305
Simon Gibbs
- 11.1 Digital Media and Multimedia   305
- 11.2 Multimedia Systems and Multimedia Programming   306
- 11.3 Multimedia Frameworks   308
- 11.4 A Multimedia Framework Example — Components   309
- 11.5 Video Widgets — A Programming Example   313
- 11.6 Summary   317

12 Gluons and the Cooperation between Software Components   321
Xavier Pintado
- 12.1 Introduction   321
- 12.2 An Overview of Cooperation Patterns   324
- 12.3 Requirements for a Financial Framework   333
- 12.4 Gluons   338
- 12.5 Gluons and the Financial Framework   341
- 12.6 Conclusion   347

Index   351

Contributors

Dr. Costas Arapis, GMD, Abtl. VMSD, Schloß Birlinghoven, D-53757 Sankt Augustin, GERMANY. *E-mail:* arapis@viswiz.gmd.de

Dr. Eduardo Casais, Forschungszentrum Informatik (FZI), Haid-und-Neu-Straße 10-14, D-76131 Karlsruhe, GERMANY. *E-mail:* casais@fzi.de

Prof. Panos Constantopoulos, Institute of Computer Science, Foundation for Research and Technology — Hellas, Science and Technology Park of Crete, Vassilika Vouton, P.O. Box 1385, GR-71110 Heraklion, Crete, GREECE. *E-mail:* panos@ ics.forth.gr

Dr. Laurent Dami, Centre Universitaire d'Informatique, Université de Genève, 24, rue Général-Dufour, CH-1211 Genève 4, SWITZERLAND. *E-mail:* dami@cui.unige.ch

Dr. Vicki de Mey, Apple Computer, Inc., One Infinite Loop, MS 301-4I, Cupertino, CA 95014, UNITED STATES. *E-mail*: vicki@apple.com

Dr. Martin Dörr, Institute of Computer Science, Foundation for Research and Technology — Hellas, Science and Technology Park of Crete, Vassilika Vouton, P.O. Box 1385, GR-71110 Heraklion, Crete, GREECE. *E-mail:* doerr@ ics.forth.gr

Dr. Simon Gibbs, GMD, Schloß Birlinghoven, D-53757 Sankt Augustin, GERMANY. *E-mail*: Simon.Gibbs@gmd.de

Dr. Dimitri Konstantas, Centre Universitaire d'Informatique, Université de Genève, 24, rue Général-Dufour, CH-1211 Genève 4, SWITZERLAND. *E-mail:* dimitri@cui.unige.ch

Prof. Oscar Nierstrasz, Institut für Informatik (IAM), Universität Bern, Neubrückstrasse 10, CH-3012 Bern, SWITZERLAND. *E-mail:* oscar@iam.unibe.ch

Dr. Michael Papathomas, Lancaster University, Computing Department, Lancaster LA1 4YR, UNITED KINGDOM. *E-mail*: michael@computing.lancaster.ac.uk

Dr. Xavier Pintado, Centre Universitaire d'Informatique, Université de Genève, 24, rue Général-Dufour, CH-1211 Genève 4, SWITZERLAND. *E-mail:* pintado@cui.unige.ch

Prof. Dennis Tsichritzis, GMD, Schloß Birlinghoven, D-53757 Sankt Augustin, GERMANY. *E-mail*: dt@castle.gmd.de

Up-to-date information concerning the authors is also available on the World Wide Web at: http://iamwww.unibe.ch/~oscar/OOSC/

Foreword

Perhaps, "Going Beyond Objects" should be the subtitle of this volume, as a large portion of the contents departs from the early and popularly perceived image of "Objects."

The object-oriented programming paradigm has now been firmly accepted in the software community as offering the most powerful and promising technology for software development currently available, and its expressiveness and modelling power have been much appreciated. But, one of the greatest promises it made in its early stage was a dramatic improvement in the ease of software composition and reuse, which is yet to be achieved. (People are sometimes entangled with webs of class hierarchies.) And the research continues.

About ten years ago, Dennis and Oscar, moving from Toronto, founded the Object Systems Group at the University of Geneva, and started a number of research projects to extend the object-oriented paradigm in various ways. It did not take more than a couple of years for the group to become the most active and visible research centre of object-oriented technology in Europe. In the mean time, part of the group became involved in a large ESPRIT project called ITHACA which aimed at producing an application development environment based object-oriented technology. This volume presents, in a written form, the fruits of the group's ten-year research and development, as directed by Dennis' clear philosophy on research and innovation. The group attacked real problems and problems firmly based on reality. Dennis' early career as a recursive function theorist, taught by Alonzo Church in Princeton, also encouraged foundational work in the group, and some chapters in this volume represent it.

"Beyond Objects" was the title of the panel discussion at the European Conference on Object-Oriented Programming (ECOOP'91), which was organized by Oscar Nierstrasz and Dennis Tsichritzis in Geneva in July, 1991. They already had clear visions of where we/they should go from the "Objects" that only partially fulfil the early promise. One of their visions was the "Component-Based" approach for software construction. Future software construction for flexible open application should be performed by composition and configuration of plug-compatible software components that generalize objects, agents and functions. Oscar and Laurent explain this approach in the first chapter of this volume.

Now in the mid 90's, advanced researchers are struggling to go beyond "Objects" in search for better software development approaches. Intelligent Agents, Coordination Languages, Integration of Constraints and Objects, Component-Based Development ... The contributions in this volume offer valuable clues and suggestions to those who wish go beyond "Objects."

University of Tokyo, January 1995   Akinori Yonezawa

Preface

Object-oriented technology has been with us since the mid 1960s, but has begun to have a significant industrial impact only since the mid 1980s. There are both good and bad reasons for adopting the technology, and even the success stories suggest that it is not so easy to introduce object-oriented techniques where they were not practised before. Some of the questionable reasons for "going OO" are:
- "Object-oriented programming is a better kind of structured programming" — perhaps, but structured programming methods won't help you very much in developing object-oriented applications. Object-oriented programming is not just structured programming wearing a new hat.
- "We'll be able to build applications more quickly because objects are reusable" — there can be a huge gap between software written in an object-oriented language and a truly reusable framework of object classes. Frameworks are hard to develop, and not always easy to use.
- "It will be easier to sell our products if we can tell our customers that they are object-oriented" — the cost and risk of adopting object-oriented technology can be very high, and should not be taken lightly.

Still, there are good reasons for adopting object-oriented technology: so far it appears to offer the best means to cope with complexity and variation in large systems. When families of similar systems must be built, or single systems must undergo frequent changes in requirements, object-oriented languages, tools and methods offer the means to view such systems as flexible compositions of software components. It may still require a great deal of skill to build flexible systems that can meet many different needs, but at least object-oriented technology simplifies the task.

Object-Oriented Software Composition adopts the viewpoint that object-oriented technology is essentially about *composing* flexible software applications from software *components*. Although object-oriented languages, tools and methods have come a long way since the birth of object-oriented programming, the technology is not yet mature. This book presents the results of a series of research projects related to object-oriented software composition that were carried out within the Object Systems Group at the University of Geneva, or by partners in collaborative research projects, during a period of about ten years. As such, this book is an attempt to synthesize and juxtapose ideas that were developed by a group of people working closely together over several years.

Although many different topics are treated, by presenting them together, we intend to show how certain ideas and principles are closely related to software composition, whether one considers programming language design, formal specification, tools and environments, or application development. Common threads running throughout the book include *plug compatibility* as a way of formalizing valid ways of composing components, *active objects* as being fundamental to the development of open systems, *protocols* as a necessary aspect of plug-compatibility for active objects, *higher-order functional composition* as complementary to object composition, and *evolution* of objects and object frameworks as an essential aspect to capture in the software lifecycle.

This book should appeal to researchers and practitioners familiar with object-oriented technology, who are interested in research trends related to software composition. Although this book was not designed as a textbook, it would be suitable for an advanced seminar on object-oriented research. Individual chapters can be read independently. The order of presentation has been selected mainly to illustrate a progression of ideas from programming language design issues to environments and applications. Not only is the "Geneva view" of object-oriented development presented, but considerable effort has gone into placing the work in context, and several of the chapters contain extensive surveys of related work.

The Object Systems Group was founded by Dennis Tsichritzis in 1985, after he had spent several years directing research in the area of Office Information Systems. At the time, it became clear that (1) object-oriented modelling was essential to modelling office systems, but these models were not yet well developed, and (2) prototypes of advanced office tools would be easier to develop using object-oriented tools and techniques, but the technology was not available. These two observations led us to conclude that, since object-orientation was a critical factor for the construction of advanced and complex applications, we should concentrate on developing this technology rather than carrying on research in office systems with inadequate tools and methodological support.

The first chapter of this book summarizes the relationship between object-oriented approaches and component-oriented development, and surveys the principle research problems in the design of programming languages, tools, environments and methods to support compositional development.The distinction between objects and components is discussed in detail, and the impact of compositional development on software lifecycles is introduced. An important theme that runs through this book is the notion that the role of a *component engineer* — as a person who is responsible for defining component frameworks — must be explicitly represented in the software lifecycle. Although this book focuses on technological issues, there is a progression of concerns from programming languages and systems towards tools, frameworks and methods.

The first two research projects of the group focused on programming language issues. *Hybrid* was an early attempt to integrate classes and inheritance with other, "orthogonal" features such as strong-typing, concurrency and persistence. *Knos* were active objects that could migrate from computer to computer within a local area network, and dynamically change their behaviour according to rules triggered by internal conditions or the state of a communications blackboard. *Knos* bear close comparison to what are now known as "intelligent agents." The work on *Hybrid* ultimately led to more detailed investigations by Michael Papathomas into the relationship between concurrency and reuse (chapter 2), and by Dimitri Konstantas into distribution support for flexible open systems (chapter 3). The

Preface

work on *Knos* led to fundamental work by Eduardo Casais into more disciplined forms of evolution of object-oriented libraries and to new techniques to reorganize class hierarchies (chapter 8).

This initial phase of experimentation allowed us to gain essential insight into both the theoretical and practical issues of object systems. As a first consequence, the group's interest in the formal aspects of programming language semantics and the specification of object systems became deeper, and led to work by Michael Papathomas and Oscar Nierstrasz on notions of "plug compatibility" for active objects (chapter 4), by Costas Arapis on modelling and reasoning about temporal aspects of collaborating object systems (chapter 5), and by Laurent Dami on new models of compositionality, extensibility and subtyping for objects (chapter 6).

In parallel with these theoretical investigations, the group developed new interests in the area of software tools and development environments. Eugene Fiume, who was visiting from the University of Toronto, and Laurent Dami in 1988 developed a prototype of a "temporal scripting language" for animated objects. This was the group's first foray into applying object-oriented technology to the domain of multimedia applications. The notion of a "script" as a high-level specification of coordination amongst a set of prepackaged objects became a key theme in the group at the time, though it was not clear how the idea could be carried over from the domain of animation to software objects in general.

At about this time we became involved in ITHACA, a large Technology Integration Project of the European Community's ESPRIT programme. The lead partner was Nixdorf Informationssysteme (later Siemens-Nixdorf) in Berlin, and other partners included Bull (Paris), Datamont (Milan), TAO — Tècnics en Automatitzaciò d'Oficines (Barcelona) and FORTH—the Foundation of Research and Technology, Hellas (Heraklion). The goal of the project was to produce a complete, application development environment based on object-oriented technology, including a state-of-the-art fourth-generation persistent object-oriented programming language and its associated tools, and a set of application "workbenches" to support development in a selected set of domains. A key component of ITHACA was the "software information base" (SIB) that was to serve as a repository for all reusable software artefacts (see chapter 7, by Panos Constantopoulos and Martin Dörr). The SIB was intended to drive application development from requirements collection and specification (according to stored domain knowledge and requirements models), through design (according to reusable generic designs), all the way to implementation (according to reusable software components and frameworks). The key insight of this approach is that the potential for reuse offered by object-oriented technology lies not only in libraries of object classes, but runs through the entire software development process. To exploit this potential, however, one needs more than object-oriented languages and tools: the software lifecycle must reflect the role of reuse; the analysis and design methods must reflect the new lifecycle; the project management strategy must support the lifecycle and the methods; and some form of software information system is needed to store and manage the reusable artefacts.

Our contribution to ITHACA was more specifically to develop a "visual scripting tool" for dynamically configuring applications from visually presented software components.

We developed a first prototype, called VST, in which the notions of ports and "plug-compatibility," and the idea that a script could be packaged up as a component, emerged naturally. Eventually we came to realize the term "script" carried too much semantic baggage from other domains in which timing was a concern (such as animation). More to-the-point was the view of an application as a *composition* of software components, and so we began to speak of *visual composition* rather than "scripting." A framework for visual composition was elaborated and realized by Vicki de Mey as part of the ITHACA project (chapter 10).

An important aspect of a software information system is a convenient interface for navigation. Whereas traditional browsers based on class hierarchies display software artefacts only according to fixed relationships, an *affinity browser* dynamically adapts its presentation according to changing notions of affinity between entities. New techniques were developed by Xavier Pintado and incorporated into a prototype (chapter 9).

Within ITHACA, object technology was applied to the areas of office systems and public administration. In Geneva, we also explored its application to the domains of multimedia systems and financial applications. A multimedia laboratory was built up over several years, and was used as an experimental platform for a multimedia framework. The framework, designed by Simon Gibbs, allowed heterogeneous hardware and software multimedia components to be encapsulated as objects that could be connected according to a standard set of paradigms (chapter 11). One of the uses of the visual composition tool developed within ITHACA was its application to the multimedia framework, thus allowing one to compose multimedia objects interactively instead of having to code C++ programs to glue them together explicitly.

A second framework for the visualization of real-time financial data was designed and realized by Xavier Pintado. In this framework, a complementary approach was taken to visual composition. Instead of requiring that components provide standard plug-compatible interfaces, the bindings between components are encapsulated as *gluons* (chapter 12).

Various themes run through this book. The dominant theme is that flexible, open applications should be seen not only as object-oriented constructions, but as *compositions of plug-compatible software components*. The distinction between objects and components, and the notion of plug-compatibility must be specified with care. A second theme is that *concurrency and distribution are fundamental*, but that integration of concurrency and other dynamic aspects into the object model of a programming language poses various technical difficulties. New computational models are needed that take behavioural aspects of objects to be fundamental rather than orthogonal. A third theme is that development of open systems should be *framework-driven*, and that this in turn requires new lifecycles, methods and tools. In particular, the development of component frameworks by component engineers is an evolutionary process, which must be supported by software information management tools. Application developers similarly need appropriate tools that facilitate instantiation of applications from frameworks and component libraries.

Our research on object systems resulted in a number of Ph.D. theses (by Casais, Arapis, Papathomas, Konstantas, de Mey, Dami and Pintado), produced between 1991 and 1994, which form the basis for seven chapters of this book. Since most of the authors have now

Acknowledgements xvii

left the group, the book also represents the end of a cycle (and the beginnings of new ones). Work on high-level coordination languages, on distributed object systems, and on financial frameworks is continuing in Geneva, whereas some of the other research directions are being pursued at new locations.

It is a hopeless task to try to indicate such a moving target as current activities in a medium as archival as a book. Up-to-date information on the activities of the Object Systems Group can be found on the World Wide Web at:

> http://cuiwww.unige.ch/OSG/

More information concerning the editors and authors of this book can be found at:

> http://iamwww.unibe.ch/~oscar/OOSC/

Acknowledgements

Many more people participated in the projects reported here than could possibly contribute as authors. Marc Stadelmann and Jan Vitek implemented the first VST prototype. Betty Junod and Serge Renfer contributed to ITHACA and to other projects. Gérald Burnand, Philippe Cornu, Jean-Henry Morin, Frédéric Pot, Vassilis Prevelakis and Didier Vallet have contributed much to the group. The group also benefited greatly from the participation of several visitors, who stayed anywhere from several months to a couple of years. Jean Bell, Christian Breiteneder, Eugene Fiume, Rosario Girardi, John Hogg, Nigel Horspool, Gerti Kappel, Barbara Pernici, Claudio Trotta, Peter Wegner and Claudia Werner helped a great deal in the elaboration of our ideas.

A number of people were also invaluable in the preparation of this book. We especially thank Jiri Dvorak, Karl Guggisberg, Thilo Kielmann, Markus Lumpe, Theo Dirk Meijler, Jean-Guy Schneider, Patrick Varone and Jan Vitek for their careful reviews of several of the chapters of this book. We also thank the authors, and especially Eduardo Casais, Laurent Dami, Simon Gibbs, Dimitri Konstantas and Vicki de Mey for their contributions to chapters they did not co-author. Finally, we thank Isabelle Huber and Angela Margiotta for their help in preparing the final manuscript.

We gratefully acknowledge the financial support of the Swiss National Foundation for Scientific Research (FNRS) which sponsored a series of projects over the years. We thank the Commission for the Encouragement of Scientific Research (CERS) for their contribution to our participation in the ITHACA project. We thank the University of Geneva for providing the infrastructure and support needed to carry out the research we describe. We also thank the Union Bank of Switzerland's Ubilab research facility for its generous financial support. Finally we would like to thank our various industrial and academic partners for their stimulating support over the years.

Geneva   Oscar Nierstrasz
May, 1995   Dennis Tsichritzis

PART I

Introduction

Chapter 1
Component-Oriented Software Technology

Oscar Nierstrasz and Laurent Dami

Abstract Modern software systems are increasingly required to be open and distributed. Such systems are open not only in terms of network connections and interoperability support for heterogeneous hardware and software platforms, but, above all, in terms of evolving and changing requirements. Although object-oriented technology offers some relief, to a large extent the languages, methods and tools fail to address the needs of open systems because they do not escape from traditional models of software development that assume system requirements to be closed and stable. We argue that open systems requirements can only be adequately addressed by adopting a *component-oriented* as opposed to a purely object-oriented software development approach, by shifting emphasis away from programming and towards generalized software composition.

1.1 Introduction

There has been a continuing trend in the development of software applications away from closed, proprietary systems towards so-called open systems. This trend can be largely attributed to the rapid advances in computer hardware technology that have vastly increased the computational power available to end-user applications. With new possibilities come new needs: in order to survive, competitive businesses must be able to effectively exploit new technology as it becomes available, so existing applications must be able to work with new, independently developed systems. We can see, then, that open systems must be "open" in at least three important ways [49]:

1. *Topology*: open applications run on configurable networks.
2. *Platform:* the hardware and software platforms are heterogeneous.
3. *Evolution:* requirements are unstable and constantly change.

Object-oriented software development partially addresses these needs by hiding data representation and implementation details behind object-oriented interfaces, thus permitting multiple implementations of objects to coexist while protecting clients from changes in implementation or representation. Evolution is only partially addressed, however, since changes in requirements may entail changes in the way that the objects are structured and configured. In fact, to address evolution, it is necessary to view each application as only one instance of a *generic class* of applications, each built up of reconfigurable software components. The notion of component is more general than that of an object, and in particular may be of either much finer or coarser granularity. An object encapsulates data and its associated behaviour, whereas a component may encapsulate *any* useful software abstraction. Since not all useful abstractions are necessarily objects, we may miss opportunities for flexible software reuse by focusing too much on objects. By viewing open applications as compositions of reusable and configurable components, we expect to be able to cope with evolving requirements by unplugging and reconfiguring only the affected parts.

1.1.1 What Are Components?

If we accept that open systems must be built in a component-oriented fashion, we must still answer the following questions: What exactly are components, and how do they differ from objects? What mechanisms must programming languages and environments provide to support component-oriented development? Where do components come from in the software development lifecycle, and how should the software process and methods accommodate them?

In attempting to answer these questions, we must distinguish between methodological and technical aspects. At a methodological level, a component, we will argue, is a component because it has been *designed* to be used in a compositional way together with other components. This means that a component is not normally designed in isolation, but as part of a *framework* of collaborating components. A framework may be realized as an abstract class hierarchy in an object-oriented language [23], but more generally, components need not be classes, and frameworks need not be abstract class hierarchies. Mixins, functions, macros, procedures, templates and modules may all be valid examples of components [3], and component frameworks may standardize interfaces and generic code for various kinds of software abstractions. Furthermore, components in a framework may also be other entities than just software, namely specifications, documentation, test data, example applications, and so on. Such components, however, will not be discussed in detail in this paper: we will mainly concentrate on some technical aspects related to software components.

At a software technology level, the vision of component-oriented development is a very old idea, which was already present in the first developments of structured programming and modularity [32]. Though it obtained a new impulse through the compositional mechanisms provided by object-oriented programming languages, component-oriented soft-

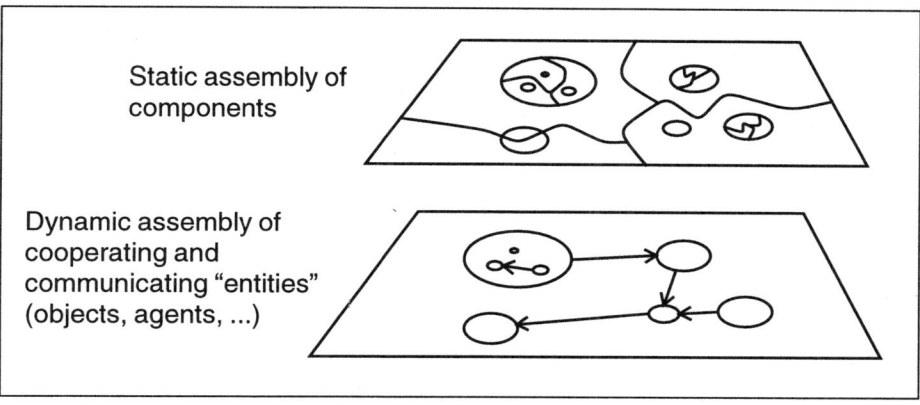

Figure 1.1 *Static and dynamic views of an application.*

ware development is not easy to realize for both technological and methodological reasons. For a programming language to support component-oriented development, it must cleanly integrate both the *computational* and the *compositional* aspects of software development. An application can be viewed simultaneously as a computational entity that delivers results, and as a construction of software components that fit together to achieve those results (figure 1.1). A component *per se* does not perform any computation, but may be combined with others so that their composition does perform useful computations, much in the way that the parts of a machine do not necessarily perform any function individually, but their composition does. The integration of these two aspects is not straightforward, however, since their goals may conflict. To take a concrete example, concurrency mechanisms, which are computational, may conflict with inheritance, which is a a compositional feature, in that implementation details must often be exposed to correctly implement inheriting subclasses [26] [31] (see chapter 2 for a detailed discussion of the issues). To complicate things even further, the distinction between "composition time" and "run time" is not always as clear as in the picture above: with techniques such as dynamic loading, dynamic message lookup or reflection, applications can also be partially composed or recomposed at run-time.

In order to achieve a clean integration of computational and compositional features, a common semantic foundation is therefore needed in which one may reason about both kinds of features and their interplay. As we shall see, the notions of *objects, functions* and *agents* appear to be the key concepts required for such a foundation. In consequence, we will adopt a definition of software component which is sufficiently abstract to range over these various paradigms.

In short, we say that a component is a *"static abstraction with plugs"*. By "static", we mean that a software component is a long-lived entity that can be stored in a software base, independently of the applications in which it has been used. By "abstraction", we mean that a component puts a more or less opaque boundary around the software it encapsulates.

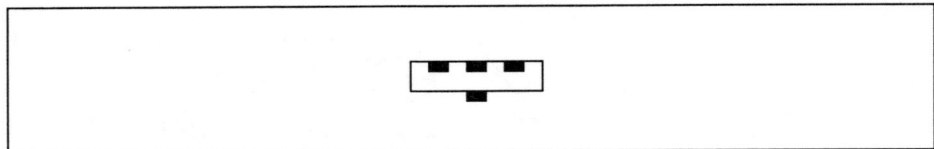

Figure 1.2 *A software component and its plugs.*

"With plugs" means that there are well-defined ways to interact and communicate with the component (parameters, ports, messages, etc.). So, seen from the outside, a component may appear as in figure 1.2: a single entity, which may be moved around and copied, and in particular may be instantiated in a particular context, where the plugs (the small black rectangles) will be bound to values or to other components. In fact, such visual representations of components can be very convenient for supporting interactive composition of applications from component frameworks (see chapter 10). *Software composition*, then, is the process of constructing applications by interconnecting software components through their plugs. The nature of the plugs, the binding mechanisms and the compatibility rules for connecting components can vary quite a bit, as we shall see, but the essential concepts of components, plugs, plug-compatibility and composition remain the same.

1.1.2 Where Do Components Come From?

Once the programming language and associated tools support the development of components, we are still left with the question, "Where do the components come from?" Although we argue that a component-oriented approach is necessary to deal with evolving requirements, it turns out that components themselves only emerge through an iterative and evolutionary software lifecycle. This is reasonable, if we consider that components are only useful as components if they can be easily used in many contexts. Before a "re-useful" component can be designed [23], one must first collect, understand and analyze knowledge about these different contexts to determine how their different needs can be addressed by some common frameworks. When component frameworks are put to use, they must be evaluated with respect to how easily they can be applied to new problems, and improvements must then be introduced on the basis of new experience. Component-oriented development is therefore a *capital-intensive activity* that treats component frameworks as capital goods (or "reusable assets"), and requires investment in component development to achieve economic benefits in the long-term [53]. This means that not only must the programming language technology and support environment address the technical requirements of component-oriented development, but the entire software process, including the analysis and design methods, must incorporate the activity of "component engineering" into the software lifecycle.

Udell, who has provocatively proclaimed the "failure of object-oriented systems to deliver on the promise of software reuse," [50] supports this view by arguing that sets of components, such as those delivered with VisualBasic are a much more successful example of software reuse than object-oriented programming. An animated discussion followed on the Internet[*] which finally came to the obvious agreement that successful software reuse is a matter of methodology and design, more than technology; so object-oriented systems cannot be taken as responsible for lack of reusability: they are more likely to help in producing reusable software, provided that the right design decisions are taken in the first place. Additional arguments on the same line can be found in [22], where various authors discuss software reuse not only in terms of technology, but above all in terms of economical, human and organizational factors.

Our position is that both software methods and development technology need to undergo some significant changes in order to take advantage of component-oriented development. We will first focus on some of the foundational issues concerning the difference between objects and components, and their integration in programming languages and environments; then we will briefly survey related technological and methodological problems to be resolved; finally, we will conclude with some prospects for the future of component-oriented development.

1.2 Objects vs. Components

Object-oriented programming languages and tools constitute an emerging software technology that addresses the development of open systems in two important ways:

1. as an *organizing principle;*
2. as a *paradigm for reuse.*

In the first case, one may view an object-oriented application as a collection of collaborating objects. The fact that each object properly encapsulates both the data and the corresponding behaviour of some application entity, and that one may only interact with this entity through a well-defined interface means that reliability in the face of software modifications is improved, as long as client–server interfaces are respected. In the second case, one may view applications as compositions of both predefined and specialized software components. Application classes inherit interfaces and some core behaviour and representation from predefined abstract classes. Interactions within an application obey the protocols defined in the generic design. Inheritance is the principle mechanism for sharing and reusing generic designs within object-oriented applications.

Despite these two significant advantages of object-oriented development, it is still true that present-day object-oriented languages emphasize *programming* over *composition*, that is, they emphasize the first view of applications to the detriment of the second. In general, it is not possible to reuse classes without programming new ones — one cannot simply compose object classes to obtain new classes in the way that one can compose

---

[*] The discussion took place during September 1994 in the newsgroup comp.object, under the subject heading "Objects vs Components."

functions to obtain new functions. Furthermore, one is either forced to define a given component as a class, whether or not the object paradigm is an appropriate one, or, if other kinds of components are supported, the list is typically *ad hoc* (for example, mixins, macros, modules, templates).

If we consider the various dimensions of programming languages supporting some notion of objects, we discover a mix of features concerned with computational and compositional issues. Wegner [54] has proposed a classification scheme with the following seven "dimensions": objects, classes, inheritance, data abstraction, strong typing, concurrency and persistence. According to the criterion that sets of features are orthogonal if they occur independently in separate programming languages, it turns out that objects, abstraction, types, concurrency and persistence are orthogonal. But this does not tell us how easy or difficult it is to cleanly integrate combinations of features within a single language.

In fact, if we consider just objects, classes and inheritance, it turns out that it is not at all straightforward to ensure both object encapsulation and class encapsulation in the presence of inheritance [47]. One way of explaining this is that classes are overloaded to serve both as templates for instantiating objects and as software components that can be extended by inheritance to form new classes. Typically, these two roles are not cleanly separated by the introduction of separate interfaces. Instead, various *ad hoc* rules must be introduced into each object-oriented programming language to determine what features of a class may be visible to subclasses. Since these rules cannot possibly take into account the needs of all possible component libraries, the net effect is that encapsulation must often be violated[*] in order to achieve the desired degree of software reusability.

A reasonably complete programming language for open systems development should not only support objects and inheritance, but also strong typing and concurrency. Types are needed to formalize and maintain object and component interfaces, and concurrency features are needed to deal with interaction between concurrent or distributed subsystems. (Fine-grain parallelism is also of interest, but is not an overriding concern.) Though types and concurrency are supposedly orthogonal to objects and inheritance, their integration is not a simple matter.

One source of difficulty for types is that objects are not simply values taken in isolation, like integers, strings, higher-order functions, or even more complex constructs such as abstract datatypes. Objects typically belong to a global context, and may contain references to other objects in that context. Furthermore, since they are dynamic entities, they may change behaviour or state, and hence the meaning of references changes over time. Hence, extracting static type information from such dynamic systems is considerably more difficult. Modelling inheritance is also problematic, due to the two different roles played by classes. Many difficulties in early attempts arose from efforts to identify inheritance and subtyping. It turns out, on the contrary, that subtyping and inheritance are best considered

---

[*] We say that encapsulation is violated if clients of a software component must be aware of implementation details not specified in the interface in order to make correct use of the component. In particular, if changes in the implementation that respect the original interface may affect clients adversely, then encapsulation is violated. If the inheritance interface cannot be separately specified, then encapsulation can be violated when implementation changes cause subclasses to behave incorrectly.

as independent concepts [1] [7]. It may even be convenient to have a separate notion of type for the inheritance interface [28].

When concurrency is also brought into the picture, the same conflicts are seen to an exaggerated degree:

1. Concurrency features may conflict with object encapsulation if clients need to be aware of an object's use of these features [45] (see chapter 2).
2. Class encapsulation may be violated if subclasses need to be aware of implementation details [26] [31].
3. Type systems generally fail to express any aspect of the concurrent behaviour of objects that could be of interest to clients (such as the requirement to obey a certain protocol in issuing requests — see chapter 4).

The source of these technical difficulties, we claim, is the lack of a sufficiently component-oriented view of objects. Components need to be recognized as entities in their own right, independently of objects. A class as a template for instantiating objects is one kind of component with a particular type of interface. An object is another kind of component with an interface for client requests. A class as a generator for subclasses is yet another kind of component with a different kind of interface. Each of these components has its own interface for very different purposes. It is possible to provide syntactic sugar to avoid a proliferation of names for all of these different roles, but the roles must be distinguished when the semantics of composition is considered.

The other lesson to learn is that each of these dimensions cannot simply be considered as an "add-on" to the others. An appropriate semantic foundation is needed in which to study the integration issues. If state change and concurrency are modelling requirements, then a purely functional semantics is not appropriate. As a minimum, it would seem that a computational model for modelling both objects and components would need to integrate both *agents* and *functions*, since objects, as computational entities, can be viewed as particular kinds of communicating agents, whereas components, as compositional entities, can be seen as abstractions, or functions over the object space. Moreover, since components may be first-class values, especially in persistent programming environments where new components may be dynamically created, it is essential that the agent and function views be consistently integrated. From the point of view of the type system, both objects and components are typed entities, although they may have different kinds of types.

1.3   Technical Support for Components

Component-oriented software development not only requires a change of mind-set and methodology: it also requires new technological support. In this section, we will review some of the issues that arise:

- What are the *paradigms* and *mechanisms* for binding components together?
- What is the *structure* of a software component?

- At which stage do composition decisions occur, i.e. how can we characterize the *composition process*?
- How do we formally model components and composition, and how can we *verify* that fragments are correctly composed?
- To which extend does a *concurrent* computational model affect software composition?

These questions obviously are interrelated; moreover, they depend heavily on the composition paradigm being used. We have argued that, ideally, a complete environment for software composition should somehow provide a combination of objects, functions and agents. So far, these paradigms have evolved quite independently. In order to combine them into a common environment, considerable care must be taken to integrate them cleanly. In the following, we examine the specific contributions of each paradigm to software composition, we discuss how they may be integrated, and we summarize the principle open research problems.

1.3.1 Paradigms for Assembling Components

Probably the most fundamental composition mechanism to mention is *functional* composition. In this paradigm one entity is first encapsulated and parameterized as a functional abstraction, and is then "activated" (instantiated) by receiving arguments that are bound to its parameters. Obviously this compositional mechanism occurs in nearly every programming environment, and is by no means restricted to functional programming languages. Many languages, however, do not allow arbitrary software entities to be treated as values, and therefore do not support functional composition in its most general form. Parameterized modules, containing variables that can be bound later to other modules, for example, are still absent from many programming languages. At the other end of the spectrum, functional languages use functional composition at every level and therefore provide *homogeneity:* any aspect of a software fragment can be parameterized and then bound to another component, thereby providing much flexibility for delimiting the boundaries of components. Furthermore, functional programming supports *higher-order* composition, i.e. components themselves are data. In consequence, composition tasks themselves can be encapsulated as components, and therefore some parts of the composition process can be automated. Finally, functional composition has the nice property of being easily verifiable, since functions can be seen externally as black boxes: under some assumptions about the parameters of a function, it is possible to deduce some properties of the result, from which one can know if that result can safely be passed to another function. Current functional programming languages have developed sophisticated type systems to check correctness of composed software [37][21].

Functional composition is a local composition mechanism, in the sense that it only involves one abstraction and the values passed as parameters. By contrast, agent environments typically use a global composition mechanism, often called a *blackboard*. A blackboard is a shared space, known by every component, in which information can be put and retrieved at particular *locations*. For systems of agents communicating through channels, the blackboard is the global space of channel names. Even without agents, global memory in traditional imperative programming also constitutes a kind of blackboard. Blackboard composition supports n-ary assemblies of components (whereas local composition mechanisms are mostly binary); furthermore, free access to the shared space imposes less constraints on the interface of components. The other side of the coin, however, is that blackboard composition systems are much more difficult to check for correctness because interaction between components is not precisely localized. As a partial remedy to the problem, blackboard composition systems often incorporate encapsulation mechanisms for setting up boundaries inside the global space within which interference is restricted to a well-known subset of components. By this means, at least some local properties of a blackboard system can be statically verified. The π-calculus [35], for example, has an operator to restrict the visibility of names; in the world of objects, *islands* [19] have been proposed as a means to protect local names and avoid certain traditional problems with aliasing.

Finally, object-oriented systems have introduced a new paradigm for software composition with the notion of *extensibility* — the possibility of adding functionality to a component while remaining "compatible" with its previous uses. Extensibility, typically obtained in object-oriented languages through inheritance or delegation, is an important factor for smooth evolution of software configurations. The delicate question, however, is to understand what *compatibility* means exactly. For example, compatibility between classes is usually decided on the basis of the sets of methods they provide, possibly with their signatures; in the context of active objects, this view does not take into account which *sequences of methods invocations* are accepted by an object. Chapter 4 studies how to capture this aspect through so-called regular types. Moreover, compatibility can be meaningful not only for classes, but for more generalized software entities; in particular, object-oriented systems based on prototypes and delegation need to understand compatibility directly at the level of objects. Chapter 6 investigates a functional calculus in which compatibility is defined at a fundamental level, directly on functions.

Figure 1.3 is an attempt to represent visually the different paradigms. Functional composition is pictured through the usual image of functions as boxes, with parameters represented as input ports and results of computation as output ports. Connections between components are established directly and represent bindings of values to formal parameters. The blackboard paradigm has an addressing scheme that structures the global space; it sometimes also uses direct connections, but in addition, components are put at specific locations, and they may establish connections with other components through their locations. Here locations are pictured as coordinates in a two-dimensional space for the purpose of the visual illustration. In practice, the common space will most often be structured by names or by linear memory addresses. Finally, extensibility is pictured by additional ports and connections added to an existing component, without affecting the features that were already present. Seen at this informal level, it is quite clear that some cohabitation of the paradigms should be possible, but it is also clear that many details need

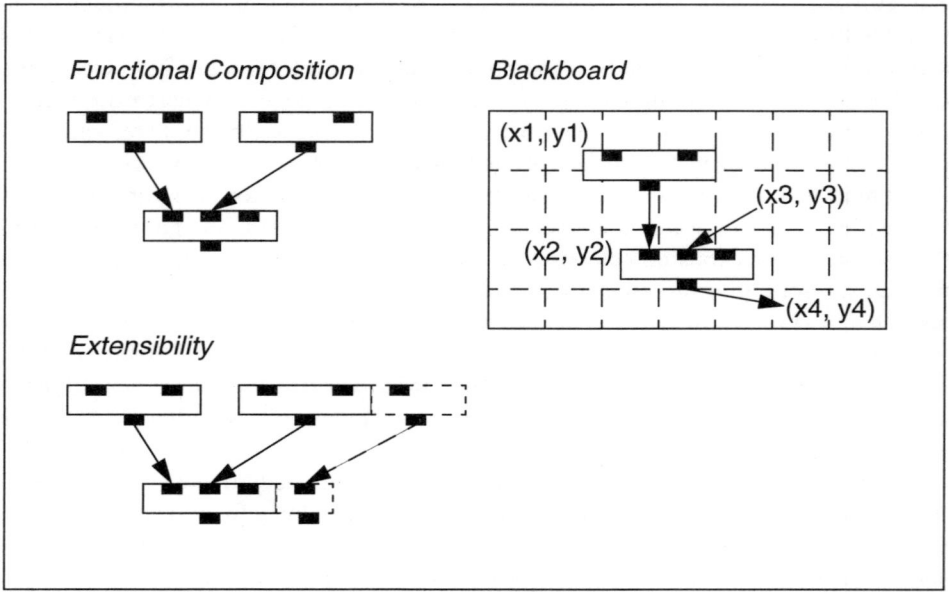

Figure 1.3 *Composition paradigms.*

careful study. The next subsections discuss the notions of components (the boxes), mechanisms (the arrows), and software configurations (the assemblies).

1.3.2 Components as Static Abstractions

In the introduction, we described components in terms of their usage: a software fragment is a component if it is designed for reuse and is part of a framework. This does not tell much about the structural aspects of a component. Some global invariants seem to be valid within any composition paradigm: components typically are *static entities*; moreover, they always consist of some kind of *abstraction*. Both notions, however, deserve more careful examination.

There are many different kinds of static software entities: procedures, functions, modules, classes and so on. In each case, they have a persistent existence independent of their surrounding context, allowing them to be manipulated and stored individually. Once assembled into a program, these static entities control the creation and evolution of dynamic entities, which in current languages are usually *not* components (procedure activations, objects, dynamic data structures). Several examples can be found, however, of dynamic entities that could be interesting as reusable software fragments, but cannot directly participate in a composition because of limitations of the software environment. For example, in most object-oriented languages the classes are static, but the objects (instances) are not. In such languages various strategies are typically used by programmers to have objects as composable entities, such as defining a class that encapsulates a single object (instance). Another strategy, heavily used in the NeXTStep environment [39], is to define complex archiving procedures so that groups of objects can be stored into files (so-called "nib" files); the corresponding files can then be composed and the resulting configuration used to recreate at run-time the collection of objects defined in the individual groups. In cases like this, where the structure of the objects composing a user interface is known statically and does not evolve at run-time, the ability to directly store objects would be much more convenient than writing programs or description files that will dynamically recreate a configuration of objects.

Another limitation to composition occurs in exactly the reverse situation: saying that components are static entities does not mean that they should be always assembled statically. Open systems have an increasing need to dynamically manipulate and exchange components, and dynamically link them with a running application. Recent languages for distributed agents such as Telescript [56] or *Obliq* [5] are good examples of this new direction. Dynamic assembly means that software can be configured at the latest stage, according to user's needs, or that several running applications can dynamically collaborate to exchange information.

The notion of a component is also closely related to that of an *abstraction*, a self-contained entity, with some kind of boundary around it, which can later be composed with other entities. A procedure is an abstraction for a sequence of instructions; a class is an abstraction for a collection of objects; a module is a set of named abstractions. The fact that abstractions have boundaries is crucial for software composition, since it provides a means for structuring software, controlling interaction between components, and verifying proper assembly. Unfortunately, most software environments impose some restrictions on the use of abstractions: boundaries cannot be drawn arbitrarily, according to user's needs, but must follow specific patterns. For example, in most object-oriented systems, boundaries cannot cross inheritance paths, i.e. a class cannot be defined without explicitly referencing its superclass. Only CLOS [27] supports a notion of inheritance through *mixins* in which the superclass need not be known and can be bound later. Full flexibility for drawing abstraction boundaries requires all software components to be treated as *first-class values* that can be passed as parameters to other components. As discussed above, the languages that are most advanced in that direction are functional languages, where "everything is a function," and functions are data. Since functional abstraction is the only abstraction mechanism, programmers have great flexibility in choosing which aspects to fix in a function definition and which aspects to leave open in parameters.

Besides treating components as values, another property of abstractions that has a great impact on compositionality is *scalability*, namely the possibility to use the same abstraction and composition mechanisms at every level of a configuration. Again this is obviously the case with functions, where an assembly of functions is a function again. The advantage is the economy of concepts, and the fact that there is no limit on the granularity of components. Through their inheritance interface, classes can be seen as scalable, since the incremental modifications of a subclass, together with the parent class, form a class again. By contrast, modules are usually not scalable: an assembly of modules is not a module itself. An environment without scalability imposes a fixed granularity of composition (modules can only be assembled into programs), and therefore restrict reusability of components. Furthermore, the absence of scalability often creates problems for formal studies of programming and composition environments, because formal theories are most successful when they can rely on a small set of universal operators. A striking example can be observed in the area of concurrency, where theoreticians typically use process calculi with scalability (a pool of agents or processes is itself a process), while most practical implementations involving concurrency clearly distinguish between a process and a system of processes.

1.3.3 The Composition Process

In traditional environments for software development the various phases for building an application are well-defined and distinct: first one has to write a collection of modules, possibly with some interdependencies, and with some dependencies to predefined modules stored in libraries; then one has to *compile* the modules, in order to generate machine code and, in strongly typed systems, to check type correctness of the modules; finally, one has to *link* the various pieces of machine code together, using a global name space to resolve all cross-references. This, of course, is the schema for compiled languages, but it accounts for the great majority of development environments in current use. Therefore, in such systems, the granularity of components seen by programmers is basically the same as the granularity of units manipulated by the development environment.

In order to get more flexible composition environments, this well-established scheme of program development has to be reviewed. There are several reasons why a component-oriented lifecycle is needed, and there are several tendencies in modern languages that demonstrate the possibility of improving the traditional three-phase assembly of software.

We discussed above the necessity for open systems to be able to dynamically link new agents into a running system. This implies that the information that is normally discarded at link-time, namely the association between global names and memory addresses, needs to be kept both in the running system and in the agent that will be added to it. In other words, even a complete system can no longer considered to be totally closed: names may be locally resolved, but they still need to be considered as potential free variables that can be linked later to a dynamic entity.

In some object-oriented systems, this is true to a further degree: not only the linkage information, but also a major part of compile-time information is required at run-time — this is necessary to implement features such as delegation or even reflection. Early advocates of object-oriented programming were often arguing in favour of the high level of flexibility offered by fully dynamic object-oriented systems, even if they admitted that such choices have a cost in terms of resources: dynamicity typically consumes more memory and more computing power than statically optimized code. Later, some thought they had found the adequate compromise with C++: use objects and classes, but compile away a maximum of information, only keeping what is strictly necessary (namely tables for dynamic binding of virtual functions); this is one of the main reasons why the C++ community grew so rapidly. Indeed, C++ has been and is very successful for a large number of applications, but one could say that the original target of proponents of object-oriented programming has shifted: C++ is being used as a replacement for C, for applications in which interaction with operating system, efficient use of resources, tractability for large-scale projects are essential. We are slowly rediscovering, however, that if flexibility, openness, fast prototyping are really important issues, then the choice of C++ is no longer justified. In the recent years, demand for qualified Smalltalk programmers has been steadily increasing, and large-scale high-level platforms for application development like *OpenStep* [40] are being based on Objective-C instead of C++; both languages differ from C++ in that they maintain full information about objects, classes and methods in the run-time environment. So the market is progressively acknowledging that efficiency is not necessarily the most important feature in any case, and that it also has its cost in terms of lack of openness and flexibility.

We are not saying that the future of software components is necessarily in fully interpreted languages, but that flexible open systems need to deal with components in many possible forms, ranging from source code to machine code through several intermediate representations, partially compiled and optimized. Some modern languages in various areas already demonstrate this tendency, and show that much progress has been done for such implementation strategies. For example, both the scripting language Perl [52] and the functional language CAML-Light [30] are compiled into an intermediate form that is then interpreted; actually, interpreted Perl programs are sometimes faster than equivalent compiled programs written in C, and the implementation of the CAML-Light interpreter is faster than compiled versions of the original CAML language! Another example is the Self language [51], which provides a very high level of run-time flexibility, and yet has efficient implementations based on the principle of *compile-by-need*: the run-time system includes a Self compiler, and methods are compiled whenever needed. Static compilation of a method in an object-oriented system is sometimes complicated, because one has to make assumptions about the context in which it will be called (taking inheritance into account); if, instead, the method is compiled at run-time, then more information is known about the context (i.e. which actual object the method belongs to), which allows for a more efficient compilation of the method. In other words, the time lost to compile the method at run-time may be quickly recovered through subsequent calls to the same method.

Ideally, the responsibility of switching between high-level, human-readable representations of components and low-level, optimized internal representations should be left to the composition environment. In practice, however, programmers still often need to guide these choices. This means that the granularity of components manipulated by the system is visible to programmers. In itself, this is not necessarily a disadvantage, but the problem is that this granularity is often identified with the granularity of logical components of a software system. In other words, programmers are forced to think in terms of "compilation units," instead of thinking in terms of "modules." Leroy [29] explained very clearly the distinction:

> *Modularization* is the process of decomposing a program in[to] small units (*modules*) that can be understood in isolation by the programmers, and making the relations between those units explicit to the programmers. *Separate compilation* is the process of decomposing a program in[to] small units *(compilation units)* that can be type-checked and compiled separately by the compiler, and making the relations between these units explicit to the compiler and linker.

Identifying the two concepts is very common, and yet is limiting, as Leroy points out in the context of the SML language [37]. Modules — i.e. logical units of a program — may be structurally much more complex than compilation units, especially if, as discussed above, one wants to be able to treat them as first-class values and to perform higher-order module combinations, either statically or even dynamically. In this respect, SML has probably the most sophisticated module system for an existing programming language, yet it does not support separate compilation. Several researchers are currently working on removing this limitation [29][16].

1.3.4 Verification of Composition

Whenever components are assembled to perform a common task, there is always an implicit contract between them about the terms of the collaboration. In order to be able to verify the correctness of a configuration, the contracts need to be made explicit and to be compared for eventual discrepancies. This issue can be addressed by a type system. However, conventional type systems cannot capture in general all the aspects of a contract, because of their limited expressiveness. Two approaches can be taken for dealing with this problem. One approach, taken by Meyer in the Eiffel language [33], is to enrich the interfaces of components with additional constraints expressing the expectations and promises of each partner in the contract. Part of the constraints are checked by the type system, and part of them are verified at run-time, each time that an actual collaboration (control passing) between two components takes place. The other approach is to improve the expressiveness of type systems. Much research has been done in this direction, especially in the area of functional programming languages. Polymorphic type inference in languages such as ML or Haskell [21] actually provides a level of security that is much higher than in a traditional language like Pascal, without putting any additional burden on the programmer. However, as soon as one leaves the functional model, such results are no longer applicable: in systems with blackboard composition (imperative programming languages, concurrent systems) one cannot infer much type information. As far as object systems are concerned, this is still an open question, examined in detail in a survey by Fisher and Mitchell [11]. The addition of subtyping makes both type inference and type checking considerably harder, so despite important progress made over the recent years, no object-oriented language with an ML-like type system has yet been developed.

To capture the recursive semantics of objects at a type level, most researchers use explicitly typed systems with either recursive types or existential quantification; such solutions have improved the state of the art for object typing, but are not likely to be applied soon in real languages, since the complexity of the resulting type expressions would probably appal most programmers not familiar with type theory. Therefore we believe that practicability of object typing will be achieved through type inference rather than through explicit typing; preliminary results in that direction are discussed in [18]. The difficult point, however, is to be able to infer types that are both "minimal" in the sense of subtyping, and "principal" in the sense of Curry type schemes (a type scheme is principal for a term if and only if it can generate all other types of that term by substitution of type variables). To our knowledge, this is still an open problem; but some recent results on principal types for objects are collected in [15].

Coming back to the problem of explicit contracts between components, we should mention another family of solutions that puts the contract, not inside components, but outside. For interlanguage composition, this is even the only possibility, since it would be quite difficult to compare contracts specified in different languages and models. An example of a contract being outside of the components is a database schema that specifies the conditions under which a common database may be accessed, and which must be respected by every program doing transactions on the database. While providing a glue between heterogeneous components, this kind of solution has the disadvantage of being quite rigid: the terms of the contract are specified from the beginning and can hardly be changed later; moreover, this approach cannot support scalability, since components are clearly distinct from configurations of multiple components. Contracts outside of components are also found in *module interconnection languages*, whose job is precisely to perform composition of software components. The amount of information handled in such languages varies from one system to the other; Goguen, for example, advocates an algebraic approach to capture semantic information about the components [13]. It should be noted, however, that module interconnection languages seem to have lost part of their importance in the literature in favour of more homogeneous approaches in which the distinction between components and component assemblies is less strict. Object-oriented approaches fall into that category, as do functional approaches to an even greater degree.

Type systems and algebraic specifications aim at verifying correctness in a machine-checkable way by statically looking at a software configuration. They belong, therefore, to the world of static semantics. By contrast, a number of techniques have been developed for studying the dynamic behaviour of programs, like denotational, algebraic, operational or axiomatic semantics. Since such techniques deal with dynamic information, and are therefore not decidable in general, they are commonly used for studying programming languages and environments rather than particular software configurations. It is therefore not our purpose here to discuss them in detail. It should be noted, however, that several of the points discussed above for the evolution of component-oriented software development will have some impact on these analysis techniques. For example, most of these semantics are compositional, but they are not modular (for denotational semantics, this is acknowledged by Mosses [38]). In the scenario of iterative compositional development, it should be possible to progressively refine the semantics of a component according to the available knowledge about its context: we know more about a component inserted into a given configuration than about this component seen in isolation. Instead of the usual distinction between static semantics, dynamic semantics, and what Jones [25] calls "binding time analysis," we should again have a whole range of intermediate steps, corresponding to the various intermediate stages of assembly.

Finally, it should be noted that traditional semantic techniques induce an equivalence relationship over software components — they have been designed to be able to state whether two components are equal or not. In the context of object-oriented programming, this is no longer sufficient, since the idea is to extend components — to produce new components that are not just "equal" to previous ones (plug-compatible), but in some sense are "better" (extended). To deal with this aspect, theoreticians of object-oriented languages have developed the notion of *partial equivalence relationships (PERs)* [4], which equates components not universally, but relative to a given type: for example the records $\{x=1, y=3\}$, $\{x=1, y=4, z=10\}$ are equivalent as type $\{x:Int\}$, but not as type $\{x:Int, y:Int\}$. An alternative approach is proposed in this book in chapter 6, in which components are this time universally related, but by a *compatibility* partial order instead of an equivalence relationship.

1.3.5 Objects as Processes

Earlier in this chapter we argued that *components* and *concurrency* are both fundamental concepts, and cannot be considered as "add-ons" to programming languages. Furthermore, the semantic issues are sufficiently subtle and complex that it is essential to have a formal object model and a semantic foundation for reasoning about all language features. What, then, should the object model look like, and what would be an appropriate semantic foundation?

Let us consider the features we would need to model in a language that supports component-oriented development:

1. *Active Objects:* objects can be viewed as autonomous agents or processes.
2. *Components:* components are abstractions, possibly higher-order, over the computational space of active objects.
3. *Composition:* generalized composition is supported, not just inheritance.
4. *Types:* both objects and components have typed interfaces, but, since objects are dynamic entities and components are static, the type system must distinguish between them.
5. *Subtypes:* subtyping should be based on a notion of "plug compatibility" that permits both objects and components to be substituted if their clients are satisfied [55].

An object model must therefore cope with both objects and components. Objects encapsulate *services*, and possess *identity, state* and *behaviour*[*]. The services are obtained through the behaviour according to some client/server *protocol*. Components, on the other hand, are *abstractions* used to build object systems, i.e., they are functions over the object/process space. Although functions are fundamental, we cannot model objects as functional entities because they are long-lived and concurrent. Since input and output are on-going, and the same input may produce different results at different times, objects are essentially non-functional. Ideally, an *object calculus* [41] would merge the operational features of a process calculus with the compositional features of the λ calculus.

Interestingly, recent progress in the study of process calculi addresses many aspects of the semantics of concurrent object-oriented systems. The original work by Milner on a Calculus of Communicating Systems (CCS) [34] resulted in a highly expressive process calculus that nevertheless could not be used to model "mobile processes" that can exchange the names of their communication ports in messages. This, of course, is essential to model objects. Work by Engberg and Nielsen [10] borrowed and adapted concepts from the λ-calculus to deal with this, and Milner [36] refined and simplified their results to produce the π-calculus, a true "calculus for mobile processes." In the meantime, Thomsen [48] developed the first "Calculus for Higher-Order Communicating Systems" (CHOCS) which essentially added term-passing to CCS. From an object systems point of view, this should allow one to model objects and components as values at run-time. Milner extended the π-calculus to a polyadic form [35], which allows one to express communication of complex messages, and he introduced a simple type system for the calculus. Following on work by Milner, Sangiorgi [46] developed a higher-order process calculus (HOπ), whose semantics can be faithfully preserved by a mapping to the unadorned π-calculus, and Hennessy [17] has developed a denotational model of higher-order process calculi. Honda [20] has also developed the ν-calculus, a process calculus based on asynchronous communication, whose semantics is obtained by a *reduction* of the features of the π-calculus. Going in the opposite direction, Dezani *et al.* [9] have investigated synchronous parallelism and asynchronous non-determinism in the classical λ-calculus. In the object-oriented community, there have been several other attempts to develop object calculi that take their initial inspiration from either process calculi or the λ-calculus, or both [8] [20] [41].

We propose that a formal model of objects and components based on recent developments in process calculi and λ-calculi should form a good basis not only for understanding and explaining abstraction and composition in a component-oriented software development method, but can actually serve as an abstract machine for developing a new generation of component-oriented languages [43] [44], much in the same way that the λ-calculus has served as a semantic foundation for modern functional programming languages.

---

[*] The distinction between "state" and "behaviour" is admittedly artificial, but is useful for conceptual reasons, since state is thought of as hidden and behaviour as visible. In fact, the notions are dual, and one can consider the "state" of an object to be its "current behaviour."

1.3.6 Summary of Research Topics

In this section we have listed some very ambitious wishes for the future of component-oriented development environments, but we have also shown that several directions already present in modern programming languages can give us some confidence about fulfilment of that program. To summarize, here are the points that we consider as most important research issues:

- Merge current notions of abstraction in process calculi, functional languages and object-oriented languages into a single notion of *component*, which should be a firstclass, storable entity equipped with the notions of parameterization (leaving some aspects of the component "open") and instantiation (ability to generate a "copy" of the component in a given run-time context), and furthermore should support scalability (possibility to encapsulate a partial configuration of components as a new component).
- Develop software manipulation tools that are able to deal with partial configurations and support an iterative assembly process, by using various levels of intermediate representations of components. Current tasks of type checking, compilation to machine code and linkage will be replaced by incremental change of intermediate representation.
- Find expressive, yet decidable type inference/partial evaluation systems, that will be able to statically decide about the correctness of a partial configuration, in a way that is transparent to (or requires minimal typing information from) programmers.

It can be seen that these research directions require a tight integration between current research being done both at a theoretical level (semantics and types of programming languages) and at a practical level (implementations, compiler/interpreter design).

1.4 Component Engineering

Once we have a language and environment that permits us to develop software component frameworks, there remains the question how these components should be developed, maintained and applied. With traditional software development, applications are in principle designed to meet very specific requirements. Component frameworks, on the other hand, must be designed to meet many different sets of requirements, and should even be built to anticipate unknown requirements.

Consider the following scenario[*] [42] for application development: an application developer has access to a *software information system (SIS)* that contains not only descriptions of available component frameworks, but domain knowledge concerning various application domains, descriptions of requirements models, generic designs, and guidelines for mapping requirements specifications in the problem space to designs and imple-

---
[*] This scenario was elaborated as part of the ITHACA project (described briefly in the preface).

mentations in the solution space (see chapter 7 for a description of a such a system). A software information system is closer in spirit to an expert system than to a repository; in fact, the principle of a SIS is that it should encode and present the knowledge acquired by a domain expert.

To use the SIS, the application developer first enters into a dialogue to identify the relevant application domain. The information pertaining to this domain can be referred to as a *Generic Application Frame (GAF)*. The GAF determines the context for application development. The next step in the dialogue is to specify the requirements. Since the GAF includes domain knowledge and requirements models, the requirements specification is largely performed according to existing patterns. The specific requirements will then lead the SIS to suggest, according to stored guidelines, generic designs and component frameworks that can be used to build the application. The guidelines may also suggest how components should be instantiated or specialized to meet specific requirements. (Chapter 10 contains a brief description of RECAST, an interactive tool for requirements collection and specification, based on this scenario.)

The process of completing requirements specifications, making design decisions and refining and composing components results in a new information structure that we will call a *Specific Application Frame (SAF)*. The SAF consists not only of the completed application, but all the information that was generated along the way. When application requirements evolve, the SIS is again used, but in this case the dialogue results in previous decisions being reconsidered and a new SAF being built from the old.

This scenario is very appealing, but suggests more questions than it answers. How is domain knowledge to be captured and represented in the SIS? How are generic designs and component frameworks developed and described? How are guidelines determined and encoded? Who is responsible for maintaining the SIS and its contents, and how are the contents evaluated and maintained? Is the scenario even realistic? How much will the SIS need to be supported by human experts? We believe it is, because successful generic applications and component frameworks do exist, but nobody knows how far this scenario can be pushed to work well in practice. Will it only work for very restricted and well-understood application domains, or is it also valid for more complex and evolving domains?

This suggests that the role of *component engineering* is fundamentally different from the more traditional role of *application development*. Although the same person may in some cases play both roles, it is important to separate them in order to keep the different sets of requirements distinct. In particular, the clients for each are very different. The clients of an application are (ultimately) the end-users, whereas the clients of a component framework are the application developers.

Why is it necessary to elevate component engineering to a distinguished activity? Should it not be possible to find reusable components by scavenging existing object-oriented applications? A plausible scenario might have application developers use traditional methods to arrive at an object-oriented design, and then search for reusable objects that would at least partially meet the specifications. The "found" objects would then be tailored to fit the task at hand.

The problem with this scenario is that you do not get something for nothing. Software components are only reusable if they have been *designed* for reuse. A repository of software objects from previous applications is like a "software junkyard" that, more likely than not, will not contain just what you are looking for. The cost of searching for and finding something that approximately meets one's needs, and the additional cost of adapting it to fit may exceed the cost of developing it from scratch. Worse, the tailored components are not maintainable, since such an approach will encourage a proliferation of hacked-up, incompatible versions of somewhat similar components, none of which is ultimately reusable. *Systematic* rather than accidental software reuse requires an investment in component framework development and in software information management [53].

1.4.1 Benefits and Risks

A component that has been designed for reuse always forms part of a framework of components that are intended to be used together, much in the way that modular furniture is made of components that can be combined in many ways to suit different needs. Clearly the development of a component framework represents an investment that must be evaluated against the expected return. The benefits can be measured in two ways: a component framework should make it easier (i) to fill (at least partially) the needs of many different applications, and (ii) to adapt a given application to changing needs. (These are also the main selling points of modular furniture.) If either or both of these requirements are present to a sufficient degree, it may be worthwhile developing a component framework, or investing in the use and possible adaptation of an existing framework.

In fact, one can easily argue that component frameworks should *always* be used: long-lived applications necessarily undergo changes in requirements with time that can be more easily met with the use of a framework, and short-lived applications must typically be developed under tight time constraints, which can also be facilitated by the use of an existing framework. The risks, however, must also be considered:

1. A steep learning curve can be associated with the use of a framework. Developers must be willing to invest time and effort into learning a framework before the benefits can be realized. The *not invented here* syndrome can be difficult to overcome.

2. Development of new frameworks is a costly and long-term activity. The long-term benefits must be justified in terms of the opportunities for recovering the investment.

3. Individual projects have short-term goals and deadlines that conflict with the long-term goals of component-engineering. Management must commit to developing a service-oriented infrastructure to support the provision of frameworks to projects [14]. If the use of frameworks introduces too much overhead, projects will not adopt them.

4. New frameworks evolve rapidly in the beginning, and may undergo several complete redesigns before they stabilize. The costs of re-engineering client applications of a redesigned framework may be quite high, though the long-term benefits of re-engineering can be significant. In principle one should not use unstable frameworks for a large base of client applications, but on the other hand, a framework will not evolve to the point that it stabilizes unless it is applied to many different kinds of applications.

The reason that each of these points can be considered a risk is that present software engineering practice actually *discourages* component-oriented development by focusing on the individual application rather than viewing it as part of a much broader software process. To address these points we need to rethink the way software is developed and introduce new activities into the software lifecycle.

If we reject the "software junkyard" model of software reuse, we can still consider it as a starting point for component engineering. A component engineer processes and digests the results of previous development efforts to synthesize (i) domain knowledge and requirements models [2], (ii) design patterns [12] and generic architectures, (iii) frameworks [24] and component libraries, (iv) guidelines to map from problem to solution domains (i.e. from requirements to designs and implementations). The result of component engineering, therefore, resembles a well-designed cookbook — it is not just a collection of prepackaged recipes, but it contains a lot of background information, generic recipes, suggestions on how to combine and tailor recipes, and advice on how to meet specific needs. The "cookbook" is intended to compensate for the fact that not everyone can afford the time and expense required to become an expert, and so the acquired expertise is reduced to a standard set of guidelines and rules. Naturally one cannot hope to answer all possible needs with such an approach, but a large class of relatively mundane problems can be addressed.

Note that component engineering is not concerned only with developing software components, but touches all aspects of software development from requirements collection and specification, through to design and implementation. The point is that the most beneficial artefacts to reuse are often not software components themselves but domain knowledge and generic designs. Software reuse is most successful if one *plans* for it in advance. By waiting until after requirements are specified and the systems are designed, many opportunities for reuse may have been wasted, and one may not even be able to find suitable components to reuse.

Component engineering can only be considered successful if the results are used to build more flexible applications. Ideally, these results actually *drive* the application development process: an application developer should be quickly positioned in the software information space to some GAF, and the activities of requirements collection and specification, application design, component selection and refinement should follow from a flexible dialog between the developer and a software information system on the basis of the contents of the GAF.

1.4.2 How to Get There from Here

However attractive such a software information system might be, little is known about how one should build one that would be successful in practice. (See chapter 7 for a discussion of some of the issues.) Good results have been achieved by introducing a so-called "Expert Services Team" of individuals who are responsible for introducing reusable assets into projects [14]. In this way, some of the domain expertise is formalized in terms of reusable assets, but the knowledge of how to apply them to particular situations remains a responsibility of this team. The hard parts remain: (i) how to identify the reusable assets applicable to a given situation (identifying the GAF), (ii) mapping the results of analysis to available architectures and designs, (iii) elaborating missing subsystems and components, (iv) adapting frameworks to unforeseen requirements.

More generally, there are various aspects of component-oriented development that can only be considered open research problems. Some of the more significant problems are:

1. *Domain knowledge engineering:* how should domain knowledge be captured and formalized to support component-oriented development?
2. *Synergy between analysis and design:* traditional software engineering wisdom would keep design issues separate from analysis, but opportunities for reuse can be missed unless one plans for it. How can analysis benefit from the knowledge that frameworks will be used in system design?
3. *Framework design:* what methods apply to framework design? Object-oriented analysis and design methods do not address the development of frameworks. Guidelines exist, but no methods [23].
4. *Framework evolution:* frameworks evolve as they stabilize. What principles should be applied to their evolution? How do we resolve the technical difficulties of maintaining applications based on evolving frameworks? [6]
5. *Reuse metrics:* traditional software metrics are of limited use in the development of object-oriented software. Less is known about measuring the cost of developing component-oriented software. How does one measure potential for reuse? The size and cost of framework-based applications? The cost of developing and maintaining reusable assets? [14]
6. *Tools and environments:* what software tools would facilitate component-oriented development? How can the software information space be managed in such a way as to provide the best possible support both for application developers and component engineers?

1.5 Conclusions

Component-oriented software development builds upon object-oriented programming techniques and methods by exploiting and generalizing object-oriented encapsulation and extensibility, and by shifting emphasis from programming towards *composition*. Present object-oriented technology is limited in its support for component-oriented development in several ways. First and foremost, the notion of a *software component* is not explicitly and generally supported by object-oriented languages. A component, as opposed to an object, is a static software abstraction that can be composed with other components to make an application. Various kinds of components can be defined with object-oriented languages, but their granularity is typically too closely linked with that of objects — in addition to classes, both more finely and coarsely grained abstractions are useful as components.

Supporting both components, as software abstractions, and objects, as run-time entities, within a common framework requires some care in integrating corresponding language features within a common framework. In particular, it is not so easy to devise a satisfactory type system that captures "plug compatibility" in all its useful forms and guises. Concurrency and evolving object behaviour pose particular difficulties, as is seen in chapters 2, 4 and 5. For these reasons, we argue, it is necessary to establish a suitable semantic foundation of objects, functions and agents that can be used to reason about software composition at all levels.

Foundational issues, though important, address only a small part of the difficulties in making component-oriented development practical. Even if we manage to produce computer languages that are better suited to expressing frameworks of plug-compatible software components, there is a vast range of technological and methodological issues to be resolved before we can expect that component-oriented development will become widespread. The most fundamental question — where do the components come from? — is the hardest to answer. In a traditional software lifecycle, application "components" are tailor-made to specific requirements. In a component-oriented approach, the activity of *component engineering* must be explicitly incorporated into the lifecycle, and supported by the software process, the methods and the tools. "Software reuse" is not something that can be achieved cheaply by arbitrarily introducing libraries or "repositories" into an existing method. In fact, rather than focusing on software reuse, we must concentrate on reuse of design, of architecture and of expertise. Component engineering is the activity of distilling and packaging domain expertise in such a way as to make component-oriented application development possible.

References

[1] Pierre America, "A Parallel Object-Oriented Language with Inheritance and Subtyping," *Proceedings OOPSLA/ECOOP '90, ACM SIGPLAN Notices*, vol. 25, no. 10, Oct. 1990, pp. 161–168.

[2] Roberto Bellinzona, Mariagrazia Fugini, Vicki de Mey, "Reuse of Specifications and Designs in a Development Information System," *Proceedings IFIP WG 8.1 Working Conference on Information System Development Process,* ed. N. Prakash, C. Rolland, B. Pernici, Como, Italy, Sept. 1–3 1993, pp. 79–96.

[3] Gilad Bracha, "The Programming Language Jigsaw: Mixins, Modularity and Multiple Inheritance," Ph.D. thesis, Dept. of Computer Science, University of Utah, March 1992.

[4] Kim B. Bruce and Giuseppe Longo, "A Modest Model of Records, Inheritance, and Bounded Quantification," in *Information and Computation*, vol. 87, 196–240, 1990.

[5] Luca Cardelli, "Obliq: A Language with Distributed Scope," preliminary draft, March 1994.

[6] Eduardo Casais, "An Incremental Class Reorganization Approach," *Proceedings ECOOP '92*, ed. O. Lehrmann Madsen, *Lecture Notes in Computer Science*, vol. 615, Springer-Verlag, Utrecht, June/July 1992, pp. 114–132.

[7] William Cook, Walter Hill and Peter Canning, "Inheritance is not Subtyping," *Proceedings POPL '90*, San Francisco, Jan. 17–19, 1990, pp. 125–135.

[8] Laurent Dami, "Software Composition: Towards an Integration of Functional and Object-Oriented Approaches," Ph.D. thesis no. 396, University of Geneva, 1994.

[9] Mariangiola Dezani-Ciancaglini, Ugo de'Liguoro, Adolfo Piperno, "Fully Abstract Semantics for Concurrent Lambda-calculus," in *Proceedings TACS '94*, *Lecture Notes in Computer Science*, vol. 789, Springer-Verlag, 1994, pp. 16–35.

[10] Uffe Engberg and M. Nielsen, "A Calculus of Communicating Systems with Label Passing," DAIMI PB-208, University of Aarhus, 1986.

[11] Kathleen Fisher and John C. Mitchell, "Notes on Typed Object-Oriented Programming," in *Proceedings TACS 94*, *Lecture Notes in Computer Science*, vol. 789, Springer-Verlag, Utrecht, 1994, pp. 844–885.

[12] Erich Gamma, Richard Helm, Ralph E. Johnson and John Vlissides, "Design Patterns: Abstraction and Reuse of Object-Oriented Design," *Proceedings ECOOP '93*, *Lecture Notes in Computer Science*, Springer-Verlag, vol. 707, 1993, pp. 406–431.

[13] Joseph A. Goguen, "Reusing and Interconnecting Software Components," in *IEEE Computer*, Feb. 1986, pp. 16–27.

[14] Adele Goldberg and Kenneth S. Rubin, *Succeeding with Objects: Decision Frameworks for Project Management*, Addison-Wesley, 1995, forthcoming.

[15] Carl A. Gunter and John C. Mitchell, *Theoretical Aspects of Object-Oriented Programming*, MIT Press, Cambridge, Mass., 1994.

[16] Robert Harper and Mark Lillibridge, "A Type-Theoretic Approach to Higher-Order Modules with Sharing," in *Proceedings POPL '95*, ACM Press, 1995, pp. 123–137.

[17] Matthew Hennessy, "A Fully Abstract Denotational Model for Higher-Order Processes," in *Information and Computation*, vol. 112(1), pp. 55–95, 1994.

[18] Andreas Hense, "Polymorphic Type Inference for Object-Oriented Programming Languages," Dissertation, Saarbrücken, Pirrot, 1994.

[19] John Hogg, "Islands: Aliasing Protection in Object-Oriented Languages," in *Proceedings OOPSLA 91*, *ACM SIGPLAN Notices*, vol. 26, no. 11, pp. 271–285, Nov. 1991.

[20] Kohei Honda and Mario Tokoro, "An Object Calculus for Asynchronous Communication," *Proceedings ECOOP '91*, ed. P. America, *Lecture Notes in Computer Science*, vol. 512, Springer-Verlag, Geneva, July 15–19, 1991, pp. 133–147.

[21] Paul Hudak, Simon Peyton Jones and Philip Wadler (eds), "Report on the Programming Language Haskell — A Non-Strict, Purely Functional Language (Version 1.2)," *ACM SIGPLAN Notices*, vol. 27, no. 5, May 1992.

[22] IEEE Software, *Software Reuse*, vol. 11, no. 5, Sept. 1994.

[23] Ralph E. Johnson and Brian Foote, "Designing Reusable Classes," *Journal of Object-Oriented Programming*, vol. 1, no. 2, 1988, pp. 22–35.

[24] Ralph E. Johnson, "Documenting Frameworks using Patterns," *Proceedings OOPSLA '92*, *ACM SIGPLAN Notices*, vol. 27, no. 10, Oct. 1992, pp. 63–76.

[25] Neil D. Jones, "Static Semantics, Types, and Binding Time Analysis," *Theoretical Computer Science*, vol. 90, 1991, pp. 95–118.

References

[26] Dennis G. Kafura and Keung Hae Lee, "Inheritance in Actor Based Concurrent Object-Oriented Languages," *Proceedings ECOOP '89*, ed. S. Cook, Cambridge University Press, Nottingham, July 10–14, 1989, pp. 131–145.

[27] Gregor Kiczales, Jim des Rivières and Daniel G. Bobrow, *The Art of the Metaobject Protocol*, MIT Press, Cambridge, Mass., 1991.

[28] John Lamping, "Typing the Specialization Interface," *Proceedings OOPSLA 93, ACM SIGPLAN Notices*, vol. 28, no. 10, Oct. 1993, pp. 201–214.

[29] Xavier Leroy, "Manifest Types, Modules, and Separate Compilation," in *Proceedings POPL'94*, ACM Press, 1994, pp. 109–122.

[30] Xavier Leroy and Pierre Weiss, *Manuel de Référence du Langage CAML*, InterEditions, 1994. Also available by WWW at http://pauillac.inria.fr/doc-caml-light/refman.html.

[31] Satoshi Matsuoka and Akinori Yonezawa, "Analysis of Inheritance Anomaly in Object-Oriented Concurrent Programming Languages," *Research Directions in Concurrent Object-Oriented Programming*, ed. G. Agha, P. Wegner and A. Yonezawa, MIT Press, Cambridge, Mass., 1993, pp. 107–150.

[32] M.D. McIlroy, "Mass Produced Software Components," *Software Engineering*, ed. P. Naur and B. Randell, NATO Science Committee, Jan. 1969, pp. 138–150.

[33] Bertrand Meyer, *Object-Oriented Software Construction*, Prentice Hall, Englewood Cliffs, NJ, 1988.

[34] Robin Milner, *Communication and Concurrency*, Prentice Hall, Englewood Cliffs, NJ, 1989.

[35] Robin Milner, "The Polyadic pi Calculus: a tutorial," ECS-LFCS-91-180, Computer Science Dept., University of Edinburgh, Oct. 1991.

[36] Robin Milner, Joachim Parrow and David Walker, "A Calculus of Mobile Processes, Part I/II," *Information and Computation*, vol. 100, 1992, pp. 1–77.

[37] Robin Milner, Mads Tofte and Robert Harper, *The Definition of Standard ML*, MIT Press, Cambridge, Mass., 1990.

[38] Peter D. Mosses, "Denotational Semantics," in ed. J. van Leuwen, *Handbook of Theoretical Computer Science*, vol. B, Elsevier, Amsterdam, 1990, pp. 575–631.

[39] *NeXTstep Reference Manual*, NeXT Computer, Inc., 1990.

[40] Next Computer, Inc. and SunSoft, Inc., *OpenStep Specification*, 1994. Available at ftp address ftp://ftp.next.com/pub/OpenStepSpec/.

[41] Oscar Nierstrasz, "Towards an Object Calculus," *Proceedings of the ECOOP '91 Workshop on Object-Based Concurrent Computing*, ed. M. Tokoro, O. Nierstrasz, P. Wegner, *Lecture Notes in Computer Science*, vol. 612, Springer-Verlag, pp. 1–20, 1992.

[42] Oscar Nierstrasz, Simon Gibbs and Dennis Tsichritzis, "Component-Oriented Software Development," *Communications of the ACM*, vol. 35, no. 9, Sept. 1992, pp. 160–165.

[43] Oscar Nierstrasz, "Composing Active Objects," *Research Directions in Concurrent Object-Oriented Programming*, ed. G. Agha, P. Wegner and A. Yonezawa, MIT Press, Cambridge, Mass., 1993, pp. 151–171.

[44] Oscar Nierstrasz and Theo Dirk Meijler, "Requirements for a Composition Language," *Proceedings of the ECOOP '94 Workshop on Coordination Languages*, ed. P. Ciancarini, O. Nierstrasz, A. Yonezawa, *Lecture Notes in Computer Science*, Springer-Verlag, 1995, to appear.

[45] Michael Papathomas and Oscar Nierstrasz, "Supporting Software Reuse in Concurrent Object-Oriented Languages: Exploring the Language Design Space," *Object Composition*, ed. D. Tsichritzis, Centre Universitaire d'Informatique, University of Geneva, June 1991, pp. 189–204.

[46] Davide Sangiorgi, "Expressing Mobility in Process Algebras: First-Order and Higher-Order Paradigms," Ph.D. thesis, CST-99-93 (also: ECS-LFCS-93-266), Computer Science Dept., University of Edinburgh, May 1993.

[47] Alan Snyder, "Encapsulation and Inheritance in Object-Oriented Programming Languages," *Proceedings OOPSLA '86, ACM SIGPLAN Notices*, vol. 21, no. 11, Nov. 1986, pp. 38–45.

[48] Bent Thomsen, "Calculi for Higher Order Communicating Systems," Ph.D. thesis, Imperial College, London, 1990.

[49] Dennis Tsichritzis, "Object-Oriented Development for Open Systems," *Information Processing 89 (Proceedings IFIP '89)*, North-Holland, San Francisco, Aug. 28–Sept. 1, 1989, pp. 1033–1040.

[50] Jon Udell, "Componentware," in *Byte*, vol. 19, no. 5, May 1994, pp. 46–56.

[51] David Ungar and Randall B. Smith, "Self: The Power of Simplicity," *Proceedings OOPSLA '87, ACM SIGPLAN Notices*, vol. 22, no. 12, Dec. 1987, pp. 227–242.

[52] Larry Wall and Randal L. Schwartz, *Programming Perl*, O'Reilly & Associates, Inc., 1990.

[53] Peter Wegner, "Capital-Intensive Software Technology," *IEEE Software*, vol. 1, no. 3, July 1984.

[54] Peter Wegner, "Dimensions of Object-Based Language Design," *Proceedings OOPSLA '87, ACM SIGPLAN Notices*, vol. 22, no. 12, Dec. 1987, pp. 168-182.

[55] Peter Wegner and Stanley B. Zdonik, "Inheritance as an Incremental Modification Mechanism or What Like Is and Isn't Like," *Proceedings ECOOP '88*, ed. S. Gjessing and K. Nygaard, *Lecture Notes in Computer Science*, vol. 322, Springer-Verlag, Oslo, Aug. 15–17, 1988, pp. 55–77.

[56] J.E. White, *Telescript Technology: The Foundation for the Electronic Marketplace,* White Paper, General Magic, Inc.

PART II

Concurrency and Distribution

Chapter 2
Concurrency in Object-Oriented Programming Languages

Michael Papathomas

Abstract An essential motivation behind concurrent object-oriented programming is to exploit the software reuse potential of object-oriented features in the development of concurrent systems. Early attempts to introduce concurrency to object-oriented languages uncovered interferences between object-oriented and concurrency features that limited the extent to which the benefits of object-oriented programming could be realized for developing concurrent systems. This has fostered considerable research into languages and approaches aiming at a graceful integration of object-oriented and concurrent programming. We will examine the issues underlying concurrent object-oriented programming, examine and compare how different approaches for language design address these issues. Although it is not our intention to make an exhaustive survey of concurrent object-oriented languages, we provide a broad coverage of the research in the area.

2.1 Introduction

Considerable research activity in the past few years has concentrated on the design of concurrent object-oriented programming languages (COOPLs). This research activity aimed at providing an integration of object-oriented and concurrent programming. The following points discuss some motivation for concurrent object-based programming:
- To augment the *modelling power* of the object-oriented programming paradigm. One goal of object-oriented programming can be seen as to model the real world directly and naturally [89]. Concurrency then adds to the modelling power by making it easier to model the inherently concurrent aspects of the real world.

- To take advantage of the *software design benefits* of object-oriented programming and the potential for *software reuse* in the development of concurrent and distributed systems. Concurrent and distributed systems are becoming more widespread and the need to develop concurrent programs is becoming more common. This is witnessed by the support provided for concurrent programming at the application level provided by modern operating systems.
- To support *sharing of distributed persistent data*. The object-oriented paradigm lends itself well for providing location transparency by encapsulating within objects access to distributed persistent data. However, as information has to be shared, access to the objects has to be scheduled in a way that avoids interference and provides support for recovering from failures in the distributed environment. Although this could be left to the language implementation, as is the case in database management systems, taking advantage of the semantics of object types to ensure atomicity has substantial benefits with respect to performance and availability. This, however, requires the use of concurrency control mechanisms for the implementation of object types[90].
- To take advantage of *parallelism* in the implementation of object classes for increased execution speeds. Data abstraction can be used to conceal parallel implementations of objects from programs that use them so as to increase their performance when run on parallel machines. Parallelizing compilers could be used to generate parallel implementations of object classes, thus avoiding the need for concurrency constructs. However, better results are generally achieved by the use of explicit parallel algorithms as implicit approaches for parallel execution uncover and exploit only a number of restricted classes of parallelism [46]. Moreover, as data abstraction hides the details of the implementation of classes, users of these classes need not be aware of their concurrent implementation.

In all of the above cases it is necessary to combine the concurrent and object-oriented programming paradigms, provide linguistic support for concurrent object-oriented programming and, ideally, exploit the reuse potential of object-oriented programming for concurrent software.

However, combining object-oriented and concurrency features has proven to be more difficult than might seem at first sight. Clearly, devising a language that has both concurrent programming and object-oriented constructs poses no problem. There has been a large number of proposals for combining object-oriented and concurrency features. However, they are not equally successful in drawing the benefits of object-oriented programming for concurrent software development. The problem is that these features are not orthogonal, and consequently they cannot be combined in an arbitrary way. Most of the research in the area is devoted to devising graceful combinations that limit the interference of features.

In this chapter we present a design space for the approaches for combining object-oriented and concurrency features and a set of criteria for evaluating the various choices. We use the criteria to evaluate some proposals and identify approaches that do not adequately support object-oriented programming as well as approaches that do achieve a graceful combination of the features.

In section 2.2 we present a design space for combining object-oriented and concurrency features with respect to several aspects of language design. In section 2.3, we discuss the issues that have to be addressed to provide the benefits of object-oriented programming. Section 2.4 examines the impact of some proposals on the integration of the programming paradigms and their potential for reuse. Finally, in section 2.5 we present our conclusions, discuss open problems and directions for further work in the area.

2.2 Design Space

We start by presenting three aspects of COOPLs that we consider for constructing the design space, and then we discuss the design choices with respect to each of these aspects. Later, in section 2.4, we will examine more closely some existing languages showing how the design of their features situate them in the design space.

2.2.1 A Design Space for Concurrent Object-Oriented Languages

We seek to evaluate language design choices with respect to the integration of their concurrency and object-oriented features and the degree to which software reuse is supported. In particular, we wish to understand how choices of concurrency constructs interact with object-oriented techniques and affect the reusability of objects. As such, our classification scheme concentrates on the relationship between objects and concurrency. We shall consider the following aspects:

- *Object models:* how is object consistency maintained in the presence of concurrency? The way objects are considered with respect to concurrent execution may or may not provide them with a default protection with respect to concurrent invocations. Furthermore, different languages may favour or enforce a particular way of structuring programs to protect objects.
- *Internal concurrency:* can objects manage multiple internal threads? This issue concerns the expressive power that is provided to objects for handling requests. Note that the execution of internal threads is also related to the protection of the internal state objects, which is determined by the choice of object model.
- *Constructs for object interaction:* how much freedom and control do objects have in the way that requests and replies are sent and received? The choice of concurrency constructs for sending and receiving messages determines the expressive power that is provided for implementing concurrent objects. Moreover, the design of constructs for conditional acceptance of messages interacts with the use of class inheritance.

In the presentation of the design space, it will become apparent that these aspects are not entirely independent: certain combinations of choices are contradictory and others are redundant or lack expressive power.

2.2.2 Concurrent Object Models

There are different ways one can structure a concurrent object-based system in order to protect objects from concurrency. A language may support constructs that favour or even enforce one particular way, or may leave it entirely to the programmer to adopt a particular model. There are three main approaches:
- *The orthogonal approach:* Concurrent execution is independent of objects. Synchronization constructs such as semaphores in Smalltalk-80 [40], "lock blocks" as in Trellis/Owl [68] or monitors as in Emerald [19] must be judiciously used for synchronizing concurrent invocations of object methods. In the absence of explicit synchronization, objects are subject to the activation of concurrent requests and their internal consistency may be violated.
- *The homogeneous approach:* All objects are considered to be "active" entities that have control over concurrent invocations. The receipt of request messages is delayed until the object is ready to service the request. There is a variety of constructs that can be used by an object to indicate which message it is willing to accept next. In POOL-T [6] this is specified by executing an explicit accept statement. In Rosette [83] an *enabled set* is used for specifying which set of messages the object is willing to accept next.
- *The heterogeneous approach:* Both active and passive objects are provided. Passive objects do not synchronize concurrent requests. Examples of such languages are Eiffel // [26] [27] and ACT++ [45]. Both languages ensure that passive objects cannot be invoked concurrently by requiring that they be used only locally within single-threaded active objects. Argus [55] provides both *guardians* (active objects) and CLU *clusters* (passive objects) [52].

2.2.3 Internal Concurrency

Wegner [87] classifies concurrent object-based languages according to whether objects are internally sequential, quasi-concurrent or concurrent:
- *Sequential objects* possess a single active thread of control. Objects in ABCL/1 [94] and POOL-T and Ada tasks [9] are examples of sequential objects.
- *Quasi-concurrent objects* have multiple threads but only one thread may be active at a time. Control must be explicitly released to allow interleaving of threads. Hybrid domains [47][70][71][72] and monitors [42] are examples of such objects.

Design Space

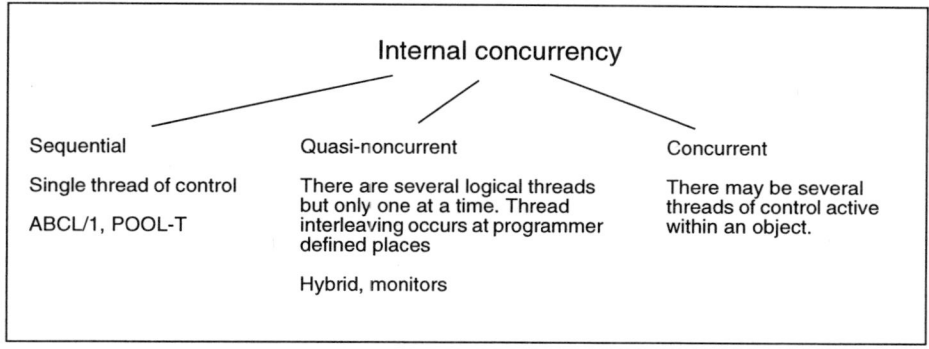

Figure 2.1 *Approaches to internal concurrency.*

- *Concurrent objects* do not restrict the number of internal threads. New threads are created freely when accepting requests. Ada *packages* and POOL-T *units* resemble concurrent objects (though they are not first-class objects). Languages like Smalltalk-80 that adopt the orthogonal object model also support concurrent objects. From the point of view of the called objects, a new local thread is effectively created whenever a method is activated in response to a message.

According to the above classification, the threads of concurrent objects are created freely when an object receives a message. However, there are languages where objects may have internally concurrent threads that are not freely created by message reception. In order to include these languages in the classification and to capture more information about the way that threads are created, we generalize the concurrent object category to include any language in which objects have concurrent threads, irrespective of the way they are created, and consider separately the issue of thread creation.

We identify three, non-exclusive ways for the creation of threads within objects as follows:

- *By message reception*: Thread creation is triggered by reception of a message. An object cannot create a thread on its own unless it can arrange for a message to be sent to it without blocking the currently executing thread. Depending on whether objects may control the creation of threads, we have the following subcategories:
  - *Controlled by the object:* The object may delay the creation of threads. For example, in the language Sina [84] a new concurrent thread may be created for the execution of a method belonging to a select subset of the object's methods only if the currently active thread executes the *detach* primitive.
  - *Unconstrained creation:* Threads are created automatically at message reception. This is the default for languages with an orthogonal object model.
- *Explicit creation*: Thread creation is not triggered by message reception but the object itself initiates the creation of the new thread. For instance, in SR [12] there is a construct similar to a "cobegin" [11] to initiate the execution of concurrent threads.

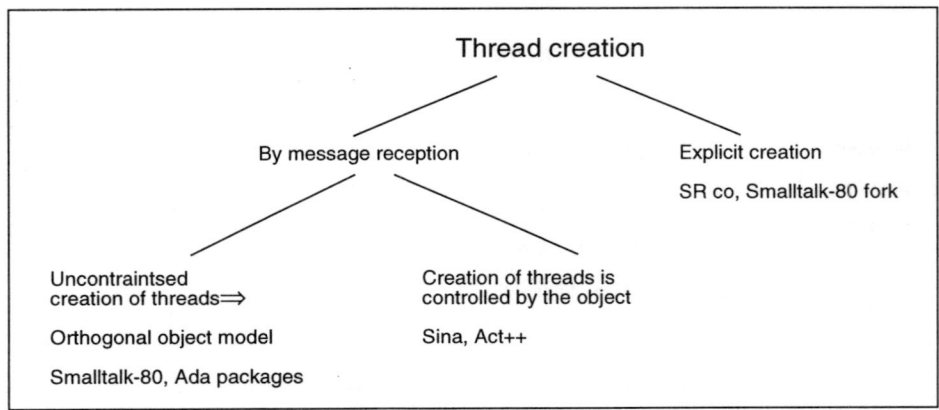

Figure 2.2 *Approaches to thread creation.*

Another way to create a new thread, in the absence of a special construct, is to call asynchronously an operation of the object. This requires, however, that such calls are not blocked at the object's interface. This approach is used in a recent version of Sina. Such calls bypass the normal method synchronization constraints as well as the request queue at the object's interface. Finally, it would also be possible to create new independent objects to call the object methods in parallel. However, this is cumbersome and it also requires some means of bypassing the message queue at the object's interface.

The *next* and *become* primitives in Rosette and ACT++ can be viewed as a controlled creation of threads, with the additional restriction that concurrent threads may not share the object's state since they execute on different "versions" of the object.

In Guide [48], an object may be associated with a set of activation conditions that specify which methods may be executed in parallel by internally concurrent threads. In the default case, as with any language following an orthogonal approach for concurrency, objects may be viewed as concurrent with unconstrained creation of threads triggered by external messages.

The creation of threads by reception of external messages or by execution of a special construct are neither mutually exclusive design choices — as illustrated by SR, which supports both — nor redundant, as we will see in section 2.3.

2.2.4 Constructs for Object Interaction

We classify these constructs with respect to the degree of control that can be exercised by objects in the client and server roles. We specifically consider *reply scheduling*, which concerns the degree of flexibility the client has in accepting a reply, and *request scheduling*, which concerns the control the server can exercise in accepting a request.

2.2.4.1 Issuing Requests

The following important issues can be identified with respect to the constructs supported for issuing requests:

- *Addressing:* How are the recipients of a request specified and determined? How and where is the reply to be sent? Flexible control over the reply destination can reduce the amount of message passing required.
- *Synchronization for requests and replies:* Can the current thread continue after issuing the request? What mechanisms are supported for matching replies to requests? How does the client synchronize itself with the computation and delivery of the reply?
- *First-class representation of requests and replies:* Do requests and replies have a first-class representation that permits them to be forged or changed dynamically? What aspects (e.g. destination, method name) can be changed dynamically?

We further discuss these issues below and present how they are addressed by different proposals.

Addressing

In most languages the recipient of a request is specified directly by using its object identifier. However, there are some proposals allowing for more flexible ways of addressing where the system determines the recipient of the request. We review some of these proposal below.

Types as Recipients in PROCOL

In PROCOL [49] [85] an object type may be used to specify the recipient of a request. In this case the potential recipients are any instance of the type that is in a state such that it may accept the request. The system determines one recipient among the set of potential recipients and delivers the request. It is important to note that this feature does not support any form of multicast; exactly one message is exchanged with the chosen recipient in a point to point fashion.

ActorSpace

ActorSpace [2] is a general model providing a flexible and open-ended approach to object communication that has been developed in the context of the actor model.

In this mode, *destination patterns* may by used to designate the recipients of a request. Patterns are matched against attributes of actors in an specified actorspace — a passive container of actors — to determine a set of potential recipients. A message may be sent by either one of two primitives: *send* or *broadcast*. The former delivers exactly one message to a recipient chosen non-deterministic by the system. The latter provides a form of multicast by delivering the request to all potential recipients.

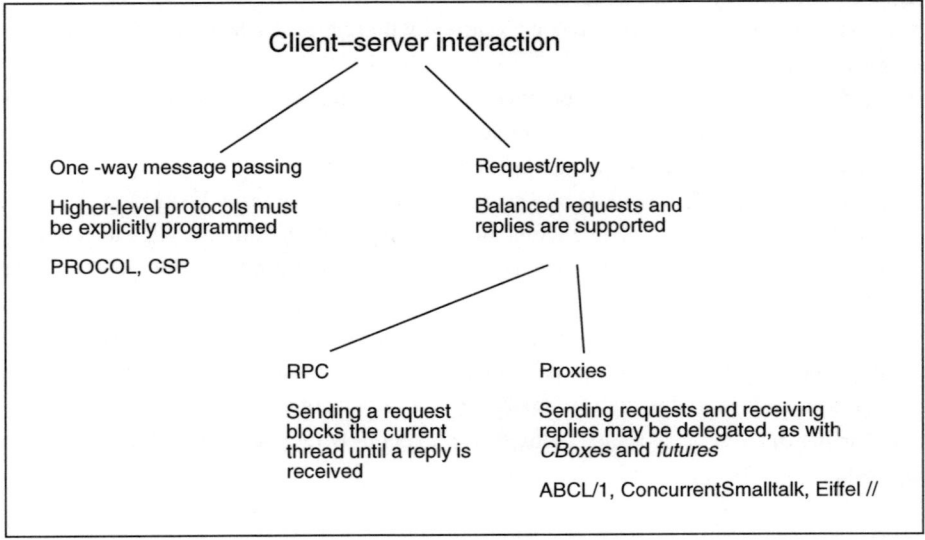

Figure 2.3 *Client–server interaction mechanisms.*

Extra flexibility is provided in this model by allowing the dynamic inclusion and removal of actors from ActorSpaces as well as by allowing the dynamic modification of actor attributes. Moreover, ActorSpaces may be nested.

Synchronization for Requests and Replies

We initially distinguish between *one-way message passing* communication primitives and constructs supporting a *request/reply* protocol. The latter provide support for object interactions where requests will be eventually matched by replies. These mechanisms vary in flexibility when sending requests and receiving replies. Strict RPC approaches enforce that requests will be matched by a reply and delay the calling thread until the reply is available. Further flexibility is provided by "proxy" objects which disassociate the sending or receiving of messages from the current thread of control. Examples of built-in proxy objects are *future variables* [94] and *CBoxes* [92].

One-Way Message Passing

Whether communication is synchronous with one-way message passing, as in CSP [43] or PROCOL [85], or asynchronous, as in actor languages, clients are free to interleave activities while there are pending requests. Similarly, replies can be directed to arbitrary addresses since the delivery of replies must be explicitly programmed.

Design Space

The main difficulty with one-way message passing is getting the replies. The client and the server must cooperate to match replies to requests. As we shall see in section 2.3, the additional flexibility and control provided by one-way message passing over request/reply based approaches can only be properly exploited if objects (i.e. servers) are implemented in such a way that the reply destination can always be explicitly specified in a request.

Remote Procedure Call

With RPC the calling thread of the client is blocked until the server accepts the request, performs the requested service and returns a reply. Most object-oriented languages support this form of interaction, though "message passing" is generally compiled into procedure calls.

Supporting RPC as the only means for object interaction may be a disadvantage when objects are sequential as we will see in the next section. Although it is trivial to obtain a reply, it is not possible to interleave activities or to specify reply addresses.

Proxies

An alternative approach that provides the client with more flexibility in sending and receiving replies is to introduce *proxies*. The main idea is to delegate the responsibility of delivering the request and obtaining the reply to a proxy. (The proxy need not be a first-class object, as is the case with *future variables* [94].) The actual client is therefore free to switch its attention to another activity while the proxy waits for the reply. The proxy itself may also perform additional computation or even call multiple servers.

If necessary, the reply is obtained by the original client by an ordinary (blocking) request. This approach, variants of which are supported by several languages [27][94][92], maintains the benefits of an RPC interface and the flexibility of one-way message passing. In contrast to one-way message passing, however, there is no difficulty in matching replies to requests.

A closely related approach is to combine RPC with one-way message passing. In ABCL/1, for example, an object that externally has an RPC interface may internally use lower-level message-passing primitives to reply by sending an asynchronous message to the client or to its proxy. The use of such facilities is further discussed in section 2.4.2.

First-Class Representation of Requests and Replies

The ability to have a first-class representation of requests and replies may enhance substantially the expressive power of a language. There is a range of aspects of requests and replies that may have a first-class representation in a language. This varies from (almost) no first-class representation at all to a full first-class representation of all aspects of requests and replies. Below we discuss how this issue is addressed in some languages that are characteristic of the various possibilities.

Minimal First-Class Representation

Apart from the method's arguments and the target, all other aspects, such as the method name and the return address, cannot be specified dynamically. This the case for languages such as POOL-T, Hybrid and Trellis/Owl. One could argue that since the target and the arguments can be specified at run-time, there is a first-class representation of some aspects and that the categorization is not accurate. In fact, in older language proposals such as CSP [43] the targets of messages were determined statically. This, however, is uncommon in more recent languages since it makes it hard to develop software libraries: a server that must be statically bound to its potential callers has a low reuse potential. A first-class representation of the target and arguments can be considered as a minimum that one should expect to find in every language.

First-Class Representation of Method Names and Reply Addresses

PROCOL supports the first-class representation of method names. The name of the method to call may be supplied as a string. This allows the method names for a request to be passed in messages or computed at run-time.

With ABCL/1 it is possible to specify dynamically and explicitly the object that is to receive the reply of a request. The benefits of the use of this feature are discussed in section 2.4.2.

Full First-Class Representation

As one would expect, full first-class representation of requests is provided in reflective languages such as ABCL/R. However, it is also provided in languages such as Smalltalk and Sina which are not fully reflective. In fact, the latter two illustrate the usefulness and the possibility of having such features in any concurrent language which is not fully reflective. Briot [23] has used the features of Smalltalk to build a several object-oriented programming models using the relative primitive concurrency features provided in the Smalltalk system. Aksit *et al.* [4] show how these features may be used to abstract and reuse several object coordination paradigms.

2.2.4.2 Accepting Requests

A main concern from the point of view of an object acting as a server is whether requests can be conditionally accepted.[*] When a request arrives, the server may be busy servicing a previous request, waiting itself for a reply to request it has issued, or idle, but in a state that requires certain requests to be delayed. We distinguish initially between conditional and unconditional acceptance of requests. Conditional acceptance can be further discriminated according to whether requests are scheduled by explicit acceptance, by activation conditions or by means of reflective computation (see figure 2.4).

---

* A secondary issue is whether further activity related to a request may continue after the reply has been sent as in the Send/Receive/Reply model [39], but this can also be seen as concern of internal concurrency where follow-up activity is viewed as belonging to a new thread.

Design Space

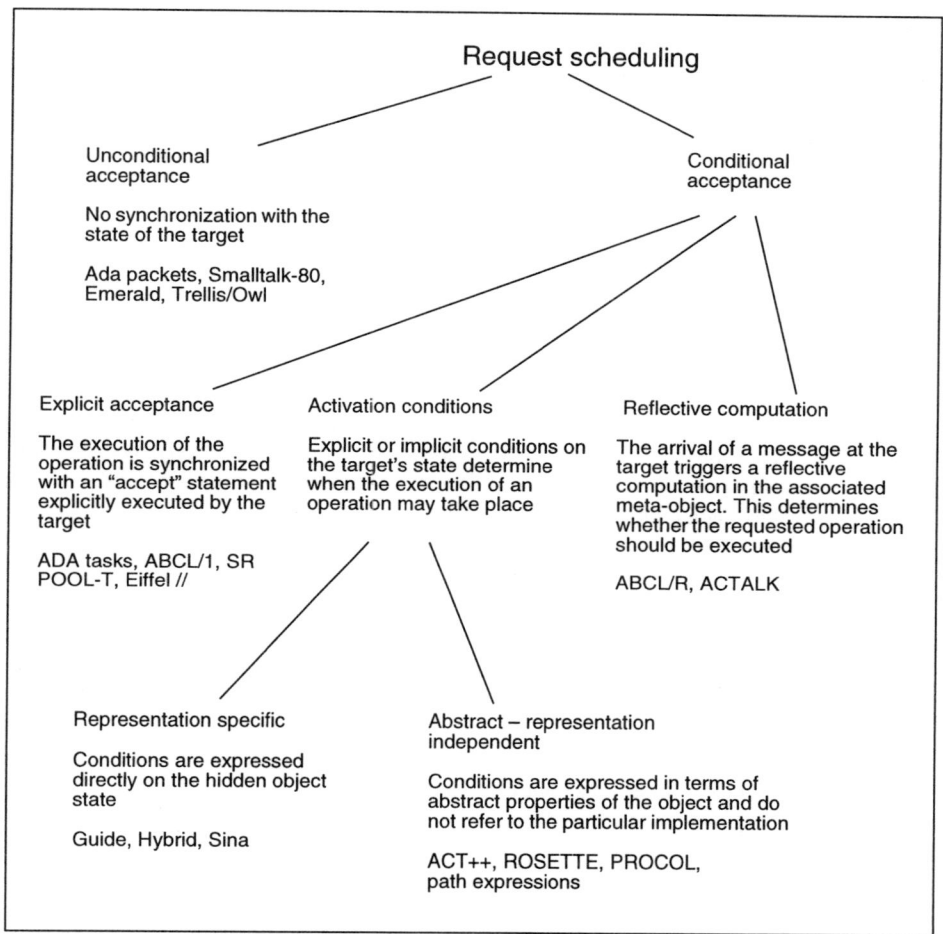

Figure 2.4 *Approaches to scheduling requests.*

Unconditional Acceptance

Unconditional acceptance of requests is illustrated by monitors [42] and by Smalltalk-80 [40] objects. The mutual exclusion that is provided by monitors could be considered as an implicit condition for the acceptance of requests. However, the mutual exclusion property is captured by viewing monitors as quasi-concurrent objects so we consider request acceptance to be unconditional. Note that message acceptance for languages with an orthogonal object model is by default unconditional.

Explicit Acceptance

With *explicit acceptance,* requests are scheduled by means of an explicit "accept" statement executed in the body of the server. Accept statements vary in their power to specify which messages to accept next. Acceptance may be based on message contents (i.e. operation name and arguments) as well as the object's state. Languages that use this approach are Ada, ABCL/1, Concurrent C, Eiffel//, POOL-T and SR. With this approach objects are typically single-threaded, though SR is an exception to this rule.

Activation Conditions

With *activation conditions*, requests are accepted on the basis of a predicate over the object's state and, possibly, the message contents. The activation condition may be partly implicit, such as the precondition that there be no other threads currently active within the object. An important issue is whether the conditions are expressed directly over a particular representation of the object's state or if they are expressed in more abstract terms. In Guide, for example, each method is associated with a condition that directly references the object's instance variables, whereas in ACT++ the condition for accepting a message is that the object be in an appropriate *abstract state* which abstracts from the state of a particular implementation. Another approach is to specify the legal sequences of message acceptance by means of a regular expression, as in path expressions [24] and PROCOL [85].

There are also some proposals such as *synchronizers* [38], *separate method arguments* [66] and *state predicates* [74], for activation conditions that depend on the state or the computation history of other objects.

A synchronizer [38] is a special object associated with a group of objects. When a method of any of these objects is called a condition in the synchronizer is evaluated. Depending on the outcome, the execution of the method may proceed, or be delayed until the condition becomes true. Synchronizers may have their own variables that are used to store information about the computation history of a group of objects.

Separate method arguments [66] can be used to constraint the execution of a method by preconditions on the argument declared as "separate." The execution of the method is delayed until the preconditions are true and the separate objects are "reserved" for the duration of the call. That is, they can only be used in the body of a method.

With state predicate notifiers [74], the execution of a method can be constrained by the notification that another object has reached a state that satisfies a *state predicate*. This feature has synchronous and asynchronous forms. In the synchronous variant, the notifying object waits until the method is executed and the method gains exclusive access to the object. In the asynchronous variant the notifying object proceeds independently.

Reflective Computation

With *reflective computation* the arrival of a request triggers a method of the server's *meta-object*. The meta-object directly then manipulates object-level messages and mailboxes as objects. This approach is followed by the language ABCL/R [86] and it is also illustrated in Actalk [23] where some reflective facilities of the Smalltalk-80 system are used to intercept messages sent to an object and synchronize their execution in a way that simulates message execution in actor-based languages.

2.3 Criteria for Evaluating Language Design Choices

So far we have presented a design space covering the most significant choices in the design of concurrency features for OOPLs, but we have said little about how the various approaches compare. Since our goal is to arrive at COOPLs that provide the advantages of object-oriented programming for the development of concurrent systems, we must first formulate our requirements as precisely as possible, before beginning to compare the approaches. We first discuss the issue of developing object classes that have high reuse potential. Then, we turn our attention to the support for reuse at a finer granularity than objects and examine the issues related to the use of inheritance and the reuse of synchronization constraints.

2.3.1 Object-Based Features — Support for Active Objects

The main issue for reuse at the object level is that concurrency in an object-oriented language should not diminish the benefits of object-based features with respect to reuse. For instance, encapsulation should still protect the internal state of objects from surrounding objects and it should still be possible to insulate objects' clients from implementation choices. This should make it possible to change the implementations without affecting the clients provided that the interfaces are maintained and that changes are, in some sense, behaviourally compatible.

Object-oriented and concurrent programming have different aims that incur different software structuring paradigms. Object-oriented programming aims at the decomposition of software into self-contained objects to achieve higher software quality and to promote reusability. Concurrent programming aims at expressing and controlling the execution, synchronization and communication of conceptually parallel activities. Its primary goal is to provide notations that are suitable for devising solutions to problems that involve the coordination of concurrent activities [11].

In order to compare language designs it is necessary to adopt a programming model for concurrent object-based programming and evaluate how well the various languages support this model. Our view regarding the way the two programming paradigms should be combined is by structuring programs as cooperating objects that exchange messages. This is similar to the way sequential object-oriented programs are structured, however, in concurrent programs objects may encapsulate one or more concurrent threads that implement their behaviour. Moreover, the operations of an object may be invoked by concurrently executing objects.

We use the term *active objects* for this programming model to emphasize that objects themselves rather than the threads that invoke their operations have the responsibility to schedule concurrent requests. Requests should be scheduled in a way consistent with the object's internal state and the possibly spontaneous execution of internal threads. The objects developed following this model are independent self-contained entities. They can be reused across applications and they may be refined to support different scheduling policies for invoked operations. The programs that use the objects should not be affected by such changes.

Although any language combining concurrent and object-oriented features could be used to develop software following this model, as will be illustrated in section 2.4, not all combinations of concurrent and object-oriented features are equally successful in supporting this programming model. Below we develop a number of requirements on the on the language features to adequately support programming following an active object model. In section 2.4 we will use these requirements to evaluate language design choices and identify the shortcomings of some approaches.

2.3.1.1 Requirements

According to the active object model discussed above, we would like languages to support the development of self-contained objects with high reuse potential. A general principle for achieving this is that reusable object classes should make minimal assumptions about the behaviour of applications that will use them. Furthermore, the choice of constructs should not constrain the possible implementations of a class. We can formulate our requirements as follows:

1. *Mutual exclusion — protecting the objects' state:* The internal state of objects should be automatically protected from concurrent invocations so that it will be possible to reuse existing objects in concurrent applications without modification.

2. *Request scheduling transparency:* An object should be able to delay the servicing of requests based on its current state and on the nature of the request. This should be accomplished in a way that is transparent to the client. Solutions that require the cooperation of the client are not acceptable from the point of view of reusability since the client then cannot be written in a generic fashion.

3. *Internal concurrency:* The concurrency constructs should allow for the implementation of objects that service several requests in parallel or that make use of parallelism in their implementation for increased execution speed in the processing of a single request. This could be done either by supporting concurrent threads within an object or by implementing an object as a collection of concurrently executing objects. Whatever approach is chosen, it is important that internal concurrency be transparent to the object's clients so that sequential implementations of objects may be replaced by parallel ones.

4. *Reply scheduling transparency:* A client should not be forced to wait until the serving object replies. In the meantime it may itself accept further requests or call other objects in parallel. It may even want replies to be directly sent to a proxy. Request

Criteria for Evaluating Language Design Choices 45

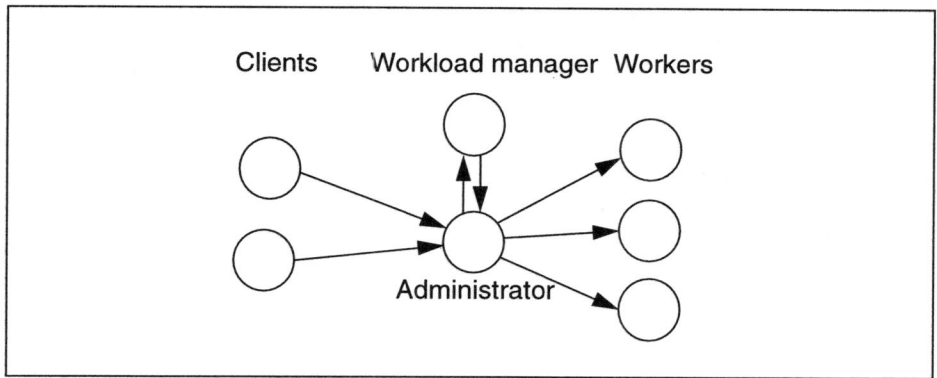

Figure 2.5 *The administrator example.*

scheduling by the client should not require the cooperation of the server since this would limit the ability to combine independently developed clients and servers.

2.3.1.2 An Example

In order to compare the design choices and their combinations with respect to the reuse requirements, we shall refer to an instance of a "generic" concurrent program structure: the *administrator* inspired by [39]. The administrator is an object that uses a collection of "worker" objects to service requests. An administrator application consists of four main kinds of components. The *clients* issue requests to the administrator and get back results. The *administrator* accepts requests from multiple concurrent clients and decomposes them into a number of subrequests. The *workload manager* maintains the status of workers and pending requests. *Workers* handle the subrequests and reply to the administrator. The administrator collects the intermediate replies and computes the final results to be returned to clients (see figure 2.5).

The administrator is a very general framework for structuring concurrent applications. For example, workers may be very specialized resources or they may be general-purpose compute servers. The workload manager may seek to maximize parallelism by load balancing or it may allocate jobs to workers based on their individual capabilities.

The components described above identify functionally distinct parts of the application that could have been developed independently and reused as indicated above to construct a new application. These components do not have to be implemented as single objects, and indeed, as we see later, depending on the constructs provided by certain languages, several objects will be necessary for realizing the desired functionality. However, it should be possible to modify the implementation of the above components without affecting the rest as if they were single objects.

The following points relate the language design requirements listed above to the reuse issues in the case of the example application:

- *Mutual exclusion:* (i) Workload manager reuse – the workload manager must be protected from concurrent requests by the administrator. There may be cases where the administrator does not invoke the workload manager concurrently. Although in such cases no protection is needed, workload managers that are not protected could not be reused in different concurrent implementations of the administrator. In such a concurrent implementation the administrator may use a collection of proxies that may invoke the workload manager concurrently. (ii) Worker reuse – workers should similarly be protected so that arbitrary objects may be used as workers with various implementations of the administrator, including concurrent ones.
- *Request scheduling transparency:* (iii) Genericity of clients, reusing the administrator with different clients — the administrator must be able to interleave (or delay) multiple client requests, but the client should not be required to take special action. In fact it should be possible to implement any object as an administrator and it should not matter to the object's clients if the serving object happens to be implemented as an administrator.
- *Internal concurrency:* (iv) Client/worker reuse — the administrator should be open to concurrent implementation (possibly using proxies) without constraining the interface of either clients or workers;
- *Reply scheduling transparency:* (v) Worker reuse — it must be possible for the administrator to issue requests to workers concurrently and to receive their replies when it chooses without special action by workers;

2.3.2 Inheritance and Synchronization

There are two main issues concerning reuse at a finer granularity than objects.
- The first is to maintain in concurrent languages the reuse potential offered by inheritance in sequential languages. Several early papers have reported difficulties in using class inheritance in COOPLs as well as in the design of languages that integrate class inheritance and concurrency constructs [19] [6] [22]. In some cases inheritance was left out as it was deemed difficult to integrate and of limited use. The need to synchronize the execution of inherited, overridden and newly defined methods, without breaking the encapsulation between classes, makes it more difficult to take advantage of class inheritance than in sequential languages. For instance, if mutexes are used for synchronizing method execution, a method defined in a subclass would have to access a mutex defined in a superclass in order to be synchronized with superclass methods. This would break encapsulation between classes. The design of concurrency constructs should be made in way to avoid such problems.
- The second is to make it possible to reuse algorithms, often called *synchronization constraints*, for scheduling the execution of methods of a class. For instance, a class may implement a synchronization algorithm that schedules its methods according to the readers and writers synchronization scheme. It would be desirable to be able to

Criteria for Evaluating Language Design Choices 47

reuse this algorithm in other classes taking into account the reader/writer property of its methods.

In most languages the reuse of synchronization constraints is achieved through class inheritance and the term *inheritance of synchronization constraints* is often used for this issue. We have chosen the term *reuse of synchronization constraints* since class inheritance is only one possible means to achieve reuse. Furthermore, it is questionable whether class inheritance should be used for this purpose. We will further elaborate on this point below. Then, we will discuss separately the requirements for supporting class inheritance and for reusing synchronization constraints.

Inheritance is often considered as the most prominent feature of object-oriented programming. The most widespread object-oriented languages such as C++, Smalltalk and Eiffel provide an inheritance mechanism that may be used for different purposes. These include: the reuse of the implementation of a class in the implementation of a new class; the specification of a type compatibility relation between a class and its parent classes, considering for type-checking purposes that instances of the class are of the same type as instances of its superclasses; finally, it may be used to express that the concept or entity modelled by the subclass is, in some sense, a refinement of the concepts or entities represented by its parent classes.

The use of a single mechanism for all these purposes can, on one hand, be a source of confusion and on the other, limit the effectiveness of the mechanism for each of these different purposes. For instance, subtypes have to be related to a class inheritance relationship even if they do not share any part of their implementation. In order to use part of the implementation of a class in a new class, all the methods have to be inherited to comply with the subtype relation that is also expressed by the inheritance link. Wegner and Zdonik [88] provide a general and in-depth discussion of inheritance as an incremental modification mechanism and illustrate its use for different purposes. Guide [48] and POOL-I [8] are concrete examples of languages with mechanisms that distinguish between the different uses of inheritance. Both languages distinguish between class inheritance as a code reuse mechanism and typing. POOL-I goes even further by also allowing the specification of behaviourally compatible classes.

In section 2.4.3 we will examine more closely the approaches for the reuse of synchronization constraints followed by different languages. This will illustrate the interactions that class inheritance may have with the reuse of synchronization constraints in these different approaches.

2.3.2.1 Class Inheritance

The issues listed below have to be addressed in order to take advantage effectively of the reuse potential of inheritance. The first two are concerned with the reuse of superclass methods. The third one concerns the use of inheritance for providing generic algorithms through the definition and refinement of *abstract classes* [36] [44].

- *Separate specification of the synchronization constraints:* If the code that implements the synchronization decisions related to the execution of methods is included

directly in methods, inherited methods typically will have to be modified to account for the synchronization constraints of the subclass [45].
- *Interface between methods and the synchronization constraints:* The separate specification of synchronization control actions and method code does not necessarily mean that the execution of methods once started should be carried out without any further interaction with the synchronization constraints. Such an approach limits the expressive power of a language. Instead, there should be a well-defined interface between methods and the synchronization constraints that allows several actions in the execution of the method to interact with the synchronization constraints associated with the various classes where it is reused.
- *Consistency with other uses of inheritance for software composition:* Apart from reusing individual methods, inheritance serves to facilitate sharing of algorithms and designs [36]. For this purpose, inheritance is paired with other features such as invocation of methods through pseudo-variables such as *self* or *super* in Smalltalk.

2.3.2.2 Reuse of Synchronization Constraints

The issues discussed below are important for evaluating and comparing the proposals for the specification and reuse of synchronization constraints:
- *Flexibility of the binding mechanism:* The mechanism that is used to apply constraints to a particular class determines the flexibility with which constraints may be reused. Depending on the mechanism, constraints are bound to exactly one class (the class where they were introduced), or to any class that inherits from the class that introduced the constraints. Additionally, method names appearing in a constraint specification may be considered as variables to be substituted at binding time with method names defined in a particular class.
- *Compositionality and extensibility:* This concerns the support provided for reusing previously defined constraints in the definition of new ones. A related issue is extending the application of constraints to methods that are introduced at a later stage.
- *Polymorphism:* The potential applicability of constraints to different classes. This is related to the binding mechanism and modularity; constraints could be specified in a way that would allow them to be applied to different classes. However, this may be impossible or inconvenient because of the absence of an appropriate binding mechanism.
- *Modifiability and locality of change:* There are circumstances where it may be desirable or necessary to change the implementation of a class or of just the synchronization constraint. Depending on the approach, this may be achieved easily through some local modification or it may require a cascade of changes in synchronization constraints. In some cases it may even be needed to modify the inheritance hierarchy. Most of the other aspects discussed above come into play when considering this issue.

2.4 Exploring the Language Design Space

We now propose to compare the various approaches to the design of COOPLs by systematically exploring the language design space and evaluating design choices against the requirements specified in the previous section. Since the various aspects of the design space are sometimes intertwined, we will find ourselves returning to common issues on occasion. Basically we will take the following course: first we briefly consider the three categories of object models; then we consider object interaction mechanisms in combination with internal concurrency; finally we explore inheritance and synchronization constraints as a topic worthy of separate study. We summarize our conclusions in section 2.4.4.

2.4.1 Object Models

By the requirement of mutual exclusion, we can immediately discount the orthogonal object model as it provides no default protection for objects in the presence of concurrent requests. The reusability of workers and workload managers is clearly enhanced if they will function correctly independently of assumptions of sequential access.

The heterogeneous model is similarly defective since one must explicitly distinguish between active and passive objects. A generic administrator would be less reusable if it would have to distinguish between active and passive workers. Similarly worker reusability is weakened if we can have different kinds of workers.

The *homogeneous* object model is the most reasonable choice with respect to reusability. No distinction is made between active and passive objects.

Note that it is not clear whether the performance gains one might expect of a heterogeneous model are realizable since they depend on the programmer's (static) assignment of objects to active or passive classes. With a homogeneous approach, the compiler could conceivably make such decisions based on local consideration — whether a component is shared by other concurrently executing objects is application specific and should be independent of the object type.

2.4.2 Object Interaction Mechanisms

Request-reply mechanisms such as an RPC-like interface provide more support for object reuse. Using our administrator example, we can see that one-way message passing has several disadvantages over RPC for reusing objects.

A concurrent client may issue several requests to the administrator before it gets a reply. In this case it is important for the client to know which reply corresponds to which request. Are replies returned in the same order as requests? In the case of synchronous message passing an additional difficulty is that the administrator may get blocked when it sends the reply until the client is willing to accept it. Requiring the client to accept the reply imposes additional requirements on the client and makes reuse more difficult. Either a different mechanism has to be supported for sending replies or proxies have to be created.

One-way message passing is also inconvenient for coping with the interaction between the administrator and worker objects. A difficulty with using one-way messages is getting the replies from workers: as there will be several workers that are invoked in parallel, as well as potentially concurrent invocations of single worker, it can be difficult for the administrator to tell which reply is associated with which request.

A solution to this problem is to create a proxy for each request. The proxy would carry out the request and then send a message to the administrator containing the worker's reply plus some extra information used for identifying the request. As with sequential RPC the administrator will also have to manage local queues for partially completed requests.

2.4.2.1 Sequential Objects

We argued that an RPC interface for objects provides better support for object reuse than one-way message passing. However, we quickly discover that if objects have a single thread of control and RPC is the only communication mechanism, the request and reply scheduling requirements of the administrator are not satisfied. We further discuss the limitation of this design choice combination below. Then we show additional mechanisms that may be used to overcome these limitations without giving up the RPC-interface or completely discarding sequential object design choice. The limitation of the combination of sequential objects ("modules" in their case) and RPC is discussed at length in [54]. However, they reach the conclusion that either the sequential object or the RPC choice should be discarded.

Limitations of the Sequential Object-RPC Combination

In particular, a sequential RPC administrator will not be able to interleave multiple clients' requests as it will be forced to reply to a client before it can accept another request. The only "solution" under this assumption requires the cooperation of the client, for example: the administrator returns the name of a "request handler" proxy to the client, which the client must call to obtain the result. In this way the administrator is immediately free to accept new requests after returning the name of the request handler. Such an approach is, however, incompatible with the requirement on request scheduling transparency since scheduling of requests by the administrator is not transparent to its clients.

Consider for instance that we would like to replace the sequential implementation of an existing object class by a parallel implementation where instances of the class act as administrators for a collection of appropriate worker objects. In accord with our requirements we would like to take advantage of encapsulation and data abstraction to replace the old implementation without having to modify the programs that used it. This, however, is not possible since, as discussed above, in order to be able to process client requests concurrently, an object, implemented as an administrator, has to have a different interface than an object having a sequential implementation.

Exploring the Language Design Space

The sequential RPC combination also provides limited support for reply scheduling by the administrator. If the administrator invokes workers directly using RPC, its single thread will get blocked until the invoked worker computes the result and returns the reply. The sequential RPC combination prevents the administrator from invoking several workers in parallel, or accepting further client requests while a worker computes the result and receiving the workers' replies at a later time.

It is also possible to have the workers cooperate with the administrator so that it does not block when delegating work to them, but such solutions require workers to be coded in a special way to implement the cooperation. This is incompatible with our requirement of request scheduling transparency, which would allow any object to be potentially used as a worker.

Using Proxies for Reply Scheduling

The limitation of the sequential RPC combination for reply scheduling can be overcome by the use of "courier" proxies used by the administrator to invoke workers. Each time the administrator needs to invoke a worker it creates an appropriate courier proxy that will invoke the worker instead. To get a worker's reply, the administrator could invoke a method of the corresponding courier or alternatively the courier could call an administrator's method when the reply becomes available.

The former alternative has the disadvantage that the administrator may get blocked if it invokes the courier too early. This may never occur with the latter approach. However, the administrator has to manage local queues for replies that are sent to it and that it cannot use immediately. Furthermore, each time a reply is returned, it should check whether all the replies needed so far for handling a client's request are available so that it may proceed with the client's request.

The use of proxy objects for carrying out requests and for storing replies is also needed in the case of one-way message passing for allowing requests to be paired with replies.

Although proxies are a general programming approach, it is cumbersome to program and use them explicitly. In fact unless the language supports classes with type parameters and a flexible manipulation of method names, a new proxy class would have to be defined for each different worker class in an administrator application.

Future variables in ABCL/1 [94], the *process* type in PAL [18] and CBox objects in ConcurrentSmalltalk [92] provide functionality which is somewhat similar to the courier proxies that were used by the administrator to call workers. These mechanisms could be used by the administrator to call workers without getting blocked and for collecting worker replies at a later time.

The advantage of these mechanisms over program-defined proxies is that they can be used for calling workers of any class. Future variables, however, are not first-class objects and so are not as flexible. For instance, a future variable cannot be sent in a message allowing a different object than the one that made the request to receive the reply.

A difficulty with built-in proxies is that the administrator may at some point in time have to get blocked and wait for a further client request or the reply to a previous worker request. Unless there exists a synchronization mechanism that allows the administrator to wait on either of these events, the administrator may get blocked to obtain a reply or request that is not available and will thus be unable to accept other requests or replies. This problem could be circumvented either by polling if a non-blocking request acceptance mechanism is supported or by additional, explicitly programmed proxies that would return the replies by invoking some administrator's operation especially provided for that purpose. This way a synchronization mechanism for selectively accepting requests would allow the administrator to be woken up either for receiving the results of a previous requests or for accepting new requests.

Still, the administrator's code may get quite involved. If there is no way to prevent being woken up by messages containing client requests or worker replies that cannot be used right away, local message queues will have to be managed by the administrator. So, it appears that built-in proxies combined with single-thread objects provide limited support for reply scheduling by the administrator since one should again rely on the use of explicitly programmed proxies.

Combining Request/Reply and One-Way Message Passing

It is also possible to relax the RPC style of communication without going all the way to supporting one-way message passing as the main communication primitive. This has the advantage that it is possible to present an RPC interface to clients and, at the same time, obtain more flexibility for processing requests by the administrator. This possibility is illustrated by ABCL/1 [94] which permits the pairing of an RPC interface at the client side with one-way asynchronous message passing at the administrator's side. Moreover, the reply message does not have to be sent by the administrator object. This provides even more flexibility in the way that the administrator may handle requests since the replies may be directly returned to the client by proxies. The following segment of code shows how this is accomplished.

The RPC call at the client side looks like:

  result := [administrator <== :someRequest arg1 ... argn] ...

A message is sent to the administrator to execute the request someRequest with arguments arg1,...,argn. The client is blocked until the reply to the request is returned and the result is stored in the client's local variable result.

At the administrator's side the client's request is accepted by matching the message pattern:

  (=> :someRequest arg1 ... argn @ whereToReply
   .... *actions executed in response to this request* ...)

When the administrator accepts this request, the arguments are made available in the local variables arg1,...,argn and the *reply destination* of the request in the local variable whereToReply. The reply destination may be used as the target of a "past type," i.e. asynchronous, message for returning the reply to the client. As a reply destination may also be passed around in messages, it is possible for another object to send the reply message to the client. This action would look like:

[whereToReply <== result]

where whereToReply is a local variable containing the reply destination obtained by the message acceptance statement shown above, and result is the result of the client's request.

Another interesting way of using the possibility to combine one-way message passing with RPC is for flexible reply scheduling by the administrator. In the previous section, on built-in proxies, we mentioned that a difficulty was that the administrator should be able to wait to accept both returned replies and further requests. A way to circumvent this problem was to use explicitly programmed proxies that would return results by invoking some operation provided by the administrator. In this way, replies were returned by requests so that a request acceptance mechanism was sufficient for allowing the administrator to wait for both requests and replies. A different approach is possible by pairing one-way messages to the RPC interface supported by workers. With this approach, the administrator may use a past type message, with itself as reply destination, for calling the workers which present an RPC interface. The replies from the workers can then be received by the administrator as any past-type message request. This allows the administrator to use the message acceptance mechanism for receiving both requests and replies.

This approach has, however, some of the drawbacks of one-way message passing: some extra work is needed in order to find out which reply message is related to what request and also that the administrator has to manage queues for replies that may not be used immediately.

2.4.2.2 Multi-Threaded Objects

Another way for allowing the administrator to service several concurrent requests is by supporting multiple concurrent or quasi-concurrent threads. A separate concurrent thread may now be used for handling each client request. However, depending on the mechanisms provided for thread creation and scheduling, it may still be necessary to resort to the solutions discussed previously in order to achieve a satisfactory level of concurrency in the processing of client requests.

We consider in turn quasi-concurrent and concurrent approaches and examine the support provided by the thread creation and scheduling mechanisms for programming administrators.

Quasi-Concurrent Approaches

A traditional example of "objects" with quasi-concurrent thread structure is provided by monitors [42] [21]. However, monitors present some well-known difficulties such as "nested monitor calls," and they unduly constrain parallelism [56] [77] [20] when used as the main modular units of concurrent programs. These limitations are due to some extent to the quasi-concurrent structure of threads. However, an approach based on monitors would also constrain concurrency among different objects because of its limited support for reply scheduling. Assuming that the administrator is a monitor, then when calling a worker the monitor would remain blocked until the invoked operation would return. This situation, called *remote delay* [53], makes it impossible for the administrator to accept further client requests or to call a second worker.

Consequently, certain object-oriented languages have adopted more flexible variations. For example, Emerald [19] uses monitors as defined by Hoare [42]. However, not all operations of an object have to be declared as monitor procedures and also several independent monitors may be used in the implementation of an object. *Lock blocks* and *wait queues* in Trellis/Owl [68] also allow for more flexible implementation schemes than if objects were identified to monitors. With this approach, however, objects in these languages are not quasi-concurrent any more.

The restricted support for concurrency among objects by monitors is not due to the quasi-concurrent structure of objects, but rather to the limited flexibility for reply scheduling. This is illustrated by the second quasi-concurrent approach we examine which by providing a more flexible reply scheduling scheme does not restrict concurrency among objects.

Hybrid [71] is another language which adopts a quasi-concurrent thread structure for objects. However, in contrast to monitors, the *delegated call* mechanism provides a more flexible reply scheduling approach that does not restrain concurrency among objects. The administrator may use the delegated call mechanism to invoke workers. In such a case a new thread may be activated in the administrator for processing another client request in the meantime.

The delegated call mechanism is satisfactory for allowing the administrator to accept further client requests while a worker is executing a previous request, thus providing support for concurrency among several client requests. However, it is of no help for allowing several workers to execute in parallel for a single client request.

This may only be done by using proxies for invoking the workers or by a construct for specifying the creation of a new quasi-concurrent thread. Such a construct was proposed in the original design of Hybrid. The newly created quasi-concurrent threads would resume each other by using delegated calls. This construct was not included in the prototype because it substantially increased the complexity of the rules for message acceptance.

Concurrent Objects

With concurrent threads it is straightforward to process several client requests concurrently by creating a new thread for processing each client request. Provided that satisfactory mechanisms are supported for constraining the creation and activation of concurrent threads, this does not result in the mutual exclusion problems of languages with an orthog-

Exploring the Language Design Space 55

onal object model. The concurrent execution that may take place is explicitly specified by the programmer and the scope of the potential interference of the concurrent threads is restricted to the state of a single object.

Provided that there is some way to suspend the execution of a concurrent thread or avoid its creation, languages that support concurrent threads provide adequate support for request scheduling and for internal concurrency to the extent that several client requests may be processed concurrently.

A different issue that is not necessarily addressed by the support for concurrent threads is the possibility to use concurrency for processing a single request. Unless the creation of multiple threads can be initiated by the object, the support for reply scheduling of concurrent threads is not sufficient for processing a request in parallel.

For example, the language Sina [84] makes it possible to use several concurrent threads within an object for processing requests; there is no direct means, however, for one of these threads to create more threads for calling the worker objects in parallel. This is done indirectly by creating a courier proxy, as described previously. It is therefore not necessarily redundant to support both multiple threads and non-blocking communication primitives.

A satisfactory way for calling workers in parallel without using proxies or asynchronous message passing is to support a construct by which more threads may be created in the object. In this case a worker can be called by each of these threads in an RPC fashion. With quasi-concurrent threads, a call to a worker should trigger the execution of another thread. In SR the code segment of the administrator that is used for issuing requests to workers in parallel would look like this:

```
co    result1 := w1.doWork(...) -> loadManager.terminated(w1)
//    result2 := w2.doWork(...) -> loadManager.terminated(w2)
oc
globalResult := computResult(result1,result2);
...
```

2.4.3 Inheritance and Reuse of Synchronization Constraints

A large body of research has concentrated on the issues of making effective use of inheritance in COOPLs as well as on the related issue of reusing synchronization constraints. We will provide a brief overview of this work. Then we will turn our attention to the issues discussed in section 2.3.2 and illustrate the issues and how they are addressed by various language designs putting particular emphasis on some points that have not received the attention they deserved in related work. More extensive presentations and systematic comparisons of the proposals for supporting inheritance and the reuse of synchronization constraints may be found in [63] [60] and [16].

2.4.3.1 A Brief Overview of Related Research

Eiffel// [26][27] and Guide [34][48] were two of the earliest proposals that attempted to combine inheritance and synchronization constraints by removing the constraints from the bodies of methods.

These approaches presented some shortcomings with respect to the ability to extend the synchronization constraints to account for new methods introduced by subclasses. The problems were independently identified by Kafura and Lee [45] and Tomlinson and Singh [83], who in turn proposed their own approaches for overcoming them. A common aspect of these proposals is that constraints are specified by associating sets of methods to abstractions of the object state in which they can be executed. The main idea was that the set of methods would be extended in subclasses with the additional methods.

Matsuoka *et al.* [62], however, showed that there existed certain cases, called *inheritance anomalies*, where new state abstractions would have to be introduced in subclasses, consequently requiring extensive redefinition of inherited methods. Matsuoka later proposed his own approach, where he retained the idea of sets of acceptable methods, and provided a combination of guards and accept sets allowing the best technique to be used for the problem at hand.

The issue of extending and combining inherited constraints was also addressed in various other proposals, notably: Synchronizing Actions [69], Scheduling Predicates [59], Ceiffel [57], Frølund's framework [37], PO [29], SINA [16] and SPN [74]. It is important to note that Synchronizing Actions and SPN are two of the very few proposals to consider the issue of suspending method execution, which is important for reply scheduling.

The language DRAGOON [13][14] supports the specification of generic synchronization constraints and provides a special inheritance mechanism separate from class inheritance of sequential aspects of classes for reusing these synchronization constraints.

Meseguer [67] has proposed a somewhat different approach for avoiding the problems related to the use of inheritance in COOPLs. He proposes to eliminate the synchronization code which causes inheritance anomalies. His language is based on a concurrent rewriting logic; the use of appropriate rewrite rules allows the specification of synchronization without introducing inheritance anomalies.

Synchronizers [38] is an approach for the specification of synchronization constraints that allows constraints to be associated to objects dynamically. An interesting point about this proposal is that constraints may depend on the state and computation history of several other objects.

2.4.3.2 Binding Mechanisms for Synchronization Constraints

The most direct way to associate synchronization constraints to methods is to specify them together as part of a class definition. Constraints defined in a class are inherited by the ordinary class inheritance mechanism. Such an approach is followed by most COOPLs, such as Guide, PO, PROCOL and ACT++, to name a few. This approach, however, has the shortcoming that it may be difficult to apply constraints to different classes. A first problem is with method names: if constraints refer to particular method names of the class in which they are defined, it will be difficult to apply them to classes where meth-

Exploring the Language Design Space

(a)
```
with SIMPLE;
class UNI_BUFFER
   introduces
      procedure PUT(I : in SIMPLE.ITEM);
      procedure PEEK (NB: out INTEGER);
end UNI_BUFFER;
```

(b)
```
class body UNI_BUFFER is
   ... definition of the instance variables and
       implementation of the operations...
end UNI_BUFFER;
```

(c)
```
behavioural class READERS_WRITERS is
   ruled WOP, ROP;
   where
      per (WOP) <=> active(WOP) + active(ROP) = 0;
      per(ROP) <=> (active(WOP) = 0) and (requested(WOP) = 0);
end READERS_WRITERS;
```

(d)
```
class READERS_WRITERS_UNI_BUFFER
   inherits UNI_BUFFER
   ruled by READERS_WRITERS
   where
      PUT => WOP,
      PEEK => ROP
end;
```

Figure 2.6 *Constraint definition in DRAGOON.*

ods have different names. Another problem comes from the use of class inheritance for reusing constraints. If one uses class inheritance to reuse the constraints, the methods defined in the class are also inherited. Below we examine some approaches that have been proposed for addressing these problems.

Genericity of Synchronization Constraints in DRAGOON

DRAGOON [13] [14] is an example of a language that supports the specification of generic synchronization constraints and of one that dissociates inheritance from the mechanism used for binding synchronization constraints to a class's methods. Generic constraints are defined as behavioural classes (b-classes). The constraints may be applied to a *sequential* class having no associated constraints, through the b-inheritance (behavioural) mechanism. This mechanism is independent from the inheritance mechanism (f-inheritance) used for sequential classes. Figure 2.6 shows an example of the use of the constraint definition and binding mechanism in DRAGOON. A class UNI_BUFFER is defined in (a) and (b) with methods PUT and PEEK used to insert a new element into the buffer and to examine the number of elements in the buffer. In (c) a generic constraint READERS_WRITERS is defined for controlling execution of the methods of a class according to the readers, and writers, scheduling policy [81]. This synchronization constraint is bound to the class UNI_BUFFER in (d) where PUT is associated with the constraints for writers and PEEK with the ones for readers.

Using the Inheritance mechanism of Beta

A similar effect for specifying and binding constraints may be achieved by using the *inner* mechanism of Beta. In Beta a method in a subclass is associated with the superclass method it specializes. Instead of the subclass method explicitly invoking the superclass method through the use of *super* mechanism, as in Smalltalk, the superclass method is *always* invoked, and subclasses may only introduce additional behaviour at the point where the keyword inner occurs. In a sense, the execution of the superclass method is wrapped around the invoked subclass method. First are executed the actions in the superclass method that precede inner, then the subclass method is executed, then the actions of the superclass method that follow inner are executed.

This feature may be combined with low-level synchronization mechanisms, such as semaphores, to implement classes that encapsulate generic synchronization policies that can be applied to methods defined in subclasses in a way similar to how it is done in DRAGOON.

Assume there is a class ReaderWriterSched (not shown) with methods reader and writer that use semaphores to implement a reader/writer scheduling policy for the methods reader and writer. This synchronization may be applied to a class SynchedBuffer with operations empty, get, put as follows:

```
SynchedBuffer: @ | ReaderWriterSched
   (# .... instance variables....
       peek:    Reader(# ...implementation of peek... #)
       get:     Writer(# ...implementation of get... #)
       put:     Writer(# ....implementation of put..#)
   #)
```

This allows the execution of peek to be constrained according the synchronization constraints of a reader, whereas get and put are synchronized according to the synchronization constraints that apply to writers. More on the use of inheritance in Beta to define generic synchronization policies can be found in [58].

Method Sets and Abstract Classes in ABCL/AP100

The *method set* feature provided in this language may be combined with abstract classes to define generic synchronization constraints that can be applied to several classes. Method sets are specified as part of class definitions, and are associated with synchronization constraints. Method sets can be inherited and modified in subclasses. Systematic use of methods sets solves the problem of applying constraints to classes with different method names. The possibility of combining method sets with abstract classes (classes where not all methods are defined) can be used to provide facilities similar to those of DRAGOON. Abstract classes, making systematic use of method sets in synchronization constraints, can be used to represent generic constraints similar to DRAGOON's b-classes. However, in contrast to DRAGOON, programmers have to use the features provided by the language in a disciplined way. Another interesting feature of this language, discussed below, is that it is possible to combine synchronization constraints.

2.4.3.3 Polymorphism and Synchronization Constraints

Polymorphism of synchronization constraints is concerned with the potential applicability of constraints to different classes provided that the language supports an appropriate binding mechanism. There are two potential deficiencies with respect to this issue in approaches for specifying synchronization. The first is related to the use of instance variables in conditions constraining the activation of methods. The second concerns the use of constraints that specify mutual exclusion among methods in languages that support intra-object concurrency.

The first deficiency, also discussed by Bergmans [16], occurs in the proposals of Frølund [37] and Matsuoka [63], and in Guide and PROCOL, to cite a few examples. In these languages the conditions that are used in their constraints reference the object's instance variables. This makes it difficult to apply the constraints to classes implemented in a way that does not require these instance variables. Moreover, it makes it difficult to change the implementation of a class without having to consider the instance variables referenced in the constraints and, eventually, modifying the constraints as well. The problem may also be more severe than just modifying the constraints of a single class, as the constraints to be modified may be used by other subclasses as well. This could cause the re-examination and adjustment of the constraints of several subclasses of the class that was modified.

Two approaches have been be followed for alleviating this problem. First, instead of accessing directly the instance variables, conditions could be specified through a function that accesses the object state indirectly. If the implementation had to be modified, only these functions would need to be modified to account for the changes in the object state. This approach is followed for this precise reason by Sina in the way conditions are specified in wait filters [16] as well as in the specification of state predicates [74]. A second approach is to use condition variables to maintain an abstract state that is separate from the actual class implementation and is used purely for synchronization purposes. This approach is followed Synchronizing Actions, DRAGOON and PO.

The second potential deficiency occurs in languages with intra-object concurrency. In several languages with intra-object concurrency, such as Guide, DRAGOON and PO, synchronization constraints specify mutual exclusion properties among methods. The main reason for imposing mutual exclusion constraints on method executions is that method implementations access common instance variables. However, a different or modified implementation of a class may use a different set of instance variables and may have different needs for mutual exclusion. Consequently, constraints that specify mutual exclusion properties among methods may find limited applicability to classes with a different implementation. Also, modifying the implementation of a class to which such constraints are attached, as discussed above for guards that reference instance variables, may cause the modification of the constraints attached to several classes. This problem, however, has not received any attention by other work in the area.

2.4.3.4 Extensibility and Compositionality

In languages such as DRAGOON, the issue of combining synchronization constraints is avoided by the way the language is designed; inheritance is not allowed among classes that are associated with synchronization constraints, r-classes, or the classes (b-classes) that are use to describe the constraints themselves. This approach has advantages and disadvantages. The separation of constraints from classes allows the use of inheritance between f-classes without having to be concerned how the associated constraints would have to be combined. The disadvantage is that there is no support for reusing constraints in the definition of new ones.

In other languages the issue of combining constraints is addressed either because class inheritance mechanism is tight up to the constraint binding mechanism or to allow constraints to be defined incrementally.

Frølund [37] proposed an approach for combining constraints of a class with those introduced in subclasses based on the view that constraints should become stricter in subclasses. The proposed approach for combining constraints supports this view by incrementally combining conditions that disable method execution. This way conditions may only become more strict in subclasses.

Matsuoka [63] provides a more elaborate way of combining constraints through modification of *method sets* and by the fact that method sets are recomputed in a subclass taking into account the full set of methods including the methods inherited from all superclasses. For instance, the method set all-except(LOCKED), where LOCKED is another method set defined elsewhere, denotes all the object's methods except the ones in LOCKED. This method set is recomputed in subclasses to account for additional methods defined in the subclass or inherited from other superclasses. Such features enable the definition of mixins that can be combined with the constraints of other classes to obtain the synchronization behaviour specified by the mixin. An example of such a mixin class is presented in [63].

A powerful way of composing synchronization constraints is also provided by wait filters in Sina. In order to get accepted, messages are matched against patterns of *wait filters*. Wait filters are associated with conditions, a form of guards, that must be true to let matching messages go through the filter. Filters can be stacked at the interface of an object and messages have to traverse all of them before being accepted by the object. Bergmans shows in [16] how this approach can be used for the locking mixin and for other constraint composition examples. The locking mixin discussed above can be realized by a class that provides a wait filter that matches all messages but unlock and is associated with a condition, Unlocked, that is true only when the object is unlocked. Lock and Unlock methods change the state of a lock object so as to render the Unlock condition false and true respec-

Exploring the Language Design Space 61

tively. A lock object can be used in the definition of another class in such a way that messages have to go through its filter first. In this way the synchronization constraint defined by lock can be reused in other classes.

PO [29] also supports the composition of constraints defined in superclasses of a class. In contrast to the proposals of Frølund and Matsuoka, where objects are single-threaded, PO constraints are designed for objects with internal concurrency. Constraints on the parallel execution of methods are partially ordered in a lattice with fully parallel execution of methods at the top and mutual exclusion among all methods at the bottom of the lattice. When incompatible constraints are inherited from different superclasses, they are compared according to this order and the more strict constraint is retained.

2.4.3.5 Combining Inheritance with Request/Reply Scheduling

In most work on the design of mechanisms for the specification and reuse of synchronization constraints, little attention has been paid to the eventuality that methods may have to be suspended halfway through their execution. However, as we discussed in section 2.4.2 this may be necessary to support reply scheduling. The possibility of suspending methods using mechanisms designed for the reuse of synchronization constraints is addressed in Synchronizing Actions [69] and in the design of the *state predicate* [74] mechanism.

Synchronizing Actions are based on multi-thread objects. The execution of a method may be suspended by calling, through *self*, another method with a pre-action such that the call is delayed. This approach may be used to support request and reply scheduling for the administrator as shown in figure 2.7. The administrator calls workers by creating proxy objects that do the actual call. After creating a proxy the administrator thread is suspended by calling the method suspend. The proxy calls the worker and when the call returns it calls the workerDone method to cause the administrator thread to be resumed. Figure 2.7 illustrates the implementation of the administrator concentrating on the synchronization aspects. Other languages that support internally concurrent objects and flexible specification of synchronization constraints, for instance Guide or Sina, could be used in a similar way. This approach, however, has some shortcomings. First, its complexity would make it difficult to use in practice. Second, it relies on the assumption that methods invoked through self are subject to the same constraints as invocations from other objects. This may not be appropriate when self is used in conjunction with inheritance to reuse algorithms defined in abstract superclasses.

The state predicate approach [74] provides a simpler and more direct way for suspending method execution based on a state predicate. The effect is similar to the one achieved by the approach discussed above. However, the resulting code is simpler as thread suspension and resumption is supported by the language and the complications deriving from the need to call the objects methods through self are avoided.

2.4.4 Summary

Below we present our observations with respect to reuse issues resulting from our exploration of language design approaches.

```
class Admin;                                        method workerDone()
concurrency_control:                                  matching (true)
   boolean worker_finished := false,                  pre { worker_finished := true }
         admin_idle := true;                          action { }
                                                      post { }
method suspend()
   matching (true)                                  method request()
   pre { admin_idle := true }                         matching ( admin_idle )
   action{                                            pre { admin_idle := false}
      self!waitWorker ()                              action {
   }                                                     do some local processing...
   post { admin_idle := false}                          request := worker_proxy.doWork();
                                                        self!waitWorker ();
method waitWorker()                                     ...some more processing...
   matching (worker_finished );                      }
   pre { worker_finished := false;admin_idle := false   post { admin_idle := true };
   }
   action { }
   post { };
```

Figure 2.7 *Request/reply scheduling with synchronization constraints.*

Object-Based Features

- *Homogeneous object models promote reuse:* Concurrent applications can safely reuse objects developed for sequential applications; efficiency need not be sacrificed.
- *Sequential objects with strict RPC are inadequate:* Request scheduling and internal concurrency can only be implemented by sacrificing the RPC interface; the solution is either to support concurrent threads or to relax the strict RPC protocol.
- *One-way message passing is expressive but undesirable*: Since higher-level request-reply protocols must be explicitly programmed, development and reuse of objects is potentially more error-prone.
- *Acceptance of concurrent requests is handled well either by concurrent threads or by explicit request/reply scheduling.*
- *Issuing concurrent requests is handled well by one-way message passing, by proxies or by internal concurrency:* The combination of both concurrent threads and non-blocking communication primitives may be appropriate for handling the separate issues of accepting and issuing concurrent requests.
- *Built-in proxies* used by *sequential objects* with non-blocking request issuing mechanisms provide adequate support for reply scheduling but are weak at combining reply and request scheduling.
- *Both concurrent objects and multi-object approaches are useful for internal concurrency:* These approaches for internal concurrency are both useful for different purposes. Concurrent threads make it easy to implement objects that may service several concurrent requests that do not modify the objects state. Multi-object approaches are

interesting when the implementation of a new object class, with internal concurrency, may be realized by using several concurrently executing instances of existing object classes.

Inheritance and Synchronization Constraints

- *Synchronization constraints should not be hardwired in methods:* If the synchronization code that schedules the execution of methods is hardwired in methods, it will be necessary to modify the method code in order to meet the constraints of other classes.
- *Multiple threads are needed to cope with reply scheduling:* To support reply scheduling it is important to be able to suspend the execution of a method. However, it seems difficult to do this if synchronization code is kept separate from methods to support inheritance.
- *Method suspension and resumption should be taken into account by synchronization constraints*: Taking into account the suspension of method execution by the mechanism that implements the synchronization constraints makes it simpler to program reply scheduling problems without compromising the reusability of methods.
- *Specification of mutual exclusion may lead to non-polymorphic constraints*: Mutual exclusion properties of methods are often related to the way methods access instance variables. Such constraints may thus not be applicable to classes with different instance variables or in which methods access instance variables in a different way. Including mutual exclusion specifications in constraints makes them less reusable.
- *It is advantageous to separate the reuse of constraints from inheritance.* It is easier to reuse synchronization constraints is they are specified generically and if their application to different classes is not accomplished through class inheritance.

2.5 Conclusion

Integrating concurrency and object-oriented programming is not as easy as it may seem at a first sight. There is no major difficulty in introducing both object-oriented and concurrency features in a single language. However, arbitrary combinations of concurrency and object-oriented features do not allow programmers draw the benefits of object-oriented programming for the development of concurrent systems. These difficulties have fostered substantial research in the past few years in the design of languages that gracefully integrate both kinds of features. However, the interference of the features occurs in several aspects of language design and the various proposals are not equally successful in all these aspects.

In this chapter we have discussed a number of issues that should be addressed in various aspects of language design, and we have formulated some criteria to use in evaluating design choices. We have used these criteria to evaluate various proposals, and we have illustrated the issues by examining specific languages. The languages discussed were chosen to illustrate particular points rather than to present a complete survey of all existing proposals. It was not our intention to compare individual languages; other issues not discussed in this chapter would have to be considered in such an endeavour. Different considerations come in to play, for example, when designing a language for rapid prototyping or a language for programming embedded systems.

We have presented some guidelines for the design of languages that support the basic object-oriented features promoting reuse. Although these seem to be necessary conditions more is needed to achieve reuse at a larger scale. These are research issues which are discussed in other chapters. The further development and the use of techniques for reuse at a larger scale for developing concurrent systems may provide more criteria for evaluating language features and may result in more requirements on language design.

References

[1] Gul Agha, *ACTORS: A Model of Concurrent Computation in Distributed Systems*, MIT Press, Cambridge, Mass., 1986.

[2] Gul Agha and C. J. Callsen, "ActorSpace: An Open Distributed Programming Paradigm," *Proceedings 4th ACM Conference on Principles and Practice of Parallel Programming, ACM SIGPLAN Notices*, vol. 28, no. 7, 1993, pp. 23–323

[3] Alfred V. Aho, Ravi Sethi and Jeffrey D. Ullman, *Compilers Principles, Techniques and Tools*, Addison-Wesley, Reading, Mass., 1986.

[4] Mehmet Aksit, Ken Wakita, Jan Bosch, Lodewijk Bergmans and Akinori Yonezawa, "Abstracting Object Interactions Using Composition Filters," *Proceedings of the ECOOP '93 Workshop on Object-Based Distributed Programming*, ed. R. Guerraoui, O. Nierstrasz, M. Riveill, *Lecture Notes in Computer Science,* vol. 791, Springer-Verlag, 1994, pp. 152–184

[5] Pierre America, "Inheritance and Subtyping in a Parallel Object-Oriented Language," *Proceedings ECOOP '87*, ed. J. Bézivin, J-M. Hullot, P. Cointe and H. Lieberman , *Lecture Notes in Computer Science,* vol. 276, Springer-Verlag, Paris, 1987, pp. 234–242.

[6] Pierre America, "POOL-T: A Parallel Object-Oriented Language," in *Object-Oriented Concurrent Programming*, ed. A. Yonezawa and M. Tokoro, MIT Press, Cambridge, Mass., 1987, pp. 199–220.

[7] Pierre America, "A Behavioural Approach to Subtyping in Object-Oriented Programming Languages," in *Proceedings of the Workshop on Inheritance Hierarchies in Knowledge Representation and Programming Languages*, Viareggio, Italy, Feb. 1989, pp. 141–156.

[8] Pierre America and Frank van der Linden, "A Parallel Object-Oriented Language with Inheritance and Subtyping," *Proceedings OOPSLA'90, ACM SIGPLAN Notices*, vol. 25, no. 10, ACM Press, Oct. 1990, pp. 161–168.

[9] American National Standards Institute, Inc., *The Programming Language Ada Reference Manual*, *Lecture Notes in Computer Science,* vol. 155, Springer-Verlag, 1983.

[10] S. Andler, "Predicate Path Expressions," in *Proceedings of 6th ACM POPL, ACM SIGPLAN Notices*, 1979.

[11] Gregory R. Andrews and Fred B. Schneider, "Concepts and Notations for Concurrent Programming," *ACM Computing Surveys,* vol. 15, no. 1, March 1983, pp. 3–43.

[12] Gregory R. Andrews, R.A. Olsson and M. Coffin, "An Overview of the SR Language and Implementation," *TOPLAS,* vol. 10, no. 1, Jan. 1988, pp. 51–86.

[13] Colin Atkinson, Stephen Goldsack, Andrea Di Maio and R. Bayan,"Object-Oriented Concurrency and Distribution in DRAGOON," *Journal of Object-Oriented Programming,* March/April 1991.

References

[14] Colin Atkinson, *Object-Oriented Reuse, Concurrency and Distribution*, Addison-Wesley/ACM Press, 1991.

[15] Henri E. Bal, J.G. Steiner and Andrew S. Tanenbaum, "Programming Languages for Distributed Computing Systems," *ACM Computing Surveys*, vol. 21, no. 3, Sept. 1989, pp. 261–322.

[16] Lodewijk Bergmans, "Composing Concurrent Objects," Ph.D. Thesis, University of Twente, 1994.

[17] Ted Biggerstaff and C. Richter, "Reusability Framework, Assessment and Directions," *IEEE Software*, vol. 4, no. 2, March 1987, pp. 41–49.

[18] Anders Bjornerstedt and Stefan Britts, "AVANCE: An Object Management System," *Proceedings OOPSLA'88, ACM SIGPLAN Notices*, vol. 23, no. 11, San Diego, Nov. 1988, pp. 206–221.

[19] Andrew Black, Norman Hutchinson, Eric Jul and Henry Levy, "Object Structure in the Emerald System," *Proceedings OOPSLA'86, ACM SIGPLAN Notices*, vol. 21, no. 11, Nov. 1986, pp. 78–86.

[20] Toby Bloom, "Evaluating Synchronisation Mechanisms," in *Proceedings of the Seventh Symposium on Operating System Principles*, ACM-SIGOPS, Dec. 1979.

[21] Per Brinch Hansen, "The Programming Language Concurrent Pascal," *IEEE Transactions on Software Engineering*, vol. SE-1, June 1975, pp. 199–207.

[22] Jean-Pierre Briot and Akinori Yonezawa, "Inheritance and Synchronisation in Concurrent OOP," *Proceedings ECOOP 87*, Paris, June 1987, BIGRE, no. 54, June 1987, pp. 35–43.

[23] Jean-Pierre Briot, "Actalk: A Testbed for Classifying and Designing Actor Languages in the Smalltalk-80 Environment," in *Proceedings ECOOP 89*, ed. S. Cook, British Computer Society Workshop Series, Cambridge University Press, 1989.

[24] Roy H. Campbell and A.Nico Habermann, *"The Specification of Process Synchronisation by Path Expressions," Lecture Notes in Computer Science,* vol. 16, Springer-Verlag, New York, 1974, pp. 89–102.

[25] Luca Cardelli and Peter Wegner, "On Understanding Types, Data Abstraction, and Polymorphism," *ACM Computing Surveys*, vol. 17, no. 4, Dec. 1985, pp. 471–523.

[26] Denis Caromel,"A General Model for Concurrent and Distributed Object-Oriented Programming," *Proceedings ACM SIGPLAN OOPSLA 88 workshop on Object-Based Concurrent Programming, ACM SIGPLAN Notices*, vol. 24, no. 4, April 1989, pp. 102–104.

[27] Denis Caromel, "Concurrency and Reusability: From Sequential to Parallel," *Journal of Object-Oriented Programming*, Sept./Oct. 1990.

[28] William Cook, "A Proposal for Making Eiffel Type-Safe," in *Proceedings ECOOP 89*, ed. S. Cook, British Computer Society Workshop Series, Cambridge University Press, 1989.

[29] Antonio Corradi and L. Leonardi, "Parallelism in Object-Oriented Programming Languages," *Proceedings of IEEE International Conference on Computer Languages*, March 1990, New Orleans, IEEE Computer Society Press, pp. 261–270.

[30] P. Courtois, F. Heymans and D. Parnas, "Concurrent Control with Readers and Writers," *Communications of the ACM*, vol. 14, no. 10, Oct. 1971, pp. 667–668.

[31] Brad J. Cox, *Object Oriented Programming: An Evolutionary Approach*, Addison-Wesley, Reading, Mass., 1986.

[32] Stefano Crespi Reghizzi, G. Galli de Paratesi and S. Genolini, "Definition of Reusable Concurrent Software Components," *Lecture Notes in Computer Science*, vol. 512, Springer-Verlag, July 1991, *Proceedings of ECOOP 91*, Geneva, pp. 148–166.

[33] S. Danforth and Chris Tomlinson, "Type Theories and Object-Oriented Programming," *ACM Computing Surveys*, vol. 20, no. 1, March 1988, pp. 29–72.

[34] Dominique Decouchant, Sacha Krakowiak, M. Meysembourg, Michel Rivelli and X. Rousset de Pina, "A Synchronisation Mechanism for Typed Objects in a Distributed System," *Proceedings ACM SIGPLAN OOPSLA 88 workshop on Object-Based Concurrent Programming, ACM SIGPLAN Notices*, vol. 24, no. 4, April 1989, pp. 105–107.

[35] L. Peter Deutsch, "Reusability in the Smalltalk-80 Programming system," in *IEEE Tutorial on Software Reusability, 1987.*

[36] L. Peter Deutsch, "Design Reuse and Frameworks in the Smalltalk-80 system," in *Software Reusability*, ed. T. J. Biggerstaff and A. J. Perlis, vol. 2, ACM Press, 1989, pp. 57–71.

[37] Svend Frølund, "Inheritance of Synchronization Constraints in Concurrent Object-Oriented Programming Languages," *Proceedings ECOOP 92*, ed. O. Lehrmann Madsen, *Lecture Notes in Computer Science*, vol.615, Springer-Verlag, Utrecht, June/July 1992, pp. 185–196.

[38] Svend Frølund and Gul Agha, "A Language Framework for Multi-Object Coordination," *Proceedings ECOOP' 93, Lecture Notes in Computer Science*, vol. 707, July 1993, pp. 346–360.

[39] Morven Gentleman, "Message Passing Between Sequential Processes: the Reply Primitive and the Administrator Concept," *Software—Practice and Experience*, vol. 11, 1981, pp. 435–466.

[40] Adele Goldberg and David Robson, *Smalltalk-80: The Language and its Implementation*, Addison-Wesley, Reading, Mass., 1983.

[41] C. A. R. Hoare, "Proof of correctness of data representations," *Acta Informatica*, vol. 1, Feb. 1972, pp. 271–281.

[42] C. A. R. Hoare, "Monitors: An Operating System Structuring Concept," *Communications of the ACM*, vol. 17, no. 10, Oct. 1974, pp. 549–557.

[43] C. A. R. Hoare, "Communicating Sequential Processes," *Communications of the ACM*, vol. 21, no. 8, Aug. 1978, pp. 666–677.

[44] Ralph E. Johnson and Brian Foote, "Designing Reusable Classes," *Journal of Object-Oriented Programming*, June/July 1988, pp. 22–35.

[45] Dennis G. Kafura and Kueng Hae Lee, "Inheritance in Actor Based Concurrent Object-Oriented Languages," in *Proceedings ECOOP' 89*, ed. S. Cook, British Computer Society Workshop Series, Cambridge University Press, 1989.

[46] Alan H. Karp, "Programming for Parallelism," *IEEE Computer*, 1987, pp. 43–577

[47] Dimitri Konstantas, Oscar M. Nierstrasz and Michael Papathomas, "An Implementation of Hybrid," in *Active Object Environments,* ed. D. Tsichritzis, Centre Universitaire d'Informatique, University of Geneva, 1988, pp. 61–105.

[48] Sacha Krakowiak, M. Meysembourg, H. Nguyen Van, Michel Riveill, C. Roisin and X. Rousset de Pina, "Design and Implementation of an Object-Oriented Strongly Typed Language for Distributed Applications," *Journal of Object-Oriented Programming*, vol. 3, no. 3, Sept./Oct. 1990, pp. 11–22

[49] Chris Laffra, "PROCOL: A Concurrent Object Language with Protocols, Delegation, Persistence and Constraints," Ph.D. thesis, Erasmus University, Rotterdam, 1992.

[50] Butler W. Lampson and D.D. Redell, "Experience with Processes and Monitors in Mesa," *Communications of the ACM*, vol. 23, no. 2, 1980, pp. 105–117.

[51] Henry Lieberman, "Using Prototypical Objects to Implement Shared Behavior in Object Oriented Systems," *Proceedings OOPSLA '86, ACM SIGPLAN Notices*, vol. 21, no. 11, Nov. 1986, pp. 214–223.

[52] Barbara Liskov, Alan Snyder, Robert Atkinson and Craig Schaffert, "Abstraction Mechanisms in CLU," *Communications of the ACM*, vol. 20, no. 8, Aug. 1977, pp. 564–576.

[53] Barbara Liskov and S. Zilles, "Programming with Abstract Data Types," *Proceedings of the ACM Symposium on Very High Level Languages, ACM SIGPLAN Notices*, vol. 9, no. 4, 1974, pp. 50–59.

[54] Barbara Liskov, Maurice Herlihy and L. Gilbert, "Limitations of Synchronous Communication with Static Process Structure in Languages for Distributed Computing," in *Proceedings of the 13th ACM POPL*, St Petersburg, Fla., 1986.

[55] Barbara Liskov, "Distributed Programming in Argus," *Communications of the ACM*, vol. 31, no. 3, 1988, pp. 300–313.

[56] A. Lister, "The Problem of Nested Monitor Calls," *ACM Operating Systems Review*, July 1977, pp. 5–7.

References

[57] Peter Löhr, "Concurrency Annotations for Reusable Software," *Communications of the ACM*, vol. 36, no. 9, Sept. 1993, pp.81–89.

[58] Ole Lehrmann Madsen, Birger Møller-Pedersen and Kristen Nygaard, *Object-Oriented Programming in the Beta Programming Language*, Addison-Wesley, Reading, Mass., 1993.

[59] Ciaran McHale, Bridget Walsh, Sean Baker and Alexis Donnelly, "Scheduling Predicates," *Proceedings of the ECOOP'91 workshop on Object-Based Concurrent Computing*, ed. M. Tokoro, O. Nierstrasz and P. Wegner, *Lecture Notes in Computer Science*, vol. 612, 1992, pp. 177–193.

[60] Ciaran McHale, Bridget Walsh, Sean Baker and Alexis Donnelly, "Evaluating Synchronisation Mechanisms: The Inheritance Matrix," Technical Report, TCD-CS-92-18, Department of Computer Science, Trinity College, Dublin 2, July 1992, (presented at the ECOOP'92 Workshop on Object-Based Concurrency and Reuse).

[61] Pattie Maes, "Concepts and Experiments in Computational Reflection," in *Proceedings OOPSLA'87, ACM SIGPLAN Notices*, vol. 22, no. 12, Dec. 1987.

[62] Satoshi Matsuoka, Ken Wakita and Akinori Yonezawa, "Analysis of Inheritance Anomaly in Concurrent Object-Oriented Languages," (Extended Abstract), *Proceedings of OOPSLA/ECOOP'90 workshop on Object-Based Concurrent Systems, ACM SIGPLAN Notices*, 1990.

[63] Satoshi Matsuoka, Kenjiro Taura and Akinori Yonezawa, "Highly Efficient and Encapsulated Re-use of Synchronisation Code in Concurrent Object-Oriented Languages," *Proceedings OOPSLA'93, ACM SIGPLAN Notices*, vol. 28, no. 10, Oct. 1993, pp. 109–129

[64] Bertrand Meyer, *Object-Oriented Software Construction*, Prentice Hall, New York, 1988.

[65] Bertrand Meyer, "Reusability: The Case for Object-Oriented Design," IEEE Software, vol. 4, no. 2, March 1987, pp. 50–64.

[66] Bertrand Meyer, "Systematic Concurrent Object-Oriented Programming," *Communications of the ACM*, vol. 36, no. 9, Sept. 1993, pp. 56–80.

[67] José Meseguer, "Solving the Inheritance Anomaly in Object-Oriented Programming," in *Proceedings ECOOP'93, Lecture Notes in Computer Science*, vol. 707, ed. O.M. Nierstrasz, Springer-Verlag 1993.

[68] J. Eliot B. Moss and Walter H. Kohler, "Concurrency Features for the Trellis/Owl Language," *Proceedings of ECOOP '87*, BIGRE, no. 54, June 1987, pp. 223–232.

[69] Christian Neusius, "Synchronizing Actions," *Proceedings of ECOOP'91, Lecture Notes in Computer Science*, vol. 512, Springer-Verlag, July 1991, pp. 118–132.

[70] Oscar Nierstrasz, "Active Objects in Hybrid," *Proceedings OOPSLA'87, ACM SIGPLAN Notices*, vol. 22, no. 12, Dec. 1987, pp. 243–253.

[71] Oscar Nierstrasz, "A Tour of Hybrid — A Language for Programming with Active Objects," *Advances in Object-Oriented Software Engineering*, ed. D. Mandrioli and B. Meyer, Prentice Hall, 1992, pp. 167–182.

[72] Michael Papathomas and Dimitri Konstantas, "Integrating Concurrency and Object-Oriented Programming: An Evaluation of Hybrid," in *Object Management,* ed. D. Tsichritzis, Centre Universitaire d'Informatique, University of Geneva, 1990, pp. 229–244.

[73] Michael Papathomas, "Concurrency Issues in Object-Oriented Languages," in *Object Oriented Development,* ed. D. Tsichritzis, Centre Universitaire d'Informatique, University of Geneva, 1989, pp. 207–245.

[74] Michael Papathomas, "State Predicate Notifiers: A Concurrent Object Model," Lancaster University Report, April 1994.

[75] David L. Parnas, "A Technique for Software Module Specification with Examples," *Communications of the ACM*, vol. 15, no. 5, May 1972, pp. 330–336.

[76] David L. Parnas, "On the Criteria to be Used in Decomposing Systems into Modules," *Communications of the ACM*, vol. 15, no. 12, Dec. 1972, pp. 1053–1058.

[77] David L. Parnas, "The Non-Problem of Nested Monitor Calls," *ACM Operating Systems Review*, vol. 12, no. 1, 1978, pp. 12–14.

[78] Geoffrey A. Pascoe, "Encapsulators: A New Software Paradigm in Smalltalk 80," in *Proceedings of OOPSLA '86, ACM SIGPLAN Notices*, Sept. 1986.

[79] Alan Snyder, "Encapsulation and Inheritance in Object-Oriented Programming Languages," ACM SIGPLAN Notices, vol. 21, no. 11, Nov. 1986, pp. 38–45.

[80] Bjarne Stroustrup, *The C++ Programming Language*, Addison-Wesley, Reading, Mass., 1986.

[81] T. J. Teorey and T. B. Pinkerton, "A Comparative Analysis of Disk Scheduling Policies," *Communications of the ACM*, vol. 15, no. 3, March 1972, pp. 177–184.

[82] Tom Thompson, "System 7.5: A Step Toward the Future," *Byte*, August 1994.

[83] Chris Tomlinson and Vineet Singh, "Inheritance and Synchronisation with Enabled Sets," *Proceedings OOPSLA '89, ACM SIGPLAN Notices*, vol. 24, no. 10, Oct. 1989, pp. 103–112.

[84] Anand Tripathi and Mehmet Aksit, "Communication, Scheduling, and Resource Management in Sina," *Journal of Object-Oriented Programming*, Nov./Dec. 1988, pp. 24–36.

[85] Jan Van Den Bos and Chris Laffra, "PROCOL: A Parallel Object Language with Protocols," *Proceedings OOPSLA '89, ACM SIGPLAN Notices*, vol. 24, no. 10, Oct. 1989, pp. 95–102.

[86] Takuo Watanabe and Akinori Yonezawa, "Reflection in an Object Oriented Concurrent Language," ACM SIGPLAN Notices, vol. 23, no. 11, 1988, pp. 306–315.

[87] Peter Wegner, "Dimensions of Object-Based Language Design," in *Proceedings OOPSLA '87, ACM SIGPLAN Notices*, vol. 22, Orlando, Florida, Dec. 1987, pp. 168–182.

[88] Peter Wegner and Stanley B. Zdonik, "Inheritance as an Incremental Modification Mechanism or What Like Is and Isn't Like," in *Proceedings ECOOP'88, Lecture Notes in Computer Science*, vol. 322, Springer-Verlag, 1988, pp. 55–77.

[89] Peter Wegner, "Concepts and Paradigms of Object-Oriented Programming," *ACM OOPS Messenger*, vol. 1, no. 1, August 1990.

[90] William E. Weihl, "Linguistic Support for Atomic Data Types," *ACM Transactions on Programming Languages and Systems*, vol. 12, no. 2, 1990.

[91] Rebecca J. Wirfs-Brock and Ralph E. Johnson, "Surveying Current Research in Object-Oriented Design," *Communications of the ACM*, vol. 33, no. 9, Sept. 1990, pp. 104–123.

[92] Yasuhiko Yokote and Mario Tokoro, "Concurrent Programming in ConcurrentSmalltalk," in *Object-Oriented Concurrent Programming*, ed. M. Tokoro, *MIT Press*, Cambridge, Mass., 1987, pp. 129–158.

[93] Yasuhiko Yokote and Mario Tokoro, "Experience and Evolution of ConcurrentSmalltalk," in *Proceedings OOPSLA '87, ACM SIGPLAN Notices*, vol. 22, Orlando, Florida, Dec. 1987, pp. 168–182.

[94] Akinori Yonezawa, Etsuya Shibayama, T. Takada and Yasuaki Honda, "Modelling and Programming in an Object-Oriented Concurrent Language ABCL/1," in *Object-Oriented Concurrent Programming*, ed. M. Tokoro, *MIT Press*, Cambridge, Mass., 1987, pp. 55–89.

Chapter 3
Interoperation of Object-Oriented Applications

Dimitri Konstantas

> **Abstract** One of the important advantages of the object-oriented design and development methodology is the ability to reuse existing software modules. However the introduction of many programming languages with different syntax, semantics and/or paradigms has created the need for a consistent inter-language interoperability support framework. We present a brief overview of the most characteristic interoperability support methods and frameworks allowing the access and reuse of objects from different programming environments and focus on the interface bridging object-oriented interoperability support approach.

3.1 Reusing Objects from Different Environments

One of the problems that people face when travelling from one country to another concerns the operation of electric appliances, like electric razors and coffee machines. A person living in Switzerland, for example, travelling to Germany will not be able to "plug in" and use his coffee machine as he is used in doing when back home. The reason is simply that the "interfaces" for connecting to the electricity distribution network, that is the plug of the appliance and the wall socket, are different. Our traveller will need to employ a small inexpensive adaptor in order to bridge the differences of the "interfaces". But things are not always that simple. If the same person is travelling to North America he will discover that not only is his (Swiss) plug different from the (North American) wall socket, but also that the electricity voltage differs. Fortunately also in this case a simple solution exists: the use of a transformer that will convert the North American voltage (110 V) to the Swiss standard (220 V).

In object-oriented programming where the reuse of objects is highly encouraged we face similar problems when we wish to access or reuse objects that are programmed in different programming languages. A programmer implementing an application in C++ cannot easily (re)use (if at all) objects and code written in Smalltalk [5] or even replace, without resorting to extensive reprogramming, a C++ object with some other one performing the same function but under a different interface. What we need are concepts similar to the electricity transformer and plug adaptor that will allow us to bridge the differences between the interfaces and paradigms of objects programmed in different languages.

In general we can classify the problems of bridging the differences between objects into three categories. The first category includes the computation differences between the objects, like the low-level data representations; the second category includes the syntactic particularities of the object interfaces, like the operation names and the required parameters; the third category includes the differences of the semantic and functional behaviour of the objects, like the representation of a collection of objects as an array or as a linked list. We will refer to the bridging of all these differences for the reuse and access of objects written in one or more languages as the *interoperability support* problem.

Interoperability is the ability of two or more entities, such as programs, objects, applications or environments, to communicate and cooperate despite differences in the implementation language, the execution environment or the model abstractions. The motivation in the introduction of interoperability support between entities is the mutual exchange of information and the use of resources available in other environments.

During the past few years several approaches have been taken for the introduction of interoperability support. We classify these approaches in two ways. First depending on the way that they solve the interface differences' problem and second on the point at which the interoperability support is handled.

For the first classification, interface differences, we identify two general categories:
- The *interface bridging* approaches bridge the differences between interfaces. They are characterized by the notions of offered and requested interface and define an interface transformation language. The interface transformation language requires the existence of two interfaces and allows one to express how the offered (requested) interface can be transformed to the requested (offered) interface. Note that the interface transformation language is programming language dependent.
- The *interface standardization* approaches standardize the interface under which a service (functionality) is offered. They are characterized by an interface definition language that allows one to express in a programming language independent way a specific interface. From the abstract definition of an interface a compiler will produce the necessary stub-interface in the implementation language selected. The compiler will always generate the same stub-interface for the selected target programming language.

For the second classification depending on the point at which interoperability support is handled, we also identify two categories:

- The *procedure-oriented interoperability* approaches that handle interoperability at the point of the procedure call.
- The *object-oriented interoperability* approaches that handle interoperability at the point of the object.

In the rest of this chapter we present a brief overview of some representative projects from different interoperability approaches, discussing their advantages and disadvantages, and describe in detail the object-oriented interoperability approach of the Cell framework [12].

3.2 Procedure-Oriented Interoperability

The problem of interface matching between offered and requested services has been identified by many researchers [6][15][18][21][22][25][26] as an essential factor for a high-level interoperability in open systems (see also chapter 12). Nevertheless, most of the approaches taken in the past are based on the remote procedure call (RPC) paradigm and handle interoperability at the point of procedure call. We call this type of interoperability support approach *procedure-oriented iteroperability (POI)*. In POI support it is assumed that the functionality offered by the server's procedures matches exactly the functionality requested by the client. Thus the main focus of the interoperability support is the *adaption* [21] of the actual parameters passed to the procedure call at the client side to the requested procedures at the server side.

3.2.1 Interface bridging

An example of this approach is the one taken in the *Polylith* system [21]. The basic assumption of the approach is that the interface requested by the client (at the point of the procedure call) and the interface offered by the server "fail to match exactly". That is the offered and requested parameters of the operation calls differ. A language called *NIMBLE* has been developed that allows programmers to declare how the actual parameters of a procedure call should be rearranged and transformed in order to match the formal parameters of the target procedure. The supported parameter transformations include coercion of parameters, e.g. five integers to an array of integers, parameter evaluation, e.g. the transformation of the strings "male" and "female" to integer values, and parameter extensions, i.e. providing default values for missing parameters. The types of the parameters that are handled are basic data types (integers, strings, Booleans, etc.) and their aggregates (arrays or structures of integers, characters, etc.). The programmer specifies the mapping between the actual parameters at the client side and the formal parameters at the server side using NIMBLE and the system will then automatically generate code that handles the transformations at run-time.

3.2.2 Interface standardization

Whereas NIMBLE focuses on bridging the differences between the offered and requested service interfaces, the *Specification Level Interoperability (SLI)* support of the *Arcadia* project [25] focuses on the generation of interfaces in the local execution environment through which services in other execution environments can be accessed. The major advantage of SLI is that it defines type compatibility in terms of the properties (specification) of the objects and hides representation differences for both abstract and simple types. This way SLI will hide, for example, the fact that a stack is represented as a linked list or as an array, making its representation irrelevant to the interoperating programs sharing the stack. In SLI the specifications of the types that are shared between interoperating programs are expressed in the *Unifying Type Model (UTM)* notation. UTM is a unifying model in the sense *"that it is sufficient for describing those properties of an entity's type that are relevant from the perspective of any of the interoperating programs that share instances of that type"*[25]. SLI provides a set of language bindings and underlying implementations that relate the relevant parts of a type definition given in the language to a definition as given in the UTM. With SLI the implementer of a new service will need to specify the service interface with UTM and provide any needed new type definitions for the shared objects and language bindings that do not already exist. In doing so the user will be assisted by the *automated assistance tools* which allow him or her to browse through the existing UTM definitions, language bindings and underlying implementations. Once a UTM definition for a service has been defined the *automated generation tool* will produce the necessary interface in the implementation language selected plus any representation and code needed to affect the implementation of object instances. This way the automated generation tool will always produce the same interface specification from the same UTM input. However, SLI can provide different bindings and implementations for the generated interface allowing a service to be obtained from different servers on different environments, provided that they all have the same UTM interface definition.

An approach similar to SLI has been taken in the *Common Object Request Broker Architecture* (CORBA) [18] of the Object Management Group (OMG). The Object Request Broker (ORB) *"provides interoperability between applications on different machines in distributed environments"*[18] and it is a common layer through which objects transparently exchange messages and receive replies. The interfaces that the client objects request and the object implementations provide are described through the *Interface Definition Language (IDL)*. IDL is the means by which a particular object implementation tells its potential clients what operations are available and how they should be invoked. An interface definition written in IDL specifies completely the interface and each operation's parameters. The IDL concepts are mapped accordingly to the client languages depending on the facilities available in them. This way, given an IDL interface, the IDL compiler will generate interface stubs for the client language through which the service can be accessed using the predefined language bindings.

3.2.3 Advantages and Disadvantages

Although the above approaches can provide interoperability support for a large number of applications, they have a number of drawbacks that severely restrict their interoperability support. The first drawback is the degeneration of the "interface" for which interoperability support is provided to the level of a procedure call. A service is generally provided through an interface that is composed of a set of interrelated procedures. What is of importance is not the actual set of the interface procedures but the overall functionality they provide. By reducing the interoperability "interface" to the level of a procedure call, the interrelation of the interface procedures is lost, since the interoperability support no longer sees the service interface as a single entity but as isolated procedures. This will create problems in approaches like Polylith's that bridge the differences between the offered and requested service interface, when there is no direct one-to-one correspondence between the interface's procedures (interface mismatch problem).

Interoperability approaches like SLI and CORBA, on the other hand, do not suffer from the interface mismatch problem, since the client is forced to use a predefined interface. Nevertheless, the enforcement of predefined interfaces (i.e. sets of procedures with specified functionality) makes it very difficult to access alternative servers that provide the same service under a different interface. This is an important interoperability restriction since we can neither anticipate nor we can enforce in an open distributed environment the interface through which a service will be provided. With the SLI and CORBA approaches, the service's interface must also be embedded in the client's code. Any change in the server's interface will result in changes in the client code.

Another restriction of the above interoperability approaches is that they require the migration of the procedure parameters from the client's environment to the server's environment. As a result only *migratable* types can be used as procedure parameters. These are the basic data types (integers, strings, reals, etc.) and their aggregates (arrays, structures, etc.), which we call *data types*. Composite non-migratable abstract types, like a database or keyboard type, cannot be passed as procedure parameters. This nevertheless is a reasonable restriction since the above approaches focus in interoperability support for systems based on non-object-oriented languages where only data types can be defined.

The need for allowing non-migratable objects as parameters to operation calls was identified in the CORBA and a special data type was introduced called *object reference*. CORBA object references are data types that encapsulate a handle to a (non-migratable) object and are globally valid. However object references are a low level primitives which must be explicitly referenced and de-referenced by the server and the client. A higher-level primitive allowing direct access to object is clearly needed if we wish to have consistent access in an object-oriented environment.

3.3 Object-Oriented Interoperability

Although procedure-oriented interoperability provides a good basis for interoperability support between non-object-oriented language based environments, it is not well suited for a high level interoperability support for environments based on object-oriented languages. The reason is that in an object-oriented environment we cannot decompose an object into a set of independent operations and data and view them separately, since this will mean loss of the object's semantics. For example, a set of operations that draw a line, a rectangle and print characters on a screen, have a different meaning if they are seen independently or in the context of a window server object where the rectangle can represent a window into which the characters that represent the user/machine interactions are printed. In object-oriented environments it is the overall functionality of the object that is of importance and not the functionality of the independent operations. We call this type of interoperability where the semantics of the objects as a whole are preserved *object-oriented interoperability (OOI)*.

3.3.1 Interface Bridging

An example of interface bridging in object-oriented interoperability is the one provided by the Cell framework [12] (where the concept of OOI was also introduced). The Cell is a framework for the design and implementation of "strongly distributed object-based systems". The purpose of the Cell is to allow objects of different independent object-based systems to communicate and access each other's functionality regardless of possible interface differences. That is, the same functionality can be offered with a different interface from different objects found either on the same or on different environments. The bridging of the interface differences is done via the *Interface Adaption Language (IAL)*. From the specification given in the IAL a compiler generates the required stub objects that support the requested interface and translate the incoming operation invocations to the invocations of the target object interface.

A more detailed presentation of the Cell interoperability approach is given in section 3.5.

3.3.2 Interface Standardization

The most important example of interface standardization in object-oriented interoperability is version 2 of CORBA. In contrast to the first version of CORBA, which was oriented towards C and C procedure calls, the second version is oriented towards a C++ environment and objects. Otherwise the functionality of CORBA and the basic elements are the same as described in section 3.2.2.

3.3.3 Summary

Object-oriented interoperability is a generalization of procedure-oriented interoperability in the sense that it will use, at its lower levels, the mechanisms and notions of POI. However OOI has several advantages over POI. First of all it allows the interoperation of applications in higher-level abstractions, like the objects, and thus supports a more reliable and consistent interoperation. A second advantage is that it supports fast prototyping in application development and experimentation with different object components from different environments. The programmer can develop a prototype by reusing and experimenting with different existing objects in remote (or local) environments without having to change the code of the prototype when the reused object interfaces differ. A last advantage is that since OOI is a generalization of POI, it can be used to provide interoperation between both object-oriented and conventional (non-object-oriented) environments. Furthermore when IB-OOI support is used for non-object-oriented environments it provides a more general frame than POI and can also handle cases where the requested and offered service interfaces do not match.

In table 3.1 we give a summary of the different approaches presented above and their position in the two classifications.

	Procedure-oriented interoperability (POI)	Object-oriented interoperability (OOI)
Interface standardization (IS)	SLI, CORBA v. 1	CORBA v. 2
Interface bridging (IB)	NIMBLE	Cell

Table 3.1 *Classification of interoperability support approaches.*

3.4 Comparison of Interoperability Support Approaches

The interface bridging approaches provide a more general solution than the interface standardization approaches for the access and reuse of objects from different programming environments since they do not enforce any specific interface. The application designer can choose the interface that he wants to use for accessing a service and use it for accessing not only the target server but also alternative servers offering the same service under different interfaces.

Another advantage of the interface bridging approaches is that they make no assumptions about the existence and semantics of types in the interoperating environments. Each type, even the simplest and most banal integer type, must be explicitly related to a type on the remote environment. This way they provide flexibility in the interconnection of diverse environments based on different models and abstractions.

One of the disadvantage of the interface bridging approaches comes from the fact that they do not enforce a common global representation model for expressing the interoperability bindings. Each execution environment is free to choose its own language. As a result the interoperability interface adaption specifications for a server need to be defined independently by the programmer for each execution environment in an interface adaption language that is specially tailored for the programming languages of the two environments. However, bilateral mappings can offer a higher flexibility when the interoperating languages support special features. For example, a common interface definition language, like the CORBA IDL, does not include the notion of a *transaction*; thus, even when the interoperating languages support transactions, like Argus [16] and KAROS [4], their IDL-based interoperation will not be able to use transactions.

Object-oriented interoperability and procedure-oriented interoperability approaches cannot be directly compared since they are designed for different programming environments: the first for object-oriented environments and the second for non-object-oriented environments. Nevertheless OOI is a generalization of POI using at its lower levels the same mechanisms as POI. Thus the major advantage of OOI over POI is that it can be applied as well to both types of programming environments and serve as bridge between object-oriented and non-object-oriented environments.

Although the interface bridging and interface standardization approaches are distinct in the way they approach the interoperability problem, they are not exclusive. An interoperability support system can very well support both approaches and give the programmers maximum flexibility in the reuse and access of objects in different programming environments. As an example we can consider CORBA which is an interface standardization interoperability support system. In a large CORBA-based open distributed system it will be difficult for all service providers to agree on a common interface for the servers they develop. As a result a number of different server interfaces will be available providing the same or similar services. However, applications being developed to access a specific server interface will not be able to access any other server even if the interface differences are minor. In addition, since it is not possible to anticipate the interfaces of future servers, applications will not be able to take advantage of newer, more advanced services. What is needed is to introduce interface bridging interoperability support. This can be easily done with the introduction of an *interface adaption* service that will allow a client to adapt its requested service interface to a specific offered interface and dispatch the service requests accordingly.

3.5 Interface Bridging — Object-Oriented Interoperability

We identify two basic components necessary for the support and implementation of interface bridging OOI (IB-OOI): *interface adaption* and *object mapping*. Interface adaption provides the means for defining the relations between types on different execution environments based on their functionality abstraction, and object mapping provides the runtime support for the implementation of the interoperability links.

3.5.1 Terminology

In the rest of this section we use the term *client interface* to specify the interface through which the client wishes to access a service, and the term *server interface* to specify the ac-

Interface Bridging — Object-Oriented Interoperability

tual interface of the server. In addition we will use the term *node* to specify the execution environment of an application (client or server), e.g. the Hybrid [7] execution environment or the Smalltalk [5] execution environment. In this sense a node can span over more than one computer, and more than one node can coexist on the same computer. Although we will assume that the client is in the *local* node and the server in the *remote* node, local and remote nodes can very well be one and the same. By the term *parameter* we mean the operation call parameters *and* the returned values, unless we explicitly state differently. Finally we should note that by the term *user* we mean the physical person who interacts and maintains the interoperability support system.

3.5.2 Interface Adaption

In a strongly distributed environment [24] a given service will be offered by many servers under different interfaces. As a result a client wishing to access a specific service from more than one server will have to use a different interface for each server. Although we can develop the client to support different interfaces for the accessed services, we might not always be able to anticipate all possible interfaces through which a service can be offered, or force service providers to offer their services via a specific interface. IB-OOI approaches this problem by handling all interface transformations, so that a client can use the same interface to access all servers offering the same service. The interface adaption problem consists of defining and realizing the bindings and transformations from the interface that the client uses (requested interface), to the actual interface of the service (offered interface).

Ideally we would like to obtain an automatic solution to the interface adaption problem. Unfortunately in the current state of the art this is not possible. The reason is that we have no way of expressing the semantics of the arbitrary functionality of a service or an operation in a machine-understandable form. In practice the best we can do is describe it in a manual page and choose wisely a name so that some indication is given about the functionality of the entity. Nevertheless, since nothing obliges us to choose meaningful names for types, operations or their parameters, we cannot make any assumptions about the meaning of these names. Furthermore even if the names are chosen to be meaningful, their interpretation depends in the context in which they appear. For example a type named *Account* has a totally different meaning and functionality when found in a banking environment and when found in a system administrator's environment. Thus any solution to the interface adaption problem will require, at some point, human intervention since the system can automatically deduce neither which type matches which, nor which operation corresponds to which, or even which operation parameter corresponds to which between two matching operations. What the system can do is assist the user in defining the bindings, and generate the corresponding implementations.

We distinguish three phases in providing a solution to the interface adaption problem. In the first phase, which we call the *functionality phase,* the user specifies the type or types on the remote environment providing the needed functionality (service). The system can assist the user in browsing the remote type hierarchy and retrieving information describing the functionality of the types. This information can be manual pages, information extracted from the type implementation or even usage examples.

In the second phase, which we call the *interface phase*, the user defines how the operations of the remote type(s) should be combined to emulate the functionality represented by the client's operations. This can a be a very simple task if there is a direct correspondence between requested and offered operations, or a complicated one if the operations from several remote types must be combined in order to achieve the needed result. As in the functionality phase the system can assist the user by providing information regarding the functionality of the operations.

The third phase is the *parameter phase*. After specifying the correspondence between the requested and remote interface operations the user will need to specify the parameters of the remote operations in relation to the ones that will be passed in the local operation call. This might require not only a definition of the correspondence between offered and requested parameters, but also the introduction of adaption functions that will transform or preprocess the parameters. The system can assist the user by identifying the types of the corresponding parameters, reusing any information introduced in the past regarding the relation between types and standard adaption functions, and prompt the user for any additional information that might be required.

3.5.2.1 Type Relations

In IB-OOI we distinguish three kinds of type relations, depending on how the local type can be transformed to the remote type. Namely we have *equivalent, translated* and *type matched* types.

Migrating an object from one node to another means moving both of its parts, i.e. data and operations, to the remote node, while preserving the semantics of the object. However, moving the object operations essentially means that a new object type is introduced on the remote node. This case is presently of no interest to IB-OOI since we wish to support interoperability through the reuse of existing types. Thus in IB-OOI, migrating an operation call parameter object means moving the data and using them to initialize an instance of a pre-existing equivalent type. This is a common case with data types, like integers, strings and their aggregates, where the operations exist on all nodes and only the data need to be moved. In IB-OOI when this kind of a relation exists between a type of the local node and a type of the remote node we say that the local type X has an *equivalent* type X´ on the remote node.

Although data types are the best candidates for an equivalence relation, they are not the only ones. Other non-data types can also exist for which an equivalent type can be found on a remote node. For example, a raster image or a database type can have an equivalent type on a remote node and only the image or database data need to be moved when migrating the object. In general, two types can be defined as equivalent if their semantics and structure are equivalent and the transfer of the data of the object is sufficient to allow the migration of their instances. In migrating an object to its equivalent on the remote node, the IB-OOI support must handle the representation differences of the transferred data. In

Interface Bridging — Object-Oriented Interoperability

this sense the *type equivalence* of IB-OOI corresponds to *representation level interoperability* [25].

In an object-oriented environment we are more interested in the semantics of an object rather than its structure and internal implementation. For example, consider the Hybrid [17] type string and the CooL[*] [1] type ARRAY OF CHAR. In the general case the semantics of the two types are different: the string is a single object, while the ARRAY OF CHAR is an aggregation of independent objects. Nevertheless when in CooL an ARRAY OF CHAR is used for representing a string, it becomes semantically equivalent and can be transformed to a Hybrid string, although the structure, representation and interfaces of the two types are different. In IB-OOI this type relation is defined as *type translation*.

Translation of the local type to the remote type is done with a user-definable translation function. This way the particularities of the semantic equivalence can be handled in a case-specific way. The user can specify different translations according to the semantics of the objects. For example, if the local node is a CooL node and the remote a Hybrid node, then we can define two different translations for an ARRAY OF CHAR — the first when the ARRAY OF CHAR represents a character string and is translated to a string, and the second when the ARRAY OF CHAR represents a collection of characters that need to be treated independently and which is translated to a Hybrid array of integer (in Hybrid characters are represented via integers).

Type translation can be compared to specification level interoperability, where the interoperability support links the objects according to their specifications. Nevertheless, type translation is more flexible than SLI since it allows multiple translations of the same type according to the specific needs and semantics of the application.

A local type for which bindings to a remote type or types have been defined, as a solution to the interface adaption problem (i.e. bindings and transformations from the interface that the client uses, to the actual interface of the service), is said to be *type matched* to the remote node. We can have two kinds of type matched types: multi-type matched and uni-type matched types. Multi-type-matched types are the ones that are bound to more that one type on the remote node, when for example one part of the requested functionality is offered from one type and another part from a second type, and uni-type matched types are the ones that are bound to a single type on the remote node.

The target of IB-OOI is to allow access to objects on remote nodes. The basic assumption being that the object in question cannot be migrated to the local node. However, the access and use of the remote object will be done with the exchange of other objects in the form of operation call parameters. The parameter objects can, in their turn, be migrated to the remote node or not. Parameter objects that cannot be migrated to the remote node are accessed on the local node via a type match, becoming themselves servers for objects on the remote node.

Type relations are specific to the node for which they are defined and do not imply that a reverse type relation exists, or that they can be applied for another node. For example, if the local node is a Hybrid node and the remote is a C++ node, the Hybrid type boolean has

---

[*] CooL is a an object-oriented language designed and implemented in the ITHACA ESPRIT [20] project

as equivalent in the C++ node an int (integer) (Booleans in C++ are represented by integers), while the reverse is, in general, false.

3.5.2.2 To Type-Match or not to Type-Match?
Type matching is a general mechanism for interoperability support and can be used in all cases in place of equivalence and translation of types. However, the existence of translation and equivalence of types is needed for performance reasons since accessing objects through the node boundary is an expensive operation. If an object is to be accessed frequently on the remote node, then it might be preferable to migrate it, either as equivalent or translated type. For example, it is preferable to migrate "small" objects, like the data types, rather than access them locally. Nevertheless the user always has the possibility of accessing any object locally, even an integer if this is needed, as might be the case with an integer that is stored at a specific memory address which is hard-wired to an external sensor (like a thermometer) and which is continuously updated. This can be done by defining a type match and using it in the parameter's binding definitions.

A typical scenario we envisage in the development of an application with IB-OOI support is the following. The user (application programmer) will first define a set of type matchings for accessing objects on remote nodes. These will be used in the development of the application prototype. When the prototype is completed the user will measure the performance of the prototype and choose for which types a local implementation is to be provided. For these types an equivalency or translation relation will also be established, possibly on both nodes, so that they can be migrated and accessed locally. This way the performance of the prototype will be improved. This process can be repeated iteratively until the performance gains are no longer justifiable by the implementation effort.

One of the major advantages of the IB-OOI approach is that in the above scenario the application prototype will not be modified when local implementations of types are introduced[*] and the type relations change. The new type relations are introduced in the IB-OOI support and do not affect the application programs.

3.5.3 Object Mapping

Whereas interface adaption maintains the static information of the interoperability templates, object mapping provides the dynamic support and implementation of the interoperability links. We distinguish two parts in object mapping: the static and the dynamic. The static part of object mapping is responsible for the creation of the classes that implement the interoperability links as specified by the corresponding type matching. The dynamic part, on the other hand, is responsible for the instantiation and management of the objects used during the interoperation.

---

[*] With the exception of a possible recompilation if dynamic linking is not supported.

3.5.3.1 Inter-Classes and Inter-Objects

The essence of object mapping is to dynamically introduce in the local node the services of servers found on other nodes. This, however, must be done in such way so that the access of the services is done according to the local conventions and paradigms. In an object-oriented node this will be achieved with the instantiation of a local object that represents the remote server, which in IB-OOI we call an *inter-object*. An inter-object differs from a *proxy*, as this is defined in [23], in three important respects. First in contrast with a proxy, an inter-object and its server can belong to different programming and execution environments and thus they follow different paradigms, access mechanisms and interfaces. The second difference is that while a proxy provides the only access point to the actual server, i.e. the server can be accessed *only* via its proxies, this is not the case with inter-objects. Objects on the same node with the server can access it directly. An inter-object simply provides the gateway for accessing the server from remote nodes. Finally, while a proxy is bound to a specific server, an inter-object can dynamically change its server or even access more than one server, combining their services to appear as a single service on the local node.

An inter-object is an instance of a type for which a type match has been defined. The class (i.e. the implementation of a type) of the inter-object is created by the object mapper from the type match information and we call it an *inter-class*. An inter-class is generated automatically by the object mapper and it includes all code needed for implementing the links to the remote server or servers.

3.5.3.2 Dynamic Support of the Object Mapping

After the instantiation of an inter-object and the establishment of the links to the remote server, the controlling application will start invoking the operations of the inter-object, passing other objects as parameters. IB-OOI allows objects of any type to be used as parameters at operation calls. The object mapper will handle the parameter objects according to their type relations with the remote node. This way objects for which an equivalent or translated type exists on the remote node will be migrated, while objects for which a type match exists will be accessed through an inter-object on the remote node.

In the case where no type relation exists for the type of a parameter object, the object mapper will invoke the type matcher and ask the user to provide a type relation. This way type relations can be specified efficiently, taking into account the exact needs and circumstances of their use. In addition the dynamic definition of type relations during run-time relieves the user from the task of searching the implementation type hierarchy for undefined type relations. Also the incremental development and testing of a prototype becomes easier since no type relations need to be defined for the parts of the prototype that are not currently tested.

3.6 Interface Adaption

Expressing the relations and transformations between two (or more) interfaces can be done using a language which we call *Interface Adaption Language (IAL)*. IAL, just like the existing interface definition languages (like the CORBA IDL) that allow the expression of an interface in an abstract language independent way, allows the expression of the relations and transformations required for the adaption of one interface to another in an abstract language independent way.

An IAL for the object-oriented interoperability support of the Cell framework prototype [8][9][11] was designed and implemented at the University of Geneva. The main goal of the Cell framework is to allow the objects of a node transparently to access and use services found on other heterogeneous nodes using the OOI support. IAL allows the user to express the interface relations between object types of the different nodes. The syntax of the IAL is very similar to the Hybrid language syntax [7][10][17], in which the Cell prototype was implemented.

In the rest of this section we give an overview of the implemented IAL using examples for the adaption of interfaces between Hybrid object types and CooL [1] object types. A complete description of IAL can be found in [13].

3.6.1 Type Relations

A type relation in IAL is defined for a specific remote cell which is identified by its name. For the examples given below we assume that the local Hybrid cell is named HybridCell and the remote CooL cell is named CooLCell. The general syntax of a type relation on the Hybrid cell is

    IdOfRemoteCell :: <TypeRelation> ;

where TypeRelation can be either equivalent, translated or type matched and IdOfRemoteCell is the id of the remote cell, which in the case of the CooL cell is CooLCell.

3.6.1.1 Equivalent and Translated types

In both CooL and Hybrid, integers and Booleans are equivalent types. On the Hybrid cell this is expressed as

    CooLCell :: integer => INT ;
    CooLCell :: boolean => BOOL ;

Although the notion of a *string* exists in both languages, in CooL, strings are represented as arrays of characters while in Hybrid they are *basic data types*. Thus the relation between them is of a translated type

    CooLCell :: string +> ARRAY OF CHAR : string2arrayOfChar ;

In the CooL cell the corresponding definitions will be:

    HybridCell :: INT => integer ;
    HybridCell :: BOOL => boolean ;
    HybridCell :: ARRAY OF CHAR +> string : arrayOfChar2string ;

In the definition of translated types we specify a translation function, like string2arrayOfChar and arrayOfChar2string, which performs the data translation.

Interface Adaption

```
type windowServer : abstract {
   newWindow : (integer #{ : topLeftX #}, integer #{ : topLeftY #},
                integer #{ : botRightX #}, integer #{ : botRightY #}) -> integer #{: windowId #} ;
   newSquareWin : (integer #{ : topLeftX #}, integer #{ : topLeftY #}, integer #{ : side #} )
                -> integer #{ : windowId #} ;
   refreshDisplay : (display ) -> boolean ;
   readCoordinates : ( mouse, keyboard, touchScreen, integer #{ : scaleFactor #} ) -> point ;
   windowSelected : (mouse, keyboard, touchScreen ) -> integer ;
} ;
```

Figure 3.1 *Hybrid type windowServer.*

3.6.1.2 Type-Matched Types.

A type can be matched to either a single remote type or to a collection of remote types (*multi-type match*). For example, if we have on the local Hybrid cell a type windowServer, which is matched to the type WINDOW_CONTROL of the remote cell, the type match will be expressed as

   CooLCell :: windowServer -> WINDOW_CONTROL {<operation bindings>*} ;

while a multi-type match will be expressed as

   CooLCell :: windowManager -> < WINDOW_CONTROL, SCREEN_MANAGER >
               { <operation bindings>} ;

When an object of the local nucleus in its attempt to access a service creates an instance of a type-matched type (an inter-object), a corresponding instance of the target type will be instantiated on the remote cell. However, there are cases where we do not want a new instance to be created on the remote cell but we need to connect to an existing server. In IAL this is noted with the addition of @ at the of remote type name:

   CooLCell :: personnel -> PERMANENT_PERSONEL_DB @ { <operation bindings>} ;

3.6.2 Description of the Running Example

In order to describe the IAL syntax we use as examples a Hybrid type windowServer and a CooL type WINDOW_CONTROL. The Hybrid windowServer defines in the Hybrid cell the interface through which a window server is to be accessed (requested interface), while the CooL WINDOW_CONTROL provides an implementation of a window server (offered interface). For simplicity we assume that the operation names of the two types describe accurately the functionality of the operations. That is, the operation named newWindow creates a new window, while the operation get_Position returns the position pointed to by the pointing devices.

The Hybrid type windowServer (figure 3.1) has five operations. Operations newWindow and newSquareWin return the id of the newly created window or zero in case of failure. Op-

---
* The syntax of the operation bindings is described in detail in section 3.6.3.

```
TYPE WINDOW_CONTROL =
  OBJECT
    METHOD create_win ( IN botRightX : INT, IN botRightY : INT,
        IN topLeftX : INT, IN topLeftY : INT, IN color : INT ) : INT
    METHOD redisplay_all (IN display : DISPLAY) : INT
    METHOD get_Position (IN inDevices : IO_DEVICES, IN scaling : INT) : POSITION
    METHOD select_Window (IN position : POSITION) : INT
  BODY
  ...
  END OBJECT
```

Figure 3.2 *CooL type WINDOW_CONTROL.*

eration refreshDisplay returns true or false, signifying success or failure. Operation readCoordinates returns the coordinates of the active point on the screen as read from the pointing devices and operation windowSelected returns the id of the currently selected window or zero if no window is selected.

The CooL type WINDOW_CONTROL (figure 3.2) has four methods. The methods create_win and select_Window return the id of the newly created window and of the window into which the specific position is found, or −1 in case of an error. Method redisplay_all returns 0 or 1, signifying failure or success, and method get_Position returns the position pointed by the I/O devices (i.e. keyboard, mouse, touch-screen) as adapted by the scaling factor.

3.6.3 Binding of Operations

Although type WINDOW_CONTROL provides all the functionality that type windowServer requires, this is done via an interface different to the one that windowServer expects. In general in the IAL we anticipate two levels of interface differences — first in the required parameters (order, type, etc.) and second in the set of supported operations, i.e. different number of operations with aggregated, segregated or slightly[*] different functionality. The resolution of these differences corresponds to the parameter and interface phases of the interface adaption definition.

3.6.3.1 Parameter Phase

Assuming that the functionality of the provided operation corresponds to the requested functionality, the differences between the parameters passed to the local operation call (offered parameters) and of the parameters required by the remote operation (requested parameters) can fall into one or more of the following categories:

- *Different order of parameters.* For example, the first parameter of the local operation might correspond to the second on the remote operation.

---

[*] The term is used loosely and it is up to the user to define what is a "slight" difference in functionality.

Interface Adaption

- *Different representation of the information held by the parameter.* For example a boolean condition TRUE or FALSE can be represented locally by an integer while on the remote operation the string "TRUE" or "FALSE" might be expected.
- *Different semantic representation of the information.* For example if we have a Hybrid array with ten elements indexed from 10 to 19, an equivalent array in CooL will be indexed 1 to 10. Thus an index, say 15, of the Hybrid array should be communicated as 6 to the CooL cell.
- *Different number of parameters.* The requested parameters might be more or less than the offered ones. In this case the parameters offered might include all information needed or more information might be required.

The IAL anticipates all the above differences and allows the user to specify the needed transformations for handling them.

Migrated parameters

In our example we consider first the operations newWindow and create_win which have the same functionality specification. The binding of newWindow to create_win is expressed in IAL as follows:

   newWindow : create_win($3, $4, $1, $2, 17) ^ RET ;

Operation newWindow offers four parameters which are identified by their position with a positive integer ($1 to $4). Method create_win will be called with these parameters transposed. Its first parameter will be the third passed by newWindow, the second will be the fourth and so on. The fifth parameter of create_win is an integer that specifies the colour of the new window. This information does not exists in the offered parameters. Nevertheless, in this case, we can use a default value using a integer literal, like in the example the number 17. The returned value from create_win, noted as RET in IAL, is passed back to the Hybrid cell and becomes the value that newWindow will return.

In the above operation binding definition we assume that a relation for the CooL and Hybrid integers exists. That is we assume that on the Hybrid cell we have

   CooLCell :: integer => INT ;

and on the CooL cell

   HybridCell :: INT => integer ;

This way migration of the parameters and returned values will be handled automatically.

Operation newSquareWin does not exist in the interface of WINDOW_CONTROL but its functionality can be achieved by operation create_win called with specific parameter values. That is we can have

   newSquareWin : create_win (bottomRX($1, $3), bottomRY($2, $3), $1, $2, 17) ^ RET;

where functions bottomRX and bottomRY are adaption functions. Adaption functions are user-defined functions, private to the specific interface adaption. They provide the means through which the user can adapt the offered parameters to a format compatible to the requested parameters. They can be called with or without parameters. The parameters to be passed to the adaption functions can be any of the offered parameters or even the result of another adaption function. In the type matching definition of the IAL the adaption functions are included at the end of the interface adaption definition between @{ and @}. Thus for the previous example we have the following adaption functions:

```
@{
    bottomRX : (integer : topLeftX, side ) -> integer ;
        { return (topLeftX + side ) ; }
    bottomRY : (integer : topLeftY, side ) -> integer ;
        { return (topLeftY - side ) ; }
@}
```

The adaption functions will be invoked locally (i.e. in our example, in the Hybrid cell) and their result will be passed as parameter to the remote call (create_win). An adaption function is effectively a private operation of the inter-class and as such it can access its instance variables or other operations.

Mapped Parameters

When the parameter cannot be migrated to the remote cell, i.e. when there is no corresponding equivalent or translated type, it should be accessed on the local cell. This will be done via a *mapping* of a remote object to the local parameter according to an existing type match. In our example this will need to be done for the refreshDisplay operation and redisplay_all method.

The parameter passed to refreshDisplay is an object of type display which cannot be migrated to the CooL cell. Thus it must be accessed on the Hybrid cell via a mapping on the CooL cell. For this a type match must exist on the CooL cell to the Hybrid display type.

```
HybridCell :: DISPLAY -> display { .... } ;
```

This way the binding of refreshDisplay to redisplay_all is expressed as

```
refreshDisplay : redisplay_all ( $1 : display <- DISPLAY ) ^ int2bool(RET) ;
```

meaning that the first parameter of the method redisplay_all will be an object mapped to the first parameter passed to the operation refreshDisplay, according to the specified type match on the CooL cell. In addition the returned value of redisplay_all, which is an integer, is transformed to a Boolean via the adaption function int2bool which is defined as follows:

```
@{
    int2bool : ( integer : intval ) -> boolean ;
        { return ( intval ~=? 0); }
@}
```

Multi-type mapped parameters

In IAL we also anticipate the case where the functionality of a type is expressed by the composite functionality of more than one type on the remote cell. In our example this is the case for the CooL type IO_DEVICES, which corresponds to the composite functionality of the Hybrid types mouse, keyboard and touchScreen.

```
HybridCell :: IO_DEVICES -> < keyboard @, mouse @, touchScreen @ > { ... } ;
```

Object Mapping   87

Note that in this example the IO_DEVICES inter-object will be connected to the existing keyboard, mouse and touchScreen objects on the Hybrid cell.

The definition of multi-type match operation bindings is similar to that of single type match bindings, but with the definition of the operation's type. If, for example, we assume that type IO_DEVICES has a method read_keyboard which corresponds to the operation readInput of the Hybrid keyboard type, the binding would be expressed as

    read_keyboard : keyboard.readInput (...) ^ ... ;

In fact this syntax is the general syntax for the definition of an operation binding and can be used in both single- or multi- type matchings. Nevertheless for simplicity in single-type matchings the definition of the corresponding type can be omitted since there is only one type involved.

In our example, the binding of the Hybrid operation readCoordinates to the operation get_Position will be expressed as

    readCoordinates : get_Position (
            < $2, $1, $3 > : < keyboard, mouse, touchScreen > <- IO_DEVICES,
            $4) ^ RET

assuming that we have on the CooL cell the relation

    HybridCell :: POSITION +> point ;

3.6.3.2 Interface Phase

When defining the operation bindings between two types from different environments there will be cases where the functionality of the local operation is an aggregation of the functionality of more than one remote operation. Adapting a requested operation interface to an offered one might require anything from simple combinations of the operations up to extensive programming. In order to simplify the user's task, IAL allows the definition of simple operation combinations in the type match specification. For example, the functionality of the Hybrid operation windowSelected can be obtained with the combination of the CooL methods get_Position and select_Window. The operation binding is thus:

    windowSelected : select_Window (WINDOW_CONTROL.get_Position (
        < $2, $1, $3 > : < keyboard, mouse, touchScreen > <- IO_DEVICES, $4)) ^ RET ;

This defines that the method get_Position will first be called on the remote CooL cell and its result will not be returned to the calling Hybrid cell but it will be used as the first parameter to the select_Window method. Since the result of the get_Position method is not returned to the Hybrid cell, there is no need for a type relation of the CooL type POSITION to exist on the Hybrid cell.

3.7 Object Mapping

Whereas interface adaption provides the means to express in an implementation language-independent way the relations between heterogeneous interfaces, object mapping provides the required language-dependent run-time interoperability support. The first task

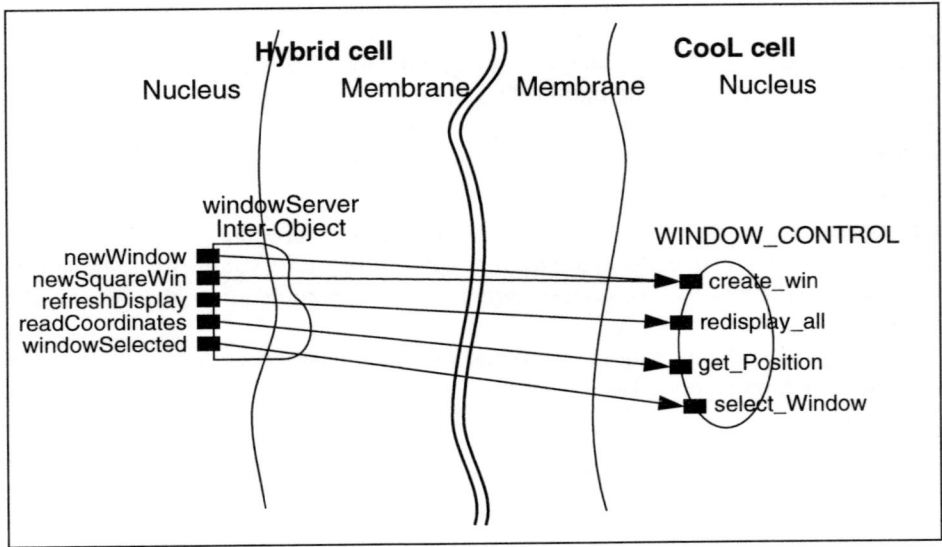

Figure 3.3 *Object mapping.*

of object mapping is to generate from the interface adaption specifications the inter-classes at the client side. Instances of an inter-class provide the client with the requested service interface and their principal task is to forward the operation invocation to the target server according to the specified interface transformations and adaptions.

In the following we describe the functionality of object mapping via the previously described example of interface adaption between the Hybrid WindowServer and the CooL WINDOW_CONTROL. In figure 3.3 we present the binding between the operations of the Hybrid inter-object and the CooL server and describe the actions taken when an operation of the windowServer inter-object is called. For our example we consider the operation readCoordinates, which is called with four parameters — a keyboard object, a mouse object, a touchScreen object and an integer (figure 3.4) — and which is bound to the method get_Position.

```
readCoordinates : get_Position (
                  < $2, $1, $3 > : < keyboard, mouse, touchScreen > <- IO_DEVICES,
                  $4 ) ^ RET
```

From the four parameters passed to operation readCoordinates, the first three (keyboard, mouse and touchScreen) cannot be migrated to the CooL cell but must be accessed locally via a multi-type match of the CooL type IO_DEVICES. The fourth parameter is an integer for which an equivalent type exists on the CooL cell and thus it can be migrated to it. The object mapping server will thus instantiate on the CooL cell two objects: an inter-object of type IO_DEVICES connected to the Hybrid objects keyboard, mouse and touchScreen, and an INT object initialized to the value of the integer parameter (figure 3.5).

Object Mapping

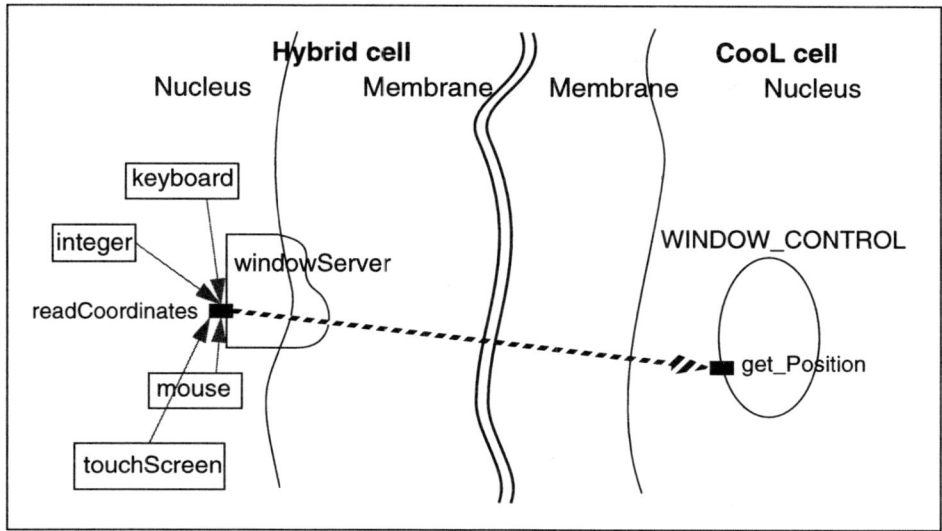

Figure 3.4 *Operation call forwarding.*

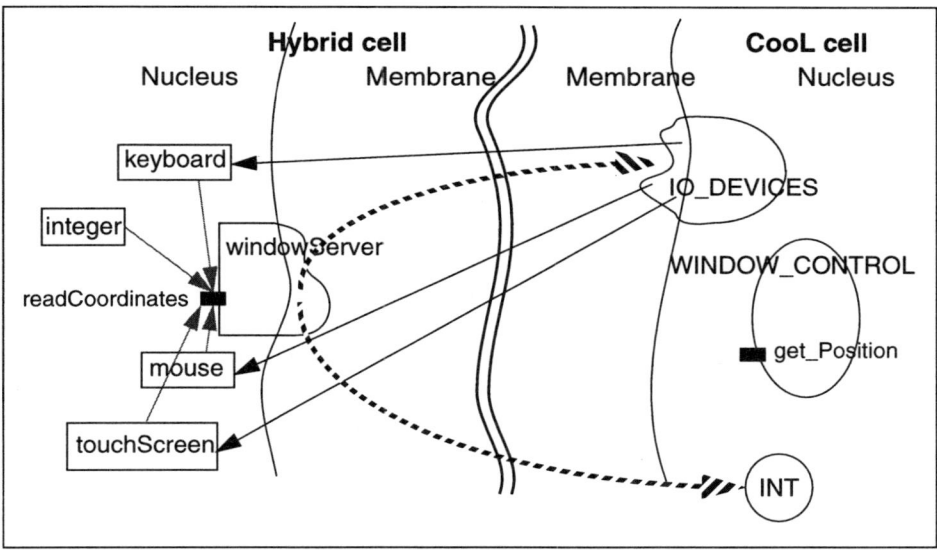

Figure 3.5 *Parameter transfer.*

When the transfer of the parameters has been completed the object mapping server will proceed with the invocation of the remote operation. The operation get_Position will be invoked with the IO_DEVICES inter-object and the INT object (figure 3.6) as parameters. The

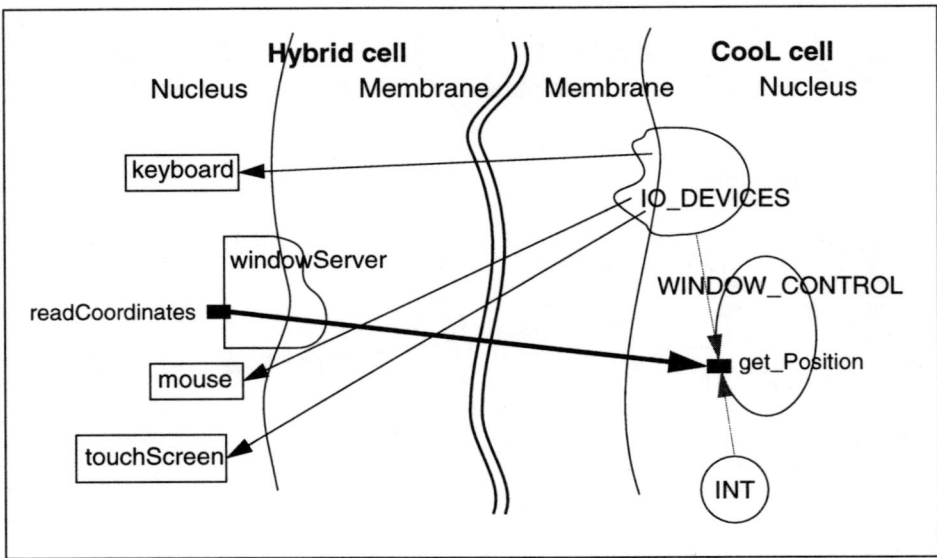

Figure 3.6 *Remote operation invocation.*

result, an object of type POSITION, will then need to be returned to the Hybrid caller. Because for the CooL type POSITION there exists a translation to the Hybrid type point, the object mapping server will instantiate an object of type point on the Hybrid cell which will be initialized to the translated value of the POSITION object. This object will be the result returned to the caller of the readCoordinates operation.

During the transfer of parameters the object mapping server might encounter a type for which no type relation has been defined. For example, it might be that on the CooL cell there is no type relation for the type IO_DEVICES. In this case when the instantiation of an IO_DEVICES inter-object is requested, the type-matching server will dynamically request the definition of the type match. The user will be required to define on the fly a type match for the IO_DEVICES type. Once this is done the object-mapping server will resume the transfer of the parameters. This way an application can be started even without any type relations defined. The object-mapping server will prompt the user to define all needed type relations during the first run of the application.

3.8 Conclusions and Research Directions

One of the important advantages of object-oriented design and development methodology is the ability to reuse existing software modules. However, the introduction of many programming languages with different syntaxes, semantics and paradigms severely restricts the reuse of objects programmed in different programming languages. Although *adhoc*

Conclusions and Research Directions

solutions can be given to solve specific inter-language reuse cases, different interoperability support methods provide the framework for consistent inter-language access and reuse of objects.

We classify the interoperability support approaches in two ways: first depending on the way that they solve the problem of the different interfaces, and second on the point at which the interoperability support is handled. For the first classification we distinguish the *interface standardization* approaches, which standardize the interface under which a service (functionality) is offered, and the *interface bridging* approaches, which bridge the differences between interfaces. For the second classification we distinguish the *procedure-oriented interoperability* approaches, which handle interoperability at the point of the procedure call, and the *object-oriented interoperability* approaches, which handle interoperability at the point of the object.

From the above approaches the interface bridging object-oriented interoperability (IB-OOI) approach is the most flexible one since it does not impose predefined interfaces and can be applied equally well to both object-oriented and non-object-oriented environments. The Cell framework, which we describe in detail, provides an example of the IB-OOI approach.

Because the IB-OOI is by no means incompatible with other interoperability approaches, its ideas and concepts can be incorporated into other interoperability frameworks, e.g. the CORBA, and significantly enhance their openness and interoperability support. Furthermore the flexibility and generality of the IB-OOI ideas can provide a framework for the solution of software integration and software evolution problems related to legacy systems.

3.8.1 Openness of Interoperability Platforms

One of the major disadvantages of existing interoperability frameworks, the most prominent of which is CORBA, is that they are *closed to themselves*. That is, client and server applications interacting via the interoperability platform must be implemented making use the specific platform interfaces. As a result, taking CORBA as an example, existing applications cannot be incorporated in the CORBA "world" (non-CORBA clients cannot use CORBA services, and non-CORBA servers cannot offer their services to CORBA clients), nor can CORBA applications be moved to a non-CORBA environment.

Designing an interface adaption service for CORBA that will allow C++, for example, client applications to access CORBA services via their IDL interface will significantly enhance the openness and acceptability of CORBA and will allow almost any application to take advantage of the services CORBA offers.

3.8.2 Interoperability and Legacy System Migration

One of the major problems that companies are facing due to the rapid advances of the computer software and hardware technologies is the migration of their legacy systems to a new platform. Most of the given solutions are *adhoc* case-dependent solutions; only recently has some kind of methodology started appearing [2][3]. However, although the problem of legacy system migration is in effect an interoperability problem, it has not been recognized as such. The reason is that most of the work and research done in the area of interoperability support focuses on the interoperability support of new applications using the interface standardization approach and does not consider existing legacy applications.

A prominent framework for the support of legacy system migration can be provided with the interface bridging object-oriented interoperability (IB-OOI) approach. A smooth incremental migration of a legacy system can be achieved by identifying its components and their interfaces and using an IB-OOI support to replace the legacy components with new ones, which most probably have a different interface [14]. This way new components can be incrementally added to the system without affecting the remaining legacy ones.

References

[1] Denise Bermek and Hugo Pickardt, "HooDS 0.3/00 Pilot Release Information," ITHACA.SNI.91.D2#4, Deliverable of the ESPRIT Project ITHACA (2705), 28 Aug. 1991.

[2] Thomas J. Brando and Myra Jean Prelle, "DOMIS Project Experience: Migrating Legacy Systems to CORBA Environments," Technical Report, The MITRE Corporation, Bedford, Mass., 1994.

[3] Michael L. Brodie and Michael Stonebraker, "DARWIN: On the Incremental Migration of Legacy Information Systems," DOM Technical Report, TR-0222-10-92-165, GTE Laboratories Inc., March 1993.

[4] Rachid Guerraoui, *Programmation Repartie par Objets: Etudes et Propositions*, Ph.D. thesis, Universite de Paris-Sud, Oct. 1992.

[5] Adele Goldberg, *Smalltalk-80*, Addison-Wesley, Reading, Mass. 1984.

[6] Yoshinori Kishimoto, Nobuto Kotaka, Shinichi Honiden, "OMEGA: A Dynamic Method Adaption Model for Object Migration," Laboratory for New Software Architectures, IPA Japan, Working Paper, April 1991.

[7] Dimitri Konstantas, Oscar Nierstrasz and Michael Papathomas, "An Implementation of Hybrid," in *Active Object Environments*, ed. D. Tsichritzis, Centre Universitaire d'Informatique, University of Geneva, 1988, pp. 61–105.

[8] Dimitri Konstantas, "Cell: A Model for Strongly Distributed Object Based Systems," in *Object Composition* ed. D. Tsichritzis, CUI, University of Geneva, 1991, pp. 225–237.

[9] Dimitri Konstantas, "Design Issues of a Strongly Distributed Object Based System," *Proceedings of 2nd International Workshop for Object-Orientation in Operating Systems (I-WOOOS '91)*, IEEE, Palo Alto, Oct. 17–18, 1991, pp. 156–163.

[10] Dimitri Konstantas, "Hybrid Update," in *Object Frameworks*, ed. D. Tsichritzis, Centre Universitaire d'Informatique, University of Geneva, 1992, pp. 109–118.

[11] Dimitri Konstantas, "Hybrid Cell: An Implementation of an Object Based Strongly Distributed System," *Proceedings of the International Symposium on Autonomous Decentralized Systems ISADS '93*, Kawasaki, Japan, March 1993.

[12] Dimitri Konstantas, "Cell: A Framework for a Strongly Distributed Object Based System," Ph.D. thesis No. 2598, University of Geneva, May 1993.

References

[13] Dimitri Konstantas, "Object-Oriented Interoperability," *Proceedings ECOOP '93*, ed. O. Nierstrasz, *Lecture Notes in Computer Science*, vol. 707, Springer-Verlag, Kaiserslautern, Germany, July 1993, pp. 80–102.

[14] Dimitri Konstantas, "Towards the Design and Implementation of a Safe and Secure Interoperability Support Layer in CHASSIS," CHASSIS SPP project technical report, University of Geneva, March 1994.

[15] Jintae Lee and Thomas W. Malone, "How Can Groups Communicate when they use Different Languages? Translating Between Partially Shared Type Hierarchies," *Proceedings of the Conference on Office Information Systems*, March 1988, Palo Alto, CA.

[16] Barbara Liskov, Dorothy Curtis, Paul Johnson and Robert Scheifler, "Implementation of Argus," in *Proceedings of the 11th ACM Symposium on Operating Systems Principles*, ACM, Austin, Tex., Nov. 1987, pp. 111–122.

[17] Oscar Nierstrasz, "A Tour of Hybrid — A Language for Programming with Active Objects," *Advances in Object-Oriented Software Engineering*, ed. D. Mandrioli, B. Meyer, Prentice Hall, 1992, pp. 167–182.

[18] Object Management Group and X Open, *The Common Object Request Broker: Architecture and Specification*, Document Number 91.12.1 Revision 1.1

[19] Object Management Group, *Object Management Architecture Guide*, OMG TC Document 92.11.1, Revision 2.0, Sept. 1992.

[20] Anna-Kristin Pröfrock, Dennis Tsichritzis, Gerhard Müller and Martin Ader, "ITHACA: An Integrated Toolkit for Highly Advanced Computer Applications," in *Object Oriented Development*, ed. D. Tsichritzis, Centre Universitaire d'Informatique, University of Geneva, July 1989, pp. 321–344.

[21] James M. Purtilo and Joanne A. Atlee, "Module Reuse by Interface Adaption," *Software Practice & Experience,* vol. 21 no. 6, June 1991.

[22] Ken Sakamura, "Programmable Interface Design in HFDS," *Proceedings of the Seventh TRON Project Symposium*, Springer-Verlag, Tokyo, 1990.

[23] Marc Shapiro, "Structure and Encapsulation in Distributed Systems: The Proxy Principle," *6th International Conference on Distributed Computing Systems*, Boston, Mass., May 1986.

[24] Peter Wegner, "Concepts and Paradigms of Object-Oriented Programming," *ACM OOPS Messenger*, vol. 1, no. 1, Aug. 1990, pp. 7–87.

[25] Jack C. Wileden, Alexander L. Wolf, William R. Rosenblatt and Peri L. Tarr, "Specification Level Interoperability," *Communications of ACM*, vol. 34, no. 5, May 1991.

[26] Daniel M. Yellin and Robert E. Strom, "Interfaces, Protocols, and the Semi-Automatic Construction of Software Adaptors," proceedings of the 9th annual conference on *Object Oriented Programming Systems, Languages and Applications — OOPSLA'94*, Portland, Oreg., 23–27 Oct. 1994.

Annex I: Interface Adaption Language

typeMatchDef	: remoteCellId '::' typeMatch ';'
typeMatch	: localType '->' remoteTypes typeMatchSpec | localType '=>' remoteType [':' transFunction] | localType '+>' remoteType [':' transFunction]
remoteTypes	: '<' remoteTypeList '>'
remoteTypeList	: remoteType ['@'] [',' remoteTypeList]
typeMatchSpec	: '{' operMatchList '}' [adaptDefList]
adaptDefList	: '@{' Program '@}' [adaptDefList]
operMatchList	: operMatch [operMatchList]
operMatch	: localOpName ':' remoteOpDef '(' argMatchList ')' '^' returnValDef ';'
remoteOpDef	: remoteType '.' remoteOpName
argMatchList	: argMatch [',' argMatchList]
argMatch	: localArgId | adaptFunct '(' localArgId ')' | localArgId ':' localType '<-' remoteType | '<' localArgIdList '>' ':' '<' localTypeList '>' '<-' remoteType | remoteOpDef '(' argMatchList ')'
returnValDef	: RET | adaptFunct '(' RET ')' | RET ':' localType '->' remoteType
localArgIdList	: localArgId [',' localArgIdList]
localTypeList	: localType [',' localTypeList]
localArgId	: '$'SMALL_INTEGER | INTEGER_LITERAL
localType	: STRING
remoteType	: STRING
remoteOpName	: STRING
remoteCellId	: STRING
transFunction	: STRING
adaptFunct	: STRING
Program	: *Program code in Native Language.*

Annex II: Type Match Definition Example

```
CooLCell :: windowServer -> WINDOW_CONTROL {
   newWindow : create_win($3, $4, S1, $2, 17 ) ^ RET ;
   newSquareWin : create_win ( bottomRX($1, $3), bottomRY($2, $3), $1, $2, 17 )
         ^ RET ;
   refreshDisplay : redisplay_all ( $1 : display <- DISPLAY ) ^ int2bool(RET) ;
   readCoordinates : get_Position
         (< $2, $1, $3 > : < keyboard, mouse, touchScreen > <- IO_DEVICES,
         $ 4 ) ^ RET
   windowSelected : select_Window (
      WINDOW_CONTROL.get_Position
         ( < $2,  $1, $3 > : < keyboard, mouse, touchScreen > <- IO_DEVICES, 1)
      ) ^ RET ;
}
@{
   bottomRX : (integer : topLeftX, side ) -> integer ;
      { return (topLeftX + side ) ; }

   bottomRY : (integer : topLeftY, side ) -> integer ;
      { return (topLeftY - side ) ; }

   int2bool : ( integer : intval ) -> boolean ;
      {
         return (intval ~=? 0) ;
      }
@} ;
```

PART III

Specification and Composition

Chapter 4

Regular Types for Active Objects*

Oscar Nierstrasz

Abstract Previous work on type-theoretic foundations for object-oriented programming languages has mostly focused on applying or extending functional type theory to functional "objects." This approach, while benefiting from a vast body of existing literature, has the disadvantage of dealing with state change either in a roundabout way or not at all, and completely sidestepping issues of concurrency. In particular, dynamic issues of non-uniform service availability and conformance to protocols are not addressed by functional types. We propose a new type framework that characterizes objects as regular (finite state) processes that provide guarantees of service along public channels. We also propose a new notion of subtyping for active objects, based on Brinksma's notion of *extension*, that extends Wegner and Zdonik's "principle of substitutability" to non-uniform service availability. Finally, we formalize what it means to "satisfy a client's expectations," and we show how regular types can be used to tell when sequential or concurrent clients are satisfied.

4.1 Introduction

Much of the work on developing type-theoretic foundations for object-oriented programming languages has its roots in typed lambda calculus. In such approaches, an object is viewed as a record of functions together with a hidden representation type [10]. While this

---

* This chapter is a revised and corrected version of a previously published paper. © ACM. *Proceedings OOPSLA '93*, Washington DC, Sept. 26 – Oct. 1, 1993, pp. 1–15. Permission to copy without fee all or part of this material is granted provided that the copies are not made or distributed for direct commercial advantage, the ACM copyright notice and the title of the publication and its date appear, and notice is given that copying is by permission of the Association for Computing Machinery. To copy otherwise, or to republish, requires a fee and/or specific permission.

view has the advantage of benefiting from a well-developed body of literature that has a great deal to say of relevance to OOP about polymorphism and subtyping — see, for example, chapter 6 of this book — the fact that objects in real object-oriented languages change state is typically dealt with in an indirect way.

The mismatch is even more acute in concurrent object-oriented languages. In such languages, "active objects" may have their own thread of control and may delay the servicing of certain requests according to synchronization constraints [20]. Such objects may furthermore require a particular protocol to be obeyed (such as an initialization protocol) for them to behave properly. Chapter 2 of this book presents a survey of such languages and a thorough discussion of issues. See also chapter 12 for an example of an object-oriented framework in which "gluons" encapsulate protocols to facilitate dynamic interconnection of components. Existing notions of object types coming from a functional setting do not address the issues of non-uniform service availability or conformance to a service protocol. (Although these issues are also relevant for passive objects and sequential OOPLs, we draw our main motivation from object-based concurrency, and so we will refer in a general way to "active" objects.)

We argue that, in order to address these issues, it is essential to start by viewing an object as a *process*, not a function. (See [26] for other reasons.) By "process" we mean an abstract machine that communicates by passing messages along named channels, as in Milner's CCS [24] or the polyadic π-calculus [25]. Processes naturally model objects since they represent pure behaviour (i.e. by message passing). Behaviour and "state" are indistinguishable in such an approach, since the current state of a process is just its current behaviour. Unfortunately there has been considerably less research done on type models for processes than for functions, and the work that has been done focuses primarily on typing *channels*, not processes (see, for example [25] [33]).

Although processes in general may exhibit arbitrary behaviour, we can (normally) expect objects to conform to fairly regular patterns of behaviour. In fact, we propose on the one hand to characterize the *service types* associated with an object in terms of types of request and reply messages, and on the other hand to characterize the *availability* of these services by *regular types* that express the abstract states in which services are available and when transitions between abstract states may take place. Services represent contracts or "promises" over the message-passing behaviour of the object: in a given state the object will accept certain types of requests over its public channels, and promises to (eventually) send a reply along a private channel (supplied as part of the request message). When providing a particular service, an object may (non-deterministically) change its abstract state to alter the availability of selected services.

Subtyping in our framework is based on a generalization of Wegner and Zdonik's "principle of substitutability" [34]: services may be refined as long as the original promises are still upheld (by means of a novel application of intersection types [5] [31]), and regular types may be refined according to a subtype relation — based on Brinksma's *extension* relation for LOTOS processes [7] — that we call "request substitutability."

In section 4.2 we shall briefly review what we mean by "type" and "subtype," and how we may understand the notion of *substitutability* in the context of active objects. In section

4.3 we introduce *service types* as a means to characterize the types of request messages understood by an object and their associated replies, and we show how *intersection* over service types provides us with a means to refine these specifications.

In section 4.4 we define *request substitutability* for transition systems and we demonstrate its relationship to failures equivalence. In section 4.5 we introduce *regular types* as a means to specify the protocols of active objects. In section 4.6 we propose to use request substitutability as a subtype relationship for regular types, and we demonstrate a simple algorithm for checking that one regular type is request substitutable for another. Next, we formalize a client's expectations in terms of *request satisfiability*, and we show how regular types relate to this notion.

In section 4.8 we summarize a number of open issues to be resolved on the way to practically applying our type framework to real object-oriented languages. We conclude with some remarks on unexplored directions.

4.2 Types, Substitutability and Active Objects

Before we embark on a discussion of what types should do for active objects, we should be careful to state as precisely as possible (albeit informally) what we believe types are and what they are for. Historically, types have meant many things from templates for data structures and interface descriptions, to algebraic theories and retracts over Scott's semantic domains. We are interested in viewing types as *partial specifications of behaviour* of values in some domain of discourse. Furthermore, types should express things about these values that tell us how we may use them safely. Naturally, we would also like these specifications to (normally) be statically checkable.

Subtyping is a particular kind of type refinement. The *interpretation* of a type for some value space determines which values satisfy the type. A subtype, then, is simply a stronger specification and guarantees that the set of values satisfying the subtype is a *subset* of those that satisfy the supertype. If T is a type (expression) and $\mathcal{U}$ is some universal value space of interest, then we shall write x:T to mean x satisfies T, and $[\![T]\!]$ to mean $\{\, x \mid x{:}T \,\}$ (i.e. where $\mathcal{U}$ is understood). Another type S is a subtype of T, written S≤T, if x:S $\Rightarrow$ x:T, i.e. $[\![S]\!] \subseteq [\![T]\!]$.

But specifically what *kinds* of properties should types specify? It is worthwhile to recall Wegner and Zdonik's principle of substitutability:

> An instance of a subtype can always be used in any context in which an instance of a supertype was expected. [34]

It is important to recognize that "can be used" implies *only* "safely," and nothing more. It does not imply, for instance, that an application in which a type has been replaced by some subtype will exhibit the same behaviour. We are not concerned with full behavioural compatibility, but only with safe usage.

What does type safety mean in an object-oriented setting? First of all, that objects should only be sent messages that they "understand." We must therefore be able to specify

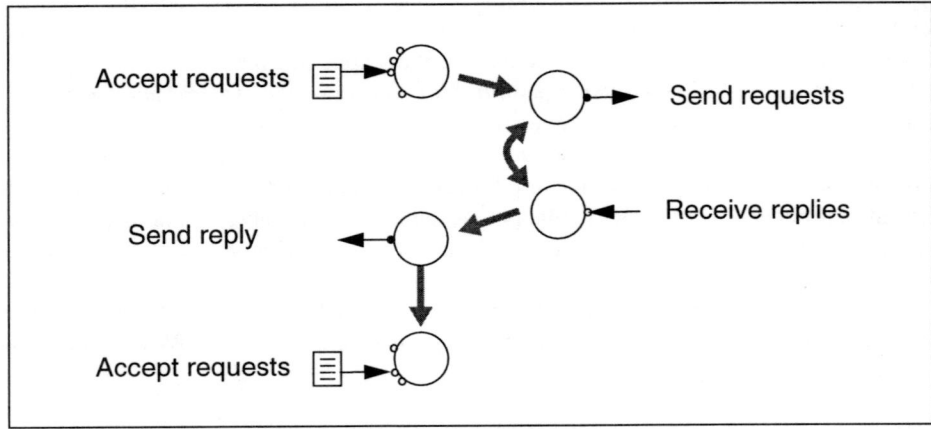

Figure 4.1 *Non-uniform service availability.*

the types of request and reply messages exchanged by objects. If we think of objects as "servers," then the services they provide are promises that they understand certain types of requests, and that, in response to a particular request, they will eventually send a certain type of reply. Subtyping of services can then be defined in a fairly conventional way, in that a subtype at least guarantees the promises of the supertype: at least the same requests are understood (possibly more) and consequent replies to those requests are guaranteed to be of the right type.

Services may not always be available, however. If requests must be sent in a certain order, or if certain services may be temporarily unavailable, then, we argue, the object's type should describe this. Type safety, in this case, means that clients (or, more generally, environments) that interact with such objects do not deadlock because of protocol errors. Type substitutability is correspondingly defined so that sequences of interactions that are valid for a supertype are also valid for a subtype. A client will never be unexpectedly starved of service because a subtype instance has been substituted.

In order to explain our type approach, we will adopt an object model that views objects as certain kinds of communicating processes [4][8][17][24]. (Although we could formalize our model in process-theoretic terms, as in, for example, [30], for the purposes of this presentation we will attempt to be rigorous and precise without being excessively formal.)

Figure 4.1 depicts an object's behaviour in an idealized fashion. The large circles represent the object in its various states and the small circles represent its communication channels, white for input and black for output. The input channels on the left side are for receiving requests. Note that the set of "enabled" input requests changes over time.

In our object model, every object receives requests along uniquely identified channels, one per request name. Each request consists of a message containing a number of arguments and a unique reply address (also a channel name). The arguments must be of the correct type. (We will not be concerned with what kinds of values may be passed, but the

Intersecting Service Types

reader may assume that any reasonable value — objects, object identifiers, channel names, etc. — is fair game.)

An object, then, accepts requests addressed to it through its (public) request channels, and it may issue requests to other objects it is acquainted with via *their* request channels. All replies, however, are communicated along *private* channels that are temporarily established by clients of requests. When an object accepts a request, it implicitly *guarantees* to (eventually) send a reply (of the correct type) to the client. This reply may be delivered by a third party to which the reply address has been forwarded. Furthermore, the object may vary the requests accepted over time by selectively listening only to certain request channels. When an object is ready to accept a message addressed to one of its request channels, we say that the request is *enabled*, and that the corresponding service is *available*. We assume that the complete set of public request channels is finite and fixed in advance for any object.

We will now separately discuss the issues of specifying types of services associated with an object (section 4.3), and specifying when those services are available (section 4.4).

4.3 Intersecting Service Types

We will start by introducing the following syntax for service types:
$S ::= \text{all} \mid \text{none} \mid M(V) \rightarrow V \mid S \wedge S$
$V ::= \text{all} \mid \text{none} \mid (V,...) \mid ...$

where M is a request name and V is a value type (i.e. types for argument and return values). "$\rightarrow$" binds more tightly than "$\wedge$". We assume that V includes some base types, the types all and none, and tuples over value types.

We will write $x : m(A) \rightarrow R$ to mean that object x may receive a value a of type A together with a reply address along a request channel x_m and will consequently promise to return a value r of type R. We may also write x.m(a) : R to say that x understands the message m(a) and returns a value of type R. We call the type expression $m(A) \rightarrow R$ a *service* of x, and we say that x *offers* this service. Note that this does not imply anything about other services that x may or may not offer.

We may refine these expressions by the *intersection* operator for types ($\wedge$). Intersection types have been studied extensively in functional settings (see [31] for a bibliography). Here we propose to assign an interpretation to them for objects in a process setting. If we write x:S1^S2, we wish that to mean precisely that x:S1 *and* x:S2. In set-theoretic terms, then:

$[\![S1 \wedge S2]\!] = [\![S1]\!] \cap [\![S2]\!]$

As specifications, we mean that both S1 and S2 are true statements about x. As we shall see, this device allows us not only to attribute sets of services to objects, but also permits us to refine their types in interesting ways.

The expressions all and none represent, respectively, the set of all objects and the empty set. That is, all tells us nothing about the services of an object, and none demands so much that no object can possibly satisfy it. (all and none are the "top" and "bottom" of our type hierarchy.)

Let us now briefly look at the subtyping properties of service types. Some facts are clear:

1. $T \leq$ all (i.e. for any value or service type T)
2. none $\leq T$
3. m(none)$\rightarrow$T = all (since no such request can ever be received)
4. $R1 \leq R2 \Rightarrow m(A)\rightarrow R1 \leq m(A)\rightarrow R2$
5. $A2 \leq A1 \Rightarrow m(A1)\rightarrow R \leq m(A2)\rightarrow R$ (i.e. a contravariant rule)

Now, considering intersections, the following are straightforward:

6. $S1 \wedge S2 \leq S1$ and $S1 \wedge S2 \leq S2$
7. $S \leq S1$ and $S \leq S2 \Rightarrow S \leq S1 \wedge S2$
8. $S1 \leq S2 \Rightarrow (S1 \wedge S2) = S1$ (follows from (6) and (7))

Now consider:

9. $m(A1)\rightarrow R1 \wedge m(A2)\rightarrow R2 \leq m(A1 \wedge A2)\rightarrow(R1 \wedge R2)$

Normally we may expect to write type expressions like:

    put(all)$\rightarrow$(Ok) $\wedge$ get()$\rightarrow$(all)

but nothing prevents us from writing:

    inc(Int)$\rightarrow$Int $\wedge$ inc(Real)$\rightarrow$Real

or even:

    update(Point)$\rightarrow$Point $\wedge$ update(Colour)$\rightarrow$Colour

If an incoming message satisfies more than one request type in the intersection, then the result must satisfy *each* of the result types. Our (informal) semantics of intersection types requires that *all* applicable service guarantees must hold. In this case, if:

    cp:ColouredPoint,

where ColouredPoint = Point$\wedge$Colour

then x.update(cp):Point *and* x.update(cp):Colour. The result, therefore, must have type ColouredPoint.

Notice that as a corollary of (9), via (6) , (4) and (7), we also have:

10. $m(A)\rightarrow(R1 \wedge R2) = m(A)\rightarrow R1 \wedge m(A)\rightarrow R2$

This also means, however, that we must take care not to intersect services with abandon. For example, suppose Int and Real are disjoint types. Then:

    size(Point)$\rightarrow$Int $\wedge$ size(Colour)$\rightarrow$Real
        $\leq$ size(ColouredPoint) $\rightarrow$ (Int$\wedge$Real)
        = size(ColouredPoint) $\rightarrow$ none

Since the two size services have contradictory result types, their intersection yields the result type none.

As a final remark, notice that type-safe covariance is naturally expressed:

update(Point) → Point ∧ update(ColouredPoint) → ColouredPoint

is a subtype of both update(Point)→Point and update(ColouredPoint)→ColouredPoint. A client supplying an instance of ColouredPoint as an argument can be sure of getting a ColouredPoint back as a result, whereas clients that supply Point arguments will only be able to infer that the result is of the more general type Point.

4.4 Request Substitutability

Service types tell us what types of requests are understood by an object and what types of reply values it promises to return, but they do not tell us *when* those services are available. In particular, we are interested in specifying when an object's request channels are enabled. The sequences of requests that an object is capable of servicing constitute the object's *protocol*. An object that *conforms* to the protocol of another object is safely substitutable for that second object, in the sense that clients expecting that protocol to be supported will receive no "unpleasant surprises."

Before tackling the issue of how to specify protocols, let us first try to formalize the appropriate substitutability relation.

According to our abstract object model, objects can do four things: accept requests, issue requests, receive replies and send replies. Since the behaviour of objects should be properly encapsulated, clients should only need to know about the first and the last of these, i.e. the requests accepted and the replies sent. If we can safely assume that an object that accepts requests promises to deliver replies according to service type specifications, then the only additional thing a client needs to know about an object's protocol is when it will accept requests. We therefore adopt an abstract view of an object's protocol that only considers *requests* received along its request channels, and *ignores all other messages*. (Later, in section 4.7, we will model clients' protocols by considering only requests issued.)

In this view we model an object as a transition system where each state of interest represents a *stable* state of the object, in which it blocks for acceptance of some set of requests. A transition takes places upon the receipt of some request and leads to a new stable state. If an object in state x can accept a request r leading to a new state x', we would write:

$$x \xrightarrow{r} x'$$

Note that we ignore all intervening communications leading to the new state. If these communications are purely internal to the object, we can view it as a closed system, but if some of these communications are with external acquaintances, then an element of non-determinism is introduced, since the transitions to new stable states may depend upon the current state of the environment. In cases like this, we feel it is correct to view the object's protocol as inherently non-deterministic, since it would be unreasonable to expect clients to monitor the environment to know the state of an object's protocol.

Clients are typically interested not just in issuing a single request, but in issuing series of related requests. Suppose s is such a sequence r1,r2,... of requests. If an object in state x can accept such a sequence, leading to state x', then we write:

$$x \stackrel{s}{\Rightarrow} x'$$

An important part of the protocol of an object is the set of sequences of requests that it may accept. This is conventionally captured by the notion of set of *traces* [8] of a transition system:

Definition 1 $traces(x) \equiv \{ s \mid \exists x', x \stackrel{s}{\Rightarrow} x' \}$.

Suppose we wish to express that an object in state x is *request substitutable* for an object in state y, which we will write x:<y. Then clearly we must have $traces(y) \subseteq traces(x)$, for if a client of y expects y to accept a sequence of requests s, and we substitute x for y, then x must accept the same sequence s. x may accept additional sequences, but since the client does not expect[*] them, they are of no concern to us.

But the inclusion of traces is not enough to guarantee request substitutability, for suppose that after a sequence of requests s, y will move to state y', but x will move to either state x' or x''. Furthermore, suppose that state x' is identical to y' — i.e. behaviour from that point on is identical — and x' permits a request r to be accepted, but x'' denies it. Then it is possible that $traces(y) \subseteq traces(x)$, but nevertheless the client may receive a nasty surprise if x is substituted for y and the request r is refused after the sequence s. Traces tell us what sequences are acceptable, but they do not tell us if they are *necessarily* acceptable! For this, we need the help of a finer notion of *failures* [8].

First, we need to define the *initials* of an object — the requests which are initially enabled:

Definition 2 $init(x) \equiv \{ r \mid \exists x', x \stackrel{r}{\rightarrow} x' \}$.

Definition 3 The set of *failures* of an object x is

$$failures(x) \equiv \{ (s,R) \mid \exists x', x \stackrel{s}{\Rightarrow} x', R \text{ is finite}, R \cap init(x') = \emptyset \}.$$

That is, (s,R) is a failure of x if x may simultaneously refuse all of the requests in the set R after accepting the sequence s. It may be the case that x will reach a state in which some or all of the requests in R will be accepted, but we know that it is *possible* that they will all be refused. (NB: It is also important that the state x' be stable for the set R to be well-defined, but we have already assumed that.)

Now, suppose that we want x:<y and we know that (s,R) is a failure of x. Furthermore, suppose that s is a sequence of requests in *traces*(y). Then a client will be satisfied *only* if it expected that (s,R) was also a failure of y. Note that if s is *not* a sequence in the protocol of y, then the client is unconcerned whether (s,R) is a failure of x or not, since it is in any

---

[*] Although we have not yet formalized clients' expectations, we are implicitly assuming here that clients are *sequential*, i.e. they only issue a single request at a time. Later, when we define *request satisfiability*, we will see how request substitutability relates to concurrent clients.

case not expected to be handled. To express this notion of *relative failures*, we need the following definition:

Definition 4 The set of *relative failures* of an object in state x with respect to an object in state y is: $failures_y(x) \equiv \{ (s,R) \in failures(x) \mid s \in traces(y)\}$.

Now we come to the definition of request substitutability:

Definition 5 An object in state x is *request substitutable* for an object in state y, written x:<y iff:
  (i) $traces(y) \subseteq traces(x)$
  (ii) $failures_y(x) \subseteq failures(y)$.

(This turns out to be identical to the *extension* relation introduced by Brinksma [7]. See also Cusack [13] for a discussion of various conformance relations, including extension, in the context of CSP [8].)

That is, a client expecting x to follow the protocol of y will expect that all sequences of requests supported by y will also be accepted by x, and that any requests refused by x after accepting one of those sequences might also have been refused by y. Note that x may (1) accept additional sequences of requests that the client does not expect and therefore will not use, and (2) may eliminate some non-determinism in y by providing *fewer* possible transitions between states. On the other hand, x may introduce new transitions and states as long as they can be explained from the viewpoint of y. In general, either x or y may have more or less states or transitions.

Note also that the set of failures of an object tells us all we need to know in order to determine request substitutability, since the traces can be derived from the failures set by projections, and relative failures can be determined from the failures of one object and the traces of another.

Proposition 1 Request substitutability is a pre-order.

Proof
  (i) :< *is reflexive*: $\forall x$, x:<x — immediate, since $failures_x(x) = failures(x)$.
  (ii) :< *is transitive*: Suppose x:<y and y:<z. Then $traces(z) \subseteq traces(y) \subseteq traces(x)$.
    Next, suppose $(s,R) \in failures_z(x)$. Then $s \in traces(z) \subseteq traces(y)$,
    so $(s,R) \in failures_y(x) \subseteq failures(y)$. But then $(s,R) \in failures_z(y) \subseteq failures(z)$,
    so we conclude x:<z. □

There exists a vast literature on process equivalences and pre-orders (see, for example, [1][14] for some interesting comparisons). Interestingly, the equivalence induces by request substitutability is the same as failures equivalence [7][8].

Definition 6 Objects in states x and y are *failures equivalent* iff $failures(x) = failures(y)$.

Proposition 2 x and y are failures equivalent iff x:<y and y:<x.

Proof
  $\Rightarrow$) $failures(x) = failures(y) \Rightarrow traces(x) = traces(y)$
    $\Rightarrow failures(x) = failures_y(x) = failures_x(y) = failures(y) \Rightarrow$ x:<y and y:<x.
  $\Leftarrow$) x:<y and y:<x $\Rightarrow traces(x) = traces(y)$.

Hence $failures_y(x) = failures(x) \subseteq failures(y)$.

By symmetry, $failures(x) = failures(y)$. □

Although failures equivalence is exactly request equivalence, the inclusion of failures sets does not imply request substitutability, nor vice versa. It suffices to consider:

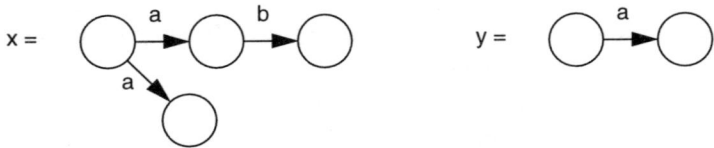

It is easy to see that x:<y (but not the reverse, since y does not permit a.b) and $failures(y) \subseteq failures(x)$ (but not the reverse, since (a.b,{a,b}) is a failure of x but not of y). See also Brinskma [7] for a detailed discussion.

4.5 Viewing Objects as Regular Processes

We now have a plausible definition of protocol conformance in terms of request substitutability — what we still need is a way to specify protocols, and a way to check that an object conforms to a protocol, or that one protocol conforms to another. In the most general case, unfortunately, request substitutability will be undecidable since failures equivalence is undecidable in general [18]. (If request substitutability were decidable, we could use its decision procedure to check if two processes were failures equivalent according to proposition 2.)

We therefore propose to specify protocols as *regular processes*, i.e. processes with a finite number of "states" or behaviours [6][11][15][23]. A regular process is essentially a finite state machine (hence the adjective "regular"), where transitions take place upon communications with other processes. We will call the specification of such a process a *regular type*, since we intend to use it to specify object protocols. It turns out that by restricting ourselves to finite state protocols, request substitutability is decidable by a simple procedure.

Furthermore, although we cannot specify all protocols exactly with a finite number of states, we can *approximate* infinite state protocols by non-deterministic regular processes. These approximations can then be used in many cases to check request substitutability.

Let us consider a few canonical examples using various kinds of "container" objects (bounded buffers, stacks, variables) each supporting (at least) put and get requests. We can associate with these objects a number of abstract states, each corresponding to a set of currently enabled requests. Since we assume that the total set of possible services is finite, a finite number of abstract states suffices to characterize all the possible combinations of enabled requests (and normally only a few of these combinations should be needed). From the client's point of view, transitions may take place when services are provided (since this is all the client may observe).

Viewing Objects as Regular Processes

First, consider a one-slot bounded buffer.

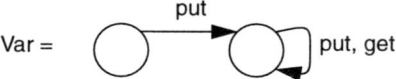
Buf =

It has two abstract states: one in which only a put is accepted, and one in which only a get is allowed. Upon accepting a put or a get request, the object changes state. We express this by the protocol (regular type) Buf.

Now consider an uninitialized variable with the protocol Var.

Var =

Its protocol requires that a put must first be requested, but then put and get requests may be interleaved arbitrarily. In this case, we see that Var:<Buf since a client that expects an object to obey the Buf protocol will never be "disappointed" if an object obeying Var is substituted. The reverse does not hold, because Buf will refuse the sequence put.get.get, whereas Var will not.

In these two cases, the transitions are deterministic, since Buf and Var are really finite state protocols.

Now consider a stack (with put and get instead of push and pop). Initially only a put is possible. Then both put and get are enabled. Further put requests will not change this, but a get may bring us back to the initial state. The corresponding regular type is specified below as NDStack.

NDStack =

It resembles Var except that after a get, we do not necessarily know what state we are in. Clearly, such a description is an approximation because we are attempting to express the service availability of a deterministic process (the object) by means of a non-deterministic one (the regular type).

We can try to add another intermediate state, as in NDStack2:

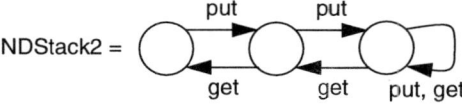
NDStack2 =

but after two put requests and a get we again do not know what state we are in. In fact, we would need an infinite number of states to describe completely the Stack protocol.

As we argued before, however, non-determinism is inherent in some protocols, because objects are not, in general, closed systems. Furthermore, the non-deterministic regular types are still useful to us. We can determine, for example, that an object conforming to the NDStack regular type also conforms to Buf since NDStack:<Buf.

Choosing a simple *and* readable syntax for specifying regular types is somewhat problematic. For the purpose of this chapter we will opt for simplicity. We specify a regular type by a pair, (x_1,E) consisting of a finite system of equations E of the form:

$E = \{ x=t, ... \}$

where x_1 is a distinguished start state, and the t are regular type expressions of the form:

$t ::= r.x \mid t + t$

r is a request name and x is a state name. Every x used in E must have exactly one defining equation in E (except for nil, which stands for a dead state with no transitions). Regular types have the following interpretation as transition systems:

1. $init(\text{nil}) = \emptyset$
2. $r.\text{nil} \xrightarrow{r} \text{nil}$
3. $x = t \in E \Rightarrow r.x \xrightarrow{r} t$
4. $t1 \xrightarrow{r1} t1' \Rightarrow t1+t2 \xrightarrow{r1} t1'$
5. $t2 \xrightarrow{r2} t2' \Rightarrow t1+t2 \xrightarrow{r2} t2'$

With this simple syntax, then, we could specify the various regular types we have seen as follows:

   Buf = (b1, { b1=put.b2, b2=get.b1 })
   Var = (v1, { v1=put.v2, v2=put.v2+get.v2 })
   NDStack = (s1, { s1=put.s2, s2=put.s2+get.s2+get.s1 })
   NDStack2 = (s1, { s1=put.s2, s2=put.s3+get.s1,
                     s3=put.s3+get.s2+get.s3 })

At this point the reader may wonder why we cannot simply use regular expressions to specify regular types. The reason is that regular expressions stand for regular *languages*, i.e. sets of strings, not regular processes. Regular expressions can consequently tell us about the traces of a transition system but not its failures. Consider, for example, the regular types Var and NDStack. If we consider any state to be a valid final state, then they recognize exactly the same regular language, namely:

$\varepsilon + \text{put}.(\text{put}+\text{get})^*$

But this does not tell us that after accepting a put followed by a get, NDStack may *refuse* another get, whereas Var never will. (A similar argument is elaborated in [16] to introduce the difference between language and process equivalence.) For precisely the same reason, it is *not* generally possible to convert a non-deterministic regular process into a deterministic one without losing information.

4.6 Subtyping Regular Types

We now propose to use request substitutability as a *subtyping* relationship over regular types. We are justified in this since we have shown that request substitutability is a preorder, so if Var:<NDStack and NDStack:<Buf, then we can conclude that Var:<Buf.

Subtyping Regular Types

The fact that regular types have finite states means that a simple algorithm exists for checking the subtype relationship (not surprisingly, the algorithm is similar to that for checking equivalence of finite state automata [2]). To derive the algorithm, we must introduce a multi-state variant of request substitutability. First let us extend $init()$ and $\rightarrow$ to work with sets of states:

Definition 7 $init(X) \equiv \{ r \mid \exists x \in X, x', x \stackrel{r}{\rightarrow} x' \}$.

Definition 8 $X \stackrel{r}{\rightarrow} X'$ iff $X' = \{ x' \mid \exists x \in X, x \stackrel{r}{\rightarrow} x' \}$.

Note in particular that $\rightarrow$ for sets of states is a *function*, not just a relation. In effect, we are turning a non-deterministic transition system into a deterministic one in the traditional way by expanding single states into sets of reachable states [2].

Now let us consider the following definition:

Definition 9 A set of object states X is *multi-state request substitutable* for a set of states Y, written X:<<Y, iff:

    (i) $init(Y) \subseteq init(X)$

    (ii) $\forall x \in X, \exists y \in Y, init(y) \subseteq init(x)$

    (iii) $\forall r \in init(Y)$, if $X \stackrel{r}{\rightarrow} X'$ and $Y \stackrel{r}{\rightarrow} Y'$, then X':<<Y'.

Condition (i) guarantees that all transitions possible from some state of Y are also possible from some state of X. Condition (ii) says that any failure possible in some state of X can be explained by a failure of some corresponding state of Y (some y has the same or fewer initial transitions possible). Condition (iii) is simply the recursive case.

Proposition 3 $\{ x \} :<< \{ y \} \Leftrightarrow x : < y$.

Proof

$\Rightarrow$) Suppose that $\{ x \} :<< \{ y \}$, then $traces(y) \subseteq traces(x)$ by 9(i) and 9(iii).

Next, suppose $(s,R) \in failures_y(x)$. Then $\exists x', x \stackrel{s}{\Rightarrow} x', init(x') \cap R = \emptyset$ and $\exists y', y \stackrel{s}{\Rightarrow} y'$, $init(y') \subseteq init(x')$ by 9.ii and 9.iii so $(s,R) \in failures(y)$ and $failures_y(x) \subseteq failures(y)$ hence x:<y.

$\Leftarrow$) Similar argument in reverse. □

Note that this result is independent of whether we restrict our attention to finite state transition systems or not. If the sets of reachable states are finite, however, i.e. if x and y are regular types, then proposition 3 provides us with a simple procedure to check whether x:<y by simply generating all the sets of states reachable from {x} and {y} by transitions in $traces(y)$ and checking conditions 9(i) and 9(ii) for all the comparable sets. Since the state space is finite, the set of reachable state sets must also be finite, and so the comparison must terminate in finite time.

The following iterative algorithm suggests itself: we maintain a LIST of comparable sets of states and possible transitions, of the form (X, Y, R), where X and Y are the sets of states of x and y reachable from some common trace s of y, and R is the set of possible transitions (requests) from Y that the algorithm must traverse. We follow each possible request to new comparable state sets until we have exhausted all transitions and checked all comparable state sets, or until we fail to satisfy one of the conditions in definition 9.

1. Verify that $init(y) \subseteq init(x)$, else FAIL
2. Add $(\{x\},\{y\},init(y))$ to LIST
3. If possible, select some (X,Y,R) from LIST where R is not empty, else SUCCEED
4. Select some r in R and replace (X,Y,R) by $(X,Y,R\setminus\{r\})$ in LIST
5. Compute X' and Y', where $X \xrightarrow{r} X'$ and $Y \xrightarrow{r} Y'$
6. If (X',Y',R') for some R' is already in LIST, then go to step 3, else continue
7. If $init(Y') \subseteq init(X')$, then continue, else FAIL
8. If for each $x_i \in X'$ there exists some $y_j \in Y'$ such that $init(y_j) \subseteq init(x_i)$, then continue, else FAIL
9. Add $(X',Y',init(Y'))$ to LIST and go to step 3.

Note that steps 2 and 7 guarantee that X' generated in step 5 will never be empty.

Since there is a finite number of reachable sets X and Y to compare, the algorithm clearly terminates. In the worst case, there will be $(2^n-1)\times(2^m-1)$ comparisons (i.e. the size of LIST), where n and m are the number of states reachable from x and y respectively, but normally there will be far fewer, since not all subsets of states will be generated, and not all possible combinations will need to be compared. In the special case that one compares two deterministic regular types, the maximum number of comparisons is just $n\times m$, but may be even as little as m (in case of success, that is).

Let us briefly look at an example that compares Buf to the regular type of a stack that supports an additional swap operation:

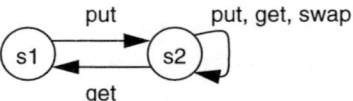

NewNDStack = (s1, { s1=put.s2,
      s2=put.s2+get.s2+get.s1+swap.s2 })

We wish to check whether NewNDStack:<Buf. We start with: ({s1},{b1},{put}). Both s1 and b1 permit a put, and they have the same requests enabled, so we can add this to our list:

({s1},{b1},{put})

The only possible transition is put, so we remove it from LIST and generate: ({s2},{b2},{get}). s2 enables at least the requests that b2 enables, so we add this to our list:

({s1},{b1},{~~put~~})
({s2},{b2},{get})

Now only a get is possible, so we generate: ({s1,s2},{b1},{put}). We verify that s1 and s2 each enable at least the requests of b1 and add this to our list:

({s1},{b1},{~~put~~})
({s2},{b2},{~~get~~})
({s1,s2},{b1},{put})

Request Satisfiability

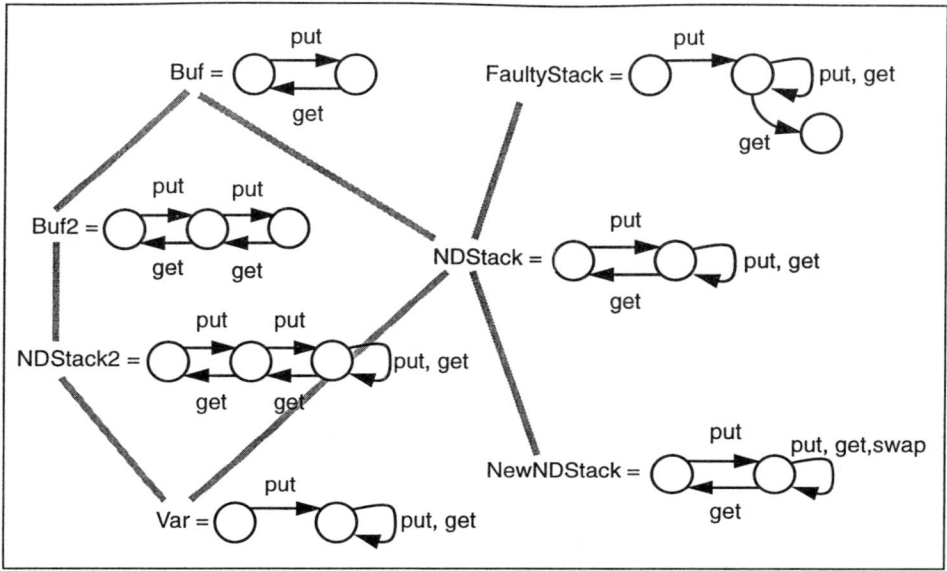

Figure 4.2 *Some subtype relationships between regular types.*

Now we can perform a put, but this just generates ({s2},{b2},{get}), which is already represented in the list. There is nothing left to check, so we SUCCEED. (In the reverse direction we would quickly FAIL in step 7 after a single put because b2 enables neither put nor swap.) Note that the total number of comparisons (3) is far less than the worst case possible (9).

Note that NewNDStack is request substitutable for Buf even though it is, in a sense, *less* deterministic than Buf. The key point is that it is safe to use wherever we are expecting Buf-like behaviour.

Figure 4.2 shows the subtype relationships between a few of the regular types we have seen. Curiously, NDStack and NDStack2 are not related (to see why, consider the sequence put.get.get, which is in *traces*(NDStack) but not in *traces*(NDStack2), and the failure (put.put.get,{get}), which is in *failures*(NDStack), but not in *failures*(NDStack2)).

4.7   Request Satisfiability

Up to now our discussion has focused on the protocols of service providers. Request substitutability tells us when an object obeying some protocol can be safely substituted by some second object, assuming that the first object satisfies the client's expectations. But we have not yet formalized what it means to satisfy a client. It turns out that we need to define a new relation, called *request satisfiability*, which expresses this idea.

If the protocol of a service provider expresses when its services are available, then the protocol of its client expresses when those services are requested. We propose that a client is *satisfied* if its requests are always honoured. Up to now we have implicitly assumed that clients issue at most one request at a time. In general, however, a client may issue multiple requests simultaneously (particularly if the "client" is actually an environment consisting of multiple concurrent clients) — in such cases, we do not ask that all of the requests be honoured together, just that the client be guaranteed to make progress, i.e. at least one request must always be accepted. Since the current state of the client may not necessarily be deterministic, the object must be prepared for the client to be in any one of its reachable states. The object is allowed to terminate (i.e. refuse all further requests) only if it can be sure that the client will issue no more requests. In short, we must ensure that an object can only *fail* if the client makes no more *offers*.

We can formalize this as follows:

Definition 10 The set of *offers* of a transition system c is:

$$\mathit{offers}(c) \equiv \{ (s,R) \mid \exists c', c \xrightarrow{s} c', R = \mathit{init}(c') \}.$$

So, if (s,R) is an offer of c, then we know that c may issue the sequence of requests s and then may issue the set of requests R. It is also possible that c may issue some other set of requests R', if (s,R') is also an offer of c.

Definition 11 An object x is *request satisfiable* for a client c, written $x \models c$, iff:

$$(s,R) \in \mathit{failures}(x) \cap \mathit{offers}(c) \Rightarrow R = \emptyset$$

If both client and server protocols are specified as regular types, then request satisfiability can be determined by an algorithm along the lines of the one we demonstrated for checking request substitutability.

4.7.1 Sequential Clients

How does request substitutability relate to request satisfiability? Clearly, we would expect that if $x{:}{<}y$ and $y \models c$, then $x \models c$. It turns out that if c is sequential, then this is in fact the case.

Definition 12 A client c is *sequential* if $(s,R) \in \mathit{offers}(c) \Rightarrow |R| \leq 1$.

Lemma 4 If c is sequential, then $y \models c \Rightarrow \mathit{traces}(c) \subseteq \mathit{traces}(y)$.

Proof By induction on the length of traces of c. □

Proposition 5 If c is sequential, then $x{:}{<}y$ and $y \models c \Rightarrow x \models c$.

Proof $(s,R) \in \mathit{failures}(x) \cap \mathit{offers}(c) \Rightarrow s \in \mathit{traces}(c) \subseteq \mathit{traces}(y)$
$\Rightarrow (s,R) \in \mathit{failures}_y(x) \subseteq \mathit{failures}(y) \Rightarrow R = \emptyset.$ □

We are taking advantage of the fact that c is sequential to conclude that y *completely* satisfies the expectations of c. (Note that it also suffices to require that $\mathit{traces}(c) \subseteq \mathit{traces}(y)$ for the same result to go through.) But if there are different ways of satisfying a client (particularly a concurrent one), then it is no longer true that the client will necessarily be sat-

Request Satisfiability

isfied by a request substitutable service provider. Some additional preconditions must be imposed.

4.7.2 Concurrent Clients

Let us consider a simple example of a concurrent client consisting of a producer and a consumer connected by a bounded buffer. The producer and the consumer each have their own view of the buffer, but we are interested in the requirements posed by their concurrent composition.

Presently we might separately specify expectations of the producer and consumer respectively as:

$$\text{Prod} = \bigcirc\!\!\!\circlearrowleft \text{ put} \qquad \text{Cons} = \bigcirc\!\!\!\circlearrowleft \text{ get}$$

We might write their concurrent composition as Prod&Cons, where:

$$c1 \xrightarrow{r} c1' \Rightarrow c1\&c2 \xrightarrow{r} c1'\&c2$$

and

$$c2 \xrightarrow{r} c2' \Rightarrow c1\&c2 \xrightarrow{r} c1\&c2'$$

So we can conclude:

$$\text{Prod\&Cons} = \bigcirc\!\!\!\circlearrowleft \text{ put, get}$$

Note that Prod&Cons is *not* sequential according to definition 12.

It is easy to check that Buf ⊨ Prod&Cons, since Buf never refuses both put and get. But what is the role of request substitutability now? Since we know that Var:<Buf can we necessarily conclude also that Var ⊨ Prod&Cons? Unfortunately this is not quite right. The reason is that a regular subtype may introduce additional behaviour that can perturb the client's expectations. Consider, for example, a deletable buffer:

$$\text{DelBuf} = \bigcirc \xrightarrow[\text{get}]{\text{put}} \bigcirc \xrightarrow{\text{del}} \bigcirc$$

It is clear that DelBuf:<Buf. But suppose that we now compose the producer and consumer with a malevolent object whose only goal is to try to delete the buffer:

$$\text{Del} = \bigcirc \xrightarrow{\text{del}} \bigcirc$$

Now Buf ⊨ Prod&Cons&Del but it is not the case that DelBuf ⊨ Prod&Cons&Del. In the first case only Del will be starved out because Buf provides no delete operation, but the client as whole will still be satisfied since Prod&Cons continues to make progress.

In the second case, however, the delete operation may succeed, then causing the client as a whole to deadlock, and thus remain unsatisfied.

What we need to do in order to be sure that DelBuf can be safely substituted for Buf is to *restrict* its behaviour to that allowed by Buf:

Definition 13 $x/Y \xrightarrow{r} x'/Y'$ iff $x \xrightarrow{r} x'$ and $Y \xrightarrow{r} Y'$.

What we mean to capture by x/Y is that some object in state x is restricted to accept only the requests allowed by a second object whose state is some y∈ Y. We do not know precisely which state the second object is in, so we keep track of the set of possible states.

Usually the initial state of the second object is known, so we will simply write x/y instead of x/{y}.

Proposition 6 $x{:}{<}y \Rightarrow x/y :< y$.

Proof
  (i) $traces(x/y) = traces(x) \cap traces(y)$. But $x{:}{<}y \Rightarrow traces(y) \subseteq traces(x)$, so $traces(x/y) = traces(y)$.
  (ii) $(s,R) \in failures(x/y) \Rightarrow \exists x', x \xrightarrow{s} x', \{y\} \xrightarrow{s} Y'$, such that $R \cap init(x') \cap init(Y') = \emptyset$
  $\Rightarrow R \cap init(x') \cap \cup\{ init(y') \mid y' \in Y'\} = \cup \{ R \cap init(x') \cap init(y') \mid y' \in Y'\} = \emptyset$.
  But $x{:}{<}y \Rightarrow \{x\} :<< \{y\} \Rightarrow \exists y' \in Y', init(y') \subseteq init(x')$
  $\Rightarrow \exists y' \in Y', R \cap init(y') = \emptyset \Rightarrow (s,R) \in failures(y) \Rightarrow failures(x/y) \subseteq failures(y)$.
  But $failures_y(x/y) = failures(x/y)$, so $x/y :< y$. □

Finally, the result we want:

Proposition 7 $x{:}{<}y$ and $y \models c \Rightarrow x/y \models c$.

Proof $x{:}{<}y \Rightarrow x/y :< y$ (by proposition 6), so $failures(x/y) \subseteq failures(y)$.
  Now $(s,R) \in failures(x/y) \cap offers(c) \Rightarrow (s,R) \in failures(y) \cap offers(c) \Rightarrow R = \emptyset$.
  Hence $x/y \models c$. □

So, for example, we can conclude that:

  DelBuf/Buf ⊨ Prod&Cons&Del

since we effectively *hide* the additional behaviour introduced by DelBuf from the client.

This is not as strong a result as we might have hoped for, but it is a natural consequence of the fact that multiple concurrent clients may interfere with one another if their expectations are not consistent. This is essentially the observation of Liskov and Wing [22] who propose a new definition of subtyping that requires view consistency. Briefly, the idea is that a type that extends the behaviour of another type may only be considered a subtype of the second if the additional behaviour can always be explained in terms of behaviour that was *already* there in the supertype.

In some cases we may get this consistency for free. Note, for example, that if the subtype's behaviour is properly included in the supertype's, in the sense that $failures(x) = failures(x/y)$, then the subtype will be request substitutable for the supertype. We must be sure, though, that the subtype behaviour is consistent with the restriction imposed by the supertype. This leads to the following result:

Open Problems

Proposition 8 If $traces(x) = traces(y)$ and $failures(x) \subseteq failures(y)$, then $y \models c \Rightarrow x \models c$.

Proof Follows from proposition 7 since
$failures(x) = failures(x/y)$. □

It may still be the case that a subtype provides additional behaviour that does *not* perturb the client. But to be sure that the subtype is truly substitutable, it is necessary to know more about the client's expectations. We have previously explored *interaction equivalence* with respect to the expectations of particular sets of observers, and found that equivalence with respect to all possible observers (also) reduces to failures equivalence [27]. We expect that *relativizing* request substitutability with respect to the expectations of specific classes of clients will lead to more general and more useful results for the case of multiple concurrent clients.

4.8 Open Problems

We have proposed service types as a means of characterizing the services an object provides, and regular types as a means to express non-uniform service availability. In both cases we have presented an approach to subtyping. Furthermore, we have formalized what it means to satisfy a client's expectations, and we have shown the role that subtyping plays in determining substitutability.

Although regular types appear to be a novel and promising approach for reasoning about some of the dynamic (type) properties of concurrent object-oriented programs, there remains much to be studied before we can claim to have a pragmatically acceptable approach for type-checking object-oriented languages. Let us briefly summarize some of these considerations.

4.8.1 Regular Service Types

So far we have treated the typing of services and their availability as orthogonal issues. Service types express types of requests and replies, and regular types tell us when requests are enabled. There is nothing to prevent us from proposing a syntax for regular service types that simply expands request names in regular types to the complete service type specification corresponding to that request. For example, an integer variable could be assigned the regular service type:

IntVar = (v1, {   v1 = put(Int)→Ok.v2,
                   v2 = put(Int)→Ok.v2 + get→Int.v2   })

Since this is somewhat verbose (the type of the put service must be given twice), it seems more desirable to keep the type specifications of services and their protocols separate.

It is conceivable, however, that the type of a service may itself change with time. In particular, the result types associated with certain requests may depend on the argument types of earlier requests (as is the case with all of the container objects we have seen). To handle this case, it would seem necessary to introduce term variables into regular types to express the dependencies between services in the protocol (i.e. à la "dependent types" [32]). It is not clear, however, what effect this would have on the determination of request substitutability.

It may also be interesting to consider bounded polymorphism in our framework, since the integration of intersection types and bounded polymorphism has been previously studied [31], but only in a functional setting. Finally, we have not considered the issue of recursively defined types, in which the regular type of an object may contain services whose argument and return types refer to the object's own type. Previous work on "F-bounded" quantification [9] addresses subtyping for such types [3], and is likely to be relevant to our framework.

4.8.2 Applying Regular Types to Object-Oriented Languages

We have presented our type model without giving any concrete interpretation for types. The objects to which we wish to assign types have been described only informally by means of a very general model of objects as transition systems. The next step would be to provide a concrete syntax for objects, either in terms of a programming language or a process calculus that can model objects in a straightforward way.

We have been working towards an *object calculus* that incorporates those features of process calculi that are most needed for expressing the semantics of concurrent object-oriented languages [28]. We intend to use the object calculus as an (executable) abstract machine for a *pattern language for (typed) active objects* [29], and assign regular types to the expressions of this language.

Since the type expressions we are dealing with can become rather unwieldy, it is especially important that we be able to do as much type *inference* as possible. In languages that directly represent abstract states of objects (such as ACT++ [20]) this job will be easier. The main difficulty will be in determining what transitions between the abstract states are possible.

We have already pointed out that objects may satisfy many different regular types, and, since regular types are only approximations, in some cases they may be refined *ad nauseam*. In order to assign regular types automatically to objects, it is necessary to generate some type assignment which is perhaps not the finest possible but which assigns at least one abstract state to every reachable subset of available services. (Recall that our first ND-Stack was such a minimal representation, whereas NDStack2 had two distinct states with the same services available.)

Another consideration, however, is whether a deterministic regular type can be assigned to an object. If such a type specification exists (e.g. Var and Buf), then this is in any case to be preferred to a non-deterministic regular type that may have less states. Such types not only completely describe service availability for an object, but are well-behaved during type-checking since the sets of reachable nodes for a given trace are always singletons. (So LIST stays small.)

4.9 Concluding Remarks

We have proposed a type framework for object-oriented languages that expresses the *services* of an object as an intersection of *service types* characterizing request and reply messages, and *non-uniform service availability* in terms of *regular types* over a finite number of abstract states associated with subsets of services. Subtyping of regular types is defined by introducing *request substitutability*, a novel pre-order over processes that has special interest for object-oriented applications. Subtyping is easy to determine for regular types, and a simple algorithm is presented. Satisfaction of client's expectations is formalized as *request satisfiability*, and we show how request substitutability relates to it.

A number of technical issues must first be resolved before the framework can be practically applied to real object-oriented languages. In particular, we seek some results that will simplify reasoning about substitutability with respect to multiple concurrent clients.

We expect that it will be easier to reason about regular types in the presence of concurrency if we interpret them either using a temporal logic or a modal process logic (such as Hennessy–Milner logic with recursion [21]). A logical characterization of the concepts we have presented will be the topic of further research.

Despite a number of open research problems, the approach seems to hold a great deal of promise, since numerous tools and algorithms exist not only for analysing properties of finite state processes [11][15][23] but also for reasoning about processes in general [12][19]. This suggests that regular types may be more generally useful for reasoning about temporal properties of concurrent objects.

We have concentrated on client–server-based protocols in which requests eventually entail replies. Can we accommodate other kinds of communication protocols (to support, for example, transactions)? If so, must we modify our model of regular types to incorporate bidirectional communications (instead of just enabling of request channels)? Can we easily accommodate *exceptions* in our framework by, for example, allowing replies to be union types?

Finally, our approach considers only objects with fixed sets of known services. Can we accommodate *reflective* objects that acquire new services with time? In such a setting, would we have to consider not only services, but also types as first-class values?

Acknowledgements

Many thanks are due to José Rolim, Didier Buchs, Laurent Dami, Michael Papathomas, and to the anonymous referees for their help and suggestions in the preparation of the original version of this work published in *OOPSLA '93*. I would also like to thank Benjamin

Pierce, Egil Andersen, William Ferreira and Patrick Varone for their careful reading of the manuscript, and for uncovering various technical errors and deficiencies.

References

[1] Samson Abramsky, "Observation Equivalence as a Testing Equivalence," *Theoretical Computer Science*, vol. 53, North-Holland, 1987, pp. 225–241.

[2] Alfred V. Aho, John E. Hopcroft and Jeffrey D. Ullman, *The Design and Analysis of Computer Algorithms*, Addison-Wesley, Reading, Mass., 1974.

[3] Roberto M. Amadio and Luca Cardelli, "Subtyping Recursive Types," *Proceedings POPL '91*, pp. 104–118.

[4] Jos C.M. Baeten and Peter Weijland, *Process Algebra*, Cambridge University Press, Cambridge, 1990.

[5] Franco Barbanera and Mariangiola Dezani-Ciancaglini, "Intersection and Union Types," in *Proceedings Theoretical Aspects of Computer Software (TACS '91)*, ed. T. Ito and A.R. Meyer, *Lecture Notes in Computer Science* 526, Springer-Verlag, Sendai, Japan, Sept. 1991, pp. 651–674.

[6] Jan A. Bergstra and J.W. Klop, "The Algebra of Recursively Defined Processes and the Algebra of Regular Processes," in *Proceedings ICALP '84*, ed. J. Paredaens, *Lecture Notes in Computer Science* 172, Springer-Verlag, Antwerp, pp. 82–95.

[7] Ed Brinksma, Giuseppe Scollo and Chris Steenbergen, "LOTOS Specifications, Their Implementations and Their Tests," *Protocol Specification, Testing and Verification VI*, ed. G. Bochmann and B. Sarikaya, North Holland, 1987, pp. 349–360.

[8] Stephen D. Brookes, C.A.R. Hoare and Andrew W. Roscoe, "A Theory of Communicating Sequential Processes," *Journal of the ACM*, vol. 31, no. 3, July 1984, pp. 560–599.

[9] Peter S. Canning, William Cook, Walter L. Hill, John C. Mitchell and Walter G. Olthoff, "F-Bounded Quantification for Object-Oriented Programming," *Proceedings of the ACM Conference on Functional Programming and Computer Architecture*, 11–13 Sept. 1989, pp. 273–280.

[10] Luca Cardelli and Peter Wegner, "On Understanding Types, Data Abstraction, and Polymorphism," *ACM Computing Surveys*, vol. 17, no. 4, Dec. 1985, pp. 471–522.

[11] Edmund M. Clarke, E. A. Emerson and A. P. Sistla, "Automatic Verification of Finite-State Concurrent Systems Using Temporal Logic Specifications," *ACM TOPLAS*, vol. 8, no. 2, April 1986, pp. 244–263.

[12] Rance Cleaveland, Joachim Parrow and Bernhard Steffen, "The Concurrency Workbench," in *Automatic Verification Methods for Finite State Systems: Proceedings*, ed. Joseph Sifakis, *Lecture Notes in Computer Science* 407, Springer-Verlag, 1989, pp. 24–37.

[13] Elspeth Cusack, "Refinement, Conformance and Inheritance," *Formal Aspects of Computing*, vol. 3, 1991, pp. 129–141.

[14] Rocco De Nicola, "Extensional Equivalences for Transition Systems," *Acta Informatica*, vol. 24, 1987, pp. 211–237.

[15] Suzanne Graf and Joseph Sifakis, "A Logic for the Specification and Proof of Regular Controllable Processes of CCS," *Acta Informatica*, vol. 23, no. 5, 1986, pp. 507–528.

[16] Matthew Hennessy, "Acceptance Trees," *Journal of the ACM*, vol. 32, no. 4, Jan. 1985, pp. 896–928.

[17] Matthew Hennessy, *Algebraic Theory of Processes*, MIT Press, Cambridge, Mass., 1988.

[18] Hans Hüttel, "Decidability, Behavioural Equivalences and Infinite Transition Graphs," Ph.D. thesis, ECS-LFCS-91-181, Computer Science Dept., University of Edinburgh, Dec. 1991.

References

[19] Paola Inverardi and Corrado Priami, "Evaluation of Tools for the Analysis of Communicating Systems," *Bulletin of EATCS*, vol. 45, Oct. 1991, pp. 158–185.

[20] Dennis G. Kafura and Keung Hae Lee, "Inheritance in Actor Based Concurrent Object-Oriented Languages," in *Proceedings ECOOP '89*, ed. S. Cook, Cambridge University Press, Nottingham, 10–14 July, 1989, pp. 131–145.

[21] Kim G. Larsen, "Proof Systems for Hennessy-Milner Logic with Recursion," in *Proceedings CAAP '88*, ed. M. Dauchet and M. Nivat, *Lecture Notes in Computer Science* 299, Springer-Verlag, Nancy, March 1988, pp. 215–230.

[22] Barbara Liskov and Jeannette Wing, "A New Definition of the Subtype Relation," in *Proceedings ECOOP '93*, ed. O. Nierstrasz, *Lecture Notes in Computer Science* 707, Springer-Verlag, Kaiserslautern, Germany, July 1993, pp. 118–141.

[23] Robin Milner, "A Complete Inference System for a Class of Regular Behaviours," *Journal of Computer and System Sciences*, vol. 28, Academic Press, 1984, pp. 439–466.

[24] Robin Milner, *Communication and Concurrency*, Prentice-Hall, 1989.

[25] Robin Milner, "The Polyadic π Calculus," ECS-LFCS-91-180, Computer Science Dept., University of Edinburgh, Oct. 1991.

[26] Oscar Nierstrasz and Michael Papathomas, "Viewing Objects as Patterns of Communicating Agents," *Proceedings OOPSLA/ECOOP '90, ACM SIGPLAN Notices*, vol. 25, no. 10, Oct. 1990, pp. 38–43.

[27] Oscar Nierstrasz and Michael Papathomas, "Towards a Type Theory for Active Objects," ACM OOPS Messenger, Proceedings OOPSLA/ECOOP '90 Workshop on Object-Based Concurrent Systems, vol. 2, no. 2, April 1991, pp. 89–93.

[28] Oscar Nierstrasz, "Towards an Object Calculus," in *Proceedings of the ECOOP '91 Workshop on Object-Based Concurrent Computing*, ed. M. Tokoro, O. Nierstrasz and P. Wegner, *Lecture Notes in Computer Science* 612, Springer-Verlag, 1992, pp. 1–20.

[29] Oscar Nierstrasz, "Composing Active Objects," *Research Directions in Concurrent Object-Oriented Programming*, ed. G. Agha, P. Wegner and A. Yonezawa, MIT Press, Cambridge, Mass., 1993, pp. 151–171.

[30] Michael Papathomas, "A Unifying Framework for Process Calculus Semantics of Concurrent Object-Oriented Languages," in *Proceedings of the ECOOP '91 Workshop on Object-Based Concurrent Computing*, ed. M. Tokoro, O. Nierstrasz and P. Wegner, *Lecture Notes in Computer Science* 612, Springer-Verlag, 1992, pp. 53–79.

[31] Benjamin C. Pierce, "Intersection Types and Bounded Polymorphism," *Conference on Typed Lambda Calculi and Applications*, March 1993, pp. 346–360.

[32] Simon Thompson, *Type Theory and Functional Programming*, International Computer Science Series, Addison-Wesley, 1991.

[33] Vasco T. Vasconcelos and Mario Tokoro, "A Typing System for a Calculus of Objects," *Object Technologies for Advanced Software, First JSST International Symposium, Lecture Notes in Computer Science*, vol. 742, Springer-Verlag, Nov. 1993, pp. 460–474.

[34] Peter Wegner and Stanley B. Zdonik, "Inheritance as an Incremental Modification Mechanism or What Like Is and Isn't Like," in *Proceedings ECOOP '88*, ed. S. Gjessing and K. Nygaard, *Lecture Notes in Computer Science* 322, Springer-Verlag, Oslo, Aug. 15–17, 1988, pp. 55–77.

Chapter 5
A Temporal Perspective of Composite Objects

Constantin Arapis

Abstract For the development of object-oriented applications, the description of temporal aspects of object behaviour often turns out to be an important issue. We present a collection of notions and concepts intended for the description of the temporal order in which messages are sent to and received from an object. We also propose notions for the description of the temporal order of messages exchanged between cooperating objects related with *part-of* relationships. Using propositional temporal logic as the underlying formalism of our approach, we show how to verify the consistency of object specifications.

5.1 Introduction

The increasing popularity of object-oriented systems [7] [12] [18] [22] over the past decade, within both the research and commercial/industrial computer science communities, have promoted the use of the object-oriented approach for requirements analysis and system design. Thus, several object-oriented analysis and design methodologies [4] [5] [6] [15] [20] [21] [23] [24] are currently available to assist the early phases of the object-oriented application development process.

An important activity during object-oriented design often turns out to be the description of temporal aspects of object behaviour. Indeed, the design of many applications may contain objects whose behaviour exhibits important temporal traits. As Booch states [4] "for some objects, this time ordering of operations is so pervasive that we can best formally characterize the behaviour of an object in terms of a finite state machine." It must be stressed that even for applications which are not designed for processing temporal information, their development requires several objects whose behaviour exhibits important temporal aspects. Yet the description of temporal properties of objects, either considered in isolation or in cooperation with other objects, is not exclusively relevant to concurrent environments. Often, the description of temporal properties of objects is deemed critical and even mandatory in sequential environments.

5.1.1 Specifying Temporal Aspects of Object Behaviour

A number of object-oriented design methodologies [4] [20] [21] integrate notions and concepts for the description of temporal properties of objects. We will call the *temporal component* of an object-oriented design method the collection of notions and concepts intended for the description of temporal aspects of object behaviour. The underlying formalisms upon which the various temporal components of object-oriented design methodologies are founded are finite state machines (FSMs) or extensions of FSMs [13]. The preponderance of FSMs over other formalisms is attributed to the following two reasons: first, FSMs are easy to understand, and second, a FSM can be easily depicted by means of a state transition diagram.

In general, object-oriented design methodologies use FSMs in the following way: a FSM M_c models temporal aspects of the behaviour of an instance of class C. Transitions of M_c are labelled with operations that an instance of C is expected to carry out. States of M_c correspond to the various possible states of an instance of C. A transition of M_c, labelled p, from state s_1 to state s_2, models the fact that operation p can be requested of an instance o of C when the current state of o is s_1. After p is carried out, the current state of o becomes s_2. Thus, by means of FSMs, temporal aspects of object behaviour are ultimately described in terms of sequences of pairs: (state, operation).

Note that the role of the temporal component of an object-oriented design methodology is limited to the description of sequences of operations and state transitions of objects. The temporal component is not designed for specifying how an object will carry out an operation. In addition, the design and integration of a temporal component within an object-oriented design methodology should guarantee harmonious synergy between the various other parts of the methodology. The above requirement suggests that the temporal component should be complementary and orthogonal to the fundamental principles of the object-oriented approach.

We will present a temporal component which has been designed independently of any design methodology and is founded on the theory of propositional temporal logic (PTL). The aim of the temporal component is to enhance existing design methodologies lacking or offering limited support for the description of temporal properties of objects. We shall introduce the temporal component in terms of a specification model called the Temporal Specification Object Model (TSOM). The specification model blends fundamental notions of the object-oriented approach and temporal notions, thus illustrating the dependence and/or orthogonality existing between them.

In contrast with temporal components founded on FSMs, TSOM emphasizes the description of temporal properties of an object o in terms of sequences of messages which are sent to and received from o. Thus, the user is not compelled to devise states that are not necessarily relevant to the description of an object's behaviour and whose only purpose is

Introduction

to complete the FSM under development. However, TSOM provides the concept of *attribute* by means of which the user may introduce states he considers relevant for the description of an object's behaviour and may also describe the various conditions that should be verified for enabling state transitions to occur.

Another important point that TSOM emphasizes is the description of the temporal order of messages exchanged between a collection of cooperating objects related by *part-of* relationships. The temporal order of messages exchanged between a composite object and its constituent objects provides a temporal perspective of what has been called the behavioural composition of objects. Promoted as a fundamental feature of object-oriented design methodologies, behavioural composition consists of combining and coordinating the functionality of existing objects to create new objects [8] [14] [19]. A composite object in TSOM encapsulates and coordinates a collection of objects that cooperate in order to reach some goal or perform some task. The composite object plays the role of a coordinator taking into account the various temporal properties and constraints specified for constituent objects. Furthermore, TSOM enables an incremental specification of object coordination. In particular, a composite object may become a constituent of another composite object, which in turn may become a constituent of another composite object, and so on.

5.1.2 Design Choices for TSOM

First and foremost, let us justify our decision for TSOM to be founded on a formal theory rather than developing a temporal component founded on some informal basis, for example a natural language. Establishing a formal basis upon which a temporal component is founded permits us not only to test the consistency of the various notions it integrates but also to test the consistency of user-provided specifications. Indeed, the early detection and correction of design errors is critical for the whole application development activity. Failing to correct design errors causes their harmful effects to be amplified and disseminated throughout the subsequent stages of the application development process.

From a number of candidate formalisms the language of PTL appears as the most suitable formalism for TSOM. Indeed, temporal properties can be very easily specified by means of PTL formulas. Formalisms like FSMs and Petri nets have been characterized as low level in the following sense: by means of FSMs and Petri nets we can specify how a system operates and then verify which properties are satisfied by the modelled system. In temporal logic the contrary is done. The desirable properties of a system are specified first. A system satisfying the specified properties is derived subsequently.

Another important argument in favour of PTL is the fact that it has been used as a foundation for various investigations performed in the area of concurrent systems, concerning the synthesis of a collection of parallel communicating processes [9] [17]. Synthesis of communicating processes bears many similarities with object behaviour composition: the collection of communicating processes can be seen as a collection of cooperating objects which should be synchronized in order to perform a particular task. We have borrowed the main ideas proposed for synthesizing communicating processes from [17] whilst we have adapted and tailored them when necessary to meet our specific needs.

We have acknowledged the verification of specifications to be an important and even a mandatory activity of the design process. However, verifying specifications is in general a difficult and lengthy process carried out without computer assistance. Automated support for the verification of specifications, relieving users from laborious and error-prone procedures, has been selected among the most important requirements. An appealing property of PTL is the existence of algorithms for testing the satisfiability of a temporal logic formula [2] [16] [17]. These algorithms may be used in a straightforward manner to provide an automated procedure for verifying the consistency of object specifications. The decidability of PTL outweighed substantial arguments for choosing a more powerful formalism, in particular predicate temporal logic [1]. Since the satisfiability test of predicate temporal logic is no longer decidable the design of an automated procedure for verifying specifications could be seriously compromised.

5.1.3 Layout

In the following section we provide a brief introduction to the temporal logic system we shall be using. In section 5.3 we describe the specification of temporal properties of objects in TSOM. Section 5.4 presents the verification procedure of object specifications. The last section presents our concluding remarks.

5.2 Propositional Temporal Logic

PTL is an extension of propositional logic (PL) in which atomic propositions have time-varying truth value assignments. The time-varying truth value assignment is obtained by associating each time-point with a *world*. A world is a particular interpretation in the sense of classical PL. Thus, the truth value of an atomic proposition p at instant t would be the truth value assigned to p in the world associated with t.

Several temporal logical systems have been developed. They differ in the properties attributed to time, i.e. whether it is discrete or continuous, with or without start or end points, or viewed as containing linear or branching past and future. The logical system we shall use considers time to be discrete, with a starting point, and linear [11].

Another important extension characterizing PTL is the collection of temporal operators which, in addition to the usual operators of PL, are used for forming PTL formulas. Different collections of temporal operators may be encountered depending on the logical system used. The logical system we have chosen to use has the following temporal operators:

   □ f   called the *always* in the *future* operator, meaning that f is satisfied[*] in the current and all future worlds,

---

[*] We say that an atomic proposition p or a formula f is satisfied in a world w if p or f is assigned the truth value true in w.

Propositional Temporal Logic

◊ f   called the *eventually* in the *future* operator, meaning that f is satisfied in the current or in some future world,

○ f   called the *next* operator, meaning that f is satisfied in the next world,

f_1 $\mathcal{U}$ f_2 called the *until* operator, meaning that either f_1 is satisfied in the current and all future worlds or f_1 is satisfied in the current and all future worlds until the world when f_2 is satisfied.

The first three operators are unary, while the last is binary. Note that for the *until* operator we do not claim f_2 will eventually be satisfied in some future world. The above operators deal only with future situations. We can extend the system with symmetric operators for the past:

■ f   called the *always* in the *past* operator, meaning that f is satisfied in the current and all previous worlds,

♦ f   called the *eventually* in the *past* operator, meaning that f is satisfied in the current or in some past world,

● f   called the *previous* operator, meaning that the current world is not the starting point and f is satisfied in the previous world,

▶ f   called the *weak-previous* operator, meaning that either f is satisfied in the previous world or the current world is the starting point; the weak previous operator has no symmetric future operator and has been included because of our assumption that time has a starting point,

f_1 $\mathcal{S}$ f_2 called the *since* operator, meaning that either f_1 is satisfied in the current and all past worlds or f_1 is satisfied in the current and all past worlds since the world when f_2 was satisfied.

Figure 5.1 illustrates the meaning of each temporal operator over the time axis τ. A time-point t which is labelled with a PTL formula f means that f is satisfied at t. Operators until and since require two alternative time axes for representing their meaning, so each pair of time axes is enclosed within a rectangular box.

5.2.1 Syntax of PTL

Given:

1. $P = \{p_1, p_2, p_3, \ldots\}$ the set of atomic propositions
2. non-temporal operators: $\neg, \wedge, \vee, \Rightarrow, \Leftrightarrow$
3. temporal operators: □, ◊, ○, $\mathcal{U}$, ■, ♦, ●, ▶, $\mathcal{S}$

formulas are formed as follows:

1. An atomic proposition is a formula.
2. If f_1 and f_2 are formulas then

    (f_1), $\neg f_1$, $f_1 \wedge f_2$, $f_1 \vee f_2$, $f_1 \Rightarrow f_2$, $f_1 \Leftrightarrow f_2$ are formulas, and
    □ f_1, ◊ f_1, ○ f_1, f_1 $\mathcal{U}$ f_2, ■ f_1, ♦ f_1, ● f_1, ▶ f_1, f_1 $\mathcal{S}$ f_2 are formulas.

3. Every formula is obtained by application of the above two rules.

128   A Temporal Perspective of Composite Objects

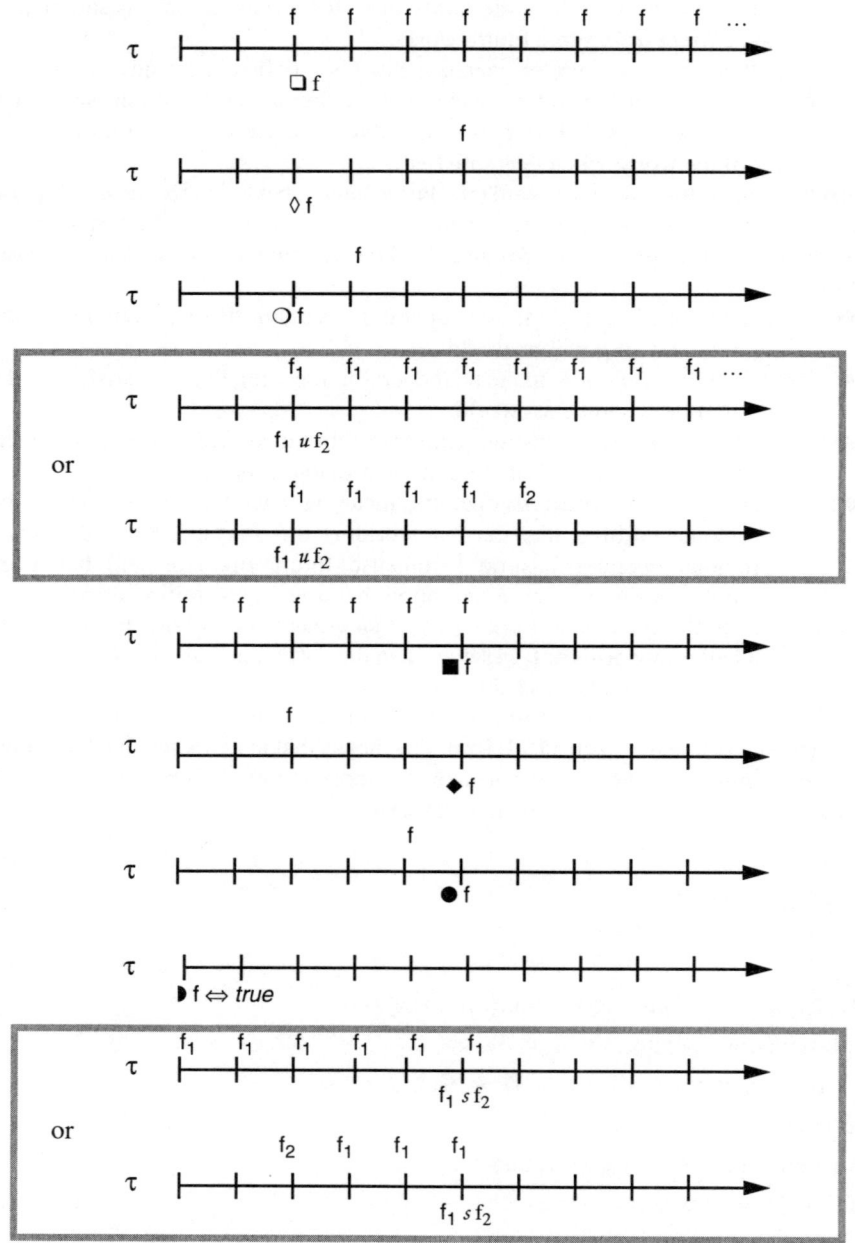

Figure 5.1 *The meaning of temporal operators over the time axis.*

Propositional Temporal Logic

Examples of well-formed formulas (wff) of PTL include:

$$\Box((p \wedge q) \vee r)$$
$$\Box(p \Rightarrow \blacklozenge q)$$
$$\bigcirc(r \, \mathcal{U} \, (p \wedge q))$$

The first wff says that in all time-points either p and q are satisfied or r is satisfied. The second wff says that for any time-point t_p in which p is satisfied, q must have been satisfied in some time-point t, $t \leq t_p$. The last wff says that from the next time-point t_{next} either r is satisfied for all time-points $t \geq t_{next}$ or there exists a time-point $t_{p \wedge q}$, $t_{p \wedge q} \geq t_{next}$, where $q \wedge p$ is satisfied and for all t, $t_{next} \leq t < t_{p \wedge q}$, r is satisfied.

5.2.2 Semantics of PTL

The time-varying truth value assignment of atomic propositions and the time-based meaning attributed to temporal operators leads to a definition of the notion of satisfiability where the truth or falsity of PTL formulas is evaluated over sequences of worlds. To be more precise, let $\sigma = w_0, w_1, w_2, w_3, \ldots$ be an infinite sequence of worlds, each $w_i \in W$ being an element of the powerset 2^P, W the set of all worlds and P the set of atomic propositions.

The satisfiability of a formula f in a world $w_i \in W$ of a sequence σ is denoted by $(\sigma, w_i) \vDash f$ and can be deduced by the following rules:

$(\sigma, w_i) \vDash p$	iff	$p \in w_i$
$(\sigma, w_i) \nvDash p$	iff	$p \notin w_i$
$(\sigma, w_i) \vDash f_1 \wedge f_2$	iff	$(\sigma, w_i) \vDash f_1$ and $(\sigma, w_i) \vDash f_2$
$(\sigma, w_i) \vDash f_1 \vee f_2$	iff	$(\sigma, w_i) \vDash f_1$ or $(\sigma, w_i) \vDash f_2$
$(\sigma, w_i) \vDash \neg f_1$	iff	not $(\sigma, w_i) \vDash f_1$
$(\sigma, w_i) \vDash f_1 \Rightarrow f_2$	iff	$(\sigma, w_i) \vDash (\neg f_1) \wedge f_2$
$(\sigma, w_i) \vDash f_1 \Leftrightarrow f_2$	iff	$(\sigma, w_i) \vDash (f_1 \Rightarrow f_2) \wedge (f_2 \Rightarrow f_1)$
$(\sigma, w_i) \vDash \Box f_1$	iff	$\forall j, j \geq i, (\sigma, w_j) \vDash f_1$
$(\sigma, w_i) \vDash \Diamond f_1$	iff	$\exists j, j \geq i, (\sigma, w_j) \vDash f_1$
$(\sigma, w_i) \vDash \bigcirc f_1$	iff	$(\sigma, w_{i+1}) \vDash f_1$
$(\sigma, w_i) \vDash f_1 \, \mathcal{U} \, f_2$	iff	either $\forall j, j \geq i, (\sigma, w_j) \vDash f_1$
		or $\exists j, j \geq i, (\sigma, w_j) \vDash f_2$ and $\forall k, i \leq k < j, (\sigma, w_k) \vDash f_1$
$(\sigma, w_i) \vDash \blacksquare f_1$	iff	$\forall j, 0 \leq j \leq i, (\sigma, w_j) \vDash f_1$
$(\sigma, w_i) \vDash \blacklozenge f_1$	iff	$\exists j, 0 \leq j \leq i, (\sigma, w_j) \vDash f_1$
$(\sigma, w_i) \vDash \bullet f_1$	iff	$i > 0$ and $(\sigma, w_{i-1}) \vDash f_1$
$(\sigma, w_i) \vDash \blacktriangleright f_1$	iff	$i > 0$ and $(\sigma, w_{i-1}) \vDash f_1$ or $i = 0$
$(\sigma, w_i) \vDash f_1 \, \mathcal{S} \, f_2$	iff	either $\forall j, 0 \leq j \leq i, (\sigma, w_j) \vDash f_1$
		or $\exists j, 0 \leq j \leq i, (\sigma, w_j) \vDash f_2$ and $\forall k, j < k \leq i, (\sigma, w_k) \vDash f_1$

A formula f is *initially satisfied* or simply *satisfied* by a sequence σ iff $(\sigma, w_0) \vDash f$. A formula f is *satisfiable* iff there exists a sequence satisfying f. Such a sequence is a *model* of f. A formula is *valid* iff it is satisfiable by all possible sequences.

In order to check the satisfiability of PTL formulas we can use one of the tableau-based algorithms presented in [2] [16] or [17]. Such algorithms we will call *satisfiability algorithms*. The algorithm takes as input a formula F and outputs a graph representing all models satisfying F. Such a graph we will call a *satisfiability graph*. If F is not satisfiable the algorithm signals that it is unable to produce a graph.

The main idea of the algorithm presented in [2] consists of building up the satisfiability graph in the following way. Start with an initial node labelled with the input formula F. For the initial node and all other nodes the following procedure is applied until no more nodes remain unprocessed. The formula labelling a node N is decomposed into disjunctive normal form, each disjunct being of the form:

current-instant-formula ∧ ○ next-instant-formula ∧ ● previous-instant-formula

The previous-instant-formula specifies what should have been verified the previous time-point. For any node N′ from which an edge points to N, the formula labelling N′ should satisfy previous-instant-formula. Otherwise node N and all edges pointing to N should be deleted. The next-instant-formula specifies what should be verified the next time point. Let N′′ be the node labelled with next-instant-formula. If there exists no node labelled with next-instant-formula then a new node N′′ is created with label next-instant-formula. Then an edge from N to N′′ labelled with current-instant-formula is introduced in the graph. The current-instant-formula specifies what should be verified the current time-point and is always a formula of PL. Thus edges are labelled with formulas of PL while nodes are labelled with formulas of PTL. The following remark ensures that the process stops. When transforming a formula f into disjunctive normal form, each conjunct within a disjunct is a conjunction of either subformulas of f or negated subformulas of f. Thus the maximum number of nodes that possibly will be generated equals the number of formulas that are conjunctions of either subformulas of F or negated subformulas of F.

Given a satisfiability graph corresponding to a formula F, a possible model μ of F is identified by traversing the graph. Initially μ is empty. Starting at the initial node, each time an edge is traversed, a world satisfying the formula labelling that edge is concatenated to the sequence of worlds forming the model μ. In general, several worlds may satisfy a formula but a single world should be chosen to be concatenated in μ. In other words, a formula labelling an edge identifies a world w_i of some model μ. The formula labelling each node identifies the rest of the sequence of worlds of μ, that is w_{i+1}, w_{i+2}, ... Note that the graph produced from the satisfiability algorithm may not be minimal in the sense that the models of the input formula could be identified with a graph with less nodes and edges.

The satisfiability graph corresponding to the formula □ ((p ∧ q) ⇒ ○ r) is shown in figure 5.2. Each node is divided into two parts: the lower part of the node contains the formula in disjunctive normal form equivalent to the formula labelling the upper part of the node. The node drawn with a thick line is the initial node. Note that the current-instant-formula is missing from the second disjunct of the formula labelling the lower part of the initial node. In such cases any non-contradictory PL formula can be taken as the current-instant-formula. We use the symbol ⊥ to denote any non-contradictory PL formula. The various worlds satisfying the formulas labelling the edges of the satisfiability graph are:

Propositional Temporal Logic 131

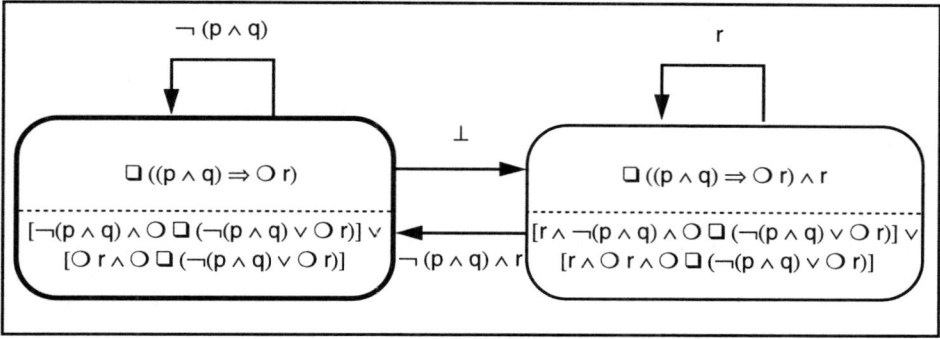

Figure 5.2 Satisfiability graph corresponding to the formula □ ((p ∧ q) ⇒ ○ r).

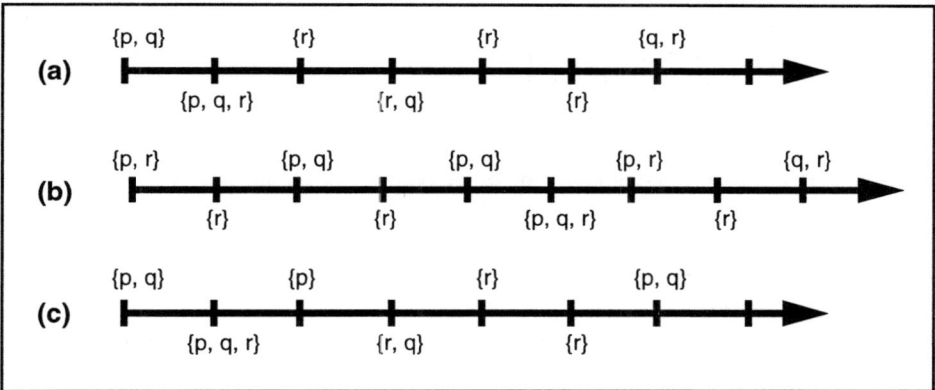

Figure 5.3 Sequences (a) and (b) satisfy □((p ∧ q) ⇒ ○r); Sequence (c) does not satisfy □((p ∧ q) ⇒ ○r)).

[{p}, {q}, {r}, {p, r}, {q, r}]   satisfy the formula ¬ (p ∧ q),
[{r}, {p, r}, {q, r}, {p, q, r}]   satisfy the formula r,
[{r}, {p, r}, {q, r}]   satisfy the formula ¬ (p ∧ q) ∧ r,
[{p}, {q}, {r}, {p, q}, {p, r}, {q, r}, {p, q, r}]   satisfy ⊥

Each world is represented by enclosing within curly brackets the atomic propositions having truth value true and assuming that all other propositions have truth value false.

Figure 5.3 shows three sequences of worlds relative to the formula □ ((p ∧ q) ⇒ ○ r). Sequences (a) and (b) satisfy the formula □ ((p ∧ q) ⇒ ○ r). Sequence (c) does not satisfy □ ((p ∧ q) ⇒ ○ r). The world which causes the sequence to be excluded from the set of models of □ ((p ∧ q) ⇒ ○ r) is the third one in which the atomic proposition r is not satisfied while in the previous world the formula (p ∧ q) was satisfied.

5.3 The Specification of Temporal Properties

In TSOM objects are intended for modelling the various entities of an application. Each object is associated with a unique object identifier (oid) permitting one to identify the object independently of its behaviour and the values of its instance variables. An object communicates with other objects by sending and receiving messages. Messages sent from an object (sender) to another object (receiver) may be interpreted as requests for the receiver to perform some task or simply as requests to send back some information to the sender. The reaction of the receiver may result in a modification of its internal state, a number of messages being sent to other objects, the return of a value to the sender, or some combination of the above cases. The internal state of an object stored in its instance variables and how it reacts to messages is assumed to be hidden from other objects.

Although we qualify TSOM as object-oriented, the notion of inheritance is not part of it. TSOM is the object-based part of the specification model presented in [2] and [3]. We shall not discuss any further the absence of inheritance in TSOM. However, the interested reader is referred to [2] where the notions of role and role playing can replace, at the specification level, the notion of inheritance.

We distinguish between *elementary objects* and *composite objects*. The difference between the two kinds of objects lies in the definition of their structural aspects. An elementary object is defined independently of other objects. A composite object consists of references to one or several elementary objects or composite objects. When a composite object o references an object z we say that z is a *component* of o. Note that a composite object is not the exclusive owner of its components. A component may be shared among several composite objects.

Objects are instantiated from classes. A class definition comprises the following items:

- *Public messages*, which can be sent to and received from an instance of the class. To indicate whether a message is to be sent to (*incoming message*) or received from (*outgoing message*) an instance, the message identifier is suffixed with a left ← or right → arrow respectively. In an object-oriented system, the effect of an incoming message defined in a class C would be implemented by an operation defined in C. The effect of an outgoing message msg of C is expected to be implemented by an operation defined in another class C´. The definition of msg as outgoing message in C simply affirms that an instance of C will send message msg to an instance of C´.

- *Attributes* of an instance o store values representing either abstract states or simply characteristic aspects which o wishes advertise to other objects. Each attribute is associated with a finite domain from which it can be assigned values. For example, in a class CAR two attributes can be defined, speed and engine_status with associated domains {stopped, moving_slowly, moving_fast} and {turned_on, turned_off} respectively.

- *Public constraints* describe the set of legal sequences of public messages and attribute-value assignments.

The Specification of Temporal Properties

- *Components* identify the parts of a composite object. Each component κ is associated with a class C, noted κ: C, requiring the value of κ to be a reference to an instance of C.
- *Component messages* which can be exchanged between the composite object and its components. As with public messages we distinguish between incoming and outgoing component messages.
- *Component constraints* describe the set of legal sequences of public messages, component messages and attribute-value assignments.
- *Implementation* is the part of the class definition containing the various programs implementing the behaviour of instances of the class.

All items listed above, with the exception of attributes, should be present in the definition of a composite object class. Items *components*, *component messages* and *component constraints* are absent from the class definition of elementary objects. In the remainder of this section we will describe in more detail each of the above items with the exception of the *implementation* item.

5.3.1 Public Messages

An example of a class definition of elementary objects is given in figure 5.4. Class CTRL_TOWER models the control tower of an airport. Public messages req_take_off and req_land have been defined as incoming messages. They model requests for taking off and landing which can be addressed to the control tower by some object. Messages perm_take_off and perm_land have been defined as outgoing messages. They model permissions for taking off and landing which are granted to those objects that had previously made a corresponding request to the control tower.

In most object-oriented systems it is recommended for *suppliers* of classes to hide outgoing messages of objects from their *clients*[*]. We decided to allow the definition of outgoing messages in an object's interface to ease the design of objects cooperating on the basis of asynchronous communication. Indeed, many real-world situations are naturally modelled as a collection of objects asynchronously communicating between them. Thus asynchronous communication has been reported as an important object cooperation technique which should be directly supported by object-oriented design methodologies. Defining an outgoing message msg for an object o implies that o is expected to cooperate with some object z which defines msg as an incoming message and to which o will send msg. Most often, o is informed which object will be the receiver of msg, by assigning the oid of z to some parameter of an incoming message of o.

The ability to include outgoing messages among public messages of a class C does not imply that all messages exchanged with an instance o of C have to be defined as public. Only messages that are part of the interface of o should be included in the list of public

---

[*] For a class C, we use the term *supplier* for naming the person who has defined and implemented C. We use the term *client* for indicating the person or object using the services of C.

```
class CTRL_TOWER {
    public messages
        req_take_off ←, req_land ←,
        perm_take_off →, perm_land →
    public constraints
        req_take_off ∨ req_land;
        ☐ (req_take_off ⇒ (◊ perm_take_off));
        ☐ (req_land ⇒ (◊ perm_land));
    implementation
        req_take_off (perm_receiver: oid, ...)
        { ... };
        req_land (perm_receiver: oid, ...)
        { ... };
        ...
}
```

Figure 5.4 *Class CTRL_TOWER modelling the lifecycle of a control tower of an airport.*

messages. For example, assuming that o is an instance of CTRL_TOWER, the four public messages defined in class CTRL_TOWER are all meaningful for clients of o. The implementation of o could use a hidden component, plane_list, having the functionality of type LIST. The usefulness of plane_list would be to represent the list of aeroplanes that have made a request for taking off or landing and for which the corresponding permission has not been yet granted. In contrast with the collection of public messages of CTRL_TOWER, messages exchanged between o and plane_list, like insert_into_list and delete_from_list, are meaningless for clients of o and should not appear in the list of public messages of class CTRL_TOWER.

5.3.2 Public Constraints

Public constraints associated with a class are specified in a language resembling PTL. More precisely, for a class C, we associate with each public message p an atomic proposition p in PTL. We model the fact that a public incoming (outgoing) message p is sent to (received from) an instance of C at time-point t by associating with t a world where p is satisfied. Mapping messages to atomic propositions implies that the distinction between incoming and outgoing messages is essentially informative for the user since it is neither captured nor enforced in PTL. However, the relevance for distinguishing between the two kinds of messages will be fully appreciated when the notion of composite object is described in detail.

Concerning the specification of constraints we assume that only one message at a time can be sent to or received from an object. In other words, in each world of a sequence of worlds we require that exactly one atomic proposition is satisfied and all others are unsat-

The Specification of Temporal Properties

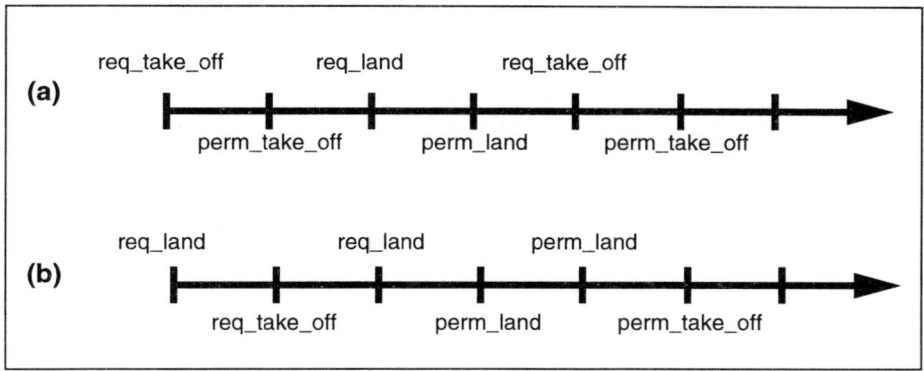

Figure 5.5 *Sequences of public and state messages relative to the class CTRL_TOWER.*

isfied. Assuming that n messages msg_i are defined in a class, the above requirement is expressed in PTL with the formula:

$$\Box ((\bigvee_{1 \leq k \leq n} msg_k) \wedge (\bigwedge_{1 \leq i \neq j \leq n} \neg(msg_i \wedge msg_j)))$$

Public constraints defined in class CTRL_TOWER (figure 5.4) formally describe the behaviour of a control tower. Let o be an instance of CTRL_TOWER. The first constraint says that the first message to be sent to o must be either req_take_off or req_land. The second constraint says that whenever message req_take_off is sent to o, then sometime in the future message perm_take_off will be received from o. The last constraint says that whenever message req_land is sent to o, then sometime in the future message perm_land will be received from o. Figure 5.5 shows two sequences of public messages satisfying the temporal constraints defined in class CTRL_TOWER.

Class CTRL_TOWER constitutes an example of a class definition expecting to cooperate with its clients on the basis of asynchronous communication. Indeed, an instance o of CTRL_TOWER will send message perm_land to those objects whose oid has been assigned to some parameter, e.g. perm_receiver, of the incoming message req_land. Similarly, the parameter perm_receiver of req_take_off will be used for determining the receivers of perm_take_off messages. Note, however, that the above relationships involving senders and receivers of messages, and parameters of messages cannot be described in PTL and therefore they cannot be explicitly specified in the constraint definition language we are proposing. They have to be annotated as comments. Nevertheless, in the case of composite objects (see below), messages exchanged with internal components are prefixed with the identifier of the involved component, thus allowing at least some form of constraint specification on internal messages.

Whether public constraints associated with a class are or are not violated is the responsibility of both the supplier and the client. For example, not receiving message perm_take_off from an instance CTRL_TOWER after having sent message req_take_off is the

```
class PLANE {
    public messages
        land ←, take_off ←;
    public constraints
        take_off;
        □(take_off ⇒ (○ land));
        □(land ⇒ (○ take_off));
    implementation
        ...
}
```

Figure 5.6 *Specification of class PLANE.*

responsibility of the supplier. Consider now the class definition PLANE (figure 5.6), modelling the lifecycle of an aeroplane. Its public constraints require the two incoming messages take_off and land to be sent to an instance o of PLANE alternately, the first message being take_off. In this case it is the responsibility of the client to ensure that take_off and land messages will be send to o in the specified order.

5.3.3 Shifting from Local Time to Global Time

Public constraints specify the temporal behaviour of an object o in *local time*, i.e. time-points are identified with messages that are sent to and received from o. However, the specification of public constraints in local time does not take into account that o may cooperate with a collection of objects. More precisely, o may become a component of a composite object, the various cooperating objects being the composite object and its components. In that case, between any pair of messages defined in o, one or several messages defined in other cooperating objects may be interleaved. In other words, public constraints of o should have been specified in *global time* in which case time-points are identified with messages that are sent to and received from any of the cooperating objects. Fortunately, constraints specified in local time can be easily transformed to constraints in global time in such a way that their initial meaning is "preserved." The transformation of public constraints from local time to global time is called *universalization* and will be formally described in subsection 5.4.2.1. There are two reasons for preferring the definition of public constraints in local time rather than the definition in global time. First, it is easier to specify constraints in local time than in global time, and second, the resulting constraints are simpler and easier to understand.

Even though the universalization of constraints preserves their initial meaning, sometimes the user wishes to specify a constraint directly in global time rather than in local time. TSOM provides the user with such a facility. Enclosing a formula or a subformula f within angle brackets "<" and ">" excludes f from the transformation process of universalization.

The Specification of Temporal Properties

```
class PLANE {
    attributes
        pl_status: {operational, maintenance};
    public messages
        land ←, take_off ←;
    public constraints
        pl_status := (operational ∨ maintenance);
        □(take_off ⇒ ((pl_status == operational) ∧ ○ land));
        □(land ⇒ (● take_off ∧ ○ ((pl_status := maintenance) ∨ take_off)));
        □((pl_status == maintenance) ⇒ (○ (pl_status := operational)));
    implementation
        ...
}
```

Figure 5.7 *Enhanced version of class definition PLANE.*

Let us elucidate with an example of both the usefulness for providing the above facility and the meaning of "preserves" in the definition of universalization. Consider the constraint □ (p ⇒ ○ q) defined in a class C requiring every message p to be *immediately* followed by message q. The universalization of the above constraint would require after p, the next message *among those defined in C* to be q, yet permitting zero or more messages msg_i to be interleaved between p and q, provided that messages msg_i have not been defined in C. Thus when specifying a formula □ (p ⇒ ○ q) in public constraints, its meaning in global time would be the second one, i.e. the meaning corresponding to its universalized version. However, specifying the constraint □ <(p ⇒ ○ q)> will ensure, *even in global time*, that every message p be *immediately* followed by message q, without allowing any message be interleaved between p and q.

5.3.4 Attributes

Figure 5.7 presents a more elaborate version of the class PLANE presented in subsection 5.3.2 (figure 5.6). Its definition includes an attribute pl_status with associated domain {operational, maintenance}. Value maintenance is assigned to pl_status during a maintenance period for the aeroplane. Value operational assigned to pl_status indicates that the aeroplane can travel.

The main reason for providing attributes in class definitions is to enhance the readability of constraints and ease their specification. Indeed, attributes are very useful when we want to express the fact that one or several actions on a particular object can be undertaken depending on the current values of one or several attributes of that object.

Let o be an instance of PLANE. The first of the public constraints says that the attribute pl_status should be assigned either the value operational or the value maintenance[*]. The second constraint says that whenever o receives message take_off the value of pl_status should be operational and the next message to be sent to o should be land. The third constraint says that o may receive message land if the previous message received is take_off. In addition, whenever message land is received, then either the next message to be sent to o should be take_off or the attribute pl_status should be assigned the value maintenance. In other words, after a flight the aeroplane can either continue travelling or begin a maintenance period. The last constraint says that if the value of attribute pl_status is maintenance, then the next action should be the assignment of value operational to pl_status.

In order to treat attributes and messages within the same framework we associate with each value val belonging in the domain of attribute at a message assign_at_val. Let us call these messages *assignment messages*. Sending the assignment message assign_at_val to an object o models the assignment of value val to the attribute at of o. Thus, whenever an assignment of the form at := val appears within constraint definitions, it is intended as a shorthand for the assignment message identifier assign_at_val. In addition, whenever a test equality of the form at == val_i appears within constraint definitions it is intended as a shorthand for the formula

$$(\blacklozenge \text{ assign\_at\_val}_i) \wedge (\neg (\vee_{1 \leq i \neq j \leq n} \text{assign\_at\_val}_j) \, S \, \text{assign\_at\_val}_i)$$

where $\{val_1, ..., val_n\}$ is supposed to be the domain associated with at. This expresses that at a given instant the current value of attribute at is val_i.

What differentiates an assignment message from a public message is that the sender and receiver of an assignment message should be the same object. It is not possible for two objects to exchange any assignment message, which implies that values of attributes defined in an object o can only be updated by o itself. Attribute-value updates constitute an example where the supplier of a class C is responsible for providing an implementation of C that satisfies the temporal order of attribute assignment defined in C's public constraints.

Figure 5.8 shows two sequences of public and assignment messages relative to the class PLANE. The first is a legal sequence satisfying the temporal constraints in figure 5.7. The second is an illegal sequence since message take_off follows the assignment of value maintenance to attribute pl_status thus violating the second and fourth public constraints.

5.3.5 Components

An example of a class definition of a composite object modelling the flight of an aeroplane is given in figure 5.9. Class FLIGHT contains three components: pl, ctt and ctl. Component pl is constrained to be assigned an instance of PLANE modelling the aeroplane making a trip. Components ctt and ctl are constrained to be assigned instances of CTRL_TOWER.

---

* If y is an attribute with associated domain $\{x_1, ..., x_n\}$ then
$y := (x_1 \vee ... \vee x_k)$ with $k \leq n$ is a shorthand for $y := x_1 \vee ... \vee y := x_k$ and
$y == (x_1 \vee ... \vee x_k)$ with $k \leq n$ is a shorthand for $y == x_1 \vee ... \vee y == x_k$
":=" is used for assigning a value to an attribute
"==" is the test-equal-value operator

The Specification of Temporal Properties

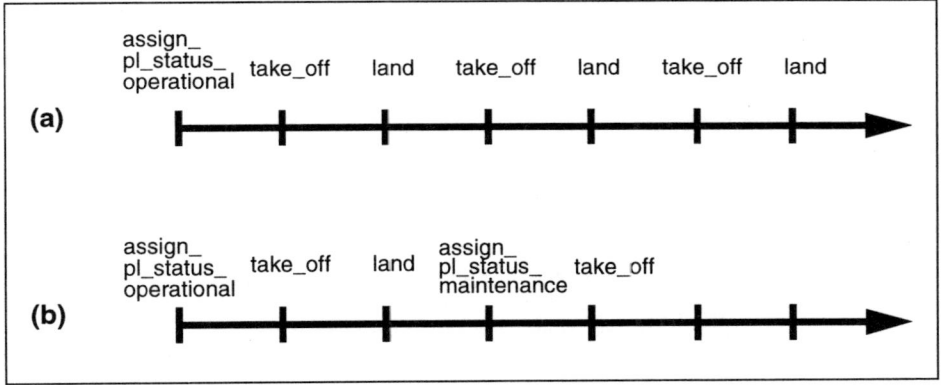

Figure 5.8 Sequences of public and state messages relative to the class PLANE ((a) legal sequence; (b) illegal sequence).

They represent the control towers of airports from which the plane respectively takes off and lands.

Even though an object w may be a shared component of several composite objects, w cannot be referenced from two different components κ_1 and κ_2 of the same composite object. Indeed, PTL does not permit us to distinguish whether the sender or receiver of a message referenced by components κ_1 and κ_2 is the same object or not. Thus TSOM assumes that different components of a composite object reference distinct objects.

Let us call the *environment* of a composite object o the set of all objects existing at a given point in time excluding o and its components. Public messages, attributes and public constraints are considered to be the interface of a composite object for its environment. Public messages are exchanged between the composite object and the environment of the composite object. Public constraints may not contain component message identifiers; they describe the behaviour of a composite object as if the communication between itself and its components has been filtered out. For example, an instance o of FLIGHT may receive messages start_flight and displ_report from its environment. The effect of the start_flight message would be to set up a cooperation between the aeroplane and the two control towers necessary for an aeroplane to make a trip. The effect of the displ_report message would be to display a complete report once the flight has been completed. Messages start_flight and displ_report can be sent to o depending on the current abstract state of o. Domain values of attribute fl_status model the various abstract states of o, which are: comp_pb when there is a problem encountered with some of o's components and the flight cannot be carried out; ready when there is no problem with any of o's components and the coordination process between components can be started; started when the plane has taken off but not yet landed; completed when the plane has landed.

```
class FLIGHT {
    attributes
        fl_status: {comp_pb, ready, started, completed};
    public messages
        start_flight ←, displ_report ←
    public constraints
        fl_status := (ready ∨ comp_pb)
        ☐ (start_flight ⇒
            [(fl_status == ready) ∧ ○ ((fl_status := started) ∧
                ((fl_status == started) 𝒰 (fl_status := completed)))]);
        ☐ (displ_report ⇒ (fl_status == completed));
        ☐ ((fl_status == (completed ∨ pl_maintenance)) ⇒
            ¬ (fl_status := (started ∨ comp_pb ∨ ready ∨ completed)));
    components
        ctt: CTRL_TOWER;
        ctl: CTRL_TOWER;
        pl: PLANE;
    component messages
        ctt$req_take_off →, ctt$perm_take_off ←,
        ctl$req_land →, ctl$perm_land ←,
        pl$take_off →, pl$land →;
    component constraints
        ...
    implementation
        perm_take_off(sender: oid, ...)
        { ... };
        perm_land(sender: oid, ...)
        { ... };
        ...
}
```

Figure 5.9 *Class FLIGHT modelling the flight of an aeroplane.*

5.3.6 Component Messages

Component messages are exchanged between the composite object and its components. The definition of each component message msg should indicate the component which is the sender or receiver of msg. This is achieved by prefixing the message identifier with the component identifier and separating the two identifiers with the character "$". For example, the definition of component message ctt$req_take_off means that message req_take_off can be sent from an instance of FLIGHT to component ctt. In addition, assuming the component definition κ: C, each incoming (outgoing) component message κ$msg, should match an outgoing (incoming) public message msg defined in class C. For example, for the definition of the incoming component message ctl$perm_land ← in class FLIGHT, the outgoing message perm_land → should appear in the list of public messages of class CTRL_TOWER.

Implementing a component incoming message κ$msg would require certifying that the sender of msg is κ, therefore necessitating a comparison between the sender's oid and κ's oid. However, in most object-oriented systems, the sender of a message is not known to the receiver of the message. A simple solution for identifying the sender of an incoming component message κ$msg ← would be the assignment of the sender's oid to a particular parameter of msg. In particular, for any outgoing public message msg defined in a class C, it would be a good practice to anticipate a parameter for the sender of msg. Indeed, a component definition κ: C in a class CC enables the definition of the incoming component message κ$msg ←. The implementation of msg in CC needs the oid of the sender of msg. An example of the above strategy is illustrated with the implementation of messages perm_take_off and perm_land in class FLIGHT (Figure 5.9). Message perm_take_off (perm_land) uses the parameter sender for identifying the sender of the message while expecting instances of CTRL_TOWER to assign their oid to sender when sending perm_take_off (perm_land).

5.3.7 Component Constraints

Component constraints specify the legal sequences of public and component messages exchanged between the composite object, components of the composite object and the environment of the composite object. For all component messages the composite object is involved either as sender or receiver. A direct communication between two components of a composite object cannot be defined. From the above restriction it becomes obvious that a composite object acts as a coordinator for its components. Temporal dependencies involving different components must be described by means of messages exchanged with the composite object. Component constraints in figure 5.10 describing the communication between an instance o of FLIGHT and o's components pl, ctl and ctt, constitute an example of such a dependency.

The first component constraint requires attribute fl_status to be initialized either with value ready or pl_maintenance depending on the value assigned to the attribute pl_status of component pl. More precisely, fl_status will be initialized to ready (comp_pb) if pl_status is assigned value operational (maintenance). The second constraint says that message start_flight may be sent to o if the current value of fl_status is ready. In addition, if start_flight is sent to o then the next instant component message req_take_off should be sent to component ctt from the composite object. The purpose of the communication between the composite object and component ctt is to grant permission to take off. Once the permission to take off is granted, the command to take off for the aeroplane is issued from the composite object. This is expressed by the third component constraint. It says that whenever message perm_take_off is received from component ctt, then the next message to be sent is take_off with sender the composite object and receiver pl. In addition, attribute fl_status is assigned value started immediately after message pl$take_off has been sent to pl. The fourth and fifth

```
class FLIGHT {
    ...
    component constraints
        ((pl$pl_status == operational) ⇒ (fl_status := ready)) ∧
            ((¬ (pl$pl_status == operational)) ⇒ (fl_status := comp_pb));

        ☐ (start_flight ⇒ ((fl_status == ready) ∧ ○ ctt$req_take_off));
        ☐ (ctt$perm_take_off ⇒ ○ (pl$take_off ∧ ○ (fl_status := started)));

        ☐ ((fl_status == started) ⇒ ◊ ctl$req_land)));
        ☐ (ctl$perm_land ⇒ ○ (pl$land ∧ ○ (fl_status := completed)));

        ☐ (displ_report ⇒ (fl_status == completed));
        ☐ ((fl_status == (completed ∨ pl_maintenance)) ⇒
            ¬ (fl_status := (started ∨ comp_pb ∨ ready ∨ completed)));
    ...
}
```

Figure 5.10 *Component constraints of class FLIGHT.*

component constraints specify an analogous communication between the composite object and component ctl. More precisely, the fourth constraint requires that component message req_land to be sent to ctl sometime in the future after the value of fl_status is started. The fifth constraint specifies that once the permission to land is granted (component message perm_land is sent to the composite object from component ctl), the command to land (component message pl$land) for the aeroplane is issued from the composite object. In addition, for indicating that the aeroplane has landed the value completed is assigned to attribute fl_status. The sixth constraint says that message disp_report may be sent to o if the current value of fl_status is completed. Finally, the last component constraint ensures that once fl_status has been assigned one of the values comp_pb or completed it cannot be later updated.

Let us now clarify the rationale for introducing both public constraints and component constraints in composite object class definitions. To test consistency of a composite object's specification, the specification of the temporal behaviour of its components must be taken into account. As we will describe in the next section, this is achieved by testing the satisfiability of the logical conjunction of public constraints of components and component constraints of the composite object. Taking the conjunction of public constraints without regard to component constraints of a component v of a composite object o permits irrelevant details of the eventual composition of v from other objects to be abstracted away. If o is in turn a component of a composite object z, the satisfiability of the conjunction of component constraints of z and public constraints of o should be tested in order to confirm either the consistency or inconsistency of z's specifications.

Figure 5.11 depicts the use of public and component constraints for composing objects. Ovals represent class definitions. An edge labelled $\mathcal{K}$ connecting a class C with a class C´

The Specification of Temporal Properties

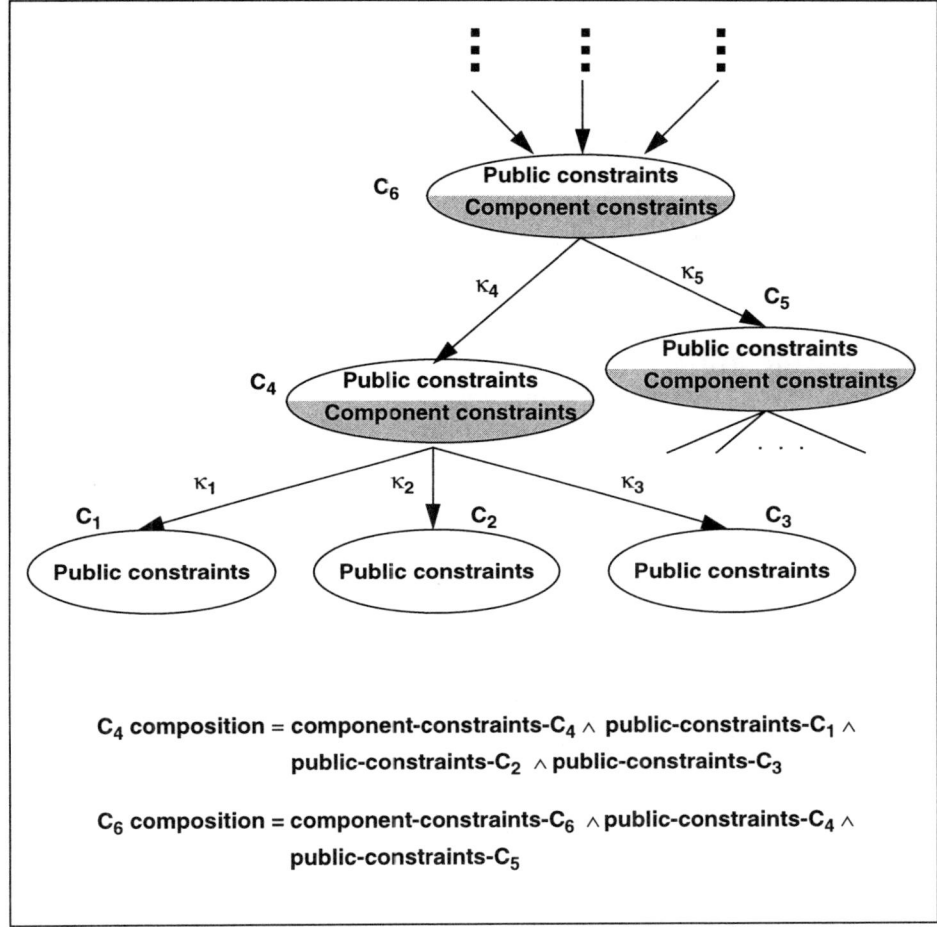

Figure 5.11 *Using public and component constraints to compose objects.*

indicates that component $\kappa: C'$ is defined within the definition of C. For class C_4 the conjunction of component constraints of C_4 with public constraints of classes C_1, C_2 and C_3 should be made. Then for the composition of C_6 the conjunction of public constraints of classes of C_4 and C_5 with the component constraints of C_6 should be made.

The above schema of object composition requires public and component constraints of the same object to be related by some compatibility rule. In fact, we must ensure that for any sequence σ satisfying component constraints there exists a sequence σ' of public messages satisfying public constraints such that when component messages are eliminated from σ we get a sequence identical to σ'. We will call the above compatibility rule between component constraints and public constraints of the same composite object the *corre-*

spondence property. The correspondence property requires us to verify the validity of the formula:

component constraints ⇒ universalized public constraints

The universalization of public constraints is necessary for taking into account that one or several component messages can be interleaved between any pair of public messages. In other words the universalization of public constraints corresponds to a shift from local time to global time. In this case time-points in local time are identified with the composite object's public and assignment messages whereas time-points in global time are identified with the composite object's component, public, and assignment messages.

5.4 Verification

To verify the consistency of object specifications we make the following assumptions concerning the object model of TSOM. Each class C owns an infinite number of oids. An oid o becomes an instance of C when it receives the predefined message create_C. An instance o of C is deleted when o receives the predefined message delete_C. The deletion of o is modelled by restricting o to only be able to accept delete_C messages.

5.4.1 Verification of Elementary Objects

The consistency of a class definition C, from which elementary objects are instantiated, can be verified by giving as input to the satisfiability algorithm the formula:

$$(\neg (\text{delete\_C} \vee m_1 \vee \ldots \vee m_n) \; \mathcal{U} \; \text{create\_C}) \wedge \qquad (4.1)$$

$$\Box \, (\text{create\_C} \Rightarrow \bigcirc \text{public\_constraint\_C}) \wedge \qquad (4.2)$$

$$\Box \, (\text{create\_C} \Rightarrow (\bigcirc \Box \neg \text{create\_C})) \wedge \qquad (4.3)$$

$$\Box \, (\text{delete\_C} \Rightarrow \bigcirc \text{delete\_C}) \qquad (4.4)$$

In the previous formula $m_1, \ldots, m_n$ is assumed to be the set of public and assignment messages defined in C[*]. public_constraint_C stands for the conjunction of constraints defined in class C. Conjunct (4.1) says that no public message nor the delete_C message can be sent to an object prior to its creation. Conjunct (4.2) says that after the creation of an object its public constraints must be verified. Conjunct (4.3) forbids an object to be created more than once. Finally conjunct (4.4) ensures that after accepting a delete_C message, an object will then only be able to accept further delete_C messages.

For a class C we will name LCpublic_C[†] the conjunction of (4.1), (4.2), (4.3) and (4.4). The output of the satisfiability algorithm corresponding to the formula LCpublic_C determines the consistency of C. If no graph is produced, the definition of C is inconsistent. If a satisfiability graph is produced, the definition of C is consistent. This satisfiability graph

---

[*] Assignment messages are indirectly defined via attribute definitions.
[†] LCpublic stands for lifecycle according to public constraints.

Verification

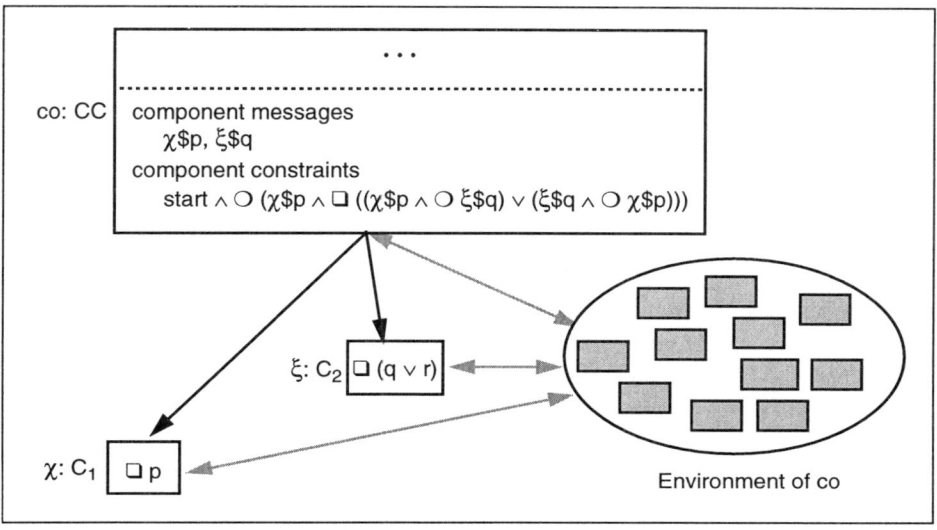

Figure 5.12 *A composite object and component specifications.*

then represents all legal sequences of public and assignment messages that can be sent to and received from an instance of C.

5.4.2 Verification of Composite Objects

To describe the verification of a composite object's specification let us assume the situation presented in figure 5.12. An object is depicted by a rectangle. A rectangle corresponding to an elementary object is labelled with a formula describing its public constraints. Rectangles corresponding to composite objects are divided into two horizontal parts. The upper part is used for listing the public constraints of the composite object. The lower part is used for listing the list of component messages and component constraints.

A grey arrow connecting two rectangles is drawn when the two objects are assumed to exchange messages. A black arrow connecting two rectangles x and y, leaving x and leading to y, is drawn when y is a component of x. Thus co in figure 5.12 is assumed to be a composite object having two components χ and ξ. Let components χ and ξ be assigned instances of classes C_1 and C_2 respectively. co is assumed to be an instance of CC.

Component constraints of co say that the first message to be sent to co must be the public message start. Immediately after the reception of start, messages p and q should be sent to components χ and ξ alternately, starting with a p message. Public constraints of components are very simple. Component χ expects always to receive message p. Component ξ expects always to receive either message q or message r.

The basic idea for testing the consistency of a composite object's specification is to give as input to the satisfiability algorithm the conjunction of the object's and its components' specifications. If a class definition CC contains the definitions of components κ_i: C_i, $i = 1, \ldots, n$, the input to the satisfiability algorithm would be the formula:

$$\text{LCpublic\_C}_1 \wedge \ldots \wedge \text{LCpublic\_C}_n \wedge \text{LCcomponent\_CC} \wedge \quad (4.5)$$

$$(\neg \text{ create\_CC } \mathcal{U} \text{ create\_C}_1) \wedge \ldots \wedge (\neg \text{ create\_CC } \mathcal{U} \text{ create\_C}_n) \wedge \quad (4.6)$$

$$\square (\neg (s_1 \vee \ldots \vee s_j)) \quad (4.7)$$

Conjuncts LCpublic_C_1, ..., LCpublic_C_n specify lifecycles corresponding to components κ_i: C_i, $i = 1, \ldots, n$, respectively. Conjunct LCcomponent_CC[*] specifies the lifecycle of the composite object and stands for the formula:

$$(\neg (\text{delete\_C} \vee m_1 \vee \ldots \vee m_n) \, \mathcal{U} \text{ create\_CC}) \wedge$$

$$\square (\text{create\_CC} \Rightarrow \bigcirc \text{ component\_constraint\_CC}) \wedge$$

$$\square (\text{create\_CC} \Rightarrow (\bigcirc \square \neg \text{ create\_CC})) \wedge$$

$$\square (\text{delete\_CC} \Rightarrow \bigcirc \text{ delete\_CC}) \wedge$$

where $m_1, \ldots, m_n$ is assumed to be the list of public, assignment and component messages defined in CC and component_constraint_CC stands for the conjunction of component constraints defined in CC. Conjuncts $\neg$ create_CC $\mathcal{U}$ create_C_i, $i = 1, \ldots, n$, say that all components must have been created before the creation of the composite object. The last conjunct says that component messages not defined in CC cannot be exchanged. Thus, s_i, $i = 1, \ldots, j$, are all such messages identifiers of the form $\kappa\$msg$ such that the component definition κ: C appears in CC, msg is a public message defined in C and $\kappa\$msg$ does not appear in the list of component messages of CC.

The constraint on component creation we have expressed with conjunct (4.6) is merely introduced for expository reasons. Its omission would not represent any significant benefit for the description of object lifecycles at the specification level but additional complexity for the various formulas formalizing the notions we are proposing. Indeed, modelling situations where an object z could be created either before or after a composite object o and then z be assigned to a component of o requires the introduction of lengthy and complicated formulas.

For the composite object co in figure 5.12, the input to the satisfiability algorithm would be the formula:

$$\text{LCpublic\_C}_1 \wedge \text{LCpublic\_C}_2 \wedge \text{LCcomponent\_CC} \wedge \quad (4.8)$$

$$(\neg \text{ create\_CC } \mathcal{U} \text{ create\_C}_1) \wedge (\neg \text{ create\_CC } \mathcal{U} \text{ create\_C}_2) \wedge \quad (4.9)$$

$$\square (\neg \xi\$r) \quad (4.10)$$

Conjuncts LCpublic_C_1, LCpublic_C_2 and LCcomponent_CC correspond to components χ, ξ and to the composite object co respectively.

However, the conjunctions of formulas (4.5), (4.6) and (4.7) cannot be directly given as input to the satisfiability algorithm. A number of transformations must be applied in advance. The rationale for these transformations and their exact nature is the subject of the

---

[*] LCcomponent stands for lifecycle according to component constraints.

Verification

following subsections. The various transformations can be carried out automatically, meaning that the whole verification process can be automated.

The output of the algorithm will determine the consistency of the composite object's specification. If no graph is produced, the specification is inconsistent. If a satisfiability graph is produced, the specification is consistent. The graph produced represents all legal sequences of public, assignment and component messages exchanged between the composite object, the various components of the composite object and the environment of the composite object.

5.4.2.1 Transformations on Component Definitions

In this subsection we describe the various transformations that should be performed on conjuncts LCpublic_C_1, ..., LCpublic_C_n of formula (4.5).

Message Renaming

To achieve the matching between component messages defined for a composite object and public messages of component $\kappa: C_i$ each message msg appearing within conjunct LCpublic_C_i of (4.5) should be renamed κ\$msg. Thus, if a class specification contains the component definitions $\kappa_1: C$ and $\kappa_2: C$ (i.e. both components κ_1 and κ_2 are associated with the same class C), the component which is the sender or receiver of msg can be distinguished since msg is renamed either κ_1\$msg or κ_2\$msg. The formula resulting from that transformation will be named κ\$LCpublic_C_i. For example, according to the public constraints of component χ in figure 5.12, χ\$LCpublic_C_1 stands for the formula:

$$(\neg (\chi\$delete\_C_1 \vee \chi\$p) \; \mathcal{U} \; \chi\$create\_C_1) \wedge$$
$$\Box (\chi\$create\_C_1 \Rightarrow \bigcirc \Box \chi\$p) \wedge$$
$$\Box (\chi\$create\_C_1 \Rightarrow (\bigcirc \Box \neg \chi\$create\_C_1)) \wedge$$
$$\Box (\chi\$delete\_C_1 \Rightarrow \bigcirc \chi\$delete\_C_1)$$

Sharing Components

To take into account that component $\kappa: C_i$ may be shared between the composite object co and the environment of co, each message κ\$msg within the conjunct κ\$LCpublic_C_i, should be replaced by the formula:

$$\kappa\$msg \vee env\$\kappa\$msg \qquad (4.11)$$

Messages exchanged between a component and the environment (named *environment messages*) are prefixed with "env\$". Messages exchanged between a component and the composite object are not renamed. Replacing a message κ\$msg with the formula (4.11) implies that the sender or receiver of a message msg could be either co or an object from the environment of co. The resulting formula from that transformation is named env\$$\kappa$\$LCpublic_C_i.

For example, for component χ in figure 5.12, env\$$\chi$\$LCpublic_C_1 would stand for the formula:

$(\neg (\chi\$delete\_C_1 \vee env\$\chi\$delete\_C_1 \vee \chi\$p \vee env\$\chi\$p)\ \mathcal{U}\ env\$\chi\$create\_C_1) \wedge$

$\Box\ (env\$\chi\$create\_C_1 \Rightarrow \bigcirc \Box\ (\chi\$p \vee env\$\chi\$p)) \wedge$

$\Box\ (env\$\chi\$create\_C_1 \Rightarrow (\bigcirc \Box \neg env\$\chi\$create\_C_1)) \wedge$

$\Box\ ((\chi\$delete\_C_1 \vee env\$\chi\$delete\_C_1) \Rightarrow \bigcirc\ (\chi\$delete\_C_1 \vee env\$\chi\$delete\_C_1))$

Recall that assignment messages cannot be exchanged between objects. Therefore only environment-assignment messages can exist since a composite object cannot be the sender of an assignment message to any of its components. Thus, any assignment message κ\$msg should be simply renamed env\$κ\$msg. In addition, the composite object cannot send a creation message to a component κ: C, since components should exist before the creation of the composite object. Therefore any κ\$create_C must be simply renamed env\$κ\$create_C.

Universalization of Public Constraints of Components

Let us assume that $m_1, \ldots, m_n$ is the collection of public messages defined in a class C and that κ: C is a component definition appearing in a class definition for composite objects. Then we introduce the following shorthand expressions:

$$
\begin{aligned}
\text{public\_msg\_C} &\equiv m_1 \vee \ldots \vee m_n \vee \text{delete\_C} \\
\text{K\$public\_msg\_C} &\equiv \text{K\$}m_1 \vee \ldots \vee \text{K\$}m_n \vee \text{K\$delete\_C} \\
\text{env\$K\$public\_msg\_C} &\equiv \text{env\$K\$}m_1 \vee \ldots \vee \text{env\$K\$}m_n \vee \text{env\$K\$delete\_C} \\
\text{K\$env\_pub\_msg\_C} &\equiv \text{K\$public\_msg} \vee \text{env\$K\$public\_msg} \vee \text{K\$create\_C}
\end{aligned}
$$

The rationale for the universalization of conjunct env\$K\$LCpublic_C corresponding to component κ: C has been described in subsection 5.3.1. The universalization consists of the following transformations:

replace   p   by $\neg$ K\$env_pub_msg_C $\mathcal{U}$ p

replace $\bigcirc$ f   by $\neg$ K\$env_pub_msg_C $\mathcal{U}$ (K\$env_pub_msg_C $\wedge \bigcirc$ f)

replace $\bullet$ f   by $\neg$ K\$env_pub_msg_C $\mathcal{S}$ (K\$env_pub_msg_C $\wedge \bullet$ f)

where p is an atomic proposition and f a wff of PTL appearing within env\$K\$LCpublic_C.

Applying the universalization of env\$χ\$LCpublic_C_1 we will obtain the following formula:

$(\neg ((\neg \chi\$env\_pub\_msg\_C_1\ \mathcal{U}$

$(\chi\$delete\_C_1 \vee env\$\chi\$delete\_C_1 \vee \chi\$p \vee env\$\chi\$p))\ \mathcal{U}$

$(\neg \chi\$env\_pub\_msg\_C_1\ \mathcal{U}\ env\$\chi\$create\_C_1)) \wedge$

$\Box\ (\neg \chi\$env\_pub\_msg\_C_1\ \mathcal{U}\ env\$\chi\$create\_C_1 \Rightarrow$

$(\neg \chi\$env\_pub\_msg\_C_1\ \mathcal{U}$

$(\chi\$env\_pub\_msg\_C_1 \wedge$

$\bigcirc \Box\ (\neg \chi\$env\_pub\_msg\_C_1\ \mathcal{U}\ (\chi\$p \vee env\$\chi\$p))))) \wedge$

$\Box\ (\neg \chi\$env\_pub\_msg\_C_1\ \mathcal{U}\ env\$\chi\$create\_C_1 \Rightarrow$

$(\neg \chi\$env\_pub\_msg\_C_1\ \mathcal{U}$

$(\chi\$env\_pub\_msg\_C_1 \wedge$

$\bigcirc \Box\ (\neg \chi\$env\_pub\_msg\_C_1\ \mathcal{U} \neg env\$\chi\$create\_C_1)))) \wedge$

Verification

$\square\ ((\neg\ \chi\$env\_pub\_msg\_C_1\ \mathcal{U}\ (\chi\$delete\_C_1 \vee env\$\chi\$delete\_C_1)) \Rightarrow$
$\qquad (\neg\ \chi\$env\_pub\_msg\_C_1\ \mathcal{U}$
$\qquad\qquad (\chi\$env\_pub\_msg\_C_1 \wedge$
$\qquad\qquad\quad \bigcirc\ (\neg\ \chi\$env\_pub\_msg\_C_1\ \mathcal{U}\ (\chi\$delete\_C_1 \vee env\$\chi\$delete\_C_1))))))$

In the above formula we have used the equivalence:

$$f\ \mathcal{U}\ (f_1 \vee f_2) \Leftrightarrow (f\ \mathcal{U}\ f_1) \vee (f\ \mathcal{U}\ f_2)$$

while $\chi\$env\_pub\_msg\_C_1$ is the shorthand for the formula:

$$\chi\$delete\_C_1 \vee env\$\chi\$delete\_C_1 \vee \chi\$p \vee env\$\chi\$p \vee env\$\chi\$create\_C_1$$

5.4.2.2 Universalization of Component Constraints of Composite Objects

Let us assume that $q_1, \ldots, q_p$ are the various component messages defined in a class CC. Then we introduce the following shorthand expressions:

component_msg_CC $\equiv\ q_1 \vee \ldots \vee q_p$
msg_CC $\equiv$ public_msg_CC $\vee$ component_msg_CC $\vee$ create_CC

The universalization of conjunct LCcomponent_CC in (4.5) is required to take into account that one or several environment messages may be interleaved between a pair of component, assignment or public messages in which the composite object is either the sender or the receiver. The universalization of LCcomponent_CC consists of the following transformations:

replace $\quad$ p $\qquad$ by $\quad \neg$ msg_CC $\mathcal{U}$ p
replace $\quad \bigcirc$ f $\qquad$ by $\quad \neg$ msg_CC $\mathcal{U}$ (msg_CC $\wedge \bigcirc$ f)
replace $\quad \bullet$ f $\qquad$ by $\quad \neg$ msg_CC $\mathcal{S}$ (msg_CC $\wedge \bullet$ f)

where p is an atomic proposition and f a wff of PTL appearing within LCcomponent_CC.

5.4.2.3 Verification of the Correspondence Property

According to the shorthand expressions we have already introduced, the correspondence property for a class CC for composite objects is easily formalized by requiring the following formula to be valid:

component_constraint_CC $\Rightarrow$ (universalization of public_constraint_CC)

The universalization of public_constraint_CC consists of the following transformations:

replace $\quad$ p $\qquad$ by $\quad \neg$ public_msg_CC $\mathcal{U}$ p
replace $\quad \bigcirc$ f $\qquad$ by $\quad -$ public_msg_CC $\mathcal{U}$ (public_msg_CC $\wedge \bigcirc$ f)
replace $\quad \bullet$ f $\qquad$ by $\quad \neg$ public_msg_CC $\mathcal{S}$ (public_msg_CC $\wedge \bullet$ f)

where p is an atomic proposition and f a wff of PTL appearing within public_constraint_CC.

As an example consider a composite object for which one public message p and one component message $\kappa\$q$ have been defined, the formula $\square$ p being its public constraint and the formula

$$\square\ ((p \wedge \bigcirc\ \kappa\$q) \vee (\kappa\$q \wedge \bigcirc\ p))$$

its component constraint. The correspondence property requires us to test the validity of the formula:

$$\Box((p \wedge \bigcirc K\$q) \vee (K\$q \wedge \bigcirc p)) \Rightarrow \Box(\neg p \, \mathcal{U} \, p)$$

Using the satisfiability algorithm of PTL, the validity of the above formula is easily verified.

5.5 Concluding Remarks

We have presented a formal approach, founded on PTL, for the description of temporal aspects of an object's behaviour and its composition with other objects. An object's temporal properties are specified by means of a collection of component and public constraints. The former specify the temporal order of messages exchanged between a composite object and its components. The latter specify the behaviour of an object as if the communication between it and its internal components has been filtered out. We described an automated procedure for verifying the consistency of object specifications based on the satisfiability algorithm of PTL.

A significant source of influence for the various ideas we have presented has been the work of Manna and Wolper who investigated the composition of synchronized collections of concurrent processes [17]. For Manna and Wolper a process specification (an object in our approach) consists of a collection of PTL formulas (public constraints) describing the temporal order of its input/output communication operations (incoming/outgoing messages). The consistency of a concurrent system consisting of a synchronizer process S (a composite object) communicating with a collection of processes P_i, $1 \le i \le n$ (components of a composite object), is verified by giving as input to the satisfiability algorithm of PTL the composition of S and P_i specifications. Even though one may find strong similarities concerning both the behaviour specification of a process (object) and the verification procedure for consistency, the two approaches are characterized by different modelling prerequisites and divergent objectives. An important prerequisite emphasized in our approach is the ability of specifying composite objects having a nested structure of arbitrary depth (composite objects having components that are other composite objects). The nested structure of composite objects necessitated the distinction between public and component constraints and the validation of the correspondence property. In addition, the fact that an object may be a shared component of several composite objects led us to introduce "env" messages. None of the above modelling issues have been investigated in [17]. Finally, there is an important distinction concerning the objectives of the two approaches. In our approach we ended up with a procedure for verifying an object's temporal specifications. In [17] the satisfiability graph corresponding to the composition of S and P_i specifications is further used for deriving the synchronization parts of code of S and the P_i's. More precisely, for each process, P_i and S, Manna and Wolper derive from the set of all possible sequences of communication operations a subset which satisfies the specified constraints.

Several improvements can be envisaged for TSOM along various directions. First and foremost, there is a need for providing the specifier with assistance for translating TSOM specifications into some object-oriented language. Assessing the various alternatives for providing higher-level assistance than that of guidelines, we ended up investigating the eventuality of enriching an existing object-oriented language with constructs that would directly support most of the notions integrated in TSOM. Further evidence to support the validity of this approach is given by Nierstrasz (see chapter 4). There, a type system for object-oriented languages is proposed which enables users to describe temporal aspects of object behaviour and provides rules for analyzing the type-consistency of such descriptions. Even though the formalism upon which that type system has been developed is different from PTL, it is likely that most of the ideas and results could also be applied for PTL. Thus, the proposed type system could serve as the starting point for enhancing object-oriented languages with constructs directly supporting most of TSOM's notions.

Another important direction along which additional efforts are necessary for improving TSOM concerns the verification procedure. The satisfiability algorithm of PTL, upon which the verification procedure is based, may generate a number of nodes that grows exponentially with the number of temporal operators of the input formula. By operating the algorithm the way we have described, i.e. applying the algorithm to each object specification separately and not to the composition of all constraints of those objects participating in a whole part-of hierarchy, the size of input formulas is considerably minimized. However, the exponential nature of the satisfiability algorithm still remains a serious efficiency handicap for its computer implementation. Restricted forms of PTL may reduce the number of nodes of the satisfiability algorithm to polynomial size [10]. However, whether such restrictions of PTL are still suitable for TSOM remains to be investigated.

References

[1]   Constantin Arapis, "Temporal Specifications of Object Interactions," *Proceedings Third International Workshop on Foundations of Models and Languages for Data and Objects*, Aigen, Austria, Sept. 1991, pp. 15–35.

[2]   Constantin Arapis, "Dynamic Evolution of Object Behaviour and Object Cooperation," Ph.D. thesis no 2529, Centre Universitaire d'Informatique, University of Geneva, 1992.

[3]   Constantin Arapis, "A Temporal Logic Based Approach for the Description of Object Behaviour Evolution," *Journal of Annals of Mathematics and Artificial Intelligence*, vol. 7, 1993, pp. 1–40.

[4]   Grady Booch, *Object-Oriented Design with Applications*, Benjamin/Cummings, 1991.

[5]   Peter Coad and Edward Yourdon, *Object-Oriented Analysis*, 2nd edn., Prentice-Hall, Englewood Cliffs, 1991.

[6]   Peter Coad and Edward Yourdon, *Object-Oriented Design*, Prentice Hall, Englewood Cliffs, 1991.

[7]   Brad Cox, *Object-Oriented Programming An Evolutionary Approach*, Addison Wesley, Reading, Mass., 1987.

[8]   Vicki De Mey, Betty Junod, Serge Renfer, Marc Stadelmann and Ino Simitsek, "The Implementation of Vista — A Visual Scripting Tool," in *Object Composition*, ed. Dennis Tsichritzis, Centre Universitaire d'Informatique, University of Geneva, June 1991, pp. 31–56.

[9]   Allen Emerson and Edmund Clarke, "Using Branching Time Temporal Logic to Synthesize Synchronization Skeletons," *Science of Computer Programming*, vol. 2, 1982, pp. 241–266.

[10] Allen Emerson, Tom Sadler and Jai Srinivasan, "Efficient Temporal Reasoning," *Proceedings 16th ACM Symposium on Principles of Programming Languages*, 1989, pp. 166–178.

[11] Dov Gabbay, Amir Pnueli, Saharon Shelah and Jonathan Stavi, "On the Temporal Analysis of Fairness," *Proceedings 7th ACM Symposium on Principles of Programming Languages,* 1980, pp. 163–173.

[12] Adele Goldberg and David Robson, *Smalltalk-80: The Language and its Implementation,* Addison-Wesley, Reading, Mass., 1983.

[13] David Harel, "On Visual Formalisms," *Communications of the ACM,* vol. 31, no. 5, May 1988, pp. 514–530.

[14] Richard Helm, Ian Holland and Dipayan Gangopadhyay, "Contracts: Specifying Behavioural Compositions in Object-Oriented Systems," *Proceedings of the ECOOP/OOPSLA Conference,* Ottawa, Oct. 1990, pp. 169–180.

[15] Ivar Jacobson, *Object-Oriented Software Engineering,* Addison-Wesley, Reading, Mass., 1992.

[16] Orna Lichtenstein and Amir Pnueli, "The Glory of The Past," *Proceedings of the Workshop on Logic of Programs, Brooklyn, Lecture Notes in Computer Science,* vol. 193, Springer-Verlag, 1985, pp. 97–107.

[17] Zohar Manna and Pierre Wolper, "Synthesis of Communicating Process," *ACM Transactions on Programming Languages and Systems,* vol. 6, no. 1, June 1984, pp. 68–93.

[18] Bertrand Meyer, *Object-oriented Software Construction,* Prentice Hall, 1988.

[19] Oscar Nierstrasz, Dennis Tsichritzis, Vicki De Mey and Marc Stadelmann, "Objects + Scripts = Applications," in *Object Composition,* ed. Dennis Tsichritzis, Centre Universitaire d'Informatique, University of Geneva, June 1991, pp. 11–29.

[20] James Rumbaugh, M. Blaha, W. Premerlani, F. Eddy and W. Lorensen, *Object-Oriented Modeling and Design,* Prentice Hall, 1991.

[21] Sally Shlaer and Stephen Mellor, *OBJECT LIFECYCLES: Modeling the World in States,* Prentice Hall, Englewood Cliffs, NJ, 1992.

[22] Bjarne Stroustrup, *The C++ Programming Language,* Addison-Wesley, Reading, Mass., 1986.

[23] Anthony Wassermann, P. Pircher and R. Muller, "The Object-Oriented Structured Design Notation for Software Design Representation," *IEEE Computer,* vol. 23, no. 3, March 1990, pp. 50–63.

[24] Rebecca Wirfs-Brock, Brian Wilkerson and Laurent Wiener, *Designing Object-Oriented Software,* Prentice Hall, Englewood Cliffs, NJ, 1990.

Chapter 6

Functions, Records and Compatibility in the λN Calculus

Laurent Dami

Abstract Subtyping, a fundamental notion for software reusability, establishes a classification of data according to a compatibility relationship. This relationship is usually associated with records. However, compatibility can be defined in other situations, involving for example enumerated types or concrete data types. We argue that the basic requirement for supporting compatibility is an interaction protocol between software components using *names* instead of *positions*. Based on this principle, an extension of the lambda calculus is proposed, which combines de Bruijn indices with names. In the extended calculus various subtyping situations mentioned above can be modelled; in particular, records are encoded in a straightforward way. Compatibility is formally defined in terms of an operational lattice based on observation of error generation. Unlike many usual orderings, errors are not identified with divergence; as a matter of fact, both are even opposite since they respectively correspond to the bottom and top elements of the lattice. Finally, we briefly explore a second extension of the calculus, providing meet and join operators through a simple operational definition, and opening interesting perspectives for type checking and concurrency.

6.1 Introduction

The lambda calculus is a widely used tool for studying the semantics of programming languages. However, there are at least two categories of programming features that cannot be modelled in the lambda calculus. One is *concurrent programming*, in which the non-determinism introduced by operations taking place in parallel cannot be captured by lambda expressions. The other is *subtyping*, which plays a prominent role in object-oriented systems, and is interesting for software reuse in general. Subtyping is based on a classification of data according to collections of valid operations; an operation valid for one type is also valid for its subtypes. The term *plug compatibility* is sometimes used to express this relationship. In the lambda calculus, functional application is the only operation, and provides no support for such a classification. Therefore, the lambda calculus must be extended to deal with subtyping: the common approach is to use *records* [9][10]. In this paper we argue that subtyping does not reduce to record systems. We propose an extended lambda calculus λN (lambda calculus with names) which can encode records — and therefore objects as well — but is more general since it also supports plug compatibility on enumerated types and concrete data types.

Our calculus is based on the observation that reusability in record systems is mainly due to the use of *names* for accessing fields, instead of *positions* in simple Cartesian products; the difference is important when considering extensibility. A product type can be extended in one direction, by adding a new component in the last position: any projections valid for the original product are still valid for the extended product. In that view, the type (Int × Int) can be seen as a supertype of (Int × Int × Colour) . However, this ordering based on positions can only have a tree structure. By contrast, an ordering based on names can be any partial order. A well-known example is the ordering of various types of points in a record system:

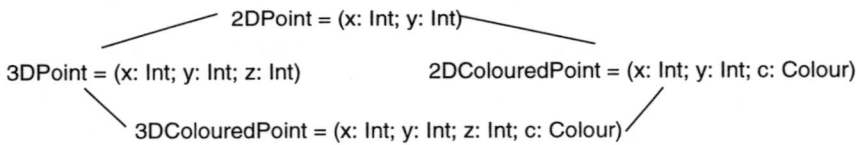

Like Cartesian products, functions use positional information to identify parameters; this is the basis for the *currying* property, which allows any function of n arguments to be encoded as a hierarchy of n lambda abstractions, with one single argument at each abstraction level. However, functions cannot be ordered in a tree structure: there is no plug-compatibility relationship between a function with three arguments and a function with only two arguments. This can be illustrated with a simple example: consider the Church encoding of Booleans and the *not* function in standard λ calculus[5]:

    True   = λt.λf.t
    False = λt.λf.f
    Not   = λb.λt.λf.b f t

and imagine we now want a three-valued logic, with an *unknown* value. We must add a new argument, and everything has to be recoded:

    $True_U$ = λt.λf.λu.t
    $False_U$ = λt.λf.λu.f
    $Unknown_U$ = λt.λf.λu.u
    Not_U = λb.λt.λf.λu.b f t u

The new encoding is incompatible with the previous one. In particular, it does not make sense to apply Not_U to True: it can only be applied to $True_U$. In a software reusability per-

Introduction

spective, this implies that any existing component producing True or False values needs to be modified to be usable with the new logic.

In order to get a compatibility relationship on functions, we propose a simple extension of the lambda calculus, inspired from records: functions are allowed to have multiple parameters *at the same abstraction level*, and those parameters are distinguished by their name. It then becomes necessary to specify which name is being bound in a functional application, but this is precisely the basis for reusability and subtyping: binding more names than those actually used by the function does no harm, and therefore a function with arguments $(x\ y)$ is compatible with a function with arguments $(x\ y\ z)$, because both can accept a sequence of bindings on names x, y and z.

A consequence of this approach is that names participate in the semantics of functions, and it is no longer possible to consider lambda expressions modulo α-equivalence (renaming of bound variables). However, α-renaming is important in the standard lambda calculus to avoid the well-known problem of name capture in substitutions. The difficulty is avoided by using *de Bruijn indices* [8] to indicate unambiguously the relationship between an applied occurrence of a variable and its corresponding abstraction level, and furthermore using names to distinguish between multiple variables at the same abstraction level. A variable, then, is a pair containing both a name and an index. The λN encoding of Booleans is:

```
True   =   λ (t, 0)
False  =   λ (f, 0)
Not    =   λλ (b, 1)(t→(f, 0))(f→(t, 0))!
```

For example, (t, 0) in True is a variable. The 0 index tells that this variable is bound by the closest abstraction level (the closest 'λ'). The other component of the pair tells that, among the parameters associated with that abstraction level, the one with name t is to be chosen. Parameter binding is done through the notation $a(x{\to}b)$, where a and b are terms, and x is a name. So in the Not function, the variable (b, 1), which refers to the outermost abstraction level, receives two bindings on parameters t and f. The exclamation mark at the end "closes" the sequence of bindings and removes an abstraction level.

As for the de Bruijn calculus, notation involving indices is convenient for machine manipulations, but hard for humans to read. Fortunately, indices can be hidden easily, by using a higher-level syntax with a simple translation function into the low-level representation. This higher-level syntax will be used for all programming examples in this chapter, while the low-level syntax is retained for presenting the semantics of the calculus. In high-level syntax, the expressions above become:

```
True   =   λ(t) t
False  =   λ(f) f
Not    =   λ(b) λ(t, f) b(t→f)(f→t)!
```

Informally, the names in parenthesis following a λ are parameters, so now they are explicitly declared instead of being implicitly recovered from indices. As an example of a derivation, consider the application of Not to True:

```
Not(b→True)!  =   (λ(b) λ (t, f) b(t→f)(f→t)!) (b→λ(t) t)!
```

The outermost binding on *b* is reduced, substituting the internal reference to *b* by True, and removing *b* from the parameter list:

$$(\lambda() \ \lambda(t, f) \ (\lambda(t) \ t)(t{\to}f)(f{\to}t)!)!$$

Then, by reducing the outermost '!', one abstraction level (one 'λ') is removed:

$$\lambda(t, f) \ (\lambda(t) \ t)(t{\to}f)(f{\to}t)!$$

The binding on *t* substitutes *t* by *f* and removes *t* from the parameter list:

$$\lambda(t, f) \ (\lambda() \ f)(f{\to}t)!$$

The binding on *f* is simply dropped, because the abstraction to which it is applied has no *f* parameter:

$$\lambda(t, f) \ (\lambda() \ f)!$$

Finally, one 'λ' is removed because of the '!':

$$\lambda(t, f) \ f$$

and although this final result declares both *t* and *f* as parameters instead of only *f*, it is equivalent to False, because its translation into low-level syntax with indices is also λ(f, 0).

Now the interesting point about this calculus is that, in order to get an augmented logic, we just write:

Unknown = λ(u) u
Not_U   = λ(b) λ(t f u) b(t→f)(f→t)(u→u)!

Not is recoded (which is normal), but we can keep the original encodings of True and False. This cannot be done in the standard lambda calculus, and is interesting for *reusability*: any other module based on the original encoding is still compatible with our new logic and does not need modification.

To the best of our knowledge, the idea of using names in a lambda calculus setting was not studied much in the literature. Two related systems are John Lamping's *unified system of parameterization* [19] and Garrigue and Aït-Kaci's *label-selective lambda calculus* [3][16]. However, both calculi treat names (or "labels") and variables as orthogonal concepts, whereas we unify them through the use of de Bruijn indices.

6.2 A Lambda Calculus with Named Parameters

It is well known that names in the standard lambda calculus are only useful to express a relationship between binding occurrences and applied occurrences of variables. Once that relationship is established, i.e. with bound variables, names can be replaced by other names through α *substitution*, or can even be removed altogether: in [8] de Bruijn proposed a modified lambda calculus in which variables are simply denoted by *indices*. A de Bruijn index is a non-negative integer expressing the distance between an applied occurrence of a variable and the abstraction level to which it refers. For example, the *not* function, written

Not   =   λb.λt.λf.b f t

A Lambda Calculus with Named Parameters

```
x, y, z ∈ Names
i, j ∈ Nat
a, b, ... ∈ Terms

a   :=   λ a              abstraction
    |    (x, i)           variable
    |    a(x→b)           bind operation
    |    a!               close operation
```

Figure 6.1 *Abstract syntax.*

in the standard calculus, becomes

   Not   =   λλλ 2 0 1

in de Bruijn notation (here we start indices with 0, while some authors start with 1; the difference is not significant). There is a straightforward translation from usual lambda expressions to their de Bruijn version. The de Bruijn notation provides a *canonical* representation: all α-equivalent lambda expressions have the same translation. Furthermore, the well-known problem of *name capture* is avoided. Both in standard and de Bruijn calculi, each abstraction level (each 'λ') introduces exactly one variable. Our proposal is to allow *several* variables at the same abstraction level. To do so, de Bruijn indices are retained, but in addition *names* are used to distinguish between different variables at the same level. This section defines the calculus; the next section shows that this extension provides support for plug-compatibility.

6.2.1 Abstract (Low-level) Syntax

Figure 6.1 presents the abstract syntax of λN. The language is built over a (finite) set of *names*.

An *abstraction* corresponds to the traditional notion of abstraction. Like in the de Bruijn lambda calculus, abstractions need not introduce names for their parameters: the connection between variables and their corresponding abstraction level directly comes from the indices associated with variables (see below).

A *variable* is a name together with a de Bruijn index. This means that an abstraction can have several parameters, all with the same index, which are distinguished by their name. The index indicates the abstraction level (which 'λ') a variable is referring to: an index of 0 refers to the closest abstraction, and higher numbers refer to farther abstraction levels.

A *bind operation* partly corresponds to the usual notion of application. However, since an abstraction may have several parameters, it is necessary to specify which of them is bound in the expression. Therefore the construct a(x->b) means: "bind b to the parameter

$$\begin{aligned}
FV_k((x, i)) &= \text{if } i = k \text{ then } \{(x, i)\} \text{ else } \{\} \\
FV_k(\lambda a) &= \{(x, i) \mid (x, i+1) \in FV_{k+1}(a)\} \\
FV_k(a(x \to b)) &= FV_k(a) \cup FV_k(b) \\
FV_k(a!) &= FV_k(a) \\
\\
FV(a) &= \bigcup_{k \geq 0} FV_k(a) \\
\\
parameters(\lambda a) &= FV_0(a) \\
\\
a \text{ closed} &\Leftrightarrow FV(a) = \{\}
\end{aligned}$$

Figure 6.2 *Free and bound variables.*

with name x in a", or, expressed differently: "substitute b for every occurrence of $(x, 0)$ in a (modulo index renumbering, as defined below)". The parameters of an abstraction may be bound separately, and in any order.

A *close operation* closes a sequence of bindings, and removes an abstraction level (removes one 'λ').

Notions of parameters, free and bound variables are as in the de Bruijn calculus; a formal definition is given in figure 6.2.

6.2.2 Reduction Rules

In the de Bruijn calculus, β-reduction involves some renumbering of indices: whenever the number of 'λ's above a subterm changes, its free variables have to be adapted in consequence. One way to express it is

$$(\lambda a)\, b \quad \to_\beta \quad \downarrow_0[a\, [0 := \uparrow_0[b]]]$$

where '$\uparrow$' (lift) is an operation incrementing all free variables by 1, '$\downarrow$' (unlift) is the reverse operation, and $a[i := b]$ is the substitution of b for all occurrences of i in a (again modulo index renumbering).

The reduction rules for λN, given in figure 6.3, are very similar, since they also involve index manipulation operations. There are two kinds of reductions, called *bind reduction* (β) and *close reduction* (γ). Basically, the operations performed by β-reduction in the standard lambda calculus have been split in two: binding reductions substitute values for variables, and close reductions "remove the lambda" and unlift the result, i.e. they remove an abstraction level. The definitions for lifting and substitution operations are given in figure 6.4

A Lambda Calculus with Named Parameters

$$(\lambda a)(x \to b) \quad \to_\beta \quad \lambda(a[(x, 0) := \uparrow_0[b]])$$
$$(\lambda a)! \quad \to_\gamma \quad \downarrow_0[a]$$

Figure 6.3 *Reduction rules.*

Lifting/Unlifting

$\uparrow_k[(x, i)]$ = if $(i < k)$ then (x, i) else $(x, i+1)$
$\downarrow_k[(x, i)]$ = if $(i < k)$ then (x, i) else if $(i = k)$ then **err** else $(x, i-1)$

$|_k [\lambda a]$ = $\lambda(|_{k+1}[a])$
$|_k [a(x \to b)]$ = $|_k[a](x \to |_k[b])$
$|_k [a!]$ = $(|_k[a])!$ where '$|$' is either '$\downarrow$' or '$\uparrow$'

err $=_{def}$ $E(x \to E)!$ where $E = \lambda\lambda (x, 1)(x \to (x, 1))!$

Substitution

$(y, j)[(x, i) := b]$ = if $((x, i) = (y, j))$ then b else (y, j)
$(\lambda a) [(x, i) := b]$ = $\lambda(a[(x, i+1) := \uparrow_0[b]])$
$(a(y \to c)) [(x, i) := b]$ = $(a[(x, i) := b])(y \to c[(x, i) := b])$
$(a!)[(x, i) := b]$ = $(a[(x, i) := b])!$

Figure 6.4 *Lifting and substitution operations.*

Careful readers will have noticed that in λN we may need to unlift a 0 index, a situation which never occurs in the de Bruijn calculus. Consider de Bruijn's β-reduction rule above: all 0 indices are substituted in a, so the expression passed to '$\downarrow$' contains no 0 index. By contrast, the λN expression $(\lambda (x, 0))!$ reduces to $\downarrow_0[(x, 0)]$, which intuitively corresponds to an error (we are trying to access a parameter that has not been bound). As a matter of fact, in such situations the definition of '$\downarrow$' yields **err**, a specific term representing errors. This will be discussed in detail in section 6.4; for the time being it suffices to know that **err** is not an additional syntactic construct, but rather is defined as a usual term in the language, with the property that further binding or close operations on **err** yield **err** again.

A binding reduction can never introduce new parameters in an abstraction, because the term passed in the substitution is lifted. Therefore if several successive bindings are done, the final result does not depend on the order of the substitutions. This amounts to say that *bindings are commutative*, i.e. expressions of the form

    $a(x \to b)(y \to c)$ and $a(y \to c)(x \to b)$

derive to the same thing, provided that x and y are *different* names. If x and y are the same name, all references to that name are substituted in the first binding, so the second binding is just ignored, and those bindings are not commutative.

6.2.3 Reduction Example

For illustrating the rules, we use again the expression Not(b→True)!. The derivation was given in an informal way in the introduction, using high-level syntax (without indices). Here, the low-level syntax is used; at each step, the lambda and the bind or close operation involved in the next reduction step are underlined.

1. (λ̲λ̲ (arg, 1) (true→(false, 0))(false→(true, 0))!)(arg̲→λ(true, 0))!
2. (λ̲λ̲ (λ(true, 0))(true→(false, 0))(false→(true, 0))!) !̲
3. λ (λ̲(true, 0))(true̲→(false, 0))(false→(true, 0))!
4. λ (λ̲(false, 1))(false̲→(true, 0))!
5. λ̲ (λ(false, 1)) !̲
6. λ (false, 0)

The final result is False. Notice at line 4 that the binding of false simply gets eliminated: this is because the abstraction (λ(false, 1)) has *no* parameter called false; it indeed uses a variable with that name, but since the index is not 0 this is a free variable, not a parameter.

At some intermediate stages (e.g. at line 2) several reductions could occur; the sequence shown here corresponds to *normal-order* reduction (choosing leftmost outermost redex first). It is therefore legitimate to ask whether a different reduction sequence would yield the same result (whether the language is confluent). The answer is *yes*, and has been established in [13]. So, as in the standard lambda calculus, results are independent from the reduction sequences through which they were obtained; furthermore, if an expression does have a result, then the normal-order reduction strategy is guaranteed to yield that result (i.e. not to diverge).

Notice that if we "forget" to supply an argument to Not before applying a close operation, as in Not!, we have the reduction

(λ̲λ̲ (arg, 1) (true→(false, 0))(false→(true, 0))!) !̲
λ **err** (true̲→(false, 0))(false→(true, 0))!
λ **err** (false̲→(true, 0))!
λ **err** !̲
λ **err**

which is equivalent to **err**, i.e. an error is produced.

6.2.4 Higher-level Syntax

Indices were necessary for defining the calculus, but are difficult to read. In order to work practically with the calculus, we will use a higher-level syntax, given in figure 6.5, in which the indices need not be explicitly written. There is a straightforward translation **T** from this syntax into the original syntax, which is formally defined in figure 6.6. In this

A Lambda Calculus with Named Parameters

$$
\begin{array}{lll}
v & := & x \qquad\qquad\qquad\qquad simple\ variable \\
  & | & \backslash v \qquad\qquad\qquad\qquad "outer"\ variable \\
  & & \\
a & := & \lambda(x_1\ ...\ x_n)\ a \qquad\ abstraction \\
  & | & v \qquad\qquad\qquad\qquad variable \\
  & | & a(x \rightarrow b) \qquad\qquad\ bind\ operation \\
  & | & a! \qquad\qquad\qquad\qquad close\ operation \\
\end{array}
$$

Figure 6.5 *Higher-level syntax.*

$$
\begin{array}{lll}
\mathbf{T}_V\ [\lambda(x_1\ ...\ x_n)\ a] & = & \lambda\ (\mathbf{T}_{V'}\ [a]) \\
\qquad where & & V' = \{(x, i+1)\ |\ (x, i) \in V\} \cup \{(x_1, 0), ..., (x_n, 0)\} \\
\mathbf{T}_V\ [\backslash...\backslash x\ ] & = & matchVar\ V\ (x, i) \qquad where\ i\ is\ the\ number\ of\ `\backslash' \\
\mathbf{T}_V\ [a(x \rightarrow b)] & = & \mathbf{T}_V\ [a](x \rightarrow \mathbf{T}_V\ [b]) \\
\mathbf{T}_V\ [a!] & = & (\mathbf{T}_V\ [a])! \\
matchVar\ V\ (x, i) & = & \text{let } J = \{j\ |\ (x, j) \in V, j \geq i\}\ \text{in} \\
 & & \qquad \text{if } (J = \{\}) \qquad \text{then } \mathbf{err} \\
 & & \qquad\qquad\qquad\qquad\quad\text{else } (x, \mathbf{min}(J)) \\
\end{array}
$$

Figure 6.6 *Translation function.*

new notation, the parameters of an abstraction are *declared* as a list of names in parenthesis. A variable is written simply as a name: the index is recovered by looking for the closest abstraction which declares the same name. In case the same name is used at several abstraction levels, and one wants to override the default variable matching scheme, the name of the variable can be preceded by a collection of backslashes. This tells the translation function to start looking for a declaration, not at the next abstraction level, but one or several levels higher (according to the number of backslashes). The parameter list following a lambda can be empty, as in

$\lambda()$ Not(arg→True)!

This is like a closure, i.e. a function that needs no arguments but is not evaluated yet (assuming a lazy interpretation as in section 6.4.1). Forcing evaluation is then done with the '!' operator.

The translation **T** from this syntax into the original syntax is like translating the standard lambda calculus into de Bruijn notation (see [12]). The first argument to the translation function is a set of currently declared variables; at each abstraction level this set is updated. The translation is defined for closed terms by taking the initially empty set of variables. Variables which are not declared at any level are translated into an error by the *matchVar* function. As an example of a translation, consider the expression

λ(x y) λ(x z) x + y + z + \x + \y + \z + \\x

(assuming that infix addition is part of the language). After crossing the two abstraction levels, the set V of declared variables is

V={(x, 1), (y, 1), (x, 0), (z, 0)}

and therefore the translation is

$\lambda\lambda$ (x, 0) + (y, 1) + (z, 0) + (x, 1) + (y, 1) + **err** + **err**

This shows how the backslash can be used to distinguish between parameters with the same name, but at different levels. Notice that x and \x are different variables, while both y and \y are translated into (y, 1), because there is no y parameter at the inner abstraction level. Furthermore, both \z and \\x are translated into **err**, because no corresponding variable declaration can be found.

6.3 The Calculus at Work

In this section we show how several common programming constructs are encoded in λN. To make the examples more appealing, we assume that integers, Booleans and strings have been added to the language, with corresponding operations (integer arithmetic, *if* expression, etc.). Such extensions are common for the lambda calculus and can be shown to be conservative, i.e. expressions in the extended language are always convertible into the original language. As a matter of fact, an encoding of Booleans has been seen already, and an encoding of integers is given in section 6.3.4. In consequence, the semantics of the language does not change. We start with a discussion on functions and recursion, just to give a clearer map of the relationship between λN and the standard lambda calculus. Then the specificity of λN, namely the encoding of extensible constructs, is demonstrated through enumerated types, concrete data types and records.

6.3.1 Functions

It can be seen easily that λN contains the usual lambda calculus. Any expression e of the pure lambda calculus can be encoded in a straightforward way, by choosing a single arbitrary name (say **arg**) to be associated with variables:

- Take the de Bruijn encoding of e.
- Replace every application MN by M(**arg**$\rightarrow$N)!, i.e. a binding of **arg** immediately followed by a close operation.
- Replace every variable i by (**arg**, i).

For example, the lambda expression λf x y. f(x + y) has de Bruijn encoding $\lambda\lambda\lambda$ 2(1+0) and becomes here

$\lambda\lambda\lambda$(arg, 2)(arg$\rightarrow$(arg, 1)+(arg, 0))!

which corresponds to

The Calculus at Work

λ(arg) λ(arg) λ(arg) \\arg(arg→\arg+arg)!

in the higher-level notation. Now how does this compare to the expression:

λ(f x y) f(arg→(x+y))!

which intuitively seems more natural? In both formulations, the arguments can be bound and the final result evaluated. The difference appears with partial bindings. When arguments are declared at the same abstraction level, as we do in the second formulation, they can be bound separately, in any order, and even if all arguments are supplied, the internal expression is not evaluated until a close operation takes place. This can be useful, as we will see later, for building lazy data structures. Furthermore, such functions are polymorphic, in the sense that any context which binds more arguments than just f, x and y will accept this abstraction without generating an error. However, if we want to do partial bindings, leaving the other arguments open, the close operation cannot be inserted, which implies that we lose the currying property, i.e. the possibility to bind one single argument and get in return another function over the remaining arguments. This is because usual functional application corresponds here to a binding *and* a close operation. When writing a function, there is therefore a choice to make about how to organize its arguments. The methodological issues involved in such choices have not been explored yet. Our choices in the coming examples are guided by some heuristics acquired during our various experiences in using the system.

6.3.2 Recursion

A fixed-point operation over a functional $\lambda(x)a$ yields a recursive function, as in the lambda calculus; however, the name x must be taken into account in the fixed-point operation. So for each name x we define a corresponding fixed-point operator

Y_x = λ(x) (λ(x) \x(x→x(x→x)!)!)(x→ (λ(x) \x(x→x(x→x)!)!))!

This is like the usual combinator Y, specialized to bind name x. It can be checked that for $f=\lambda(x)a$ we have

Y_x(x→f)! →∗ f(x→Y_x(x→f)!)!

In order to facilitate such recursive definitions we introduce some syntactic sugar: an expression with recursion over parameter x is written $\mu(x)a$ and is translated into

Y_x(x→λ(x)a)!

With this extension we can write

Factorial = μ(f) λ(arg) if (arg > 1) then arg*f(arg→(arg-1))! else 1

6.3.3 Extensible Enumerated Types and Case Selection

We already have seen an encoding of Boolean values, which is a simple enumerated type with two values. The approach can be generalized to n-ary enumerated types:

Green   =   λ(green) green
Orange   =   λ(orange) orange
Red   =   λ(red) red

Each colour in the encoding above is a kind of identity function on a particular name. The way to use such values is to perform *case selection*:

trafficLight   =   λ(colour) colour(green→Go)(orange→Stop)(red→Stop)!

Here we assume two defined driving actions Go and Stop. Depending on the colour, the appropriate driving action is chosen. Observe that case selection is just a sequence of bindings. The set of colours can be extended easily:

Blue   =   λ(blue) blue
Violet   =   λ(violet) violet
Yellow   =   λ(yellow) yellow
complement = λ(colour) colour(green→Red)(blue→Orange)(violet→Yellow)
              (red→Green)(orange→Blue)(yellow→Violet)!

so the first three colours are "reused" here in a different context, without breaking the original encoding of trafficLight. As explained in the introduction, this can *not* be done in the standard lambda calculus.

6.3.4 Extensible Concrete Data Types

A direct extension from previous section is the encoding of concrete data types. Concrete data types are built through a finite number of *constructors*, which can take arguments. Functions using such data types then have to perform case selection over the constructors. We will consider the example of natural numbers, with two constructors:

Zero   =   λ(zero) zero
Succ   =   λ(n) λ(positive) positive(pred→n)!

The names zero and positive are used to distinguish constructors. Case selection is done as with enumerated types, except that constructors with arguments must be able to pass the corresponding values to the function using the data type, so there must be a convention between the constructor and its users about which name to use for that purpose. In the case of Succ, the conventional name is pred. An example of using the data type is the addition function:

Add   =   μ(add) λ(left right) left
          (zero→right)
          (positive→λ(pred) add(left→pred)(right→Succ(n→right)!)!)!

which proceeds by decomposition of the left argument.

The encoding can be extended easily to include negative numbers as well:

Pred= λ(n) λ(negative) negative(succ→n)!

Inc= λ(n) n(zero→Succ(n→n)!)(positive→Succ(n→n)!)(negative→λ(succ)succ)!

Dec= λ(n) n(zero→Pred(n→n)!)(positive→λ(pred)pred)(negative→Pred(n→n)!)!

The Calculus at Work 165

$$\text{Add} = \mu(\text{add})\ \lambda(\text{left right})\quad \text{left}(\text{zero} \to \text{right})$$
$$(\text{positive} \to \lambda(\text{pred})\ \text{add}(\text{left} \to \text{pred})(\text{right} \to \text{Inc}(n \to \text{right})!)!)$$
$$(\text{negative} \to \lambda(\text{succ})\ \text{add}(\text{left} \to \text{succ})(\text{right} \to \text{Dec}(n \to \text{right})!)!)!$$

Again, functions using only positive numbers need *not* be recoded because of that extension.

Generally speaking, the encoding of data types given here is pretty low-level. However, syntactic sugar for data type constructors and pattern matching, as in most modern functional languages, could be added easily.

6.3.5 Records

A more interesting example of extensibility and polymorphism is the encoding of records. We extend the syntax with a record constructor and a field selection operation; the translation of these constructs is given in figure 6.7. The translation can be understood more

---
$$\mathbf{T}\,[\{x_1=a_1\ \ldots\ x_n=a_n\}] \quad = \quad \lambda(\text{sel})\ \text{sel}(x_1 \to \uparrow_0[a_1])\ldots(x_n \to \uparrow_0[a_n])!$$
$$\mathbf{T}\,[a.x] \quad = \quad a(\text{sel} \to \lambda(x)x)!$$

Figure 6.7 *Records*

easily through a comparison with the encoding of binary products (pairs) in the standard lambda calculus:

$$(a, b) = \lambda\text{sel}.\ \text{sel}\ a\ b$$
$$\text{fst} = \lambda\text{pair}.\ \text{pair}\ (\lambda\text{first}.\ \lambda\text{second}.\ \text{first})$$
$$\text{snd} = \lambda\text{pair}.\ \text{pair}\ (\lambda\text{first}.\ \lambda\text{second}.\ \text{second})$$

The encoding of a pair is a function which takes a *selector* and then binds both members of the pair to that selector. A selector is just a function taking two arguments and returning one of them, so the *fst* projection function applies a selector which extracts the first argument, while the *snd* function applies a selector which extracts the second argument. Similarly, a record in λN is a function which takes a selector, and binds all fields to corresponding named parameters in that selector. Since one abstraction level was added because of the *sel* argument, all internal fields are lifted in order to protect free variables from being captured. A selector for field x is just an identity function on that name, so a field selection operation simply binds the appropriate selector to the *sel* argument of the record. Here are some examples:

$$\{x=5\} \quad = \quad \lambda(\text{sel})\ \text{sel}(x \to 5)!$$
$$\{x=3\ y=2\} \quad = \quad \lambda(\text{sel})\ \text{sel}(x \to 3)(y \to 2)!$$
$$\{x=5\}.x \quad = \quad (\lambda(\text{sel})\ \text{sel}(x \to 5)!)(\text{sel} \to (\lambda(x)x))! \quad \to_* \quad 5$$
$$\{x=3\ y=2\}.x \quad = \quad (\lambda(\text{sel})\ \text{sel}(x \to 3)(y \to 2)!)(\text{sel} \to (\lambda(x)x))! \to_* \quad 3$$
$$\{x=3\ y=2\}.z \quad = \quad (\lambda(\text{sel})\ \text{sel}(x \to 3)(y \to 2)!)(\text{sel} \to (\lambda(z)z))! \to_* \quad (\lambda(z)z)! \quad \to \mathbf{err}$$

$$\mathbf{T}\,[\langle x_1 \ldots x_n \rangle] \;=\; \mu(rec)\lambda(x_1 \ldots x_n)\,\{$$
$$get=\{x_1{=}x_1 \ldots x_n{=}x_n\}$$
$$set=\{x_1{=}\lambda(arg)\,rec(x_1{\to}arg)(x_2{\to}x_2)\ldots(x_n{\to}x_n)!$$
$$\ldots$$
$$x_i{=}\lambda(arg)\,rec(x_1{\to}x_1)\ldots(x_i{\to}arg)\ldots(x_n{\to}x_n)!$$
$$\ldots$$
$$x_n{=}\lambda(arg)\,rec(x_1{\to}x_1)\ldots(x_i{\to}x_i)\ldots(x_n{\to}arg)!$$
$$\}$$
$$\}$$
$$\mathbf{T}\,[\langle x_1{=}a_1 \ldots x_n{=}a_n \rangle] \;=\; (\mathbf{T}\,[\langle x_1 \ldots x_n \rangle])(x_1{\to}a_1)\ldots(x_n{\to}a_n)!$$
$$\mathbf{T}\,[a\langle x := b \rangle] \;=\; a.set.x(arg{\to}b)!$$

Figure 6.8 *Updatable records.*

We see that ".x" is a polymorphic operation that can be applied to any record containing at least an x field.

The same encoding can support more general operations on records, like a form of "execute in context" operation, similar to quoted expressions in LISP or to the blocks of Smalltalk: for example an expression like

$$r.[x + y + z] \;=\; r(sel{\to}\lambda(x\,y\,z)x + y + z)!$$

asks record r to add its fields x, y and z and return the result.

Moreover recursion can be used to get recursive records:

$$\text{Seasons} = \mu(rec)\,\{\quad \begin{array}{lll} \text{spring=} & \{\text{name="spring"} & \text{next= rec.summer}\} \\ \text{summer=} & \{\text{name="summer"} & \text{next= rec.autumn}\} \\ \text{autumn=} & \{\text{name="autumn"} & \text{next= rec.winter}\} \\ \text{winter=} & \{\text{name="winter"} & \text{next= rec.spring}\} \end{array}$$
$$\}$$

so for example Seasons.autumn.next.next.name yields "spring". Seasons can be seen as a recursive record, but also as a memory with four locations. Expressions like rec.summer work as "pointers" in the memory fixed by Seasons. Here we have a flat space of memory locations, but the approach can be easily extended to define hierarchical memory spaces with corresponding fixed-point operations at different levels. Pointers in the hierarchical space simply would use variables with different indices (using the '\' syntax).

6.3.6 Updatable Records (Memories)

The next step is to define updatable records, or, seen differently, writable memories. This can be done using the previous constructs, as pictured in figure 6.8. An updatable record is a recursive function, with one named parameter for each field; internally it consists of a simple record with a *get* field, which returns the internal values, and a *set* field, which re-

Compatibility Relationship

turns a record of update functions. An update function for field x_i takes one argument *arg*, and uses recursion to return the same updatable record, in which all fields are bound to their current values except the one being updated which takes the new value. Updating a record consists of selecting the appropriate update function, and binding the new value to its *arg* parameter. Functions using this encoding are naturally polymorphic: the function

    ZeroX   = λ(aRecord) aRecord$\langle x := 0 \rangle$

can be applied to *any* record containing an x field and returns the original record, with only field x being updated.

Updatable records give full flexibility for modelling local state of objects and object identifiers. In languages using a flat domain of object identifiers, like Smalltalk or Objective-C, each object would have its own updatable record, representing local state, and then all objects would be stored in a global record, representing the space of object identifiers. Some other languages have a more complex structure: for example in C++, an object can be contained in the memory space of another object (so the implementation structure reflects the "has-a" relationship). Modelling such structures in λN would involve hierarchical updatable records, in which some fields contain sub-records.

6.3.7 Field Overwriting

The encoding presented in the previous subsection supports modification of an existing field, but not addition of new fields. An alternative approach to updatable records is to consider field overwriting. Here is how it can be done:

    r[x←a]   = λ(sel) r(sel→sel(x→a))!

This creates a new record from r in which field x has value a, whether or not x was already present in r. Observe that the encoding is based on the fact that the selector received as a parameter is immediately bound to a on name x, *without a close operation*, before being passed to the record r. This explains why any binding on x in r will be ignored. Given a field overwriting operation, it is possible to implement record concatenation "for free", following Rémy's technique [26]: one would start with an empty record

    λ(sel) sel!

and then consider each record as a "record-modifying function", adding the desired fields; such functions can be combined by functional composition.

6.4 Compatibility Relationship

Several examples of extensible and reusable constructs have been shown, but so far we have no formal definition of a compatibility relationship. In this section such a relationship is studied, through an observational classification of λN expressions. In the standard lambda calculus, the only observable property of terms is their termination behaviour:

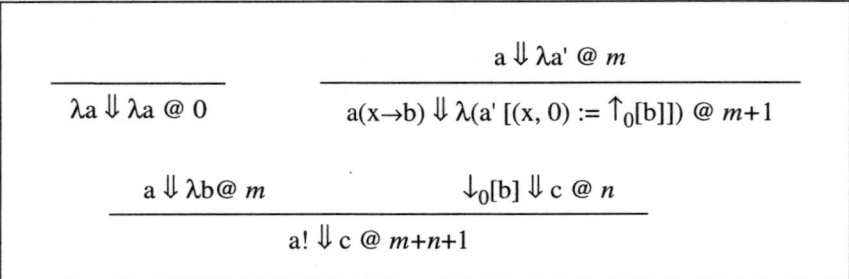

Figure 6.9 *Convergence to weak normal form.*

errors never occur, since all values are functions. Here, we have seen that errors can be generated during a computation, and therefore errors also represent a valuable observation. So, as a complement to the usual approximation ordering, which compares terms on the basis of convergence, we also consider a compatibility ordering, comparing terms on the basis of error generation. This section is mainly inspired from operational orderings in Scott Smith's work [28], who himself draws from a vast body of literature on observational relations (see for example [20][1]). However, Smith identifies errors with divergence, whereas we treat them as distinct observations.

6.4.1 Errors and Lazy Operational Semantics

Now it is time to justify our encoding of errors, as it was given in figure 6.4. The complex expression defining **err** could be written, in high-level notation, as $\mu(x)\,\lambda()\,x$, i.e. as an abstraction without any parameters, containing itself. Such a term can consume any sequence of bind or close operations, but always reduces back to itself. In a classical lambda calculus, a similar behaviour is displayed by the term

$(\lambda x.\lambda y.xx)(\lambda x.\lambda y.xx)$

which consumes any input without ever using it. Under a usual interpretation, this is just identified with the bottom element (divergence); however, in a lazy interpretation, it becomes the top element. Boudol [7] calls this an "ogre", while Abramsky and Ong [1] say "a term of order ∞". Usually the "ogre" is not considered very interesting, because it does not interact with its environment. However, this is precisely the behaviour of a run-time error: once it occurs, the "continuation" of the program is ignored, and the final result is the error. So the ogre is a natural choice for representing run-time errors. In consequence, we define in figure 6.9 a lazy convergence relation, where $a \Downarrow b\ @\ m$ means "a converges to b in m steps of computation". We simply write $a\Downarrow$ if there are a', m such that $a \Downarrow a'\ @\ m$, and $a\Uparrow$ if $\neg(a\Downarrow)$.

Compatibility Relationship

Definition 14 A term a is *erroneous* (written a?) iff it converges and any binding or close operation on it yields an erroneous term again. Formally:

$$a? \Leftrightarrow a\Downarrow \text{ and } (a!)? \text{ and } \forall b.\ (a(x \rightarrow b))?$$

Another way to state this is to say that a is erroneous iff $\forall \bar{o},\ a\bar{o}\Downarrow$, where $\bar{o}$ is a sequence of bind or close operations. We write $a_{\lnot}$ whenever $\lnot(a?)$. It is an easy exercise to check that (**err**?).

6.4.2 Approximation and Compatibility

Definition 15 The *approximation ordering*, written $\leq_{\perp}$, is

$$a \leq_{\perp} b \quad \Leftrightarrow \quad \forall C[-].\ C[a]\Downarrow \Rightarrow C[b]\Downarrow$$

where a *context* $C[-]$ is a term with "holes", which can be filled by another term a through the context-filling operation $C[a]$.

Definition 16 The *compatibility ordering*, written $\leq_{\text{err}}$, is

$$a \leq_{\text{err}} b \quad \Leftrightarrow \quad \forall C[-].\ C[b]_{\lnot} \Rightarrow C[a]_{\lnot}$$

Observe that here a and b are in reverse order in the implication. The first preorder states that whenever a converges, b also converges. The second preorder states that whenever b does not generate an error, a does not either. It may seem strange that these definitions are in opposite directions, but this corresponds to standard practice in semantic domains and subtype orderings. In semantic domains, the least defined element (representing the divergent program) is at the bottom, and more defined elements are higher up in the ordering. In type systems, the least defined type (type of anything) is usually at the top, and more refined types are lower. It can be checked, for example, that $\text{Not}_U \leq_{\text{err}} \text{Not}$, i.e. our extended version of the *not* operation for a three-valued logic, is indeed compatible with the *not* operation on Boolean values only.

In [14] we have defined similar orderings for a pure lambda calculus with records (but without extensible records), and we have shown that both orderings coincide, i.e. approxima and compatibility are the same when **err** is chosen as the top element. The proof can be transposed to λN without difficulty. So we have a formal framework for reasoning not only about equivalence of software components, as in usual semantics, but also about their plug-compatibility relationships. Some consequences of this result are discussed in the rest of this section.

6.4.3 Lattice Structure

Define $\bot = \mu(x)\, x$. This is the divergent term [observe the difference with **err** $= \mu(x)\, \lambda()\, x$]. $\bot$ is smaller than any term: a divergent term never generates an error, and never reduces to a WNF in any relevant context. On the other hand, **err** is a greatest element in both orderings, since it never diverges and is an error. This implies that the order is a *lattice* with top element **err** and bottom element $\bot$.

The fact that we get a lattice is interesting in many respects. Lattices were originally considered by Scott for solving domain equations. Then the presence of a top element was criticized, in particular by Plotkin [25], because this element fails to satisfy some intuitively natural identities about the conditional function: for example we expect a phrase like

if *a* **then** *b* **else** *c*

always to give either b or c; however, this does not hold when a is the top element, and it is not clear then what the answer should be: it could be TOP itself, or it could be the upper bound of b and c, but none of these solutions seems to make sense in usual interpretations. Therefore the semantics community moved to algebraic CPO models instead of lattices.

Since our approach is purely operational, there is no reason here to argue for or against a particular model. Nevertheless, it is worth noticing that the operational lattice has some natural properties. In particular, interpreting the top element as an error, it is quite natural that we should have

if err then *b* **else** *c* = **err**

The answer is neither b nor c, but this does not contradict our intuitive understanding of the conditional statement: if the first argument is an error, then the whole statement produces an error.

A more recent discussion about lattice models was written by Bloom [6], partially based on Plotkin's previous work. Bloom supports the view that, despite the fact that lattices are mathematically more tractable than CPOs, they have several defects when used as models for programming languages. One of his main criticisms to lattice models is that they are not single-valued: for example if we choose the second solution for the conditional statement above, namely

if TOP **then** *b* **else** *c* = *b* ⊔ *c*

we get the upper bound of b and c, which, if not TOP itself, is a "multiple value". However, the justification for taking single-valuedness as an essential criterion is not strongly established. Therefore Boudol [7] criticizes Bloom's position, and argues that under a different notion of observation, multiple values make perfect sense. Parallel functions in Boudol's paper yield a lattice model. Similarly, powerdomains used for modelling concurrency also have a lattice structure. These observations lead us to another extension of the calculus which completes the operational structure by introducing all meets and joins. Full development of these constructs would go beyond the scope of this paper; however, a brief appetizer will be given.

Compatibility Relationship

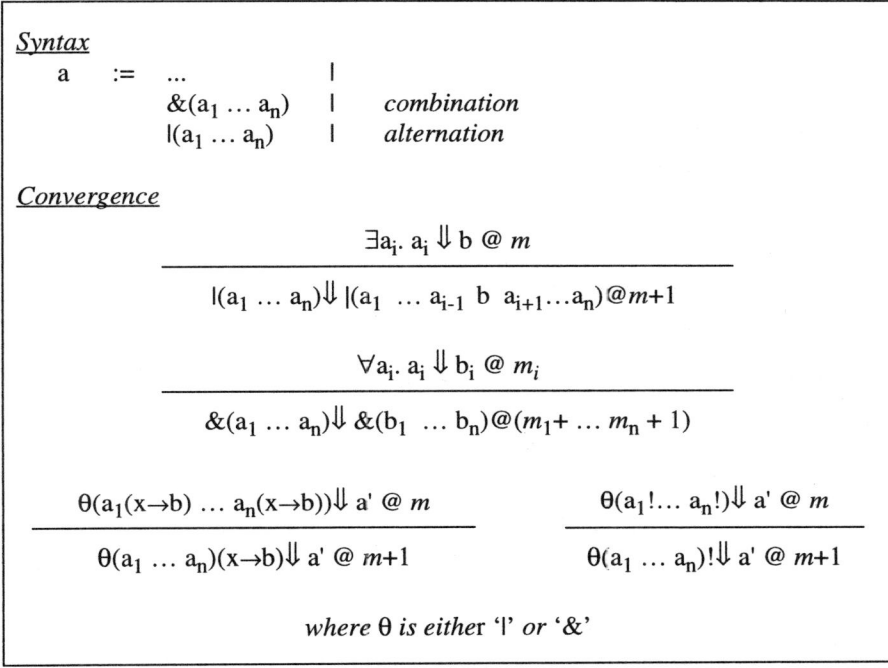

Figure 6.10 *Combinations and alternations.*

6.4.4 Meets and Joins

Figure 6.10 introduces two *n*-ary constructs called *combination* and *alternation*. The reduction rules are exactly the same for both: any binding or close operation is simply distributed to the internal members. Therefore they can be seen as an array of non-communicating processors accepting common operations, in a kind of SIMD architecture. The difference between combinations and alternations comes observationally from the definition of convergence: combinations converge if all their members converge, while alternations converge if at least one member converges. Since convergence is at the foundation of our approximation/compatibility relationship, we have the following properties:

- The combination is a *glb* (greatest lower bound, meet) operator.
- The alternation is a *lub* (least upper bound, join) operator.

This has many interesting applications, all related to various possible uses of *sets* of values.

The alternation operator can be interpreted to model non-determinism. A very similar proposal has been made by Boudol under the name *parallel functions* [7]. Boudol mainly discusses the use of parallel functions for solving the full abstraction problem (relating the operational ordering with the semantic ordering). Another application is concurrency modelling, where all possible outcomes of a computation are grouped together in an alternation, on which further processes can compute: in [13] we discuss an encoding of shared memory, processes and synchronization primitives using alternations. Yet another possibility is to interpret an alternation as a type, "containing" all its member terms. This opens very interesting perspectives for typing, since the notions of type membership and subtype relationship are both captured by the approximation/compatibility ordering, and therefore values and types are merged into one single concept. Finally, since we deal with sets of values we can directly apply Scott Smith's results [28] for proving theorems like fixed-point induction in a purely operational setting, without going to semantic domains.

Applications of the combination construct, which in a sense is an "overdeterministic" operator, are less intuitive. Remembering that **err** is the top element, combinations can be used to remove errors in a computation, by taking the lower bound of a set of values. This can be applied for operations such as *record concatenation* [10][17]. Moreover, following the idea of unifying types and values, combinations have the same properties as *intersection types*[4][24]. Interestingly, a connection between record concatenation and intersection types as also been proposed by John Reynolds in his Forsythe language[27].

6.5 Conclusion

A lambda calculus with name-based interaction has been described. A few systems using similar ideas have been mentioned in the introduction [19][16]; the original aspect of λN is the unification of names with variables through the use of de Bruijn indices. Not only is this more practical; it also allows us to directly import most of the results established for the standard lambda calculus. Extensible functions in λN are a good basis for studying reusability mechanisms (in particular inheritance and subtyping), and the economy of constructs compares advantageously to other approaches based on records ([9][17]) or extensible methods [23].

The other extension (alternations and combinations) is perhaps more venturing. It touches several hot research areas, like observational equivalences and full abstraction for lambda models [1], parallel functions [7], extensible records [17], and semantics of concurrency. Most of these issues require further investigation. An exciting challenge is to see how the π-calculus[21], also based on names, relates to λN.

The issue of typing was mentioned very briefly, and the development of a full type theory for the calculus is under investigation [13][15]. Using the term ordering as a semantic basis for types seems a promising direction, and has some similarities with type theories based on the Curry–Howard isomorphism (identification of types with logical propositions)[29], in which the usual distinction between terms and types is also blurred. Including name-based interaction in such theories would be a promising step towards an object-oriented logic, and would relate to what Aït-Kaci calls *features* [2]. Related to this, the term ordering in λN can be useful for object-oriented databases, since it gives a query language for free!

Apart from those foundational issues, there are several practical directions in which this work can be extended. One, which in fact was the original motivation for developing the calculus, is to use it for explaining the differences between various forms of inheritance and delegation in object-oriented languages. In addition, many other aspects of programming languages, like modularity, state manipulation or restricted islands of memory locations [18] can be studied in this framework. Ultimately, it is of course tempting to build higher-level syntactic constructs on top of the calculus and make it a full programming language integrating these various aspects.

Finally, it is worth considering implementation issues for this calculus, and perhaps to design a name-based abstract functional machine. As noted by Garrigue [16], names can be translated into offsets in a machine implementation; however, their combination with de Bruijn indices probably raises some technical problems. Combinations and alternations are more challenging. Evaluating a combination can be done by sequentially evaluating all of its members, but evaluating an alternation must be done in some form of parallelism, to be consistent with our notion of WNF.

Acknowledgments

I am grateful to Oscar Nierstrasz, who gave much of his time for examining this work, to Benjamin Pierce, Christian Breiteneder, John Lamping, and Jacques Garrigue, who commented earlier versions, and to Patrick Varone, who read this version carefully and helped to correct several points.

References

[1] Samson Abramsky and C.-H. L. Ong, "Full Abstraction in the Lazy Lambda Calcul," *Information and Computation*, vol. 105, 1993, pp. 159–267.

[2] Hassan Aït-Kaci and Andreas Podelski, "Towards a Meaning of LIFE," *Proceedings PLILP '91, Lecture Notes in Computer Science*, vol. 528, Springer-Verlag, 1991, pp. 255–274.

[3] Hassan Aït-Kaci and Jacques Garrigue, "Label-Selective λ-Calculus, Syntax and Confluence," *Proceedings 13th International Conference on Foundations of Software Technology and Theoretical Computer Science, Lecture Notes in Computer Science*, vol. 761, Springer-Verlag, 1993, pp. 24–40.

[4] Franco Barbanera and Mariangiola Dezani-Ciancaglini, "Intersection and Union Types," *Proceedings Symposium on Theoretical Aspects of Computer Science, Lecture Notes in Computer Science*, vol. 526, Springer-Verlag, 1991, pp. 651–674.

[5] H. P. Barendregt, *The Lambda Calculus, its Syntax and Semantics*, vol. 103 of *Studies in Logic and the Foundations of Mathematics*, North-Holland, 1985 (2nd printing).

[6] Bard Bloom, "Can LCF Be Topped? Flat Lattice Models of Typed λ-Calculus," *Information and Computation*, vol. 87, 1990, pp. 264–301.

[7] Gérard Boudol, "Lambda-Calculi for (Strict) Parallel Functions," *Information and Computation*, vol. 108, 1994, pp. 51–127.

[8] N. de Bruijn, "Lambda-Calculus Notation with Nameless Dummies, a Tool for Automatic Formula Manipulation," *Indag. Mat.*, vol. 34, 1972, pp. 381–392.

[9] Luca Cardelli, "A Semantics of Multiple Inheritance," *Information and Computation*, vol. 76, 1988, pp. 138–164.

[10] Luca Cardelli and John C. Mitchell, "Operations on Records," *Proceedings Conference on Mathematical Foundations of Programming Semantics, Lecture Notes in Computer Science*, vol. 442, Springer-Verlag, 1989, pp. 22–52.

[11] Thierry Coquand and Gérard Huet, "The Calculus of Constructions," *Information and Computation*, vol. 76, 1988, pp. 95–120.

[12] Pierre-Louis Curien, *Categorical Combinators, Sequential Algorithms, and Functional Programming*, 2nd edn., Birkhäuser, Boston, 1993.

[13] Laurent Dami, "Software Composition: Towards and Integration of Functional and Object-Oriented Approaches," Ph.D. Thesis, University of Geneva, 1994.

[14] Laurent Dami, "Pure Lambda Calculus with Records: from Compatibility to Subtyping," working paper, 1994.

[15] Laurent Dami, "Type Inference for λN, and Principal Type Schemes for Record Concatenation," working paper, 1994.

[16] Jacques Garrigue and Hassan Aït-Kaci, "The Typed Polymorphic Label-Selective λ-Calculus," *Proceedings 21st ACM Symposium on Principles of Programming Languages*, 1994, pp. 35–47.

[17] Robert Harper and Benjamin Pierce, "A Record Calculus Based on Symmetric Concatenation," *Proceedings 18th ACM Symposium on Principles of Programming Languages*, ACM Press, 1990, pp. 131–142.

[18] John Hogg, "Islands: Aliasing Protection In Object-Oriented Languages," *Proceedings OOPSLA '91, ACM SIGPLAN Notices*, vol. 26, no. 11, Nov. 1991, pp. 271–285.

[19] John Lamping, "A Unified System of Parameterization for Programming Languages," *Proceedings ACM Conference on Lisp and Functional Programming*, 1988, pp. 316–326.

[20] Robin Milner, "Fully Abstract Models of Typed λ-Calculi," *Theoretical Computer Science*, vol. 4, 1977, pp. 1–22.

[21] Robin Milner, "The Polyadic π-Calculus: A Tutorial," Tech. Report ECS-LFCS-91-180, University of Edinburgh, 1991.

[22] Robin Milner, "Elements of Interaction," (Turing Award Lecture), *Communications of the ACM*, vol. 36, no. 1, Jan. 1993, pp. 78–89.

[23] John C. Mitchell, Furio Honsell, Kathleen Fisher, "A Lambda Calculus of Objects and Method Specialization," *Proceedings 8th Annual IEEE Symposium on Logic in Computer Science*, 1993.

[24] Benjamin C. Pierce, "Intersection Types and Bounded Polymorphism," *Proceedings Conference on Typed lambda-calculi and Applications, Lecture Notes in Computer Science*, vol. 664, Springer-Verlag, March 1993, pp. 346–360.

[25] Gordon Plotkin, "Domains," Course Notes, Department of Computer Science, University of Edinburgh, 1983.

[26] Didier Rémy, "Typing Record Concatenation for Free," *Proceedings ACM POPL'92*, ACM Press, 1992, pp. 166–176.

[27] John C. Reynolds, "Preliminary Design of the Programming Language Forsythe," Technical Report CMU-CS-88-159, Carnegie-Mellon University, 1988.

[28] Scott F. Smith, "From Operational to Denotational Semantics," *Proceedings Conf on Mathematical foundations of Programming Semantics, Lecture Notes in Computer Science*, vol. 598, Springer-Verlag, 1992, pp. 54–76.

[29] Simon Thompson, *Type Theory and Functional Programming*, International Computer Science Series, Addison-Wesley, Reading, Mass., 1991.

PART IV

Software Information Management

Chapter 7
Component Classification in the Software Information Base

Panos Constantopoulos and Martin Dörr

Abstract   A key component in a reuse-oriented software development environment is an appropriate software repository. We present a repository system which supports the entire software development lifecycle, providing for the integrated and consistent representation, organization, storage, and management of reusable artefacts. The system can support multiple development and representation models and is dynamically adaptable to new ones. The chapter focuses on the facilities offered by the system for component classification, an important technique for retrieving reusable software. It is demonstrated that the inherently delicate and complex process of classification is streamlined and considerably facilitated by integrating it into a wider documentation environment and, especially, by connecting it with software static analysis. The benefits in terms of precision, consistency and ease of use can be significant for large scale applications.[*]

7.1   Introduction

Software reuse is a promising way of increasing productivity, assuring quality and meeting deadlines in software development. There are several, non-exclusive approaches to reuse, including organizational support, software libraries, object-oriented programming, AI-based methods for design reuse and process analysis.

---

[*] Work on the SIB was partly funded by the European Commission through ESPRIT project ITHACA. Partners in ITHACA were: Siemens-Nixdorf (Germany), University of Geneva (Switzerland), FORTH (Greece), Bull (France), TAO (Spain) and Datamont (Italy).

A common theme in all these approaches is that reuse concerns not only software code, but also design, requirements specifications and development processes. Supporting the communication of all these aspects of software development between the original developer and the reuser, and, furthermore, the cooperation within communities of software developers ("software communities" [14]), is a basic concern of reuse technology. Software repositories are key components in reuse-oriented software development environments [9] supporting the organization and management of software and of related information, as well as the selection and comprehension of relevant software and of development processes. In an orthogonal manner, object-oriented languages facilitate the development of reusable software components through encapsulation, data abstraction, instantiation, inheritance, genericity and strong typing. For broad, comprehensive surveys of reuse the reader is referred to [5] [18]. Krueger presents in [18] a taxonomy of reuse methods in terms of their ability to abstract, select, specialize (adapt) and integrate software artefacts.

In this chapter we assume that applications are developed using object-oriented technology, and that the software components of interest are mainly classes specified in an object-oriented programming language. As pointed out in [14], the management of large class collections introduces a number of problems concerning the representation of classes, in particular, the expression of structural and descriptive information, the representation of relationships and dependencies among classes in a collection, the selection and understanding of classes by appropriate querying and browsing facilities, and the support of class evolution.

Small to medium size collections of software classes can be organized by fairly simple schemes in the style of Smalltalk-80 [15]. Classes are hierarchically organized by inheritance and are grouped by functionality into possibly overlapping categories. The class browser allows the selection and exploration of reusable classes.

Various approaches have been proposed for addressing the selection problems arising in large collections. One such is the faceted classification scheme developed by Prieto-Diaz and Freeman [23]. In this scheme, components are classified according to six descriptors ("facets"), the values of which are hierarchically organized and on which a conceptual distance is defined. A variant of the faceted classification scheme, better suited for object-oriented software, was developed within the ESPRIT REBOOT project [17]. Other approaches to organizing software collections include: library cataloguing [16]; hypertext (DIF, [13]); object-oriented libraries (Eiffel [20], Objective-C); ER and extended models (IBM Repository [19], Lassie of AT&T [11]); and hybrid approaches (e.g. SIB [8]).

The Software Information Base (SIB) is a repository system, developed within the ESPRIT ITHACA project, that stores information about the entire software lifecycle. The SIB offers a uniform representation scheme for the various artefacts and concepts involved in the different stages of the software lifecycle; the scheme can be extended to accommodate new ones. It also supports multiple forms of presentation, depending on the tool using the particular artefact. Finally, it provides querying, browsing and filtering mechanisms for selecting and understanding artefacts, and interfaces to other software development tools.

In this chapter we first give an overview of the SIB and of its concepts in section 7.2. We examine the querying and browsing capabilities of the SIB in section 7.3. The SIB's classification scheme is described in section 7.4; section 7.5 explains how the classification of software artefacts is automated, whereas section 7.6 reports on our experiences with the SIB. We conclude with perspectives for future work.

7.2 The Software Information Base

7.2.1 General Concepts

The SIB is structured as an attributed directed graph, with nodes and links respectively representing descriptions of software artefacts (objects) and relations between them. There are three kinds of descriptions, namely:

1. requirements descriptions (RD);
2. design descriptions (DD); and
3. implementation descriptions (ID).

These descriptions provide three corresponding views of a software object:

1. an application view, according to a requirements specification model (e.g. SADT);
2. a system view, according to a design specification model (e.g. DFD); and
3. an implementation view, according to an implementation model (e.g. set of C++ classes along with documentation).

Descriptions can be simple or composite, consisting of other descriptions. The term *descriptions* reflects the fact that these entities only describe software objects. The objects themselves reside outside the SIB (e.g. in a Unix file storing a C++ program), accessible from the corresponding descriptions.

There are several kinds of relationship between descriptions or parts of descriptions serving a variety of purposes:

- *Flexibility* in *defining* or *modifying* types of artefacts and relationships, or even description models, accomplished through multiple instantiation and a series of instantiation levels.
- Classification of artefacts and relationships in *generalization/specialization* hierarchies supporting multiple strict inheritance.
- expression of *semantic* and *structural* relationships between artefacts, including aggregation, correspondence, genericity and similarity.
- expression of *user-defined* and *informal links* — including links for hypertext navigation, annotations, and for defining version derivation graphs.
- *grouping* of software artefacts descriptions into larger functional units.

An important concept in the SIB is the *application frame (AF)*. Application frames represent complete systems or families of systems and comprise (*hasPart*) at least one implementation and optional design and requirements descriptions. AFs are further distinguished into specific and generic (SAFs and GAFs) while the RDs, DDs and IDs of an AF should be considered as groupings of such descriptions (i.e. other associations).

A SAF describes a complete system (be it a linear programming package, a text processor or an airline reservation system) and includes exactly one ID. A GAF is an abstraction of a collection of systems pertinent to a particular application and includes one RD, one or more DDs and one or more IDs for each DD. Application frames play a key role in the reuse-oriented software development lifecycle envisaged in ITHACA. Generic components and applications are produced by *application engineers*. These are represented by GAFs and constitute a core of, presumably good quality, components and applications which are configured and adapted to fit particular needs by *application developers*. Such derived, specific systems are represented by SAFs. For more on the ITHACA application development methodology and the role of application frames see [10] [9].

The representation language employed in the SIB is Telos [21]: a conceptual modelling language in the family of entity–relationship models [7]. The main reason for choosing Telos over other E-R extensions, such as those used by the PCTE+ OMS or the IBM Repository Manager, MVS, is that it supports unlimited instantiation levels and treats attributes as objects in their own right (which, therefore, can also have attributes). These features account for great expressiveness and easy schema extension, and are fully exploited in the SIB.

7.2.2 Relationships Between Software Artefacts

Relationships are essential for the classification and retrieval of software artefacts. We therefore elaborate on each kind of link and indicate, when appropriate, how they support the querying and browsing activities in the SIB.

Attribution

Attribution is represented by *attribute* links. This is a general, rather unconstrained representation of semantic relations, whereby the attributes of a description are defined to be instances of other descriptions. An attribute can have zero or more values. Consider the following example:

    Description SoftwareObject with
        attributes
            author : Person
            version : VersionNumber

SoftwareObject has attributes author and version whose values are instances of Person and VersionNumber respectively. Dynamic properties, such as 'calls' relations of methods and procedures, also fall into this category.

Aggregation

Aggregation is represented by *hasPart* links. This relates an object to its components. For example:

    Description SoftwareObject with
        ...
        hasPart
            components: SoftwareObject

The components of an object have a distinct role in the function of the object and any possible changes to them affect the aggregate object as well (e.g. new version).

Classification

Classification (converse *instantiation*) is represented by *instanceOf* links. Objects sharing common properties can be grouped into classes. An object can belong to more than one class. Classes themselves are treated as generic objects, which, in turn, will be instances of other, more generic objects (so-called "meta-classes"). In fact, every SIB object has to be declared as an instance of at least one class. Effectively, an infinite classification hierarchy is established starting with objects that have no instances of their own, called tokens. Instantiation of a class involves instantiating all the associated semantic relations. Thus relations are treated as objects themselves. For example:

    Description BankIS instanceOf SoftwareObject with
        author : Panos
        version : 0.1
        components : CustomerAccounts, Credit, Investments

The attribute and hasPart links of BankIS are instances of the corresponding attribute and components links of SoftwareObject.

Classification is perhaps the most important modelling mechanism in the SIB. [33] gives a detailed account of the construction of models and descriptions in the SIB.

Generalization

Generalization (converse *specialization*) is represented by *isA* links. This allows multiple, strict inheritance of properties between classes leading to the creation of multiple generalization hierarchies. A class inherits all the attributes of its superclasses (possibly more than one — multiple inheritance); however, inherited properties can only be constrained, not overridden (strict inheritance).

Correspondence

Correspondence is represented by *correspondsTo* links. A software object can have zero or more associated requirements, design and implementation descriptions. Correspondence relations concern the identity of an object described by different descriptions and can have as parts other correspondence relations between parts of the corresponding descriptions. Correspondence links actually indicate that the descriptions they link together describe the same object from different perspectives. The correspondences of the parts need not be one-to-one. For instance, a requirements specification may correspond to more than one design and a design may have more than one alternative implementation. Similarly, a single implementation could correspond to more than one design entity. Application Frames are an important type of controlled correspondence in the SIB.

Similarity

Similarity links represent similarity relationships among software objects and provide a foundation for approximate retrieval from the SIB. Similarity has been studied in psychology [32] and AI, most relevantly to this work in case-based reasoning [4]. Within the context of object-oriented systems, similarity has been viewed as a form of generalization [34]. Alternatively, it has been interpreted as degree of affinity with respect to various relations, providing the foundation for the dynamically changing presentation of related objects within a browser (see chapter 9). Its applications include the support of *approximate* retrieval with respect to a software repository as well as the re-engineering of software systems [27].

We are primarily interested in similarity links that can be computed automatically from information that is loaded into the SIB. For added flexibility, however, user-defined similarity links are also supported. Similarity is computed with respect to similarity criteria and expressed in terms of corresponding similarity measures, which are numbers in the range [0,1]. An aggregate similarity measure with respect to a set of criteria can be obtained as a weighted aggregate function of single-criterion similarity measures, the weights expressing the relative importance of the individual criteria in the set. This measure may be symmetric or directed. For example, similarity with respect to generalization may be defined as symmetric, whereas similarity with respect to type compatibility of the parameters of two C routines may be defined as directed.

Similarity can be used to define task-specific partial orders on the SIB, thus facilitating the search and evaluation of reusable software objects. Moreover, subsets of the SIB can be treated as equivalence classes with respect to a particular symmetric similarity measure, provided all pairs of the class are more similar than a given threshold. Such similarity equivalence classes may span different application domains, thus supporting inter-domain reuse. For details on the similarity analysis of SIB descriptions see [29].

Genericity

Genericity is represented by *specialCaseOf* links. This relation is defined only between application frames to denote that one application frame is less parameterized than another. For example, a bank accounting and a hotel accounting application frame could both be derived from a more general, parametric accounting application frame.

Informal and user-defined links

When users have foreseeable needs for other types of links they can define them using the attribute definition facility of Telos. For instance, versioning can be modelled by special correspondence links labelled *derivedFrom*. Furthermore, random needs for representation and reference can be served by informal links, such as hypertext links which allow the attachment of multimedia annotations to SIB objects.

Association

Association is an encapsulation mechanism intended to allow the grouping of descriptions that together play a functional role [6]. It associates a set of descriptions with a particular symbol table:

> Association = (setOfDescriptions, symbolTable)

The contents of an association can only be accessed through the entry points supplied in its symbol table. For example, we may define as an association the descriptions that constitute a design specification for a hotel information system, or all the classes that define an implementation of that same system. The SIB itself is a global association containing all objects included in any association. Its symbol table contains all the external names of every object. Name conflicts can be resolved by a precedence rule.

Associations can be derived from other associations through queries or set operations. Furthermore, associations can be considered as materialized views. Non-materialized views, or simply *views*, differ from associations in that they cannot be updated directly, but rather, through updates of the associations which they are derived from.

7.3 Information Retrieval and User Interface

7.3.1 Querying and Browsing

The selection of software descriptions from the SIB is accomplished through the *selection tool* (ST) in terms of an iterative process consisting of retrieval and browsing steps. Browsing is usually the final and sometimes the only step required for selection. The functional difference between the retrieval and the browsing mode is that the former supports the retrieval of an arbitrary subset of the SIB and presumes some knowledge of the SIB contents, while the latter supports local exploratory searches within a given subset of the SIB without any prior knowledge. Operationally, both selection modes evaluate queries against the SIB.

The basic selection functions of the SIB are:

> *Retrieve:* Queries $\times$ Associations $\rightarrow$ $\mathcal{P}$(Descriptions $\times$ Weights)
> *Browse:* Identifiers $\times$ $\mathcal{P}$(Links $\times$ Depths) $\times$ Associations $\rightarrow$ Views

The *Retrieve* function takes as input a (compound, in general non-Boolean) query and an association, and returns a subset of the associated descriptions with weights attached, indicating the degree to which each description in the answer set matches the query. Non-Boolean queries are based on similarity. Queries are formulated in terms of the query primitives offered by the Programmatic Query Interface. A set of queries of particular significance can be preformulated and offered as menu options, thus providing maximum ease-of-use and efficiency for frequent retrieval operations.

Browsing begins with a particular SIB description which is the current focus of attention (called the *current object*) and produces a view of a *neighbourhood* of the current object within a given association. Since the SIB has a network structure, the neighbourhood of the current object is defined in terms of incoming and outgoing links of interest. Moreover, the size of the neighbourhood can also be controlled. Thus, the *Browse* function takes as input the identifier (name) of the current object, a list of names of link classes paired with depth control parameter values and an association, and determines a local view centred around the current object.

When the depth control parameters are all equal to 1, a *star view* results, showing the current object at the centre surrounded by objects directly connected to it through links of the selected types. This is the simplest and smallest neighbourhood of an object, in topological terms, with a controllable population. Effectively, the *Browse* function provides a moving window with controllable filters and size, which allows navigational search over subsets of the SIB network.

When the depth control parameters are assigned values greater than 1, *Browse* displays all objects connected to the current object via paths consisting of links of the selected types (possibly mixed), where each type of link appears in a path up to a number of times specified by the corresponding depth parameter. This results in a directed graph rooted at the current object. Finally, when the depth parameters are assigned the value ALL (infinite), the transitive closure of the current object with respect to one or more link types is displayed. Such a browse operation can display, for example, the call graph (forward or backward) of a given routine.

Queries to the SIB can be classified from a user's point of view as *explicit* or *implicit*. An *explicit* query involves an arbitrary predicate explicitly formulated in a query language or through an appropriate form interface. An *implicit* query, on the other hand, is generated through navigational commands in the browsing mode, or through a button or menu option, for frequently used, "canned" queries. Browsing commands and explicit queries can also be issued through appropriate interfaces from external tools.

7.3.2 Implementation

An application-scale SIB system has been implemented at the Institute of Computer Science, FORTH, and is available to other sites for experimentation[*] (see figure 7.1).

The user interface supports menu-guided and forms-based query formulation with graphical and textual presentation of the answer sets, as well as graphical browsing in a hypertext-like manner. A hypertext annotation mechanism is also provided. Menu titles, menu layout and domain-specific queries are user-configurable.

A forms-based interactive data entry facility is available for entering data and schema information in a uniform manner. This facility automatically adapts itself to the structure of the various classes and subclasses byemploying the schema information. Furthermore, it is customizable to application-specific tasks, such as classification of items, addition of descriptive elements, etc.

---

[*] For details, consult the WWW page for this book (see the preface).

Information Retrieval and User Interface

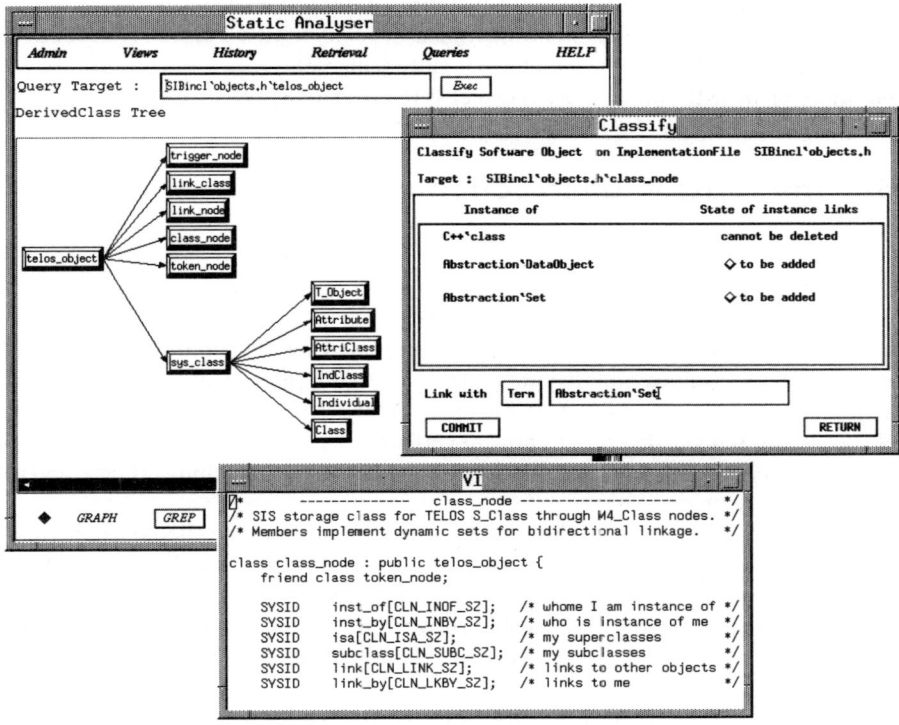

Figure 7.1 *SIB static analyzer and class management system.*

Any item in the SIB may reference a multimedia object, comprising images, video, sound or text, stored externally. The SIB recognizes such references and automatically generates calls to the appropriate presentation tools with the respective parameters, which results in a synchronous display of the multimedia object.

The SIB is optimized for referential access and large amounts of highly structured data, especially for network structures consisting of a large variety of classes, rather than relatively few classes with large populations per class (typical in a DBMS). Recursive queries on aggregational hierarchies, classification hierarchies, and retrieval of graph structures, such as flow-charts or state-transition diagrams, play a more important role than access by value conditions. A transitive closure with cycle detection of a binary tree with 1024 nodes can be retrieved in 2 seconds on a Sun SPARC Station. The performance of the SIB in look-up and traversal exceeds that of modern relational systems by one and two orders of magnitude respectively. This allows for real-time queries that would be prohibitive with traditional databases.

Data entry speed is acceptable: 10,000 references are loaded in batch mode in 3 minutes, and 500,000 in 2.5 hours on a SPARC. Both examples were measured with real application data from static analysis of a medium (30.000 code lines) and a very large application (2.5 million code lines). The theoretical capacity limit is 1 billion references. The design of the internal catalogue structures is fully scalable.

For more on the SIB, the interested reader is referred to [8] [9].

7.4 The Classification Scheme

7.4.1 Principles

Given a set of entities (objects, concepts) represented by descriptors (keywords), the grouping of those entities into disjoint classes according to some criterion of descriptor matching is called *classification*. Matching may express some kind of semantic similarity. A *classification scheme* determines how to perform classification in a given setting, prescribing the sets of descriptors and possible internal ordering, matching criteria, and rules for class assignment.

Depending on the number of descriptors used, a classification scheme can be uni- or multi-dimensional. An example of a unidimensional scheme is the Universal Decimal Classification (see [26]). In library science, multidimensional (*faceted*) classification, was introduced by Ranghanathan [25], breaking down information into a number of categories thus addressing corresponding aspects of the classified entities. These aspects are called *facets*.

Prieto-Diaz and Freeman developed a faceted classification scheme for software reuse [23] [24] in which they use six facets to describe software: *function*, *object*, *medium/ agent*, *system type*, *functional area*, and *setting*. They mainly describe component functionality, the last three facets pertaining to the internal and external environment. Each facet has a *term space*, i.e. a fixed set of legal values (*concepts*), in the sense of a controlled vocabulary, and an extensible set of *user terms*. Concepts are organized by a directed acyclic specialization relation, and terms are assigned as leaves to concepts. Subjective conceptual distances between concepts and terms are defined, to support retrieving software components by their degree of matching.

A variant of the scheme of Prieto-Diaz and Freeman was developed in the ESPRIT REBOOT project [17] [28] [22] [31]. This scheme comprises four facets, better suited for describing object-oriented components: *abstraction*, *operation*, *operates-on* and *dependency*. The first three are analogous to subject, verb and object in a natural language sentence describing component functionality, while the fourth is the counterpart of the three environmental facets of the Prieto-Diaz and Freeman scheme. The term spaces are also structured by relations such as specialization and synonymy. A conceptual distance between terms is defined, which, like that of Prieto-Diaz and Freeman, is the outcome of human assessment. Neither Prieto-Diaz and Freeman nor REBOOT relate the derivation of classification terms to the knowledge of structural dependencies between software components. In [28], however, such a connection is suggested as potentially useful.

The Classification Scheme

In the SIB classification scheme the REBOOT facets are adopted, except that facets are assigned not necessarily to a class as a whole but, rather, to the relevant parts. Specifically, the contents of the SIB classification facets are as follows:

Abstraction

Abstraction terms are nouns representing *active* object types. Typically these abstractions indicate the role that the object plays in its interactions with other objects of an application. An object-oriented software class as a whole is assigned an abstraction, such as 'String', 'Set', 'WindowSystem', 'Index' or 'NameList'. Abstraction terms do not include expressions that denote processing, such as 'String concatenation' or 'String conversion'. Since object types are assumed to be active, the Abstraction terms do not reflect processing in general either (e.g. 'String manipulation').

Operation

Operation terms are verbal types representing specific activities. The active part of a class comprises its methods. Hence we associate Operation terms with each individual method responsible for an activity, e.g. 'Solve', 'Invert', 'Lock-Unlock', 'Open-Close'. Pairs of inverse properties, such as 'Open-Close', are regarded as one term, to keep the term space small.

Operates-On

Besides operating on the class to which it belongs, a method operates on its parameters. In object-oriented design, non-trivial parameters belong to classes. (Methods may also directly access input/output devices, which may or may not be represented as objects.) Operates-On terms are nouns representing the object types acted on by methods, including Abstractions, basic data types and devices. Note that Operates-On is a superset of Abstraction and that the abstraction of a class must be a default 'Operates-On' for its own operations. Operates-On represents the role an object type plays with respect to other types.

Dependency

Dependency terms represent environmental conditions, such as hardware, operating system or language. It is good practice in software development groups to test and release complete libraries for a certain environment. Accordingly we assign Dependency terms to class libraries as a whole. The classes of the library are then indirectly linked to a dependency through the library itself. Each combination of programming language, system software and hardware forms a different environment. Dependency terms are provided in the SIB which reflect single environmental conditions, as well as combinations of those. For instance, a library tested, for example, on (SINIX ODT1.1, AT&T C++ 3.0B, SNI WX200), and (SINIX 5.41, CooL 2.1, SNI WX200) does not necessarily run on (SINIX 5.41, AT&T C++ 3.0B, SNI WX200). Such triples are terms by themselves in the SIB, the constituents of which represent their immediate higher terms. Thus retrieval is possible by the triple itself, as well as by simple terms, e.g. SINIX 5.41, Unix, C++, etc. (see figure 7.2).

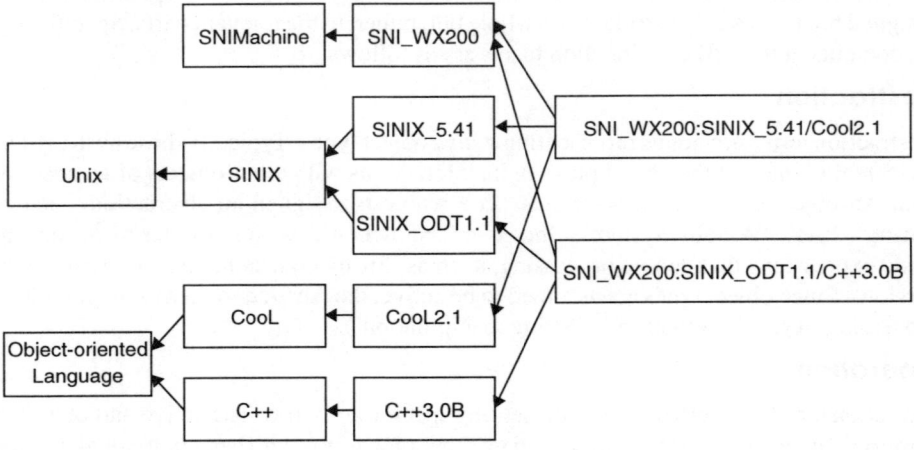

Figure 7.2 *The isA hierarchy of combinatory Dependency terms.*

7.4.2 Classification Hierarchies in the SIB

Facets are represented as meta-classes in the SIB. The terms, i.e. the values of a facet, are instances of that facet, and are therefore simple classes. The instances of those classes are the software objects sharing the functional property the term denotes. The assignment of a term to a software object is accomplished by declaring the object to be an instance of the term.

Note that facet terms reflect the *functional* role of components as they cooperate in a process, as distinguished from structural relations or user application tasks. For instance, 'C++ class', 'Menu item', 'Selection of goods, clients, or accounts' may be respectively the structural, functional and application roles of one software object. These other two roles are also very pertinent for reuse. In the SIB we take advantage of such information both independently and jointly with functional classification, as we shall see below. On the other hand, some essential functional parts of a software object are and should be hidden from the user, hence they do not have any application task associated with them.

In addition to a functional classification scheme, like the one discussed here, one can independently develop a classification scheme with respect to structural aspects of the programming language, or other criteria. Concurrent classification of software objects according to more than one scheme is supported by the SIB. Technically, the assignment of terms from several schemes is performed by multiple classification: a component is declared to be an instance of all the relevant terms.

The term space for each facet is partially ordered by a specialization/generalization relation (isA) which, in the SIB, obeys multiple strict inheritance. This organization has a

The Classification Scheme

number of advantages. It minimizes the data entry involved in describing a software component, since each term inherits all its predecessors. In addition, the probability of inconsistent classification is limited. Multiple isA relations express multiple independent properties. By contrast, simple isA relations generate pure hierarchical structures which are not flexible enough for expressing general, multifaceted relationships. If we interpret the term space as a set of classes semantically ordered by isA relations derived from their implicit properties, assuming strict inheritance of those properties, the terms lose their linguistic nature and become concepts. *Homonyms*, i.e. instances of the same word with different meanings, must then be assigned different terms. For example, spectral 'radius' and circle 'radius', law and 'order' and warehouse 'order' do not share properties. The recall of such a concept-based system is superior to a linguistic one (see [30]).

No distinction in nature is made between leaf terms and higher terms. The granularity of analysis depends very much on the breadth of the domains classified, and should be dynamically adaptable to the contents of the repository. As is generally accepted in the literature, term spaces are kept small in order to help the user become quickly acquainted with the applicable terms for a given problem. Retrieved components can subsequently be reviewed efficiently by browsing.

In order to combine discipline with linguistic flexibility in developing term spaces, synonyms are introduced. Two different words are *synonyms* if they have the same meaning, such as 'alter' and 'change' in the Unix system call manual. Preferred words are selected as terms for inclusion in the isA-structured term space. Synonyms are attached to those through the attribute category *synonym* specifically defined in the SIB. Thus access is possible by all synonymous words and term, while vocabulary control is maintained.

Multiple inheritance expresses multiplicity of nature of a term itself. For instance, 'Copy' has the properties of both 'Put' and 'Get'. We adopt the principle that for any group of terms sharing some implicit property, there should be a higher term with this property: 'Get', 'Put', 'I/O' share a property 'transfer', whereas 'Put', 'Update' share 'Modify', etc. Arbitrary decisions on term placement in a hierarchy can thus be avoided. On the other hand, as any conceptual distance or similarity is based on some sharing of properties, those notions become closely related to the higher terms structure.

Multiplicity of nature at the item level (components), not resulting from intrinsic properties of the terms, is expressed through multiple instantiation (assignment of terms), e.g. a method doing 'Lock' and 'Update'. It turns out that the benefits from the specialization (isA) structure of term spaces are fully obtained if items are only assigned to leaf terms. Nevertheless, the system is robust to a dynamic refinement of the term space, whereby leaf terms may become higher terms. Items assigned to higher terms can be treated by the retrieval query as possible candidates for all leaf terms under it, with a decreasing priority according to the number of levels between them.

The isA organization facilitates exploring, understanding and retrieving terms. Naturally, alphabetical browsing and retrieval by lexical pattern matching are also provided. Finally, a "conceptual distance" (conversely, similarity) can be defined as a suitable metric over the term space partially ordered by the isA relation [29]. The advantage of such a metric is that its computation requires no user input, as it effectively relies on the intrinsic

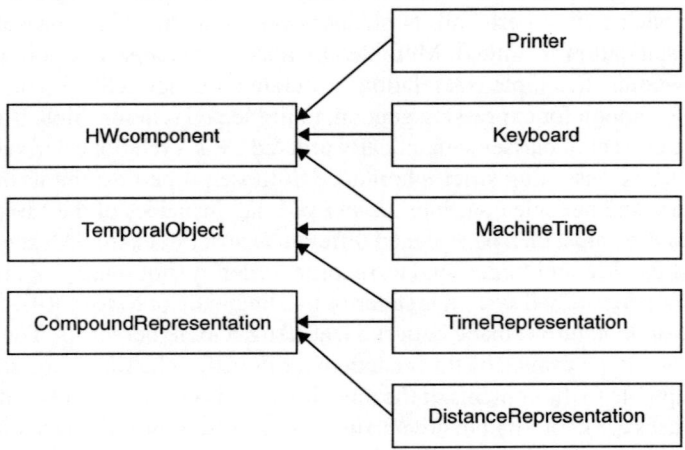

Figure 7.3 *The isA hierarchy environment of Abstraction 'TimeRepresentation'.*

properties of the common higher terms. To which degree this notion of measure can be exploited to improve or normalize the hierarchy itself is a topic of further research.

7.4.3 Example

Let us consider the abstractions of a class 'Time', which handles arithmetic with years, hours, minutes, etc. On the one hand, it has to do with the representation of time values; on the other hand, it does not relate to actual time. We therefore choose the term 'TimeRepresentation'. This term has two higher terms: 'TemporalObject', and 'CompoundRepresentation'. By 'CompoundRepresentation' we denote systems of measurement using different units for different orders of magnitude, such as miles, yards, etc. Another specialization of 'TemporalObject' is 'MachineTime'.

A 'TimeRepresentation' class may be directly used, or in conjunction with a 'MachineTime' class to measure elapsed time. This conforms to the initial intention of such a class. Note that we could easily change unit names and conversion factors between units to adapt such a class to handle miles, yards, etc. In this case we reuse the algorithm or structure of a specific solution. This property is intrinsic to a time representation module, and we express it by the higher term 'CompoundRepresentation'.

This example demonstrates how multiple inheritance can serve to bring related terms together, and how a careful analysis of implicit properties of terms may help to support reuse in ways the developer did not originally have in mind (see figure 7.3). Since the development of generic modules is regarded to be desirable for reuse, any support for detecting candidates to be generalized or parameterized is valuable.

7.5 Streamlining the Classification Process

7.5.1 Static Class Analysis

The SIB stores various kinds of structural and descriptive information about software components. In particular, at the implementation description level, it stores the results of static analysis performed by program parsers. Given a programming language, a corresponding implementation description model defines a set of entities, such as class, method, parameter, source file, and relations between these entities, such as defines, calls, user-of. The static analysis data of a given component are entered as instances of the model concepts. (This information is useful enough in its own right that a version of the SIB has been developed purely as static analyzer.) Static analysis information is also useful for streamlining the classification process.

We distinguish classification into *direct*, which is assigned explicitly to an entity, and *derived*, which is defined by means of queries. Minimizing direct classification not only saves human effort, but also improves consistency when software or term space modifications take place. Static analysis allows for an automatic mapping of information (methods, parameters, etc.) to classification facets and terms.

Abstractions are associated to classes, and Operations are associated to methods. Procedures and operators are treated like methods, if they are connected to a class via friend declarations. Otherwise, an additional class, such as 'Procedure_group' is introduced for their classification. The operations of a class are derived by queries through the links indicating the methods belonging to that class. The explicit correspondence of methods and Operations facilitates maintenance and consistency of code and classification terms. The Operates-On terms of a class are also derived, and include the abstraction of the class itself (since its methods can access its instances) and the parameter types of its methods, be they abstractions (i.e. other classes) or basic data types. (The assignment of terms representing devices, system calls, etc., to methods is done manually at present.) In a linguistic sense, Operates-On is the direct object of the Operation verb. Operates-On is at first hand a property of the method, or even more precisely of the instantiation of a specific operation in a method, and only in a wider sense a property of the class as a whole.

Dependency terms are assigned to libraries and applications. Therefore, the dependencies of a class are derived by relating library files with the classes they contain.

7.5.2 Derived Classification

A number of derivation paths are used, in either direction, depending on whether the objective is to find a class or the valid terms for a class. An example comprising all those paths is given in the next section. The following is the complete list of relevant path elements:
- From synonyms to established terms through the 'synonym of' link.

- From class terms to higher terms through the 'isA' link.
- From Abstraction terms of classes to methods as 'Operates-On' through the inverse 'has parameter' link.
- From method terms to classes through the inverse 'has method' link.
- From class terms to derived classes, in the sense of the PL, through the inverse of the 'has parent' or 'has supertype' link.
- From Dependency terms to classes through the 'Library.runs_on' – 'Library.has_file' – 'class.defined_in' path.

Note that the direct assignment of terms is done not to software classes but to more finely-grained entities (e.g. methods) that are structurally related to them. In this way it is sufficient, in most practical cases, to assign one term to each entity. Furthermore, static analysis information can support the automatic extraction of classification terms from formalized source code comments.

When creating term spaces it is important to maintain semantic links between Operation terms and Abstraction terms, in particular:

1. which legal operations belong to an abstraction; and
2. which application domain an operation term is intended for.

The first kind of constraint should naturally be represented by linking abstractions with their legal operations. Creating higher operation terms would be unnecessary. For example, Operation'truncate is an operation applicable to both strings and files. This should be indicated by links from Abstraction'file and Abstraction'string to Operation'truncate. Introducing, say, Operation'string_operations and Operation'file_operations as higher terms, to which Operation'truncate would be isA related, conveys no information on the *nature* of Operation'truncate.

The second kind of constraint introduces a problem related to homonyms. These are handled by adding prefixes to the terms, so that the homonyms effectively obtain unique names in the SIB. Besides, they preserve the homonym character in the last part of the word, which allows access by substring matching. However, great care should be taken not to create substructures in the term space on the basis of homonyms (more precisely: the homonymous parts of terms), which may prove semantically wrong. For example, a substructure including Abstraction'order along with its specializations Abstraction'warehouse_order and Abstraction'serial_order is not based on common semantics as expected. By contrast, Abstraction'warehouse_order isA Abstraction'commerce and Abstraction'serial_order isA Abstraction'memory_management are semantically correct.

7.6 Experiences

7.6.1 The Classification Process

Classification is an iterative process. The user understands the functionality of a part of a component by studying (through the browser) documentation, static analysis data, and/or the code itself, supported in each step by the SIB, matching it with terms in the term space. Term understanding is supported by the linguistic form of the term, its position in the hierarchy, text comments on its meaning, or use in the classification of similar code known to the user. The user must decide if a given term matches with the component and if the term is specific enough. If not, a new term must be introduced in agreement with a group of developers responsible for the term space maintenance. With use and experience, the upper parts of the term space become increasingly stable and complete.

A user should be aware not only of the meaning of terms, but also of their *quality* (i.e. for retrieval purposes), which leads to the need to know the principles under which terms are created. The following general criteria are proposed for selecting terms in a given domain of interest [12] [22]:

- Terms should be *well-known words*, usually technical terms or expressions, widely accepted in the software engineering community, or at least by experts in the particular domain of interest (object-oriented development).
- Terms should have *clear meanings*, relative and easily associated to the concepts conveyed by their specializations or generalizations, in the classification structure. Moreover, they should be *distinct* and precise, in order to facilitate the direct linking of the component to the corresponding classification term.
- Terms should also be *general* enough, in the sense that a term may encompass more than one specialized term in the classification structure. In other words, every term should be used to address more than one component, or a specific (under some semantic criteria), set of components. Keeping a set of terms general — therefore small enough, and expressive at the same time, thus useful for the reuse process — is one of the basic and most difficult tasks in classification. Conversely, keeping a large term space usually means confusion for suppliers and reusers of components, inconvenient browsing, poor search performance, etc.
- Redundancy should be avoided, in the sense that there should be no two terms with very close meaning in the same classification hierarchy. If this happens, then they should be related only with synonym relationship, with the most representative term present in the classification hierarchy.

As these criteria are generally conflicting, the implementation of an effective term space requires striking a judicious balance among them: a non-trivial task.

7.6.2 An Example

We draw an example from the classification developed for the Colibri class library [3] of the CooL language environment. CooL [2] is an object-oriented programming language developed at Siemens-Nixdorf within the ESPRIT ITHACA project. We demonstrate the selection and the assignment of terms, and the resulting valid terms by derivation.

Consider the following partial listing of the classes 'Date' and 'DateRepr':

```
--                              -*- Mode: Cool -*-
-- Date.t --
--
-- PURPOSE
         |    Date is an object type representing a calendar entry      |
         |    consisting of year, month, and day. This object type      |
         |    offers methods to construct, modify and actualize an      |
         |    object and to get information about an object. Further    |
         |    methods deal with arithmetic operations and               |
         |    predicates                                                |
-- TABLE OF CONTENTS
REFER Duration, Interval, time;
TYPE Date = OBJECT (   IN Year : INT,
                       IN Month : INT,
                       IN Day : INT)
-- ----------------------------------------------------------------------
-- 2. Actual Date
-- ----------------------------------------------------------------------
METHOD SetToActualDate;
         -- ---------------------------------------------------------
         -- Set this date to the actual date.
         -- ---------------------------------------------------------


-- ----------------------------------------------------------------------
-- 4. Selective access
-- ----------------------------------------------------------------------
METHOD GetYear : INT;
METHOD GetMonth : INT;
METHOD GetDay : INT;
         -- ---------------------------------------------------------
         -- Return the specific information of this date
         -- ---------------------------------------------------------


-- ----------------------------------------------------------------------
-- 5. Arithmetic operations
-- ----------------------------------------------------------------------
METHOD Add (IN Extent : Duration);
METHOD Subtract (IN Extent : Duration);
         -- ---------------------------------------------------------
         -- Add or subtract an extent from this date.
         -- ---------------------------------------------------------

END OBJECT;
-- ----------------------------------------------------------------------


--                              -*- Mode: Cool -*-
-- DateRepr.t --
--
-- PURPOSE
         |    DateRepr is a sub type of object type Date representing    |
```

Experiences

```
            |    a calendar entry...together with a format string          |
            |    containing the presentation description according to      |
            |    the C library function strftime()...                      |

-- TABLE OF CONTENTS

REFER Date, String;

TYPE DateRepr = Date OBJECT
                    (IN Year : INT,
                     IN Month : INT,
                     IN Day : INT,
                     IN Format : STRING)

-- ------------------------------------------------------------------------
-- 3. Format representation
-- ------------------------------------------------------------------------
METHOD Present : STRING;
        -- ----------------------------------------------------------------
        -- Return this date formatted with its representation
        -- ----------------------------------------------------------------

END OBJECT;
-- ------------------------------------------------------------------------
```

Classification of 'Date':

1. Object type 'Date' under Abstraction 'TimeRepresentation'.
2. Method 'SetToActualDate' under Operation 'Set-Reset' and Operates-On 'MachineTime'. This method uses internally the Unix system call 'time()'.
3. Method 'Add' and 'Subtract' under Operation 'Add-Subtract'.

'Date' is not automatically updated to the current date or machine time. Hence 'MachineTime' was not regarded as a good abstraction for it. The methods GetYear, etc., as all others not listed above, are omitted for the simplicity of the example.

Classification of 'DateRepr':

4. (4) Method 'Present' under Operation 'Convert'.

We usually classify within one term the inverse of an operation as well, since such operations belong semantically together. The method name 'Present' denotes the application task of the method, not its function within the component. We therefore prefer the term 'Convert'.

More examples on reasoning about good terms are given in [12]. We further assume that, in a previous step, the Colibri library was assigned the Dependency terms (CooL2.1, SINIX_5.41, SNI_WX200), and 'Duration' was assigned the Abstraction 'TimeRepresentation'. The classification of built-in types of the programming language, such as integer, string, etc., is initially provided in the SIB. Figure 7.4 shows all paths through which leaf terms for the CooL Object Type 'DateRepr' are derived.

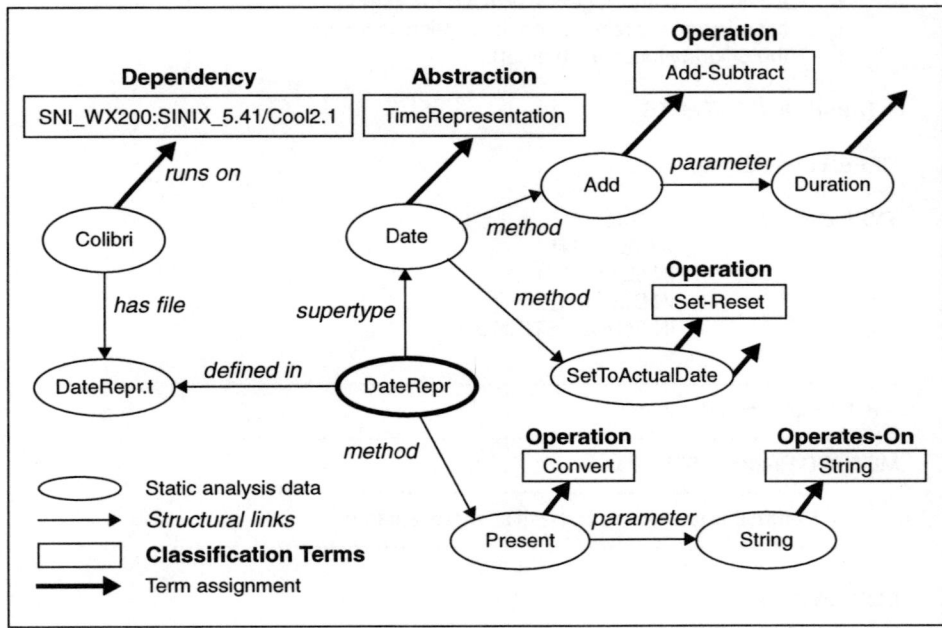

Figure 7.4 Leaf terms valid for the CooLObjectType 'DateRepr'.

The complete list of terms and synonyms for 'DateRepr', resulting from the above leaf term assignment and the term space currently in the SIB, is given in table 7.1. Notice that these terms are *all* derived. Having in mind that good object-oriented applications usually derive some tens of classes from one base class, adding few methods in each derivation step, the advantage of the SIB system for classifying large class hierarchies becomes obvious.

Once found, terms are easily attached to components or correctly integrated in the term space by using the SIB facilities. To classify a class with some twenty methods we typically spend half an hour to one hour. These times, however, vary strongly with the functionality of the class. User interface classes or mathematical classes can be much more quickly classified than some internal components or components with complex functionality. For instance, characterizing the SIB query processor in contrast to other query processors is not straightforward. Evidently, the quality and maturity of existing terminology plays an important role. These observations raise interesting issues for further work, experimental as well as on the field of terminology.

Our in-house experience with the SIB classification facilities is currently based on three cases: the class library Colibri for the CooL language environment, the C++ Extended (APEX 1.0) library [1], and classes of the SIB implementation itself. The term space for the first two examples has been fully developed. The classification of the SIB implemen-

Conclusion

Facet	Derived leaf terms	Higher terms	Synonyms
Abstraction	TimeRepresentation	TemporalObject CompoundRepresentation	Time NonDecimalSystem
Operation	Add-Subtract Set-Reset Convert	StateManipulation Arithmetic Mathematical Format	Algebraic
Operates-On	TimeRepresentation MachineTime String	TemporalObject CompoundRepresentation HWcomponent List Ordered_Collection Collection Bag	Time NonDecimalSystem CurrentTime DateFormat ComputerTime Date Calendar
Dependency	SNI_WX200:SINIX_5.41 :CooL2.1	Unix SINIX SINIX_5.41 SNIMachine SNI_WX200 CooL ObjectOrientedLanguage CooL2.1	

Table 7.1 *Terms and synonyms for the CooLObjectType 'DateRepr'.*

tation is part of an on-going work to use the SIB for its complete self-documentation. Experience reports are also expected from users outside our institute.

7.7 Conclusion

The SIB classification method defines in an objective way how terms and entities will be related. This facilitates the consistent usage of the system by a group of users in that there is a high probability that two users classifying the same object will come up with the same usage of given terms, that two users will come up with the same higher–lower term ordering of given terms, and that users retrieving objects will have the same understanding of the terms as those who have classified the objects. These properties are expected to improve considerably the recall of the system. Nevertheless, there is an intellectual investment in the creation of term spaces, well known from efforts to create thesauri in other domains as well. A good term space incorporates a lot of experience and knowledge. As such, it should be subject to specific developments and exchange between user communities. In our opinion, this issue has not yet received enough attention in the literature.

Classification of software objects is a time-consuming task. We argue that the various derivation mechanisms offered in the SIB will reduce considerably the time needed for classification. They further improve the consistency of the code with the terms applied, in particular the maintenance of the applied terms after updates of the software objects. Both aspects are essential for the industrial usage of such a system.

The SIB is different from a series of other approaches in its data modelling capabilities, which allow it to integrate, without redundancies and in a single tool, the above classification mechanism with other organization principles, such as libraries, application frames, associations and lifecycle information in general. As an open, configurable system it is easily adapted to new methodologies and standards embedded into software production environments.

Integrating all aspects in a logically consistent way, as discussed above for static analysis and functional classification, gives rise to a bootstrapping and verification problem. The larger the population of the system, the more useful it is, the more important further organization principles and lifecycle information become, and the better the validity of their interconnections can be tested. To attract real users of the system, they must be provided from the very beginning with immediately useful functionalities and usage guidance. The reduction of manual work by importing as much information as possible from existing sources plays an important role in this context. The incremental development of further chains of functionality in the SIB, like the static analysis–functional classification presented here, is a main line of our future work.

References

[1] *C++ Extended Library*, APEX 1.0 Information brochure, Siemens Nixdorf Informationssysteme AG, Berlin, April 1992.

[2] *CooL V1.0*, Language Reference Manual, Siemens Nixdorf Informationssysteme AG, Berlin, April 1992.

[3] *CooL V1.0, CoLibri*, Reference Manual, Siemens Nixdorf Informationssysteme AG, Berlin, April 1992.

[4] Ralph Barletta, "An Introduction to Case-Based Reasoning," *AI Expert*, vol. 6, no. 8, Aug. 1991, pp. 42–49.

[5] Ted J. Biggerstaff and Alan J. Perlis, *Software Reusability,* Volume I: *Concepts and Models,* Volume 2: *Applications and Experience*, Addison-Wesley, Reading, Mass., 1989.

[6] Michael Brodie and Dzenan Ridjanovic, "On the Design and Specification of Database Transactions," in *On Conceptual Modelling: Perspectives from Artificial Intelligence, Databases and Programming Languages*, ed. Michael Brodie, John Mylopoulos and Joachim Schmidt, Springer-Verlag, New York, 1984, pp. 277–312.

[7] Peter P.-S. Chen, "The Entity-Relationship Model: Towards a Unified View of Data," *ACM Transactions on Database Systems*, vol. 1, no. 1, March 1976, pp. 9–36.

[8] Panos Constantopoulos, Martin Dörr and Yannis Vassiliou, "Repositories for Software Reuse: The Software Information Base," in *Proceedings IFIP WG 8.1 Conference on Information System Development Process*, Como, Sept. 1993, pp.285–307.

References

[9] Panos Constantopoulos, Matthias Jarke, John Mylopoulos and Yannis Vassiliou, "The Software Information Base: A Server for Reuse," *The VLDB Journal* (to appear).

[10] Valeria de Antonellis, et al., "Ithaca Object-Oriented Methodology Manual," ITHACA Report ITHACA.POLIMI-UDUNIV.E.8.6, Politecnico di Milano, 1992.

[11] Premkumar Devanbu, Ronald J. Brachman, Peter G. Selfridge and Bruce W. Ballard, "LaSSIE: A Knowledge-Based Software Information System," *Communications of the ACM*, vol. 34, no. 5, May 1991, pp. 34–49.

[12] Martin Dörr and Eleni Petra, "Classifying C++ Reusable Components," ITHACA Report ITHACA.FORTH.94.SIB.#2, Institute of Computer Science, Foundation of Research and Technology - Hellas, Jan. 1994.

[13] Pankaj Garg and Walt Scacchi, "On Designing Intelligent Hypertext Systems for Information Management in Software Engineering," *DIF, Proceedings Hypertext '87*, Nov. 1987, pp. 409–431.

[14] Simon Gibbs, Dennis Tsichritzis, Eduardo Casais, Oscar Nierstrasz and Xavier Pintado, "Class Management for Software Communities," *Communications of the ACM*, vol. 33, no. 9, Sept. 1990, pp. 90–103.

[15] Adele Goldberg, *Smalltalk-80: The Interactive Programming Environment*, Addison-Wesley, Reading, Mass., 1984.

[16] T. Hopking, C. Phillips, *Numerical Methods in Practice: Using the NAG Library*, Addison-Wesley, Reading, Mass., 1988.

[17] E. A. Karlsson, S. Sorumgard and E. Tryggeseth, "Classification of Object-Oriented Components for Reuse," *Proceedings TOOLS 7*, Dortmund, 1992.

[18] Charles W. Krueger, "Software Reuse," *ACM Computing Surveys*, vol.24, no.2, June 1992, pp. 131–183.

[19] Colin Low, "A Shared, Persistent Object Store," *Proceedings ECOOP'88*, Oslo, Aug. 1988, pp. 390–410.

[20] Bertrand Meyer, *Eiffel: the Libraries*, Prentice Hall, New York, 1990.

[21] John Mylopoulos, Alex Borgida, Matthias Jarke and Manolis Koubarakis, "Telos: Representing Knowledge About Information Systems," *ACM Transactions on Information Systems*, vol. 8, no. 4, Oct. 1990, pp. 325–362.

[22] P. Paul, "Classification of Software Components for Reuse," SIEMENS Technical Report, July 1992.

[23] Ruben Prieto-Diaz and Peter Freeman, "Classifying Software for Reusability," *IEEE Software*, vol. 4, no. 1, Jan.1987, pp.6–16.

[24] Ruben Prieto-Diaz, "Implementing Faceted Classification for Software Reuse," *Communications of the ACM*, vol. 34, no. 5, May 1991, pp. 88–97.

[25] Sarada R. Ranganathan, "Prolegomena to Library Classification," *Garden City Press*, Letchworth, Hertfordshire, 1957.

[26] Geoffrey Robinson, "UDC: A Brief Introduction," Technical Report, International Federation of Documentation, 1979.

[27] Robert W. Schwanke, "An Intelligent Tool for Re-Engineering Software Modularity," *Proceedings International Software Engineering Conference*, Austin, Tex., 1991, pp. 83–92.

[28] L.S. Sorumgard, G. Sindre and F. Stokke, "Experiences from Application of a Faceted Classification Scheme," *Proceedings 2nd International Workshop on Software Reusability 1993 (REUSE'93)*, Lucca, March 1993.

[29] George Spanoudakis and Panos Constantopoulos, "Similarity for Analogical Software Reuse: A Computational Model," *Proceedings European Conference on Artificial Intelligence*, Amsterdam, Aug. 1994.

[30] E. Svenonius, "Design of Controlled Vocabularies," *Encyclopedia of Library and Information Science*, Marcel Dekker, New York, 1989

[31] S. Thunem and G. Sindre, "Development With and for Reuse: Guidelines from the REBOOT Project," *Proceedings ERCIM Workshop on Methods and Tools for Software Reuse*, Heraklion, Crete, Oct. 1992, pp. 2–16.

[32] Amos Tversky, "Features of Similarity," *Psychological Review*, July 1977.

[33] Costis Vezerides, "The Organization of a Software Information Base for Software Reuse by a Community of Programmers," Master's Thesis, Department of Computer Science, University of Crete, May 1992.

[34] Peter Wegner, "The Object-Oriented Classification Paradigm," in Research Directions in Object-Oriented Programming, ed. Bruce Schriver and Peter Wegner, MIT Press, Cambridge, Mass., 1987.

Chapter 8
Managing Class Evolution in Object-Oriented Systems

Eduardo Casais

Abstract Software components developed with an object-oriented language undergo considerable reprogramming before they become reusable for a wide range of applications or domains. Tools and methodologies are therefore needed to cope with the complexity of designing, updating and reorganizing class collections. We present a typology of techniques for controlling change in object-oriented systems, illustrate their functionality with selected examples and discuss their advantages and limitations.

8.1 Object Design and Redesign

8.1.1 The Problem

Nowadays, it is generally assumed that the mechanisms provided by object-oriented languages — namely classification, encapsulation, inheritance and delayed binding — together with a comprehensive set of interactive programming tools, provide the basic functionality required for the large-scale production of highly reusable software components. However, software developers working with an object-oriented system are frequently led to modify extensively or even to reprogram supposedly reusable classes so that they fully suit their needs. This problem has been documented during the design of the Eiffel [31] and Smalltalk [21] hierarchies, the construction of user interfaces [20], the development of libraries for VLSI-design algorithms [2], and the development of object-oriented frameworks for operating systems [23].

The first difficulty with object-oriented development is achieving a correct initial modelling of an application domain. Because of the variety of mechanisms provided by object-oriented languages, the best choice for representing a real-world entity in terms of classes is not always readily apparent. The problem is compounded by the versatility of the inheritance mechanism, which can serve to denote specialization relationships, to enforce typing constraints, or to share implementations. Inadequate inheritance structures, missing abstractions in a hierarchy, overly specialized components or deficient object modelling may seriously impair the reusability of a class collection. Such defects must be eliminated through an evolutionary process to improve the robustness and the reusability of a library [20][22].

Even when a class collection embodies stable abstractions that have been reused successfully a number of times, repeated reorganizations of the library may still be unavoidable. Paradoxically, the high degree of reusability of a library may cause it to undergo major reorganizations when developers attempting to take advantage of its functionality stretch its range of application to new domains, thus imposing additional constraints on the library and invalidating the assumptions that drove its original design.

Software reuse also raises complex integration issues when teams of programmers share classes that do not originate from a common, compatible hierarchy. Classes may require significant adaptations, like reassigning inheritance dependencies or renaming properties, to be exchanged between different environments.

8.1.2 The Solutions

Among the approaches that have been proposed in recent years to control evolution in object-oriented systems, we identify the following general categories:
- *Tailoring* consists in slightly adapting class definitions when they do not lead to easy subclassing. Most object-oriented languages provide built-in constructs for making limited adjustments on class hierarchies.
- *Surgery*. Every possible change to a class can be defined in terms of specific, primitive update operations. Maintaining the consistency of a class hierarchy requires that the consequences of applying these primitives be precisely determined.
- *Versioning* enables teams of programmers to record the history of class modifications during the design process, to control the creation and dissemination of software components, and to coordinate the modelling of variants in complex application domains.
- *Reorganization* of a class library is needed after significant changes are made on it, like the introduction or the suppression of classes. Reorganization procedures use information on "good" library structures to discover imperfections in a hierarchy and to suggest alternative designs.

A second problem, related to class evolution, is that instances must be updated after their representation is modified. Restarting a program and discarding existing instances is not always feasible, since objects may be involved in running applications and may contain useful, long-lived information. This is especially true for environments implementing persistent objects. We consider in detail three techniques to tackle this issue:

- *Change avoidance* consists in preventing any impact from class modifications on existing instances, for example by restricting the kind of changes brought to classes.
- *Conversion* physically transforms objects affected by a class change so that they conform to their new class definition.
- *Filtering* hides the differences between objects belonging to several variants of the same class by encapsulating instances with an additional software layer that extends their normal properties.

The remainder of the chapter explains the principles behind these approaches, referring when appropriate to the research prototypes or industrial products that implement them, and illustrating their functionality with simple examples.

8.2 Class Tailoring

8.2.1 Issues

Quite often, object-oriented programming does not follow the ideal scenario where superclasses, extended with additional attributes, naturally give rise to new object descriptions. Inherited variables and methods do not necessarily satisfy all the constraints which need to be enforced in specialized subclasses [9]. Typically, one prefers an optimized implementation of a method to the general and inefficient algorithm defined in a superclass. Similarly, a variable with a restricted range may be more appropriate than one admitting any value. Tailoring mechanisms alleviate these problems by allowing the programmer to replace unwanted characteristics from standard classes with properties better suited to new applications.

8.2.2 Language Mechanisms

Object-oriented languages have always provided simple constructs for tailoring classes. We present here an overview of the tailoring mechanisms provided by the Eiffel language [30]. Similar mechanisms are available in many other programming languages.
- *Renaming* is the simplest way to effectively modify a class definition. Renamed variables and methods can no longer be referred to by their previous identifier, but they keep all their remaining properties, like their type or their argument list.
- *Redefinition* enables the programmer to actually alter the implementation of attributes. The body of a method may be replaced with a different implementation; a special undefine clause in Eiffel 3 allows the programmer to turn an inherited method into a deferred definition in a subclass. Eiffel also allows the type of inherited variables, parameters and function results to be redeclared, provided the new type is compatible with the old one. Finally, the pre- and post-conditions of a method may

be redefined, as long as the new pre-condition (or the new post-condition) is weaker (or stronger) than the original one.
- *Interfaces* are not statically defined in Eiffel. An attribute declared as private in a superclass may be made accessible in a subclass; conversely, a previously visible attribute may be excluded from the subclass interface.

The following excerpt from the Eiffel 2.1 library illustrates the use of these various tailoring mechanisms. Notice the changes in class interfaces, the redefinition of the variable parent and the renaming and overriding of the operations for creating tree objects.

```
--
--   Trees where each node has a fixed number of children (The number of children is
--   arbitrary but cannot be changed once the node has been created).
--
class FIXED_TREE [T]
    export
        start, finish, is_leaf, arity, child, value, change_value, node_value,
        change_node_value, first_child, last_child, position, parent, first, last,
        right_sibling, left_sibling, duplicate, is_root, islast, isfirst, go, go_to_child,
        delete_child, change_child, attach_to_parent, change_right, change_left,
        wipe_out
    inherit
        ...
    feature
        parent   :     FIXED_TREE [T];
        Create (n : INTEGER; v : T) is ...
            --  Create node with node_value v and n void children.
        end; -- Create
        ...
    end -- class FIXED_TREE

--
--   Binary trees.
--
class BINARY_TREE [T]
    export
        start, finish, is_leaf, arity, child, value, change_value, node_value,
        change_node_value, left, right, has_left, has_right, has_both, has_none,
        change_left_child, change_right_child
    inherit
        FIXED_TREE [T]
        rename
            Create as fixed_Create, first_child as left, last_child as right
        redefine
            parent
    feature
        parent   :     like Current;
        Create (v : T) is
            --  Create tree with single node of node value v
        do
            fixed_Create (2, v)
```

Class Tailoring

```
            ensure
                node_value = v;
                right.Void and left.Void
            end; -- Create
            ...
        end -- class BINARY_TREE [T]
```

Sometimes, adaptations cannot be limited to local class adjustments; global changes to the hierarchy are required. Objective-C provides a mechanism where a user-defined class can "pose" as any other class in the hierarchy [33]. When the "posing" class is installed in the system, it shadows the original definition. Objects depending on the "posed" class, whether by inheritance or by instantiation, do not have to be changed; the method dispatching scheme guarantees that a message sent to an object of the posed class actually results in invoking a procedure in a posing object. The posing class may override any method of the posed class and define additional operations; it has access to all original, now shadowed, properties.

8.2.3 Evaluation

Tailoring techniques are useful in performing small adjustments on a class collection. The overriding of inherited attributes enables the programmer to escape from a rigid inheritance structure that is not always well-suited to application modelling. It facilitates the handling of exceptions locally and does not require the factoring of common properties into numerous intermediate classes. Tailoring mechanisms correspond to constructs of object-oriented languages; consequently, they can be implemented efficiently within compilers.

On the other hand, overreliance on tailoring may quickly lead to incomprehensible structures overloaded with special cases, which are, as far as persistent object-oriented systems are concerned, difficult to manage efficiently with current database technology. Introducing exceptions in a hierarchy destroys its specialization structure and obscures the dependencies between classes since a property cannot be assumed to hold in every object derived from a particular definition. Renaming and interface redeclaration may completely break down the standard type relations between classes. When signature compatibility is not respected, or when the semantics of a method can be radically altered, polymorphism becomes impossible; an instance of a class may no longer be used where an instance of a superclass is allowed. Changing attribute representations also cancels the benefits of code sharing provided by inheritance.

If tailoring is allowed, one must be wary of developing a collection of disorganized classes. Exceptions should not only be accommodated, but also integrated into the type hierarchy when they become too numerous to be considered as special cases [10]. Unfortunately, the techniques we have described in this section do not really help detect design flaws in object descriptions.

8.3 Class Surgery

8.3.1 Issues

Whenever changes are brought to the modelling of an application domain, corresponding modifications must be applied to the classes representing real-world concepts. These operations disturb a class hierarchy much more profoundly than tailoring: instead of overriding some inherited properties when new subclasses are defined, the structure of existing classes themselves must be revised. Because of the multiple connections between class descriptions, care has to be taken so that the consistency of the hierarchy is guaranteed.

This problem also arises in the area of object-oriented databases, where it has been extensively investigated [3][4][27][32][35]. There, the available methods determine the consequences of class changes on other definitions and on existing instances, as well, so that possible integrity violations can be avoided. These methods can be broken down into a number of steps:

1. The first step consists of determining a set of integrity constraints that a class collection must satisfy. For example, all instance variables should bear distinct names, no loops are allowed in the hierarchy, and so on.

2. A taxonomy of all possible updates is then established. These changes concern the structure of classes, like "add a method", or "rename a variable"; they may also refer to the hierarchy as whole, as with "delete a class" or "add a superclass to a class".

3. For each of these update categories, a precise characterization of its effects on the class hierarchy is given and the conditions for its application are analyzed. In general, additional reconfiguration procedures have to be applied in order to preserve schema invariants. It is for example illegal to delete an attribute from a class C if this attribute is really inherited from a superclass of C. If the attribute can be deleted, it must also be recursively dropped from all subclasses of C.

4. Finally, the effects of schema changes are reflected on the persistent store; instances belonging to modified classes are converted to conform to their new description.

We base our discussion on class surgery mainly on the research performed around the object-oriented database systems GemStone, ORION, O_2 and OTGen, although evolutionary capabilities based on this technique have been proposed for many other systems. We defer the description of instance conversion techniques to the section on change propagation.

8.3.2 Schema Invariants

Every class collection contains a number of integrity constraints that must be maintained across schema changes. These constraints, generally called schema invariants in the literature, impose a certain structure on class definitions and on the inheritance graph.

Class Surgery

- *Representation invariant.* This constraint states that the properties of an object (attributes, storage format, etc.) must reflect those defined by its class.
- *Inheritance graph invariant.* The structure deriving from inheritance dependencies is restricted to form a connected, directed acyclic graph (so that classes may not recursively inherit from themselves), possibly restricted to be a tree, and having as root a special predefined class usually called OBJECT.
- *Distinct name invariant.* All classes, methods and variables must be distinguished by a unique name.
- *Full inheritance invariant.* A class inherits all attributes from its superclasses, except those that it explicitly redefines. Naming conflicts occurring because of multiple inheritance are resolved manually, or by applying some default precedence scheme.
- *Distinct origin invariant.* No repeated inheritance is admissible in ORION and O_2: an attribute inherited several times via different paths appears only once in a class representation.
- *Type compatibility invariant.* The type of a variable (or of a method argument) redefined in a subclass must be consistent with its domain as specified in the superclass. In all systems this means that the new type must be a subclass of the original one.
- *Type variable invariant.* The type of each instance variable must correspond to a class in the hierarchy.
- *Reference consistency invariants.* GemStone guarantees that there are no dangling references to objects in the database; instances can only be deleted when they are no longer accessible. OTGen requires that two references to the same object before modification also point to the same entity after modification.

Schema invariants supported by four object-oriented database systems are summarized in table 8.1.

8.3.3 Primitives for Class Evolution

Updates to a schema are assigned to a relevant category in a predetermined taxonomy. Every definition affected by these modifications must then be adjusted. If the invariant properties of the inheritance hierarchy cannot be preserved, the transformation of the class structure is rejected. Schema evolution taxonomies are compared in table 8.2.

- *The insertion of an attribute*, whether it is a variable or a method, is an operation that must be propagated to all subclasses of the class where it is initially applied, in order to preserve the full inheritance invariant. When a naming or a type compatibility conflict occurs, or when the signature of the new method does not match the signature of other methods with the same name related to it via inheritance, one either disallows the operation (as in O_2 and GemStone), or resorts to conflict resolution rules. In all systems, instances of all modified schemas are assigned an initial value for their additional variables that is either specified by the user or the special nil value.

Schema invariants	GemStone	O_2	ORION	OTGen
Representation	✓			
Inheritance graph	✓	✓	✓	✓
Distinct name		✓	✓	✓
Full inheritance	✓	✓	✓	✓
Distinct origin		✓	✓	
Type compatibility	✓	✓	✓	✓
Type variable				✓
Reference consistency	✓			✓

Table 8.1 *Schema invariants of four object-oriented database systems. Some constraints (like the representation invariant) are implicit in most models.*

- *Deleting an attribute* is allowed only if the variable or method is not inherited. Because of the full inheritance and representation invariants, the attribute must also be dropped from all subclasses of the definition where it is originally deleted. If a subclass, or the class itself, inherits another variable or a method with the same name through another inheritance path, this new attribute replaces the deleted one. Of course, all instances lose their values for deleted attributes. O_2 forbids the suppression of attributes if the operation results in naming conflicts or in type mismatches with other attributes.
- *Attribute renaming* is forbidden if the operation gives rise to ambiguities in the class or in its subclasses, or, in GemStone, if the attribute is inherited.
- The *type* of a variable (or of a method argument) can rarely be arbitrarily modified because of the subtype relations imposed by the compatibility invariant. In ORION and GemStone, the domain of a variable can be generalized. GemStone also allows a variable to be specialized, except if the new domain causes a compatibility violation with a redefinition in a subclass. Operations that are neither specializations nor generalizations are not supported; moreover, type changes are not propagated to subclasses. Instances violating new type constraints have their variables reset to nil.
- Properties like the default value of a variable or the body of a method can also be modified. Changing the origin of an attribute is an operation supported only in ORION. It serves to override default inheritance precedence rules and is logically handled as a suppression followed by the insertion of an attribute. In addition, ORION provides operations to update shared variables and special aggregation links.
- *Adding a class* to an existing hierarchy is a fundamental operation for object-oriented programming, and, as such, it appears in all systems examined here. Connecting a

Scope of change	GemStone	O_2	ORION
Instance variables			
add a variable	✓	✓	✓
remove a variable	✓	✓	✓
rename a variable	✓	✓	✓
redefine the type of a variable	✓	✓	✓
change the inheritance origin			✓
change the default value			✓
modify other kinds of variables			✓
Methods			
add a method		✓	✓
remove a method		✓	✓
rename a method		✓	✓
redefine the signature		✓	
change the code		✓	✓
change the inheritance origin			✓
Classes			
add a class	✓	✓	✓
remove a class	✓	✓	✓
rename a class		✓	✓
modify other class properties	✓		
Inheritance links			
add a superclass to a class		✓	✓
remove a superclass		✓	✓
change superclass precedence			✓

Table 8.2 *A comparison of schema evolution taxonomies.*

new class to the leaves of a hierarchy is trivial — possible conflicts caused by multiple inheritance are solved with standard precedence rules. GemStone allows for inserting a class in the middle of an inheritance graph, provided the new class does not initially define any property: this basic template may be subsequently augmented by applying the attribute manipulation primitives described in the preceding pages. With O_2, a new class may be connected to only one superclass and one subclass initially. The definition must specify how inherited attributes are superseded, and these redeclarations must comply with subtyping compatibility rules.

- *Removing a class* causes inheritance links to be reassigned from the class's superclasses to its subclasses. All instance variables that have the deleted class as their type are assigned the suppressed class's superclass as their new domain. GemStone assumes that a class which is being discarded no longer defines any property and that no associated instances exist in the database. O_2 forbids class deletion if it results in dangling references in other definitions, if instances belonging to the class still exist, or if the deletion leaves the inheritance graph disconnected.
- *Renaming a class* is allowed only if the new identifier is unique among all class names in the inheritance hierarchy. As with attributes, each object model may define supplementary class properties, such as the indexable classes in GemStone, and their corresponding manipulation primitives.
- *Adding a superclass* to a schema is illegal if the inheritance graph invariant cannot be preserved. In particular, no circuits may be introduced in a hierarchy. The consequences of this operation are analogous to those of introducing attributes in a class.
- *The deletion of a class S* from the list of superclasses of a class C must not leave the inheritance graph disconnected. O_2 provides a parameterized modification primitive that enables the programmer to choose where to link a class that has become completely disconnected from the inheritance graph (by default, it is connected to OBJECT). One may also specify whether the attributes acquired through the suppressed inheritance link are preserved and copied to the definition of C. In most other systems, if S is the unique superclass of C, inheritance links are reassigned to point from the immediate superclasses of S to C. In the other cases, C just loses one of its superclasses; no redirection of inheritance dependencies is performed. Of course, the properties of S no longer pertain to the representation of C, nor to those of its subclasses. The primitives for suppressing attributes from a class are applied to convert the definition of all classes and instances affected by this change.
- *Reordering inheritance dependencies* results in effects similar to those of changing the precedence of inherited attributes.

8.3.4 Completeness, Correctness and Complexity

Three issues have to be addressed to ensure that class surgery captures interesting capabilities:

- *Completeness*: does the set of proposed operations actually cover all possibilities for schema modifications?
- *Correctness*: do these operations really generate class structures that satisfy all integrity constraints?

- *Complexity*: is it possible to detect violations of schema invariants and subsequently regenerate a schema conforming to these invariants in an efficient way?

The first two problems have been studied in the context of the ORION methodology, where it has been demonstrated that a subset of its class transformation primitives exhibits the desired qualities of completeness and, partially, of correctness. In contrast, the Gem-Stone approach does not strive for completeness; only meaningful operations that can be implemented without undue restrictions or loss of performance are provided. An interesting result is provided by the O_2 approach, where it is shown that although a set of basic update operations may be complete at the schema level (i.e. all changes to a class hierarchy can be derived from a composition of these essential operations), this same set may not be complete at the instance level, when changes are carried out on objects and not on classes. For example, renaming an attribute is equivalent to deleting the attribute and then reintroducing it with its new name; if the same sequence of operations is applied to a variable of an object, the information stored in the attribute is lost.

Ensuring correctness of class changes is much more difficult than it appears at first sight. Since a method implementation may depend on other methods and variables, one cannot consider the deletion of one attribute in isolation. This operation may have far-reaching consequences if an attribute is excluded from a class interface. Similarly, introducing a new method in a class may raise problems because the code of the method may refer to attributes that are not yet present in the class definition and because of implicit changes in the scope of attributes. If the method supersedes an inherited routine, subclasses referring to the previous method may become invalid. Not surprisingly, maintaining behavioural consistency across schema changes is an undecidable problem [39]. Dataflow analysis techniques, like those that are used by some compilers to check for type violations in object-oriented programs, can help detect the parts of the code that become unsafe because of schema updates, but they are typically pessimistic and might reject legal programs as incorrect [14]. Enriching the set of schema invariants to detect more (semantical) inconsistencies requires careful selection to avoid turning an efficient test procedure for constraint satisfiability into an NP, or even an undecidable problem [26][39]. As a consequence, all aforementioned systems capture relatively simple structural constraints with their schema invariants and give little support to update methods upon class alterations [41].

8.3.5 Evaluation

Decomposing all class modifications into update primitives and determining the consequences of these operations has several advantages. During class design, this approach helps developers detect the implications of their actions on the class collection and maintain consistency within class specifications. During application development, it guides the propagation of schema changes to individual instances. For example, renaming an instance variable, changing its type or specifying a new default value usually has no impact on an application using the modified class. Introducing or discarding attributes (variables or methods), on the other hand, generally leads to changes in programs and requires the reorganization of the persistent store — although the conversion procedure can be deferred in some situations.

Depending on its modelling capabilities and on the integrity constraints, an object-oriented programming environment may provide different forms of class surgery. It is easy to envision a system where class definitions are first retrieved with a class browser and then modified with a structured editor where each editing operation corresponds to a schema manipulation primitive like those of ORION or GemStone [32]. Such an environment would nevertheless fall short of providing fully adequate support for the design and evolution processes. Class surgery forms a solid and rigorous framework for defining "well-formed" class modifications. In this respect, it improves considerably over uncontrolled manipulations of class hierarchies that are more or less the rule with current object-oriented programming environments. But, it limits its scope to local, primitive kinds of class evolution. It gives no guidance as to when the modifications should be performed and does not deal with the global management of multiple, successive class changes carried out during software development.

8.4 Class Versioning

8.4.1 Issues

Ensuring that class modifications are consistent is not enough; they must also be carried out in a disciplined fashion. This is of utmost importance in environments where a number of programmers collectively reuse and adapt classes developed by their peers made available in a shared repository of software components. The early experiences with the Smalltalk system demonstrated that the lack of a proper methodology for controlling the extensions and alterations brought to the standard class library quickly resulted in a disastrous situation. The incompatibilities between variants of the same class hierarchy were sufficient to hinder the further exchange of software, or at least to severely reduce its portability.

In the case of single-user environments, the exploratory way of programming advocated by the proponents of the object-oriented approach requires some support so that software developers may correct their mistakes by reverting to a previous stable class configuration. When experimenting with several variants of the same class, to test the efficiency of different algorithms, for example, care has to be taken to avoid mixing up class definitions and dependencies.

Because *adhoc* techniques do not scale well for large, distributed programming environments, current approaches favour a structured organization of software development and a tighter control of evolution based on class versioning. Versioning basically consists in checkpointing successive and in principle consistent states of a class structure. The creation and manipulation of versions raises complex issues:

Class Versioning

- How is version management organized with respect to software development?
- How does one distinguish between different versions of the same class?
- What are the circumstances that justify the creation of new versions, and how is this operation carried out?
- What can be done to handle the relations between different and perhaps incompatible versions?

8.4.2 The Organization of Version Management

An environment for version management is divided into several distinct working spaces, each one providing a specific set of privileges and capabilities for manipulating different kinds of versions [15][24]. Three such domains are generally recognized in the literature:
- A private working space supports the development activities of one programmer. The information stored in the programmer's private environment, in particular the software components he or she is currently designing or modifying, is not accessible to other users.
- All classes and data produced during a project are stored in a corresponding domain that is placed under the responsibility of a project administrator. They are made available to all people cooperating in the project, but remain hidden from other users, since they cannot yet be considered as tested and validated.
- A public domain contains all released classes from all projects, as well as data on their status. This information is visible to all users of the system.

It is natural to associate one kind of version with each working space:
- Released versions appear in the public domain. They are considered immutable and can therefore neither be updated nor deleted, although they may be copied and give rise to new transient versions.
- Working versions exist in project domains and possibly private domains. They are considered stable and cannot be modified, but they can be deleted by their owner, i.e. the project administrator or the user of a private domain. Working versions are promoted to released versions when they are installed in the public repository; they may give rise to new transient versions.
- A transient version is derived from any other kind of version. It belongs to the user who created it and it is stored in his or her private domain. Transient versions can be updated, deleted and promoted to working versions.

The principal characteristics of version types are summarized in table 8.3.

A typical scenario begins when a project is set up to build a new application. The programmers engaged in the development, copy from the public repository class definitions they want to reuse or modify for the project. These definitions are added to their private environments as transient versions. Each programmer individually updates these classes and perhaps creates other definitions (via usual subclassing techniques) in the domain as

Characteristics of version types	Transient	Working	Released
Location			
public domain			✓
project domain		✓	
private domain	✓	✓	
Admissible operations			
update	✓		
delete	✓	✓	
Origin			
from a transient version by	derivation	promotion	
from a working version by	derivation		promotion
from a released version by	derivation		

Table 8.3 *Principal characteristics of version types. Some systems consider only two kinds of versions (transient and released) and two levels of domains (private and public) for managing their visibility.*

additional transient versions. In order to try different designs for the same class, or to save the result of the programming activity, programmers may derive new transient versions from those they is currently working on, while simultaneously promoting the latter to working versions. When a programmer achieves a satisfactory design for a software component, he or she installs it as a working version in the project domain. Of course, these working versions can subsequently be copied by colleagues and give rise to new transient versions in their respective environments. Once software components have reached a good stage of maturity in terms of reliability and design stability, they are released by the project administrator and made publicly available in the central repository.

Since all operations for version derivation and freezing are done concurrently, careful algorithms are required to ensure that the system remains consistent. Fortunately, all updates are applied to local, transient objects, and not directly to global, shared definitions. As a consequence, concurrency control does not have to be as elaborate as traditional database transaction mechanisms and can use simpler checkin/checkout or optimistic locking techniques.

Class Versioning 215

8.4.3 Version Identification

Class identity is an essential problem to deal with. It is no longer enough to refer to a software component by its name, since it might correspond to multiple variants of the same class. An additional version number, and possibly a domain name, must be provided to identify a component unambiguously [24]. When the version number is absent from a reference, a default class is assumed. Typical choices for resolving the dynamic binding of version references include:

- The very first version of the class referred to.
- Its most recent version. The idea behind this decision is that this version can be considered the most up-to-date definition of a class. This is a good solution to bind version references in interactive queries in object-oriented databases.
- Its most recent version at the time the component which made the reference was created. This is the preferred option for dealing with dynamic references in class definitions.
- A default class definition specified by the administrator in charge of the domain. This definition, called a generic version, can be coerced to be any element in a version derivation history.

The default version is first searched for in the domain where the reference is initially discovered to be unresolved; the hierarchy of domains is then inspected upward until the appropriate definition is found. Thus, to bind an incomplete reference to a class made in a project domain (i.e. a reference consisting only in the class name, without additional information), the system first examines the class hierarchy in the current domain; if this domain does not contain the class definition referred to, the search proceeds in the public repository. No private domain is inspected, for stable versions are not allowed to refer to transient versions that could be in the process of being revised. Similarly, dynamic references to classes in the public domain cannot be resolved by looking for unreleased components in a project domain. Naturally, dynamic binding can be resolved at the level of a private domain for all classes pertaining to it.

If only the most recent version gives rise to new versions, there is in principle no need for a complex structure to keep track of the history of classes: their name and version number suffice to determine their relationship to each other. The situation where versioning is not sequential, i.e. where new versions derive from any previous version, requires that the system record a hierarchy of versions somewhat similar to the traditional class herarchy. When a version is copied or installed in a domain, the programmer decides where to connect it in the derivation hierarchy. AVANCE provides an operation to merge several versions of the same class. With this scheme, the derivation history takes the form of a directed acyclic graph [8].

The information on derivation dependencies is generally associated with the generic version of a class version set. Version management systems like IRIS and AVANCE implement a series of primitives for traversing and manipulating derivation graphs [5][8]. Programmers can thus retrieve the predecessors and the successors of a particular version;

obtain the first or the most recent version of a class on a particular derivation path; query their status (transient, released, date of creation, owner); determine which version was valid at a certain point in the past and bind a reference to it; freeze or derive new versions, etc.

The management of versions and related data obviously entails a significant storage and processing overhead. This is why in most systems one is required to explicitly indicate that classes are versionable by making them subclasses of a special class from which they inherit their properties of versions — that is often called Version, as in AVANCE and IRIS.

8.4.4 Versioning and Class Evolution

It is evidently impossible to delegate full responsibility to the system for determining when a transient version should be frozen and a new transient one created, or if a component should be released. Such actions must be based on design knowledge that is best mastered by the software developers themselves. Thus, the automatic generation of new versions triggered by update operations on object definitions is a scheme that has found limited application in practice.

Another difficulty arises because of the superimposition of versioning on the inheritance graph. For example, when creating a new variant for a class should one derive new versions for the entire tree of subclasses attached to it as well? A careful analysis of the differences between two successive versions of the same class gives some directions for handling this problem [8].

- If the interface of a class is changed, then new versions should be created for all classes depending on it, whether by inheritance (i.e. its subclasses) or by delegation (i.e. classes containing variables whose type refers to the now modified definition).
- If only non-public parts are changed, like the methods visible only to subclasses (such methods are called "protected methods" in C++), the type of its variables, or its inheritance structure, then versioning can be limited to its existing subclasses.
- If only method implementations are changed, no new versions for other classes are required; this kind of change is purely internal and does not affect other definitions.

For reasons analogous to those exposed above, some approaches prefer to avoid introducing a possibly large number of new versions automatically and rely instead on a manual procedure for re-establishing the consistency of the inheritance hierarchy. The users whose programs reference the class that has been updated are simply notified of the change and warned that the references may be invalid. Two strategies are commonly adopted to do this: either a message is directly sent to the user, or the classes referencing the modified object definition are tagged as invalid. In the latter case, class version timestamps are frequently used to determine the validity of references [15]. Thus, a class should never have a "last modification" date that exceeds the "approved modification" date of the versions referring to it. When this situation occurs, the references to the class are considered inconsistent, since recent adaptations have been carried out on the component, but have not yet been acknowledged on its dependent classes. It is up to the programmer to determine the effects of the class changes on other definitions and to reset the approved revision timestamp to indicate that the references have become valid again.

Building consistent configurations of classes and instances, and maintaining compatibility between entities belonging to different versions is a major issue and an object-oriented system should provide support for dealing with this aspect of version management. Application developers may want to view objects instantiated from previous class versions as if they originated from the currently stable version, or they may want to prohibit objects from older versions from referring to instances of future variants. We describe in more detail how to achieve these effects in the section devoted to update propagation.

8.4.5 Evaluation

Versioning is an appealing approach for managing class development and evolution. Recording the history of class modifications during the design process has several benefits. It enables the programmer to try different paths when modelling complex application domains and it helps avoid confusion when groups of people are engaged in the production of a library of common, interdependent classes. Versioning also appears useful when keeping track of various implementations of the same component for different software environments and hardware platforms. Besides, the hierarchical decomposition of the programming environment into workspaces, the attribution of precise responsibilities to their administrators, and the possibilities afforded by this kind of organization (e.g. the separation of the long-term improvement of reusable components from the short-term development of new applications) are considered to be particularly valuable for increasing the quality and efficiency of object-oriented programming [38].

The main drawback of versioning techniques resides in the considerable overhead they impose on the development environment. Programmers have to navigate through two interconnected structures, the traditional inheritance hierarchy and the version derivation graph. They have to take into account a greater set of dependencies when designing a class. The system must store all information needed for representing versions and their reciprocal links, and implement notification. Moreover, methods for version management still lack some support for design tasks: at what point does a version stop being a variant of an existing class to become a completely different object definition?

In spite of their overhead, class and object versioning techniques have proved invaluable in important application domains like CAD/CAM, VLSI design and office information systems. They have therefore been integrated into several object-oriented environments, including Orwell [38], AVANCE [7], ORION [3] and IRIS [19].

8.5 Class Reorganization

8.5.1 Issues

The lessons drawn from the construction of collections of reusable classes have led to the formulation of some principles that serve to improve object-oriented libraries [22].

The first principle is to make sure that components are really polymorphic. This can be achieved in a number of ways:

- Adopt a uniform terminology for related classes and standardize the methods making up their interface [31].
- Eliminate code that explicitly checks the type of an object. Rather than introducing case statements to execute some actions on the basis of an object's class, one should invoke a standard message in the object and let it carry out the appropriate actions.
- Decrease the number of arguments in a method, either by splitting the method into several simpler procedures, or by creating a class to represent a group of arguments that often appear together. A method with a reduced number of parameters is more likely to bear a signature similar to some other method in a different class. Both methods may then be given the same name, thus increasing interface standardization.

A second set of rules aims to increase the degree of abstraction and generality of classes:

- Factorize behaviour common to several classes into a shared superclass. Introduce abstract classes (with deferred methods) if convenient, to avoid attribute redefinitions.
- Minimize the accesses to variables to reduce the dependency of methods on the internal class representation [29]. This can be achieved by resorting to special accessors instead of referring directly to variables.
- Ensure that inheritance links express clear semantic relationships such as specialization, or even better, relationships with known mathematical properties like conformance or imitation [40].

Finally, reorganizations should improve the modularization of functionality in a library:

- Split large classes into smaller, cohesive classes that are more resilient to change.
- Separate groups of methods that do not interact. Such sets of methods represent either totally independent behaviour or different views of the same object, which are perhaps better represented by distinct classes.
- Uncouple methods from global attributes or internal class properties by sending messages to parameters instead of to self or to instance variables.

These guidelines are very general; the problem is therefore to formulate these empirical rules rigorously and to make them amenable to a subsequent automation.

8.5.2 Refactoring

8.5.2.1 Issues and Techniques

Refactoring is an approach that extends basic class surgery primitives with advanced redesign mechanisms [23]. Refactoring is based on an object model that is specifically tailored to represent and manipulate the rich structure of components developed with an object-oriented programming language. The schema invariants of class surgery are extended with additional constraints for preserving behaviour, and the preconditions for modification operations are made more precise or more restrictive to avoid introducing behaviour and referential inconsistencies in a class collection. The approach proposed in [34] is intended to support refactoring specifically for C++ libraries. Four important operations are discussed in detail.

- Distributing the functionality of a class over multiple subclasses by splitting methods along conditional statements. Let us consider a hypothetical class that checks the rights of users to access a system during weekends and normal working days:

```
class ACCESS-CONTROL
    methods
        CheckPrivileges
            begin
                -- some general code ...
                if date = Sunday or date = Saturday then
                    -- restricted access on week-ends ...
                else
                    -- usual checks during normal working days ...
                end-if
            end CheckPrivileges; ...
    end;
```

ACCESS-CONTROL is specialized in as many classes as there are branches in its CheckPrivileges method; CheckPrivileges is itself decomposed so that, in each subclass, it contains only the code corresponding to one branch of the original conditional statement. The common part of all CheckPrivileges variants is left in ACCESS-CONTROL.

```
class ACCESS-CONTROL
    methods
        CheckPrivileges
            begin
                -- some general code ...
            end CheckPrivileges; ...
    end;
class CONTROL-WEEK-END
    inherit ACCESS-CONTROL;
    methods
        CheckPrivileges
            begin
                super.CheckPrivileges;
```

```
                        -- restricted access on week-ends ...
                    end CheckPrivileges; ...
            end;
        class CONTROL-WORKING-DAYS
            inherit ACCESS-CONTROL;
            methods
                CheckPrivileges
                    begin
                        super.CheckPrivileges;
                        -- usual checks during normal working days ...
                    end CheckPrivileges;
            end;
```

- Creating an abstract superclass. This operation analyses two classes, extracts their common properties, which are placed in a new component, and then makes both initial classes subclasses of the new definition. The extraction of similarities between two classes is not performed automatically and relies on heuristics to detect common structures in method signatures and implementations. Additional renaming of variables and methods, reordering of method parameters and transformations of method implementations may be carried out to achieve a satisfactory result. However, contrary to the incremental reorganization algorithm described in section 8.5.4.3, refactoring does not propagate through the inheritance graph.
- Transforming an inheritance relation into a part-of relation. The following example shows a class SYMBOL-TABLE that inherits functionality from HASH-TABLE.

```
        class HASH-TABLE
            methods
                Insert ...
                Delete ...
        end;
        class SYMBOL-TABLE
            inherit HASH-TABLE; ...
        end;
```

Rather than being a subclass of HASH-TABLE, SYMBOL-TABLE can refer to an instance of HASH-TABLE via a part-of relation. This requires severing the inheritance link between both classes, introducing a variable of type HASH-TABLE in SYMBOL-TABLE, and adding a series of procedures in SYMBOL-TABLE for delegating the invocations of methods previously inherited from HASH-TABLE to this new variable. In our simplified example, the refactoring does not change the superclass. In general, it may be necessary to introduce special operations in the superclass to encapsulate accesses to its variables, and to change the methods declared in the subclass so that they manipulate these variables through these operations.

```
        class SYMBOL-TABLE
            variables
                store           :       HASH-TABLE; ...
            methods
                Insert (...)
```

Class Reorganization 221

```
            begin
                store.Insert (...);
            end Insert;
        Delete (...)
            begin
                store.Delete (...);
            end Delete; ...
    end;
```

- Reshuffling attributes among classes. This operation is intended to improve the design of classes representing aggregations, where a component of an aggregation can only belong to or be referred to by one object. Redistributing variables denoting aggregation elements in a behaviour-preserving way is feasible only when several strong conditions on referencing patterns are satisfied. References to the migrated variables are updated or replaced with invocations to appropriate accessors.

8.5.2.2 Evaluation

Refactoring is one of the most interesting approaches for providing software developers with high-level, intuitive operations supporting complex redesign activities. Refactoring embodies some of the empirical guidelines derived from actual experience with class evolution; it would therefore be appealing to integrate such a toolkit of operations in an editing and browsing environment. This approach is not without limitations though; the decision to carry out specific refactorings, the optimization goals and the selection of the classes to modify are left entirely up to the programmer. Thus, refactoring exhibits the same shortcomings as class surgery. The automatic approaches discussed in the following sections are based on systematic strategies that are probably more adequate in the context of large, complex libraries. As with any other restructuring method, refactoring faces intractability problems when trying to achieve all possible transformations or to preserve behaviour. For example, all interesting situations where a method could be split among subclasses cannot be detected, and, in fact, the conditional expressions considered are only of a very elementary nature.

8.5.3 Restructuring Interattribute Dependencies

8.5.3.1 Issues

Avoiding unnecessary coupling between classes and reducing interattribute dependencies are two important prerequisites for well-designed objects. Two major issues have to be addressed:

- What are the inferior or "harmful" dependencies?
- How can unsafe expressions be automatically replaced with adequate constructs?

A possible solution to this problem has been proposed by Lieberherr *et al.* [29] under the name of "Law of Demeter", together with a small set of techniques for mechanically transforming object definitions so that they comply with this law [12].

8.5.3.2 The Law of Demeter

The Law of Demeter distinguishes three types of interattribute dependencies and three corresponding categories of relationships between class definitions:

- A class C_1 is an *acquaintance class* of method M in class C_2, if M invokes a method defined in C_1 and if C_1 does not correspond to the class of an argument of M, to the class of a variable of C_2, to C_2 itself, or to a superclass of the aforementioned classes.
- A class C_1 is a *preferred-acquaintance class* of method M in C_2, if C_1 corresponds to the class of an object directly created in M or to the class of a global variable used in M.
- A class C_1 is a *preferred-supplier class* of method M in C_2, if M invokes a method defined in C_1, and if C_1 corresponds to the class of a variable of C_2, or to the class of an argument of M, to C_2 itself, to a superclass of the aforementioned classes, or to a preferred-acquaintance class of M.

The "class form" of the law states that methods may only access entities belonging to their preferred-supplier classes. The "object form" of the law does not consider the classes a method depends on, but rather the objects this method sends messages to. In this context, a preferred-supplier object is an instance that is either a variable introduced by the class where the method is defined, or an argument passed to the method, or an object created by the method, or the pseudo-variable self (identifying the object executing the method). The "object form" of the law prohibits references to instances that are not preferred-suppliers of a method. In its *weak* version, the law considers the classes of inherited variables (or the variables themselves, in the "object form" of the law) as legitimate preferred-suppliers. The *strict* version does not consider the classes of inherited variables (or inherited variables) as legitimate preferred-suppliers.

8.5.3.3 Application and Examples

We illustrate the main reorganization aspects dealt with by the Demeter approach for a group of simple object descriptions [12][29]. Let us consider the following partial class definitions:

```
class LIBRARY
    variables
        Catalog              :    CATALOG; ...
    methods
        Search-book (title : STRING) returns LIST [BOOK]
            begin
                books-found    :    LIST [BOOK];
                books-found := Catalog.Microfiches.Search-book (title);
                books-found.Merge (Catalog.Optical-Disk.Search-book (title));
                return (books-found);
            end Search-book; ...
end;

class CATALOG
    variables
        Optical-Disk         :    CD-ROM;
```

```
            Microfiches        :    MICROFICHE; ...
    end;
class CD-ROM
    variables
        Book-References   :    FILE [BOOK]; ...
    methods
        Search-book (title : STRING) returns LIST [BOOK]
            begin
                book              :    BOOK;
                books-found       :    LIST [BOOK];
                books-found.New ();
                Book-References.First ();
                loop
                    exit when Book-References.End ();
                    book := Book-References.Current ();
                    if title.Equal (book.Title) then
                        books-found.Add (book)
                    end-if;
                    Book-References.Next ();
                end loop;
                return (books-found);
            end Search-book; ...
    end;
class MICROFICHE
    variables
        Book-References   :    FICHES [BOOK]; ...
    methods
        Search-book (title : STRING) returns LIST [BOOK] ...
    end;
class BOOK
    variables
        Title             :    STRING; ...
    end;
```

These definitions obviously do not conform to the law: the method Search-book in LIBRARY accesses internal components of Catalog (the attributes Microfiches and Optical-Disk); it sends messages to these variables and receives as a result objects that are neither components of LIBRARY nor instances of a preferred-supplier class of LIBRARY. We also note that the algorithm for retrieving all references stored on the optical disk manipulates the internal structure of books to find whether their title matches a specific search criterion.

It is clear that the details of scanning microfiche and CD-ROM files to find a particular reference should be delegated to the CATALOG class. This makes the querying methods of LIBRARY immune to alterations in the internal structure of the catalogue — for example the replacement of the microfiches with an additional CD-ROM file. In doing so, we have to take care that LIST [BOOK], the type of the result of methods Search-book in MICROFICHE and CD-ROM, is not a preferred-supplier of CATALOG. The introduction of the auxiliary method Merge-refs in CATALOG solves this problem and makes the dependency between classes CATALOG and LIST [BOOK] explicit. Finally, ensuring the proper encapsulation of

BOOK objects requires that their variables be manipulated through special-purpose accessors; CD-ROM is adjusted accordingly.

```
class LIBRARY
    variables
        Catalog              :    CATALOG; ...
    methods
        Search-book (title : STRING) returns LIST [BOOK]
            begin
                return (Catalog.Search-book (title));
            end Search-book; ...
end;

class CATALOG
    variables
        Microfiches          :    MICROFICHE;
        Optical-Disk         :    CD-ROM; ...
    methods
        Search-book (title : STRING) returns LIST [BOOK]
            begin
                return (self.Merge-refs (Microfiches.Search-book (title),
                                        Optical-Disk.Search-book (title)));
            end Search-book;
        Merge-refs (microfiche-refs : LIST [BOOK]; cd-rom-refs : LIST [BOOK])
            returns LIST [BOOK]
            begin
                return (microfiche-refs.Merge (cd-rom-refs));
            end Merge-refs; ...
end;

class CD-ROM
    variables
        Book-References      :    FILE [BOOK]; ...
    methods
        Search-book (title : STRING) returns LIST [BOOK]
            begin
                books-found      :    LIST [BOOK];
                books-found.New ();
                Book-References.First ();
                loop
                    exit when Book-References.End ();
                    if title.Equal (self.RefTitle (Book-References.Current ()))
                        then books-found.Add (Book-References.Current ());
                    end-if;
                    Book-References.Next ();
                end loop;
                return (books-found);
            end Search-Book;
        RefTitle (reference : BOOK) returns STRING
            begin
                return (reference.Get-Title);
```

```
                        end GetRefTitle; ...
            end;
        class BOOK
            variables
                Title           :       STRING; ...
            methods
                Get-Title returns STRING
                    begin
                        return (Title);
                    end Get-Title; ...
            end;
```

8.5.3.4 Evaluation
The Law of Demeter nicely captures some issues dealing with encapsulation and coupling; although a fully formal model that would mathematically justify its underlying assumptions is still lacking [36], its application to the design of modular class libraries has been found to be beneficial [29]. However, putting the Law of Demeter into practice raises several difficulties [36]. It cannot be completely enforced with languages, such as CLOS or Smalltalk, that allow expressions to be constructed dynamically and then executed at run-time. In general, the "class form" of the law does not seem to be fully effective for untyped languages; since objects are untyped, violations of the law cannot be discovered by a static inspection of the source code, but must be monitored during program execution.

As far as typed languages are concerned, applying the Demeter principles is not always straightforward either. First, there are some special cases where the spirit of the Law of Demeter is violated, although all the dependencies formally respect all the Demeter rules stated in section 8.5.3.2. Fortunately, such anomalies are rare and occur only in very contrived situations. More importantly, the law requires significant enhancements and reformulation to handle language peculiarities correctly; for example, translating the law of Demeter into equivalent terms for C++ is far from trivial, because of the hybrid model of this language and the need to take constructs like friend functions into account.

8.5.4 Restructuring Inheritance Hierarchies

8.5.4.1 Issues
A frequent problem during the design of inheritance hierarchies is that programmers overlook intermediate abstractions needed for establishing clean subclassing dependencies, and develop components too specialized to be effectively reusable. Several approaches have been proposed to automate the detection and correction of such defects in inheritance hierarchies. They are distinguished by the way they address a few fundamental issues:
- What is the scope of the reorganization applied to an inheritance graph?
- What are the criteria driving the reorganization?
- What properties are preserved across reorganizations?

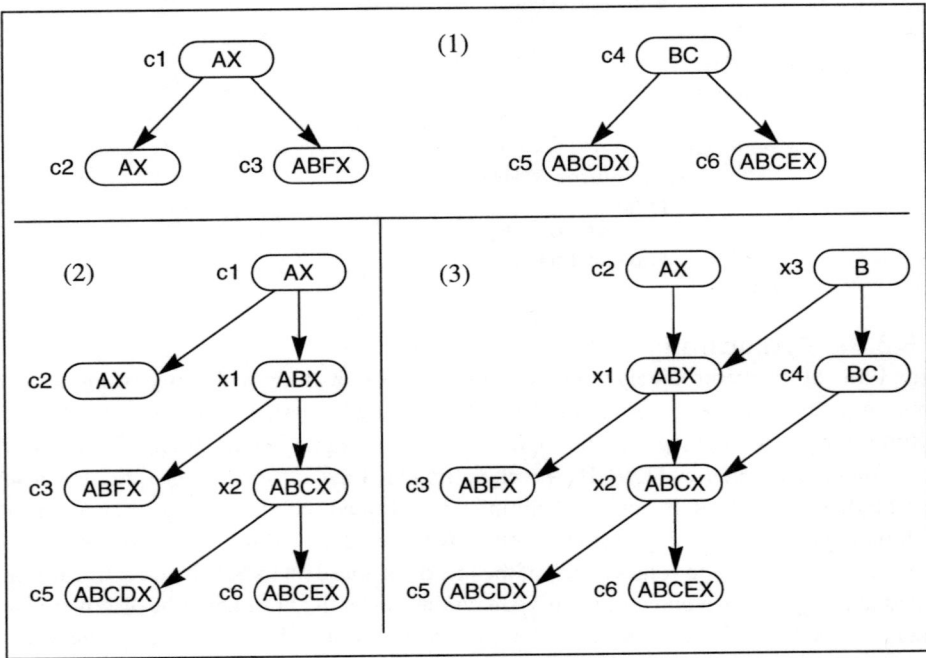

Figure 8.1 *Reorganizing a redundant, non-connected hierarchy (1); capital letters represent attributes. (2): after applying the Demeter algorithm; (3): after applying the algorithm described in [12]. Class c2 is the concrete counterpart of abstract class c1; similar definitions are merged in (3), but not in (2). Class c4 is preserved in (3), but considered as superfluous in (2).*

The differences between inheritance reorganization methods are best summarized by grouping these approaches into global and incremental reorganization techniques.

8.5.4.2 Global Reorganization

Global reorganization approaches produce optimal inheritance graphs, without attribute redundancy and with a minimum number of classes and inheritance links, from pre-existing hierarchies (figure 8.1). These techniques can be fully automated. They work globally, analyzing and recasting an entire class collection at a time.

The approach proposed in the context of the Demeter project is based on a formalism that distinguishes between abstract classes, which can be inherited but not instantiated, and concrete classes, which can be instantiated but cannot be used as superclasses. Classes correspond to the vertices in a graph. The edges of the graph denote either inheritance relationships between classes, or part-of relationships between classes and their (typed) attributes [28]. This model forms the basis for global reorganization algorithms whose goal is to optimize the structural characteristics of an inheritance graph (i.e. to minimize the

number of classes and relations in a library). Redefinitions and attribute structures are not taken into account. The formal properties of these algorithms have been investigated in detail [28]:
- Transforming a hierarchy to suppress redundant part-of edges, i.e. forcing classes to inherit common attributes from a shared superclass, is in P.
- Minimizing the overall number of edges is NP-complete. When the final hierarchy is actually a tree, efficient (polynomial) algorithms exist for optimizing the hierarchy.

A different method is based on an object model that allows classes to inherit from concrete superclasses [12]. The corresponding algorithm proceeds by flattening all class definitions present in a hierarchy, then factoring out common structures, relinking all class definitions through inheritance, and finally eliminating redundant inheritance links and auxiliary class definitions. Contrary to the Demeter approach, this algorithm does preserve all definitions that actually differ in the library before the reorganization, it takes redefinitions into account and it can be tailored to avoid repeated inheritance in the final hierarchy.

None of the global algorithms deal with interattribute dependencies or with the preservation of behavioural properties. Global algorithms do not always produce identical results because of their varying assumptions and goals — as is shown clearly in figure 8.1.

8.5.4.3 Incremental Reorganization

Adding a subclass is a major step in the development of an object-oriented library, warranting an evaluation, and possibly an improvement of the hierarchy. The evaluation can be restricted to the relationships between the new class and its superclasses, and the reorganization can be limited to the location where the new class is introduced. The incremental factorization algorithm proposed in [11] is driven by the analysis of redefinition patterns between a new class and its superclasses. It attempts to optimize the inheritance graph within reason while keeping the disturbances to the original library to a minimum. Behavioural properties can be maintained to a certain extent and classes present in the hierarchy before the reorganization are not deleted [12]. The algorithm transforms a hierarchy automatically to eliminate unwanted subclassing patterns, to pinpoint places requiring redesign and to discover missing abstractions. It can take into account renaming and structural transformations similar to those discussed in 8.5.2.

The incremental reorganization algorithm extracts the properties shared by several classes and isolates them in a new, common superclass. Figure 8.2 shows a fragment of the Eiffel library where class CIRCLE inherits from ELLIPSE. This subclassing operation is accompanied by a partial replacement of ELLIPSE's behaviour. Simultaneously, CIRCLE changes its superclass's interface in a way that corresponds neither to a restriction (which would be expected in a specialization relationship) nor to an extension (characteristic of subtyping relationships). A transformation of the hierarchy eliminates this unnatural subclassing pattern by inserting an intermediate definition containing the properties common to both CIRCLE and ELLIPSE, and by making these two classes subclasses of the new auxiliary node.

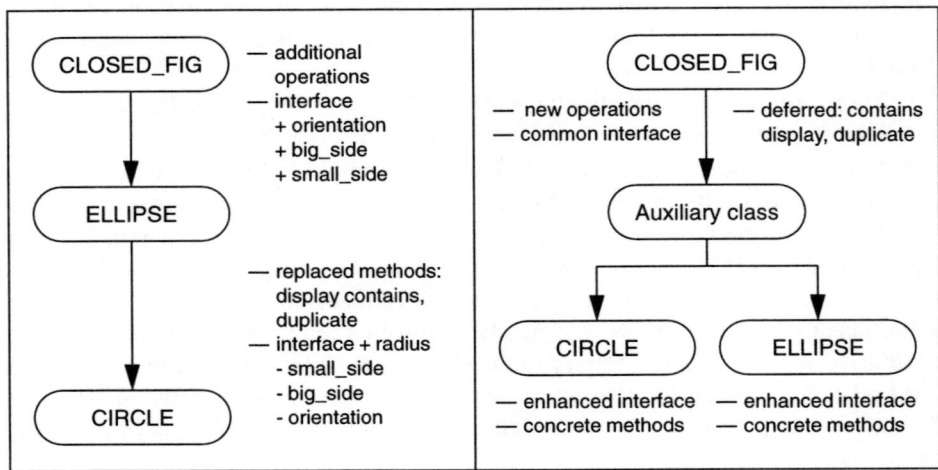

Figure 8.2 *Factorizing inheritance relationships.*

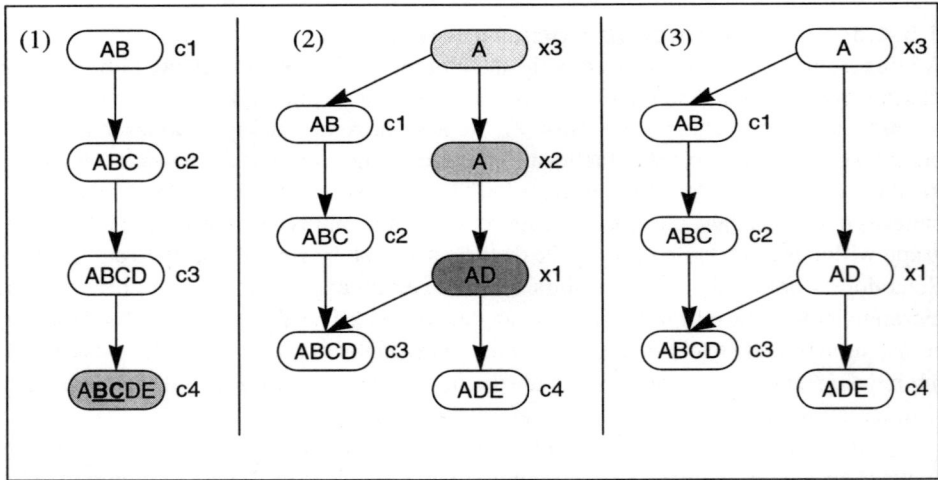

Figure 8.3 *The new class c4 rejects attributes B and C from c3; this triggers an incremental reorganization of the hierarchy whose final result is depicted in (3).*

In more complex situations, the factorization propagates as high up in a hierarchy as is needed to eliminate unwanted subclassing patterns and introduces auxiliary definitions along the way. A last simplification phase suppresses redundant auxiliary nodes and links (figure 8.3).

Class Reorganization

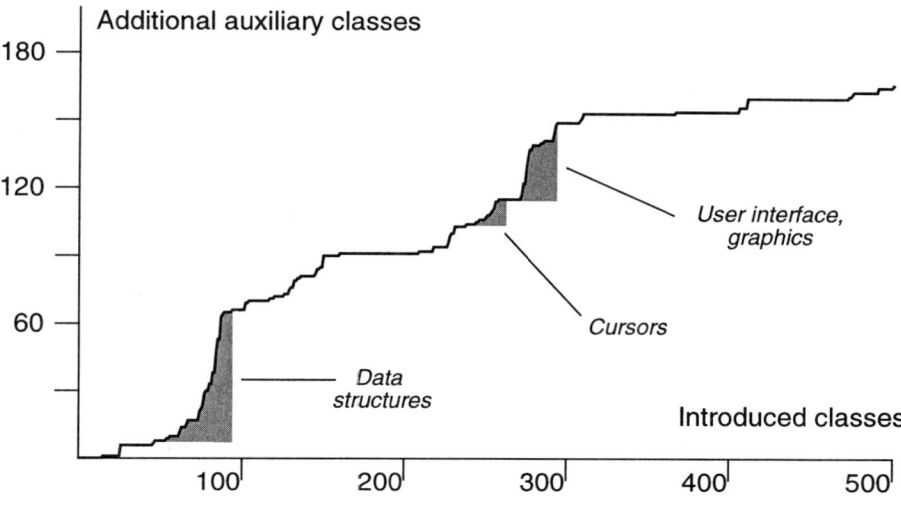

Figure 8.4 *Restructuring the Eiffel 2.3 library. A few groups of classes responsible for clustered reorganizations are highlighted. Overall, the incremental factorization of Eiffel 2.3 adds 166 auxiliary definitions to the library.*

8.5.4.4 Application of Incremental Reorganization

The incremental reorganization algorithm of [11] is one of the rare approaches whose effectiveness has been quantitatively assessed on the basis of large-scale experiments involving the reorganization of versions 2.1 and 2.3 of the Eiffel library (98 and 500 classes respectively). Starting from an empty hierarchy, Eiffel classes were added one by one to the library, triggering incremental reorganizations whenever redefinition patterns amounting to the rejection of inherited methods were detected (figure 8.4). This study brought to light several interesting results [13]:

- A large majority (63%) of the problems uncovered by the reorganization algorithm were caused by the utilization of inheritance for code sharing and by an inadequate modularization of functionality leading to other improper subclassing relationships.
- In 21% of the cases, the outcome of the reorganization corresponds to what one would expect from a manual redesign of the library. The restructuring patterns of the incremental algorithm closely match empirical observations on the evolution of object-oriented libraries [2], as well as small-scale reorganizations of a limited subset of the Smalltalk hierarchy [17].
- In 33% of the cases, the incremental algorithm detects, but is not able to correct, many actual design problems in a library that are best solved by other kinds of reorganizations, such as transforming inheritance links into part-of relationships.

- The algorithm is also useful for evaluating and comparing the quality of object-oriented libraries, especially when it is combined with other incremental techniques that are sensitive to naming patterns [13]

8.5.4.5 Evaluation

Global reorganizations are a prerequisite when the goal is to put a hierarchy into a "normal form" free from redundancy. However, global revisions may thoroughly transform a library. The results are therefore difficult to grasp and to utilize, particularly with libraries comprising hundreds of classes. Incremental factorization, on the other hand, limits its scope to the inheritance paths leading to one new class — an approach that also guarantees better performance in an interactive environment. Besides, it is doubtful that a global reorganization can achieve significant results without additional processing to extract the structural similarities between class interfaces or method signatures that are hidden because of diverging naming and programming conventions [31][34]. Maintaining behavioural properties is a problem with both global and incremental reorganizations [6][12][39] and, anyway, many design problems cannot be solved through adjustments of subclassing relationships alone. Inheritance reorganization techniques must therefore be enhanced with other methods such as refactoring to support redesign activities effectively. Automatic approaches are nevertheless essential to reduce the search space for redesign operations on large libraries to a manageable size before applying interactive, user-driven surgery or refactoring operations.

8.6   Change Avoidance

8.6.1   Confining the Effects of Evolution

In principle, modifications of class specifications must be propagated to objects instantiated on the basis of old definitions, so as to maintain the overall consistency of the system. Nevertheless, in many cases instances need not be updated or enhanced when their class is modified. Detecting when these situations arise is important, since one can then avoid the inconvenience of change propagation without giving up system consistency.

Change avoidance is easily combined with class tailoring. Tailoring operations are carried out only for the purpose of defining additional subclasses; no matter how inherited properties are overridden, the modifications appear and take effect only at the level of the subclasses performing the redeclarations. New classes obviously have no associated instances, so there is no need to care about filtering or conversion procedures. Thus, object-oriented systems avoid updating instances when subclassing operations are considered.

Several other evolution primitives exhibit no side-effects and can safely be applied without reorganizing running applications. Among the surgery operations listed in section 8.3.3, the following have no consequences on object structures:

Change Avoidance

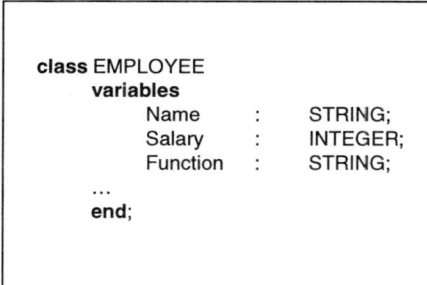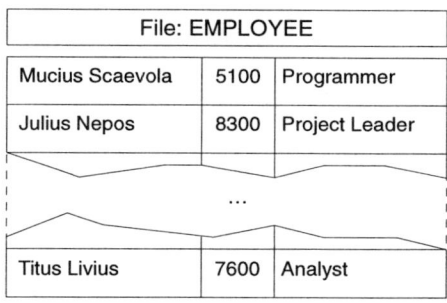

Figure 8.5 *Traditional storage technique for a hypothetical* EMPLOYEE *class.*

- Renaming classes, methods and variables only affects the description of classes, not the structure of instances, although this may not always be true for programs that explicitly manipulate class or attribute names.
- Changing the default value of a variable or a shared slot has no effect on instances, since these values pertain to the class definitions, not to the objects themselves.
- The implementation of a method can be changed freely; the code is associated and kept with a class definition, to be shared among all individual instances.
- Because no arbitrary changes to the domain of variables and arguments are allowed, one can guarantee that the values stored within existing objects remain compatible with their new type.

8.6.2 Physical Structures

A technique for confining the effects of class evolution consists of uncoupling the logical object model from its physical representation, so that instances may be implemented in a way immune to change. Transposed files exhibit such desirable characteristics [18].

In traditional database systems, the state of an object (i.e. the set of all its variables) is usually stored in one record (methods are shared and stored in a separate area). Every class of a hierarchy is associated with a file which is used as a persistent storage space for its entities, with each record of a file containing the state of a particular entity (figure 8.5). When a variable is added to a class definition, additional space must be allocated for the corresponding class and its subclasses; the instances affected by the modification are subsequently copied into the new storage zones. When a variable is suppressed from a class, special procedures are required for reclaiming unused storage space, a process that generally entails unloading and reloading entire class extents.

Transposed files associate one file with each variable of a class. Each record contains the value of the variable for a particular instance. The complete representation of a class is thus spread among several files. One reconstitutes the state of an object by first accessing

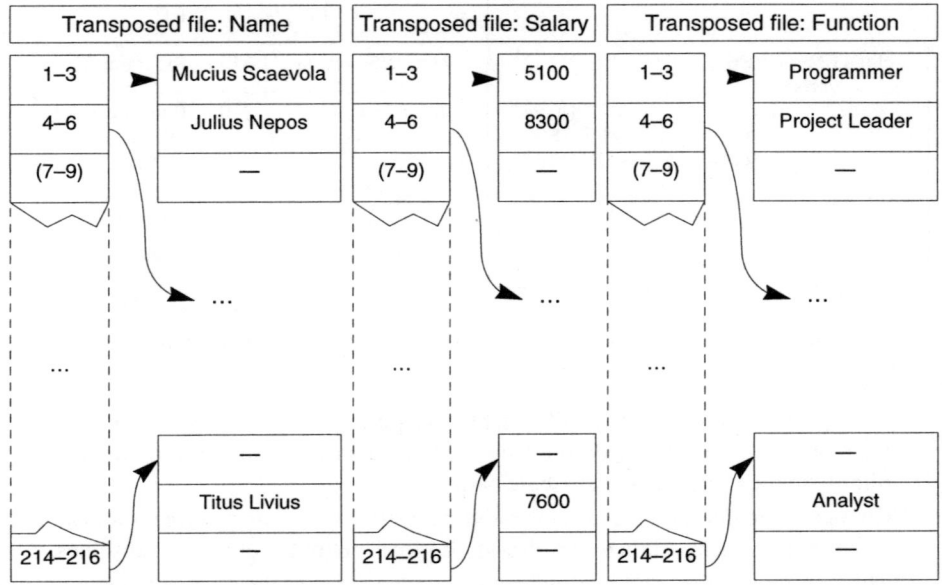

Figure 8.6 *Using a transposed file organization for storing class* EMPLOYEE. *Rank 2 contains all information relative to employee "Julius Nepos", rank 215 the data relative to "Titus Livius". No instance corresponds to ranks 7–9, so the corresponding block is not allocated.*

the values of its various variables in their respective files, and then grouping them together in the main memory for processing. All values for the variables of an object are stored in records located at the same rank in the various files; this is made possible by deriving this rank directly from the identifier assigned to every object in the system. A simple scheme is to use a pair ⟨class-identifier, rank⟩ to identify objects. Because file management systems generally allocate disk space not by records but by blocks, a level of indirection is needed to access the value of a variable. On the other hand, such a structure facilitates the insertion of objects whose identifiers are not strictly sequentially determined (blocks corresponding to unused identifiers need not be reserved), and the release of space after the last object associated with a particular block is deleted. Resource waste is therefore reduced. The diagram of figure 8.6 represents the simplified structure of a transposed file.

Transposed files provide an efficient kernel for implementing many of the class surgery primitives described in section 8.3.3, for example:

- Adding a variable to a class does not require reformatting the existing records to make room for the new attribute. Instead, an additional file is reserved to contain the supplementary variable that is initialized to some default value, such as nil or 0, for existing instances.

Conversion 233

- Suppressing a variable is achieved by deleting the corresponding file and returning all the space it occupies to the system. No compaction of the database is required.
- A subclass definition comprises all its superclass files plus some additional files. If a reorganization of the hierarchy results in the destruction of the subclass, all files for the attributes it introduces are deleted, but not those corresponding to the variables of its superclass. All instances of the subclass automatically become members of the superclass, without one having to execute any procedure to save, reformat and transfer the objects from one class to the other. The class-identifier part of all object identifiers must nevertheless be updated to remain consistent across changes.

Transposed files have proved very useful in domains such as statistical and econometric information systems. They have therefore been implemented in special-purpose database systems geared towards supporting these categories of applications. Their application in semantic and object-oriented database systems is currently a field of active research [18].

8.7 Conversion

8.7.1 Issues

Transforming all entities whose class has been modified seems like the most natural approach to dealing with change propagation. This technique implies that instances are physically updated so that their structure matches the description of the class they belong to. Two important requirements must be met:

- Because there is in general not a direct or a unique correspondence between old and new class definitions, care has to be taken to avoid losing information.
- The conversion process has to be organized in such a way that it interferes as little as possible with normal system operations.

A consequence of the first requirement is that *ad hoc* reconfiguration procedures have to be programmed to accompany automatic conversion processes whose capabilities to preserve the semantics of an application domain are evidently limited. The second requirement forces all conversion procedures to behave as atomic transactions (transformations must be applied completely to the objects involved in the conversion) and puts strong restrictions on their duration.

8.7.2 Instance Transformation

CLOS provides a good example of how automatic conversion can be enhanced by the programmer to take supplementary integrity constraints into account [25]. Conversions are performed according to the rules listed in table 8.4. CLOS deletes from objects all attributes that have been deleted in their class, including their associated accessor methods;

Old slot	New slot		
	shared	local	none
shared	preserved	preserved	discarded
local	initialized	preserved	discarded
none	initialized	initialized	—

Table 8.4 *Default conversions carried out by CLOS on objects after a class modification. A slot corresponds to a variable. Preserved slot values are left untouched. Discarded slots are removed and their values are lost. Initialized slots are assigned a value determined by the class the instance belongs to. This table is reproduced from [25].*

it adds and initializes those attributes that have been introduced in the class definition, and adapts the attributes whose status has passed from shared to local (or vice versa). These conversions are carried out by a standard function called update-instance-for-redefined-class that is inherited by every class in a hierarchy and can be customized by the programmer. Arguments such as the list of attributes added to the class, or the list of attributes discarded from the class or converted from local to shared, with their original values, are passed to this function. This allows the programmer to take proper actions to correct and augment the default restructuring and reinitialization procedures provided by CLOS, and thus to determine freely the mapping from an old to a new object schema.

The OTGen system provides a similar kind of functionality for transforming instances affected by a class modification, although this capability is presented to the user through a table-driven interface rather than as a programming feature attached to the inheritance hierarchy [27]. A table lists all class definitions whose instances have to be converted and suggests default transformations that apply, which can of course be overridden or extended by the user. The transformation operations possible with OTGen are as follows:

- Transfer objects which belong to the old class definition to the new database. Unchanged objects are simply copied from a database to another.
- Delete objects from the database if their class has been deleted.
- Initialize the variables of an object. When the old and new types of a variable are incompatible, the default action taken by OTGen consists of assigning the nil value to the variable. The user can override the standard behaviour of the system by providing its own initial values.
- Change local variables to shared variables.
- Perform context-dependent changes. One may initialize variables based on previous information stored in the objects, or partition the instances from a class into two other categories based on the information they contain.

- Move information between classes, for example by shuffling variables among classes, without losing associated information.
- Introduce new objects for classes created while updating the hierarchy and initialize their variables on the basis of information already stored in the database.

Providing a framework to handle the most common transformations certainly eases the task of the programmer. It is difficult, however, to guarantee that such a predetermined set of primitives effectively covers all possibilities for object conversion. When complex adaptations cannot be expressed with these operations, one is eventually forced to resort to special-purpose routines.

8.7.3 Immediate and Delayed Conversion

A major constraint with conversion concerns the time at which objects must be transformed.

Immediate conversion consists in transforming all objects at once, as soon as the corresponding class modifications are committed. This solution does not find much favour in practice, because it may entail the full unloading and reloading of the persistent object store, and long service interruptions if a significant number of entities have to be converted. On the other hand, this technique provides ample opportunities for optimizing the storage and access paths to objects as part of the conversion process. Immediate conversion has been implemented in the GemStone object-oriented database system [35].

Lazy conversion consists in adapting instances on an individual basis, but only when they are accessed for the first time after a class modification. This method does not incur the drawbacks of system shutdown imposed by immediate conversion at the price of degraded response time when instances are initially accessed after a class modification. Lazy conversion requires keeping track of the status of each object. When successive revisions are carried out on the same class, the system must record each associated conversion procedure, to be able to transform objects that are referenced after a long period of inactivity. Lazy conversion is nevertheless an appealing approach for applications with short-lived instances that are rapidly garbage-collected and therefore do not even need to be converted. This technique has been proposed as the standard mechanism for CLOS. A version of the O_2 system implements both techniques [41], applying immediate conversion to instances present in main memory at the time of the modification and resorting to lazy conversion for objects residing in secondary storage [4].

8.7.4 Evaluation

Conversion, and in particular lazy conversion, is a very attractive technique for propagating changes in an object-oriented system. It requires the programming of transformation functions, even when the environment supports automatic conversion, but there are no other alternatives for resolving intricate compatibility conflicts. When the conversion of instances is infeasible, scope restriction techniques borrowed from the filtering approach may prove helpful.

8.8 Filtering

8.8.1 Issues

Under some circumstances, one may not need to physically convert instances, because they have become obsolete due to class modification, or because they represent information that is not allowed to be modified for legal reasons, like accounting records. In these situations, it is preferable to ensure a partial compatibility between old and new object schemas, so that an application may still use them, but without striving to make them perfectly interchangeable.

Filtering (or screening) is a general framework for dealing with this problem. It is most often used in combination with version management. This can be done by wrapping a software layer around objects. The layer intercepts all messages sent to the enclosed object; these messages are then handled according to the object's version, to make it conform to the current or to a previous class description, or to cause an exception to pop up when an application uses an object with an unsuitable definition. Three major issues must be examined with this approach:

- How does one characterize the degree of compatibility between class versions?
- How can one map instances from a class version to another?
- How far can a filtering mechanism hide class changes from the users?

8.8.2 Version Compatibility

Fundamentally, filtering is a mechanism for viewing entities of a certain class version as if they belonged to another version of the same class. From the predecessor–successor relationship between versions, we identify two types of compatibility [1]:

- A version C_i is *backwards compatible* with an earlier version C_j if all instances of C_j can be used as if they belonged to C_i.
- A version C_i is *forwards compatible* with a later version C_j if all instances of C_j can be used as if they belonged to C_i.

In the first case, applications can use old instances as if they originated from new definitions. With the second form of compatibility, old programs can manipulate entities created on the basis of later versions.

Each class C is associated with the partial ordering of versions { C_i }. We assume that, at any point in time, some C_i is considered the valid version of class C. Building on these

Filtering

definitions, we say that a class version C_i is *consistent* with respect to version D_j of another class D ($C \neq D$) if one of the following conditions is satisfied [1]:
- D_j was the currently valid version of D when C_i was committed. This is the usual situation; C_i references up-to-date, contemporaneous properties of D.
- D_k was the currently valid version of D when C_i was committed, D_j is a later version of D, and D_k is forwards compatible with D_j. Here C_i references an obsolete definition of D, but the forwards compatibility property allows it to work with instances created according to the new schema.
- D_k was the currently valid version of D when C_i was committed, D_j is an earlier version of D, and D_k is backwards compatible with D_j. Here C_i is supposed to manipulate an up-to-date representation of D; thanks to the backwards compatibility, it is nevertheless able to use instances generated from old versions.

8.8.3 Filtering Mechanisms

The operations that cause problems when invoked on a non-compatible object can be classified in a limited number of categories. For example, deleting a method generates access violations when an object attempts to invoke the deleted method. These effects are summarized in table 8.5.

A simple way to deal with this problem is to replace each access primitive with a routine specifically programmed to perform the mapping between different class structures. Thus, for each variable that violates compatibility constraints, one provides a procedure that returns the variable's value, and another procedure for changing its value. These procedures perform various transformations, like mapping the variable to a set of other attributes [1]. For example, if the "birthday" attribute of a person class has been replaced with an "age" variable, one has to provide the following procedures to ensure backwards compatibility:
- A read accessor that determines the age of a person based on the time elapsed between the recorded birthday and the current date.
- A write accessor that stores the age of a person as a birthday, computed on the basis of the current date and the age given as argument to the accessor.

Similarly, one must define two symmetrical operations to guarantee forwards compatibility. More generally, one can define so-called substitute functions for carrying out these mappings between objects with different structures as follows:
- A *substitute read function* $RC_{ij}A(I)$ is given an instance I of version i of class C. It maps the values of a group of attributes from this object to a valid value of attribute A of version j of C. In other words, it makes instances of class version C_i appear as if they contained the attribute A of class version C_j for reading operations.
- A *substitute write function* $WC_{ij}A(I,V)$ is given an instance I of version i of class C, and a value V for attribute A of C_j. It maps the value V into a set of values for a group of attributes defined in C_i. In other words, this function makes instances of class ver-

Scope of change	Compatibility	Consequences
add a variable	backwards	undefined variable in old objects
delete a variable	forwards	undefined variable in new objects
extend variable type	backwards	writing illegal values into old objects
	forwards	reading unknown data from new objects
restrict variable type	forwards	writing illegal values into new objects
	backwards	reading unknown data from old objects
add a method	backwards	undefined method in old objects
delete a method	forwards	undefined method in new objects
extend argument type	backwards	passing illegal values to old objects
	forwards	getting unknown data from new objects
restrict argument type	forwards	passing illegal values to new objects
	backwards	getting unknown data from old objects
change argument list	backwards and forwards	similar to dropping and adding a method

Table 8.5 *Consequences of class changes. The middle column indicates which kind of compatibility is affected by a modification, the right column describes the exceptions raised when accessing an object from the old or the new class definition.*

sion C_i appear as if they could store information in attribute A, although this information is actually recorded in other variables.

A second approach favours the use of handlers to be invoked before or after a failed access to the attribute they are attached to, a technique that has been implemented in the EN-CORE system [37]. Pre-handlers typically take over when attempting to access a non-existent attribute, or when trying to assign an illegal value to it. A pre-handler may perform a mapping like those carried out by the substitute functions, coerce its argument to a valid value, or simply abort the operation. A post-handler is activated when an illegal value is returned to the invoking object; a common behaviour in this case consists in returning a default value.

8.8.4 Making Class Changes Transparent

Where should filters be defined? As originally stated, the technique based on handlers requires global modifications in all versions of the same class [37]. More precisely,

- Whenever an attribute is added to a class, pre-handlers for the attribute must be introduced in all other versions of the class.
- Pre-handlers must be added to a version that suppresses attributes of a class.
- When a version extends the domain of an attribute, corresponding pre- and post-handlers must be introduced in all other versions of the class.
- When the domain of an attribute is restricted, the class version redeclaring the attribute type must be wrapped with a pre-handler and a post-handler.

This solution is rather inelegant: it requires that old class definitions be adjusted to reflect new developments and leads to a combinatorial explosion of handler complexity.

The model of substitute functions allows one to exploit the derivation history for mapping between versions that have no direct relationships. Thus, one can map a version C_i to another version C_j if there exist either substitute functions for them ($RC_{ij}X$, $WC_{ij}X$, where X denotes an attribute of C_j), or a succession of substitute functions that transitively apply to them (i.e. there are substitute functions for mapping between C_i and C_k, then C_k and C_l and eventually C_l and C_j for example). Depending on compatibility properties, one can even relate class definitions placed in different derivation paths in a version hierarchy. Furthermore, substitute functions are defined only in the newer versions; previous class definitions remain unchanged.

When compatibility between versions cannot be achieved, one may install scope restrictions that isolate objects pertaining to different definitions from each other:

- A *forward scope restriction* makes instances from a new version inaccessible to objects from older versions.
- A *backward scope restriction* makes instances from older versions unreachable from objects of more recent versions.

Scope restrictions and compatibility relationships make it possible to partition a class extension in such a way that operations may be applied to any object regardless of its version. Naturally, interoperability decreases with such a scheme, since the entities from different versions of the same class can no longer be referred to and accessed as members of one large pool of objects.

8.8.5 Evaluation

Screening has been implemented in some systems, but its application scope there is notably reduced. ORION does not immediately convert instances affected by a class change so as to avoid reorganizing the database [3]. When an instance is fetched, and before its attributes are accessed, deleted variables are made inaccessible (after, if needed, the physical destruction of the objects they refer to). Default values are automatically supplied to account for the introduction of new properties. Rearrangements of inheritance patterns are reflected by hiding unwanted properties and supplying default values for new inherited attributes.

From our discussion, it appears that filtering cannot fulfil its objective of making class changes transparent without considerable complexity and overhead. The programmer must not only develop a series of special-purpose functions for mapping between the variants of a class, but must also accept a degradation of application performance as these handlers accumulate, replacing the originally simple and efficient accessors. In practice, this complexity does not appear fully warranted. With lazy conversion, for example, one has also to define *ad hoc* procedures for transforming entities from one version to another, but these procedures are called only once for every object. Their execution is therefore not as expensive as the systematic run-time checks and exception raising implied by screening techniques. On the positive side, filtering provides a rigorous framework for defining and dealing with compatibility issues, and it is most adequate during prototyping, when class modifications may be cancelled just after being tested. Recent approaches provide improved mechanisms derived from database views that encompass filtering techniques and that can also be suitable as modelling tools during application development [16].

8.9 Conclusion

Object-oriented development reveals its iterative nature as successive stages of subclassing, class modification and reorganization allow software engineers to build increasingly general and robust classes. We therefore expect object-oriented CASE systems to take advantage of the large spectrum of tools and techniques available to manage the various aspects of class evolution (see table 8.6).

Approach	Actual impact on instances	In charge of controlling change propagation	Implementation
change avoidance			
confinement	logical	system	side-effect free operations
storage structures	physical	system	transposed files
conversion	physical	programmer	conversion routines
filtering	logical	programmer	handlers/wrappers

Table 8.6 *The main characteristics of change propagation techniques.*

It is appealing to envision an environment where software engineers build new classes out of reusable components, tailor them to suit their needs, and launch exploratory incremental reorganizations to detect the places in their code most likely to require further revisions. Software developers may then refine the outcome of automatic reorganizations with class surgery primitives and perhaps embark on comprehensive refactoring activities. The results of different reorganizations and their subsequent adjustments are kept as

Conclusion

Approach	Scope	Phase in library development	Enforced properties
tailoring	attributes; interfaces	extension	syntactical constraints
surgery	attributes; inheritance links; classes	redesign	schema invariants
versioning	classes	extension	configuration consistency
reorganization			
refactoring	classes; attributes; method structures; inheritance links	redesign	schema invariants; preservation of behaviour
interattribute dependencies	method structures	redesign	preservation of behaviour
inheritance (global)	classes; inheritance links	redesign	preservation of class structures; global optimality of hierarchy
inheritance (incremental)	classes; inheritance links; interfaces; method structures	extension	preservation of class structures; local optimality of hierarchy; preservation of behaviour

Table 8.7 *The main characteristics of evolution management techniques. Attributes refer to methods as well as to variables; method structures correspond to the signature and the implementation of methods.*

versions of the hierarchy, that can be further modified, tested, debugged and possibly cancelled by the programmers (see table 8.7). Filtering makes it possible to test the correctness of various class definitions without having to carry out numerous conversions. When a satisfactory design for a new component and its related classes is achieved, it can be frozen and publicly released as the new version of the class library, while the other temporary versions are discarded. If necessary, instances from modified classes can then be definitely converted to conform to their new definitions.

Some approaches have been partially implemented and already appear, albeit in isolation, in some object-oriented systems; we hope that integrated tools suitable for supporting class evolution in industrial and commercial environments will become available in the near future.

References

[1] Matts Ahlsén, Anders Björnerstedt, Stefan Britts, Christer Hultén and Lars Söderlund, "Making Type Changes Transparent," SYSLAB report 22, SYSLAB-S, University of Stockholm, 26 Feb. 1984.

[2] Bruce Anderson and Sanjiv Gossain, "Hierarchy Evolution and the Software Lifecycle," in *Proceedings 2nd TOOLS Conference*, ed. J. Bézivin, B. Meyer and J.-M. Nerson, Paris, 1990, pp. 41–50.

[3] Jay Banerjee, Won Kim, Hyoung-Joo Kim and Henry F. Korth, "Semantics and Implementation of Schema Evolution in Object-Oriented Databases," *SIGMOD Record* (special issue on SIGMOD '87), vol. 16, no. 3, Dec. 1987, pp. 311–322.

[4] Gilles Barbedette, "Schema Modification in the LISPO$_2$ Persistent Object-Oriented Language," in *Proceedings 5th ECOOP Conference*, ed. P. America, *Lecture Notes in Computer Science*, vol. 512, Springer-Verlag, Geneva, 15–19 July 1991, pp. 77–96.

[5] David Beech and Brom Mahbod, "Generalized Version Control in an Object-Oriented Database," in *Proceedings of the 4th IEEE International Conference on Data Engineering*, Los Angeles, Feb. 1988, pp. 14–22.

[6] Paul L. Bergstein and Walter L. Hürsch, "Maintaining Behavioral Consistency during Schema Evolution," in *Object Technologies for Advanced Software (First JSSST International Symposium), Lecture Notes in Computer Science*, vol. 742, Springer-Verlag, Nov. 1993, pp. 176–193.

[7] Anders Björnerstedt and Stefan Britts, "AVANCE: An Object Management System," *ACM SIGPLAN Notices* (special issue on OOPSLA '88), vol. 23, no. 11, Nov. 1988, pp. 206–221.

[8] Anders Björnerstedt and Christer Hultén, "Version Control in an Object-Oriented Architecture," in *Object-Oriented Concepts, Databases, and Applications*, ed. W. Kim and F. H. Lochovsky, Frontier Series, Addison-Wesley/ACM Press, 1989, pp. 451–485.

[9] Alexander Borgida, "Modelling Class Hierarchies with Contradictions," *SIGMOD Record* (special issue on SIGMOD '88), vol. 17, no. 3, Sept. 1988, pp. 434–443.

[10] Alexander Borgida and Keith E. Williamson, "Accommodating Exceptions in Databases, and Refining the Schema by Learning from them," in *VLDB 1985 Proceedings*, ed. A. Pirotte and Y. Vassiliou, Stockholm, 21–23 August 1985, pp. 72–81.

[11] Eduardo Casais, "An Incremental Class Reorganization Approach," in *Proceedings 6th ECOOP Conference*, ed. O. Lehrmann Madsen, *Lecture Notes in Computer Science*, vol. 615, Springer-Verlag, Utrecht, June 29 – July 3 1992, pp. 114–132.

[12] Eduardo Casais, "Managing Evolution in Object-Oriented Environments: An Algorithmic Approach," Ph.D. Thesis, Université de Genève, Geneva, 1991.

[13] Eduardo Casais, "Automatic Reorganization of Object-Oriented Hierarchies: A Case Study," *Object-Oriented Systems*, vol. 1, no. 2, Dec. 1994., pp. 95–115

[14] Fabiano Cattaneo, Alberto Coen-Porisini, Luigi Lavazza and Roberto Zicari, "Overview and Progress Report of the ESSE Project: Supporting Object-Oriented Database Schema Analysis and Evolution," in *Proceedings 10th TOOLS Conference, Versailles*, ed. B. Magnusson and J.-F. Perrot, Prentice Hall, 1993, pp. 63–74

[15] Hong-Tai Chou and Won Kim, "A Unifying Framework for Version Control in a CAD Environment," in *12th VLDB Conference Proceedings*, Kyoto, 25–28 August 1986, pp. 336–344.

[16] Stewart M. Clamen, "Type Evolution and Instance Adaptation," Technical Report CMU-CS-92-113, Carnegie-Mellon University, Pittsburgh, June 1992.

[17] William R. Cook, "Interfaces and Specifications for the Smalltalk-80 Collection Classes," *ACM SIGPLAN Notices* (special issue on OOPSLA '92), vol. 27, no. 10, Oct. 1992, pp. 1–15.

[18] Thibault Estier, Gilles Falquet and Michel Léonard, "F2: An Evolution Oriented Database System," Cahiers du CUI no. 69, Centre Universitaire d'Informatique, Genève, January 1993.

[19] D. H. Fishman, J. Annevelink, D. Beech, E. Chow, T. Connors, J. W. Davis, W. Hasan, C. G. Hoch, W. Kent, S. Leichner, P. Lyngbaek, B. Mahbod, M. A. Neimat, T. Risch, M. C. Shan and W. K. Wilkinson, "Overview of the IRIS DBMS," in *Object-Oriented Concepts, Databases, and Applications*, ed. W. Kim and F. H. Lochovsky, Frontier Series, Addison-Wesley/ACM Press, 1989, pp. 219–250.

[20] Erich Gamma, "Objektorientierte Software-Entwicklung am Beispiel von ET++: Klassenbibliothek, Werkzeuge, Design," Dissertation, Universität Zürich, August 1991.

[21] Adele Goldberg and Daniel Robson, *Smalltalk-80: The Language and its Implementation*, Addison-Wesley, Reading, Mass., 1983.

[22] Ralph E. Johnson and Brian Foote, "Designing Reusable Classes," *Journal of Object-Oriented Programming*, June-July 1988, pp. 22–35.

[23] Ralph E. Johnson and William F. Opdyke, "Refactoring and Aggregation," in *Object Technologies for Advanced Software (First JSSST International Symposium), Lecture Notes in Computer Science*, vol. 742, Springer-Verlag, Nov. 1993, pp. 264–278.

[24] Randy H. Katz, "Towards a Unified Framework for Version Modelling in Engineering Databases," *ACM Computing Surveys*, vol. 22, no. 4, Dec. 1990, pp. 375–408.

[25] Sonya E. Keene, *Object-Oriented Programming in Common LISP: A Programmer's Guide to CLOS*, Addison-Wesley, Reading, Mass., 1989.

[26] Hyoung-Joo Kim, "Algorithmic and Computational Aspects of OODB Schema Design," in *Object-Oriented Dabatases with Applications to CASE, Networks and VLSI CAD*, ed. R. Gupta and E. Horowitz, Prentice Hall, 1991, pp. 26–61.

[27] Barbara Staudt Lerner and A. Nico Habermann, "Beyond Schema Evolution to Database Reorganization," *ACM SIGPLAN Notices* (special issue on OOPSLA '90), vol. 25, no. 10, Oct. 1990, pp. 67–76.

[28] Karl J. Lieberherr, Paul Bergstein and Ignacio Silva-Lepe, "From Objects to Classes: Algorithms for Optimal Object-Oriented Design," *BCS/IEE Software Engineering Journal*, July 1991, pp. 205–228.

[29] Karl Lieberherr, Ian Holland and Arthur Riel, "Object-Oriented Programming: an Objective Sense of Style," *ACM SIGPLAN Notices* (special issue on OOPSLA '88), vol. 23, no. 11, Nov. 1988, pp. 323–334.

[30] Bertrand Meyer, *Eiffel: The Language*, Object-Oriented Series, Prentice Hall, 1992.

[31] Bertrand Meyer, "Tools for the New Culture: Lessons from the Design of the Eiffel Libraries," *Communications of the ACM*, vol. 33, no. 9, Sept. 1990, pp. 68–88.

[32] Shamkant B. Navathe, Seong Geum, Dinesh K. Desai and Herman Lam, "Conceptual Design for Non-Database Experts with an Interactive Schema Tailoring Tool," in *Proceedings of the 9th Entity-Relationship Conference*, ed. H. Kangassalo, Lausanne, 8–10 Oct. 1990, pp. 3–20.

[33] *Objective-C Compiler Version 4—User Reference Manual*, StepStone Corporation, Sandy Hook, 1988.

[34] William F. Opdyke, "Refactoring Object-Oriented Frameworks," Ph.D. thesis, Department of Computer Science, University of Illinois at Urbana-Champaign, 1992.

[35] D. Jason Penney and Jacob Stein, "Class Modification in the GemStone Object-Oriented DBMS," *ACM SIGPLAN Notices* (special issue on OOPSLA '87), vol. 22, no. 12, Dec. 1987, pp. 111–117.

[36] Markku Sakkinen, "Comments on the 'Law of Demeter' and C++," *ACM SIGPLAN Notices*, vol. 23, no. 12, pp. 34–44.

[37] Andrea H. Skarra and Stanley B. Zdonik, "The Management of Changing Types in an Object-Oriented Database," in *Research Directions in Object-Oriented Programming*, ed. B. Shriver and P. Wegner, MIT Press, Cambridge, Mass., 1987, pp. 393–415.

[38] Dave Thomas and Kent Johnson, "Orwell: a Configuration Management System for Team Programming," *ACM SIGPLAN Notices* (special issue on OOPSLA '88), vol. 23, no. 11, Nov. 1988, pp. 135–141.

[39] Emmanuel Waller, "Schema Updates and Consistency," in *DOOD'91 Proceedings*, ed. C. Delobel, M. Kifer and Y. Yasunaga, *Lecture Notes in Computer Science*, vol. 566, Springer-Verlag, Dec. 1991, pp. 167–188.

[40] Franz Weber, "Getting Class Correctness and System Correctness Equivalent — How to Get Covariance Right," in *Proceedings 8th TOOLS Conference, Santa Barbara*, ed. R. Ege, M. Singh and B. Meyer, Prentice Hall, 1992, pp. 199–213.

[41] Roberto Zicari, "A Framework for Schema Updates in an Object-Oriented Database System," in *Building an Object-Oriented Database System — The Story of O_2*, ed. F. Bancilhon, C. Delobel and P. Kanellakis, Morgan Kaufmann, 1992, pp. 146–182.

Chapter 9
The Affinity Browser

Xavier Pintado

Abstract Large numbers of classes, complex inheritance and containment graphs, and diverse patterns of dynamic interaction all contribute to difficulties in understanding, reusing, debugging, and tuning large object-oriented systems. These difficulties may have a significant impact on the usefulness of such systems. Tools that help in understanding the contents and behaviour of an object-oriented environment should play a major role in reducing such difficulties. Such tools allow for the exploration of different aspects of a software environment such as inheritance structures, part-of relationships, etc. However, object-oriented systems differ in many respects from traditional database systems, and in particular, conventional querying mechanisms used in databases show poor performance when used for the exploration of object-oriented environments. This chapter defines the requirements for effective exploration mechanisms in the realm of object-oriented environments. We propose an approach to browsing based on the notion of *affinity* that satisfies such requirements. Our tool, the affinity browser, provides a visual representation of object relationships presented in terms of affinity. Objects that appear closer in the visual representation are more strongly related than objects lying farther apart. So, the intensity of a relationship is translated into distance in the visual representation that provides the support for user navigation. We provide many examples of metrics defined over the objects of an environment to illustrate how object relationships can be translated in terms of affinity so that they can be used for the exploration of an environment.

9.1 Introduction

Large numbers of classes, complex inheritance and containment graphs, and diverse patterns of dynamic interaction all contribute to difficulties in understanding, reusing, debugging, and tuning large object-oriented systems. From the inception of object-oriented environments, developers and software designers have felt the need for tools that support the process of understanding the objects, the classes and the relationships provided by their environments. For example, reuse of existing software components requires navigation and inspection of classes and how they are related. Inspection and navigation capabilities are also instrumental for the combination of instantiated objects since they allow the user to go back and forth, inspecting objects and combining them. In a similar vein, discerning global and local patterns of interaction among classes and among objects is critical for tuning and debugging.

This chapter proposes an approach to browsing for object-oriented environments based on the notion of affinity. Our tool, the affinity browser, allows for the exploration of collections of objects based on a visual representation of object relationships presented in terms of affinity. Objects that appear closer in the visual representation are more strongly related than objects lying farther apart. So, the intensity of a relationship is translated into distance in the visual representation.

Our approach displays many advantages. First, affinity browsing is not based on point-to-point navigation. The user is provided with the set of objects that lie within a given neighbourhood relative to the object currently being inspecting. The affinity browser promotes, therefore, proximity-based navigation whereby exploration proceeds by exploring first the objects that are close to the current object of interest. Second, the browser allows for the exploration of dynamically evolving relationships. The evolution of such relationships is visualized as an animation where the change in the relative position of objects conveys the change of the underlying relationships expressed in terms of affinity. Third, many different kinds of object relationships can be translated into affinity representations allowing the same exploration paradigm and the same user interface to be used to explore a large spectrum of object relationships.

This chapter is organized as follows. Section 9.1.1 addresses the problem of finding and selecting objects inside an object-oriented environment. It discusses the characteristics of object-oriented systems that may have an impact on the effectiveness of various browsing mechanisms. Section 9.1.2 surveys work related to browsing ranging from traditional graph-based browsing to graphical and spatial browsing. Section 9.2 defines the requirements for effective exploration mechanisms in the realm of object-oriented environments. Section 9.3 presents the affinity browser as a tool that satisfies such requirements. In section 9.4 we provide many examples of metrics defined over the objects of an environment to illustrate how object relationships can be translated in terms of affinity so that they can be used for the exploration of an environment

9.1.1 Object Selection

We address here the issue of selection in the object-oriented realm. Users may want, for instance, to select classes, objects, or functionality. Selection in an object-oriented environment has many problems, however. First, an application designer has only approximate selection criteria to select an appropriate reusable object class for developing his or her application. Second, the object classes and the objects in a running system have relationships that change dynamically. Third, objects are encapsulated and content selection has only very limited use.

Furthermore, object-oriented principles applied to software design seem to promote systems with object relationships that are more complex than in more traditional software environments. Many authors think that these principles will allow designers and developers to create software environments that are an order of magnitude more complex than existing software systems [19] [4].

A noteworthy supporting reason for such belief is that object-oriented design techniques seem to allow significantly better decomposition of complex problems into units of manageable complexity. First, by the virtue of encapsulation an object conceals its internal complexity and it acquires some level of autonomy. Second, incremental definition through inheritance allows for the endless refinement of object behaviour and functionality without the need to rework the whole hierarchy at each refinement step. These mechanisms, with such desirable features, allow for the implementation of models that integrate much detail both at the object level and at the level of object relationships. This intuition is further supported by experience that shows that it is quite easy to introduce complexity in the design and in the implementation of an object-oriented environment. For instance, object-oriented programming is more an activity of *wiring* together sets of objects. For the programmer or for the designer whose task is to build a system through the composition of objects it might be quite easy to combine them in many different ways — this is the producer's view. On the other hand, for a developer who wants to understand existing functionality for reuse or maintenance, it may be difficult to comprehend the large number of functional relationships that have been created — this might be the consumer's view.

Early experiences with object-oriented environments highlighted the need for tools that allow for the exploration of object relationships. The Smalltalk environment, for instance, already provided a sophisticated integrated browsing tool [12]. Interestingly enough, it has been argued that the Smalltalk browsing tool is one of the most appealing features of that environment and it is often cited as a reference. For sure, almost every programming activity on the environment relies on the browser to support navigation needed for the kind of non-linear programming promoted by object-orientation. The browser is used to code new objects, to find reusable classes and to explore object relationships.

9.1.1.1 Querying and Browsing

The two methods commonly applied for selection are querying and browsing. The methods are usually applied in a complementary manner; we query and browse in alternation, applying which method seems more appropriate at different stages of the selection process.

Querying provides fine selectivity when the structure of the information space is known and when content selection can be used. For instance, querying is the primary selection method in database systems. When querying provides good selectivity, browsing diminishes in importance. Most selected items are appropriate and we only need a crude browsing tool to inspect them.

Querying, however, can have poor results for many reasons. If the selection criteria are ill-defined and fuzzy querying does not work well, e.g. in information retrieval. If the structure of the information space changes dynamically, queries are not easy to formulate, e.g. in financial information systems. Finally, if content selectivity is difficult to exploit, querying loses a lot of selectivity power, e.g. in multimedia databases. In all these cases powerful browsing capabilities become indispensable.

9.1.1.2 Dynamically Evolving Relationships

As we already mentioned, the analysis of dynamically evolving relationships plays an important role in debugging but can also be of invaluable assistance for reuse since it helps understanding how objects are related in existing applications. However, providing support for the understanding of dynamically evolving relationships is a challenging task. In fact, traditional querying techniques usually assume a user with knowledge of the search structure that supports selection. Such an assumption usually implies structure stability since it seems unrealistic to assume user knowledge of a quickly evolving structure.

With traditional databases it is usually assumed that their information contents changes but not their structure — or at least not frequently. For example, widely used query languages such as SQL provide almost no support for selection in an environment with a changing structure. The stability of database schemes represents an advantage in terms of access to information but it makes traditional databases ill-suited for information with dynamically evolving structures.

The need to cope with dynamically evolving relationships appears in many object selection problems. For example, we may be interested in finding which are the objects that interact most frequently with a given object in order to determine its patterns of interaction. The change in the interaction patterns depending on what activities the system is performing may provide useful information about the intended role of an object. This information can be used, for instance, to assess the potential of reuse for an object in an environment that may or may not provide the same activity context.

The need for more flexibility than that provided by query mechanisms appeared also in databases. For example, Motro [20] [21] [22] describes browsing tools that allow for *navigation* in a semantic network extracted from the internal structure of a relational database, and provide capabilities for fuzzy queries. The approach has been later extended to integrate similar capabilities in an object-oriented environment [23].

9.1.2 Related Work

Because there is an observable trend towards more complex and quickly evolving information systems we need to investigate how to enhance browsing capabilities for the exploration of information systems. In this section we describe previous work related to browsing.

9.1.2.1 The Smalltalk Browser

To the best of our knowledge, the Smalltalk system was the first programming environment where exploration tools played a major role. Furthermore, the browsing concepts and mechanisms have been clearly defined [13] [12] and they are quite often cited as the historical reference to which more recent browsing tools are compared.

The Smalltalk environment provides capabilities to inspect the message interface of objects through a system view called a *browser*. Similarly, the internal state of an object can be inspected through another system view called an *inspector*. Furthermore, it is possible to obtain interface information about sets of objects through another kind of system view called a *message-set browser*. These views are generated as responses to queries such as: which classes implement a given message? Which objects send a particular message?

The main way to find out about classes in the environment is to use a system class browser. The browser presents a hierarchical view of class-related information. It presents *categories* that organize the classes within the environment, and categories that arrange messages within each class. Categories provide essentially a way of grouping classes and messages into meaningful groups.

It should be noted that in the Smalltalk environment the role of the exploration tools is not restricted to inspection. For example, an *inspector* allows users to change interactively the values of instance variables and to send messages to objects. In general, inspection tools are used for both inspection and programming purposes. For instance, the creation of a new class derived from an existing one, and the definition of new methods is also performed through the browser.

Other browsing tools have been described and implemented in various systems. The browsing mechanisms implemented in the Smalltalk environment have been a continuous source of inspiration for new browsing tools. For example, the Trellis programming environment [24] provides browsing capabilities that are quite similar to those of the Smalltalk environment [12].

The great majority of existing browsing tools allow for a *point-to-point* navigation, i.e. the navigation paths are defined by a tree or a network structure. For instance, the tree structure of the Smalltalk browser is based on classification. This approach has proven to be useful for small collections of objects. But when the number of classes becomes large users may feel lost because there is no global view and the structure cannot be rearranged to fit their intuitive perception of the object's space.

Discerning global and local patterns of interaction among classes is critical for tuning and debugging. A few authors have already identified this as an important issue and proposed adequate tools. For example, Böcker and Herczeg [1] introduce a *software oscilloscope* for visually tracking the interactions between objects in a system. The system's dynamic behaviour is inspected by placing obstacles between objects and animating the flow of messages across them. The tool focuses only on microscopic behaviour, however. Brüegge, Gottschalk and Luo [3] describe BEE++, an object-oriented application framework for the analysis of distributed applications. BEE++ is fundamentally an event processing system since it views the execution of distributed activities as streams of events. Event processing is encapsulated in a set of core base classes that are intended to be derived for customization.

Other authors such as Kleyn and Gingrich [17] focus on object behaviour issues. Their tool offers concurrently animated views of the behaviour of an object-oriented system. These views include graphs of invocations between objects. Podgursky and Pierce address the problem [30] of retrieving reusable software components based on sampled behaviour. Finally, Rubin and Goldberg [31] sketch an object-oriented design approach based on object behaviour analysis and stress the importance of exploration tools to support the design process.

9.1.2.2 Graphical and Spatial Browsing

In the late 1970s Fields and Negroponte, in a visionary paper [10], expressed the need for new clues to find data. Among the many approaches they envisioned for locating information are spatial referencing and proximity. Shortly after, Donelson [7], Bolt [2], and Herot [14] published papers about spatial management of information which apply many techniques for information exploration and inspection that will serve as a basis for future systems. They introduced the *spatial data management system* (SDMS) concept, whereby information is expressed in graphical form and presented in a spatial framework so that the information has a structure that is more obvious than in a conventional database. Herot argues that: "in this way the user can find the information he seeks without having to specify it precisely or know exactly where in the DBMS it is stored."

More recently, Caplinger [5] has described a sophisticated browsing tool with a graphical spatial interface that is, in fact, an evolution of the original SDMS idea. A further elaboration of SDMS is BEAD [6], a system for the visualization of bibliographical data. In BEAD, articles in a bibliography are represented by particles in 3-space. The system uses physically based modelling techniques to take advantage of methods for the approximation of potential fields. Interparticle forces tend to make similar articles move closer to one another and dissimilar ones move apart, so that the relationships between articles are represented by their relative spatial positions. We may also mention the N-Land system [18], which addresses the problem of visualizing higher dimension information spaces.

The growing interest on hypertext systems generalized the use of browsing as a mechanism for information access. Many things have been written recently about hypertext browsing and hypertext navigation, and we will just mention a few works that seem to deserve particular interest in the context of this work. SemNet [8] is a system for the three-dimensional visualization and exploration of large knowledge bases that promotes a hypertext-like navigation paradigm. Feiner's work addresses the problem of how to conveniently display hypertext structures [9] so as to facilitate hypertext navigation.

Another interesting approach is described by Stotts and Furuta [34]. The basic idea is to replace the usual directed graph of an hypertext system by a Petri net. Unlike a directed graph, a Petri net also allows the specification of *browsing semantics*, i.e. the dynamic properties of a reader's experience when browsing a document. So, Petri nets add to the hypertext system access control capabilities based on a formally sound mechanism. The authors describe the α-Trellis system that has been implemented to experiment with the Petri-net-based model. This approach is also discussed in [28] where it is used to explore hypertext systems with an affinity browser.

A sophisticated browsing tool with advanced capabilities for databases has been developed by Stonebraker [33], which combines query refinement techniques and browsing. Jones has described a personal filer with interesting retrieving capabilities [15]. His system, ME, is a database of files connected through links which represent weighted terms. A retrieval request is a set of terms, and a spreading activation process is used to match the files that are most relevant. Finally we cite a browsing tool for specific databases; Gedye [11] has discussed the problems associated with accessing information related to chip design, and described a browsing tool to inspect the contents of a chip design database.

9.2 Browsing Requirements

To illustrate our browsing requirements we will use a simple paradigm. Suppose we have an information base relative to a city. We need a *city browser* which can guide visitors to plan their stay. For example, suppose we arrive at a hotel and want to go to eat. We would like the city browser to help us choose a restaurant which is geographically close, within an interesting and safe walk (or a place easy to reach and park), with good food, nice surroundings, good service and within our budget.[*] It is obvious that we have multiple criteria for our choice and it will be very difficult to find a restaurant that is best in all. We need, therefore, to be guided to reach a compromise. We should also be aware that restaurants do not always advertise all their points (especially their shortcomings). They have, therefore — like encapsulated objects — hidden information which we can only get from persons that have been there.

To begin, we should point out that if the number of restaurants is small then we don't need sophisticated browsing tools. We can explore each one of them according to the multiple criteria, while keeping the rest in the back of our mind. This approach, however, breaks down when the number of objects and criteria becomes large.

The first requirement for effective browsing is a notion of locality. The browser should present us first with the choices that are *close*. Close implies a measure of distance which does not necessarily have a single interpretation. For instance it can be geographically close, public-transportation close, etc. Each definition of closeness is within a certain context. The browser should, therefore, be capable of dealing with many contexts. Each context defines a measure of affinity between the objects we are looking for, in this example city locations. We should also be in a position to change contexts in our browsing or combine contexts relating independent selection criteria.

The second requirement is that the measure of distance should be able to change dynamically. For example, time distances between locations can vary with traffic. The browser should be able, therefore, to deal with quickly changing definitions of closeness.

The third requirement is that we need a notion of set-at-a-time navigation. The browser should present us with many choices which could be pursued in the information space. There are two reasons for this requirement. First, the immediately next objects should all

---

[*] Such a system was implemented at Bell Labs for New York city restaurants.

be presented to allow other more subjective criteria to be considered. Second, if we insist on point-to-point navigation we may reach many dead-ends and be forced to backtrack. Backtracking is very confusing especially when trying to find an object according to multiple criteria.

Finally, users should be able to visualize the information space they are searching. We need, therefore, to project a multidimensional information space into a two dimensional screen. This projection should somehow preserve the definition of closeness and give a good user interface for identification of choices.

To summarize, we need a browsing capability which can incorporate:
- a multidimensional space;
- a measure of distance among objects defined according to a certain context;
- a facility for dealing with many contexts independently or in combination;
- a dynamic environment where measures can change;
- a set-of-objects-at-a-time navigation;
- visualization of contexts in two dimensions.

9.3 The Affinity Browser

We describe in this section an approach to browsing based on the concept of *affinity*. Our approach, the *affinity browser*, is a tool for the exploration of object relationships expressed as affinity between objects that fulfils the requirements discussed in section 9.2. The affinity browser is a generic browsing tool for the exploration of information systems. As a generic tool it is meant to be tailored to specific browsing activities. The tailoring is accomplished in essentially two ways. First, by defining the appropriate affinity metrics to describe object relationships of interest among the objects of the system. Second, by adding concepts and visual features that enhance the navigation guidance of the associated search space.

Most of the browsing tools that have been discussed in the previous sections support either point-to-point navigation based on hierarchical structures (e.g. the Smalltalk browser), or they rely on spatial relations for navigation. Our approach is based on the concept of affinity that can be appropriately expressed in visual terms as a spatial relationship: proximity. Objects that appear close in the representation space are more strongly related than objects that lie farther apart. A significant advantage of this approach is that a large spectrum of object relationships can be expressed in terms of affinity provided that we can devise metrics defined on the objects of the system that appropriately portray the relationships in terms of affinity.

The first step for the realization of a visual representation of a relationship among objects portrayed in terms of affinity is the choice of a metric that satisfactorily represents the relationship. The second step is the construction of a multidimensional placement of the objects based on the affinity information. The dimension of the space, the coordinates and

The Affinity Browser

the measure of distance are chosen in such a way that the position of each object conveys its relationship to the others. Objects that appear close together should have an affinity to each other. Finally, the object placement needs to be visualized in order to provide navigation support for the user. A detailed discussion of the affinity browser can be found in [28].

Affinity is a powerful conceptual relationship that humans utilize in everyday life to construct a cognitive structure over a generally loosely structured world. One of its important characteristics is that it is highly *context* sensitive. A set of objects that are close in one context can appear quite unrelated in another context. Furthermore, different views of the same set of objects relating to different contexts can be displayed simultaneously and thus complement one another. Adding new views increases, therefore, the user's understanding about these object relationships.

Once affinity is visually represented, users perform proximity-based navigation. Because users can explore different contexts, the browser should allow them to explore the system by choosing, at each step, the context that seems the most appropriate for the next move and update the other views accordingly. The set of coordinated views are called synchronized views. This capability seems convenient since objects that appear close together in one view may lie far apart in another view. Conversely, the user may wish to pursue many explorations concurrently, so the browser should also allow for independent views. These aspects will be discussed in more detail in the next section.

9.3.1 The Affinity Browser Exploration Paradigm

The intended usage of the affinity browser is the exploration of an information space assisted by visual representations of object relationships. Each such affinity can be explored through an affinity browser.

Figure 9.1 represents the typical layout of an affinity browser. Each of the round icons represents an object. The black icon in the centre of the browser is the *marked object*. The marked object is the object around which exploration recurs; users usually select, or *mark* an object, and then explore the objects in its neighbourhood. Eventually, during the exploration they will find an object that appears to be more appropriate, in which case they may select it as the new marked object.

The selection of a new marked object has two main consequences. First, the new marked object is displayed in the centre of the browser. Second, the set of objects that appear in the browser are those that correspond to the new marked object's neighbourhood. As a consequence of marking a new object, some objects may disappear from the representation while others may become visible.

In terms of exploration concepts, marking a new object corresponds to a shift in perspective. The user chooses a new navigation focal point and then explores the neighbourhood of the new marked object.

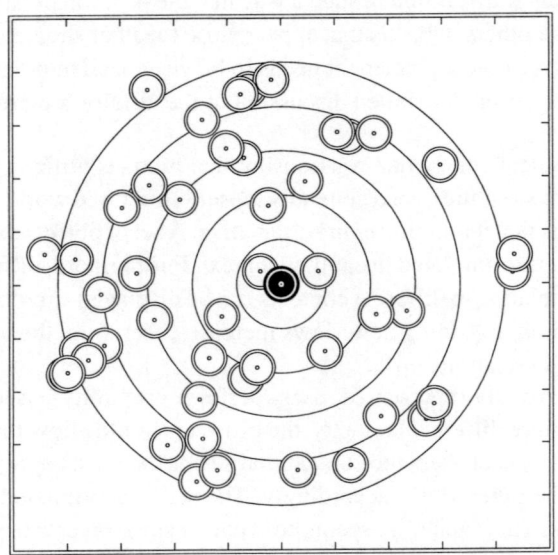

Figure 9.1 *Typical layout of an affinity browser representing an affinity context. The black icon represents the **marked object**.*

In a typical browsing session users select either an object they are acquainted with if they already have some knowledge of the information space or they selected one of the entry points that may be provided by the system.

An exploration path can be characterized by the sequence of marked objects. These may act as exploration landmarks and it may be interesting to provide a set of exploration paths that represent relevant guided tours.

9.3.1.1 Affinity Neighbourhood

An affinity browser does not usually show all the objects of an affinity context at a time. The displayed objects are those that lie within a user-defined neighbourhood of the marked object. More precisely, the neighbourhood of an object is controlled by a parameter $\varepsilon \in [0, 1]$ which represents a discriminant threshold: only the objects that have an affinity higher than ε relative to the marked object are displayed.

Alternatively, the user may specify the maximum number of objects to appear in the display. In practice this is the most commonly used way of specifying the visual neighbourhood range. The reason is that by keeping the same number of objects during exploration the user avoids situations where the system does not provide enough choices (e.g. few objects displayed), or situations where the browser presents too many choices in a cluttered display.

The Affinity Browser

The notion of set-of-objects-at-a-time navigation results from limiting the displayed objects to those that lie in the specified neighbourhood of an object. This set represents the inspection alternatives that the browser offers concurrently to the user. Although the "radius" of the neighbourhood can be changed at any time, it is an essential assumption of our approach that proximity-based navigation is a convenient exploration paradigm for most exploration or inspection tasks. Further, we see the neighbourhood restriction rather as a feature than as a limitation. Once users locate a region of interest they should be presented only with the choices that are close in its exploration context.

9.3.1.2 Synchronised Affinity Browsers

The proximity-based navigation provided by an affinity browser is mainly intended for "fine-grained" exploration. That is, once users have identified an interesting region, they explore the alternatives that are close in order to select the most appropriate. However, when users are exploring the information space "at large", local navigation alone is usually not enough.

A powerful mechanism used in human mental processes is association. For example, users proceed by association to recall entities that are close to a given entity. This mental process corresponds, in terms of browsing, to proximity-based navigation. A slightly more elaborate mental process consists of focusing on an object, exploring its neighbours, and investigating how the neighbouring objects in the present context are related in another context, and then exploring the objects that are close in the new context. This is a powerful process since it allows us to reach objects that are not closely related in the first context. Loosely speaking, we may say that exploration is based on transitive association; navigation is proximity-based but by alternating the navigation context the user can reach many other interesting objects. The mechanism that we provide to support this kind of transitive associations is the synchronization of affinity browsers. The synchronization of the affinity browsers implies that the object under inspection in one browser is also highlighted in the others. Users may pursue exploration in any of the browsers and the same path is followed in the others provided the inspected object also belongs to the latter context. We may recall here that two objects that are close in one context might not be close, or may even be unrelated, in another context. Figure 9.2 shows a set of four synchronized browsers. Synchronized views allow users to inspect objects that would otherwise be unreachable if navigation is based on just one exploration context. This stems from the fact that, in one browser objects that are not related to the marked object are normally not displayed. So, to reach non-related objects the user needs to switch to another browser for which the objects are related in the displayed context. This emphasizes the notion of navigation based on the strict neighbourhood of the marked object. However, the browsers allow users to display objects that are not directly related but are related by transitivity.

When objects are transitively related, their affinity is calculated either by a max-min transitivity rule or by a max-product rule. Refer to [28] for a detailed discussion about these operations.

Finally, the user may also explore the information space based on multiple independent browsers or a combination of synchronized and non-synchronized browsers. The syn-

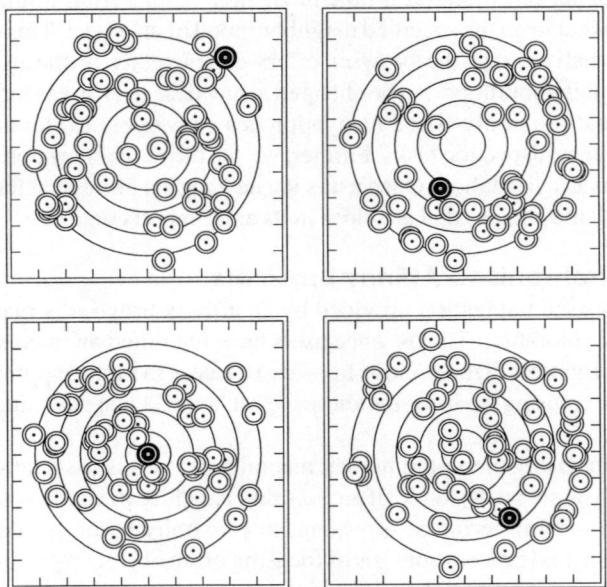

Figure 9.2 *Synchronous affinity browsers. The black icon represents the marked object. The user is performing exploration in the lower left browser where the marked object appears in the centre. Since the browsers are synchronized, the marked object is the same in all the browsers.*

chronization of the browsers is not a symmetric mechanism: saying that browser (a) is synchronized with browser (b) does not imply that browser (b) is synchronized with browser (a). To obtain two-way synchronization the user needs to specify it explicitly.

9.3.1.3 Exploration Based on Dynamically Evolving Affinity Contexts

As we stated in our browsing requirements, affinity browsers are intended to provide navigation guidance based on dynamically evolving object relationships. The browser provides such support essentially in two ways. First, it is able to track in a visual way and in interactive time-evolving relationships. Second, the browser provides for a degree of visual feedback where the movement of the visual objects gives the illusion of dynamic motion and dynamic interaction. Both aspects are addressed in more depth in [28] and [25].

One difficulty that users may find with dynamically evolving affinity contexts is that the changes in object relationships may make some objects disappear from the representation

The Affinity Browser

and others may show up due to the neighbourhood-restricted display. From our experience, this is quite cumbersome for unstable relationships that evolve at a fast pace.

9.3.2 Architectural Elements of an Affinity Browser

The architectural foundation of the affinity browser relies on an approach to software construction based on the composition of software components. Such an approach emphasizes modularity and careful study of component interfaces in order to achieve reusability and flexibility in software configuration. This flexibility is needed for the affinity browser since the idea is to provide a generic architecture that can be configured to meet the exploration requirements that a specific browser is intended to support.

9.3.2.1 Affinity Engine and View Engine

An affinity browser is comprised of two main units: the *affinity engine* and the *view engine*. The affinity engine is responsible for the management of tasks that are related to the translation of object relationships into a standard form of affinity representation.

The view engine is responsible for display and user interaction management. The affinity engine and the view engine communicate through well-defined protocols. The affinity engine often incorporates application-domain-dependent functionality in order to enhance navigation guidance with domain dependent-features. Similarly, the view engine can also incorporate visual features specific to the application domain and we frequently use this capability, in particular for financial tools.

9.3.2.2 Translucency: One Browser, Multiple Contexts

In our architecture, a browser can display multiple contexts simultaneously. This capability is made available by the view engine that supports a stack of translucent views so that the user can see through the views those that lie behind. The user can specify the desired degree of translucency from completely transparent to completely opaque. In a transparent view, no objects are visible. In an opaque view, objects hidden behind a front view do not show up. The superimposition of views is displayed with a visual effect of depth cueing: views progressively fade away from front to back.

The use of translucency is quite effective because it allows for the simultaneous exploration of many contexts on the same visual space. As a rule of thumb, in order to be useful the number of displayed views should not usually exceed four since the visual fading effect makes some views unreadable. Translucent visual layers are also effective to display domain-dependent information such as names, visual cues, transient information and alarms.

The interaction protocols between the view engine and the visual layers is well-defined, which allows the dynamic insertion of new layers into the view stack. The main advantage of having multiple views displayed in two dimensions is that lengths and distances can be compared visually, which is not usually the case when display relies on three-dimensional techniques since projection distorts distances.

9.3.3 User Interaction and Event Management

In order to conveniently support interaction with multiple superimposed visual layers, the view engine provides an event distribution mechanism through which events from many sources are distributed to the various layers that are responsible for reacting to them. When a new event is queued, it is sent first to the topmost layer, which is asked if it is interested in the event. If the layer is not interested or if the layer does not consume the event, then it is sent to the next layer in the view stack. The operation is applied recursively down the view stack until either the event is consumed or the bottom of the view stack is reached.

The order of the visual layers can be changed interactively by the user. Typically, users bring the layer with which they want to interact to the top of the stack. Furthermore, visual layers can be added to and deleted from the stack. A new visual layer is inserted, by default, at the top of the stack. Object relationships displayed in different visual layers of the same browser can be either synchronized or not, much in the same way as object relationships are displayed in different browsers.

The event distribution mechanism plays an important role in implementing coupled cooperative strategies between the visual layers. In fact, one of our design goals was to define an architecture for the view engine independent of the application domain. To achieve this goal, the interaction between the view engine and the visual layers only supports application-independent operations and not intended to be extended. We decided to provide flexibility in the way cooperation between views can be specified through an extended event distribution mechanism that acts as a messaging backbone.

The event distribution mechanism allows visual layers to communicate spontaneously or in reaction to user-initiated events. Additionally, the browser can be dynamically controlled by other applications that send events through the event distribution mechanism.

We applied the idea of external browser control to a financial application that displays real-time evolving relationships [29]. The application, which runs most of the time without user interaction, implements various display strategies aimed at highlighting important financial instruments relationships. The display and the relative position of the visual layers changes under the control of another application that monitors interesting investment opportunities. This approach to browsing control can be used to provide automatic navigation for dynamically evolving system.

To summarize, the affinity browser architecture has the following desirable characteristics for an exploration tool:

- *Versatility*. Allows users to inspect the underlying system through object relationships expressed in terms of affinity. The exploration can be based both on static or dynamic relationships, and the exploration perspective can be either local or global.
- *Composability*. Users can navigate based on multiple object relationships used independently or in combination. Multiple views can be active concurrently.
- *Extensibility*. New object relationships can be easily added to the exploration tool and combined with previously defined ones.

9.4 The Affinity Browser by Example

An intuitive way to describe the affinity browser approach is to say that we "measure" object relationships in such a way that the measurements translate the relationships into object affinities. Alternatively, we can say that we quantify a relationship in order to express it in terms of object affinity or proximity. For the affinity browser, these measurements are always performed between pairs of objects and are called metrics (refer to [28] for a formal presentation of these concepts).

As we may easily anticipate, one of the critical issues related to affinity browsing is the definition of metrics that portray interesting object relationships. We provide here a few examples of such metrics describing both static and dynamic relationships. Our main goal is to illustrate how the affinity browser can help one to understand particular aspects of an object-oriented environment, and provide typical examples of the kind of information an affinity browser is intended to provide for a system.

We first discuss metrics based on static analysis of class relationships. This kind of analysis is usually important to assess design and to understand architectural articulations; it provides insight into the relationships among classes without actually executing the code. Therefore, the information is primarily extracted by source code analysis.

Next we address the issue of extracting relationships corresponding to the dynamic behaviour of the system. We can identify interesting relationships among both classes and objects. Metrics to portray such relationships are based on dynamic analysis that consists of collecting statistical information, or simply frequency data during a system's execution.

The analysis can be performed either dynamically, in which case the display of the relationship is synchronized with the execution, or it can be off-line based on the information collected. In the latter case, the exploration phase resembles static analysis since the relationships do not evolve dynamically. It is also possible to collect data about the dynamic behaviour of the system and perform the analysis off-line. The advantage is that the analysis can be performed at the user's pace while still allowing for dynamic display.

9.4.1 Class Relationships

We discuss in this section three examples of metrics aimed at revealing class relationships. The first example deals with portraying functional commonality among classes. As a result of inheritance, derived classes inherit functionality from their base classes, and this raises the issue of the extent to which classes differ. The example discusses metrics related to this issue.

The second example deals with class acquaintances. In order to perform their tasks, the methods of a class send messages to other classes to invoke services. Patterns of interaction between a class and its environment may provide useful information about the required working environment for the class. We discuss metrics intended to reveal class acquaintances.

The third example addresses the problem of class relationships related to object *birth* and *death*. More specifically, we are interested in knowing which classes are instantiating and freeing objects. Because we are focusing here on relationships among classes, we consider that two classes are related if one class instantiates or frees objects of the other class.

It should be noted that the extraction of information for building such metrics depends considerably on the environment and on the language used to define the classes. In particular, with strongly typed object-oriented languages such as C++ and Eiffel, relationships like those of the first two examples are usually more accurately portrayed than when metrics are derived from classes implemented with weakly typed languages since, with strongly typed languages, relationships among classes are mostly statically defined.

9.4.1.1 Functional Commonality

In this example we construct a metric aimed at portraying the functional commonality among classes. For the sake of concreteness, the metric construction is illustrated with the set of classes $C = \{C_0, ..., C_8\}$ depicted in figure 9.3. Following inheritance rules, classes recursively inherit methods from their superclasses. We further assume that a class can redefine the methods inherited from its superclasses. Let $M(X)$ be a function that returns the set of methods in the interface to class X. For instance, $C_3 = \{a, b, g, h\}$. With this metric we want to convey the extent to which classes provide common functionality. The measure of affinity between two classes can, therefore, be expressed as the proportion of methods that are common to the two classes relative to the total number of the methods defined in both classes. As a candidate measure we define the affinity $A_1(X, Y)$ between class X and class Y by the function:

$$A_1(X, Y) = \frac{\text{card}(M(X) \cap M(Y))}{\text{card}(M(X) \cup M(Y))}$$

where card() is a function that returns the cardinality of a set.

Suppose now that we want to emphasize the fact that redefined functionality might differ from inherited functionality. We can modify slightly the affinity measure for the case of redefined functionality. Let m be the inherited method and m' be its redefinition. In the case where both m and m' appear in $\text{card}(M(X) \cup M(Y))$ then for the affinity calculation we consider $m = m'$ in $\text{card}(M(X) \cap M(Y))$ while in $\text{card}(M(X) \cup M(Y))$ we take $m \neq m'$. This produces a slight reduction of the affinity between classes where one redefines a method from a superclass (such as class C_1). From the affinity function we can derive the table 9.1 of pairwise affinities.

Figure 9.4 shows a view of the affinity browser depicting metric $A_1(X, Y)$ applied to the classes of figure 9.3. In figure 9.4, the highlighted class, C_4, is the *marked* item selected by the user. Therefore, the exploration is centred on it and the browser displays the items that lie inside the neighbourhood of the marked item, where the neighbourhood is defined as the set of objects for which the affinity relative to the current object is higher

The Affinity Browser by Example

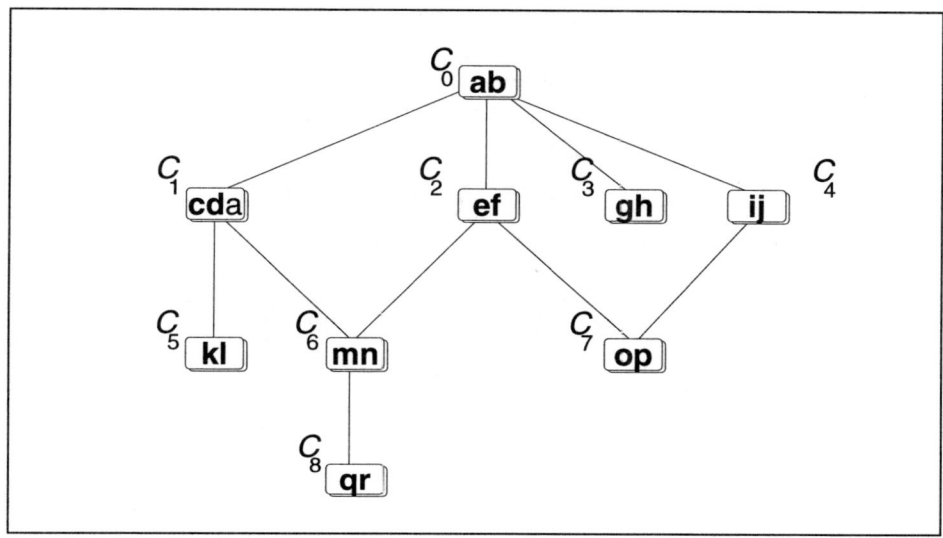

Figure 9.3 *Inheritance structure of a set of classes.*

C_1	C_2	C_3	C_4	C_5	C_6	C_7	C_8	
2/5	1/2	1/2	1/2	2/7	2/9	2/8	2/11	C_0
	2/7	2/7	2/7	2/3	4/9	2/11	4/11	C_1
		1/3	1/3	2/9	4/9	1/2	4/11	C_2
			1/3	2/9	2/11	2/10	2/13	C_3
				2/9	2/11	1/2	2/13	C_4
					4/11	2/13	4/13	C_5
						4/13	8/11	C_6
							4/15	C_7

Table 9.1 *Functional commonality: pairwise affinity.*

than a chosen value. In this case, however, due to the small number of items, they are all displayed.

9.4.1.2 Metrics Based on Binary Vectors

Many other metrics can be defined to reveal functional commonality. A particularly interesting approach relies on metrics based on binary data. The interest in using binary vectors

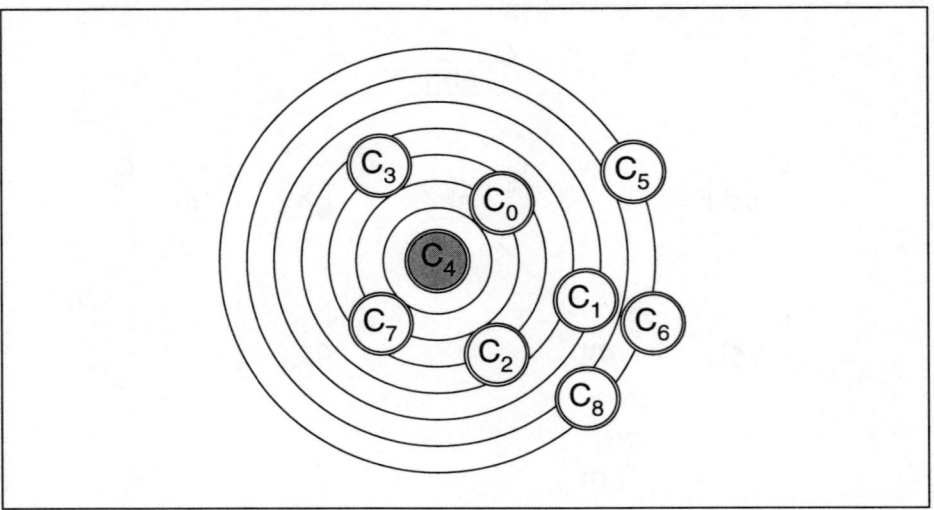

Figure 9.4 *Affinity browser display showing a set of classes.*

to build metrics is that many relationships can be expressed in terms of binary vectors to which we can apply a set of "standard" operations to measure their similarity.

In order to apply these metrics to portray functional commonality we assign to each class a binary vector of length l, where l represents the number of distinct method signatures in the system. Each entry of the vector is associated with a method signature. Referring to the set of classes depicted in figure 9.3, the binary vector takes the form:

| a | b | c | d | e | f | g | h | i | j | k | l | m | n | o | p | q | r |

Each entry contains a Boolean value that tells if the associated method signature is present or absent in the class. For example, the binary vector associated with class C_0 looks like:

| 1 | 1 | 0 | 0 | 0 | 0 | 0 | 0 | 0 | 0 | 0 | 0 | 0 | 0 | 0 | 0 | 0 | 0 |

and the vector associated with class C_6:

| 1 | 1 | 1 | 1 | 1 | 1 | 0 | 0 | 0 | 0 | 0 | 0 | 1 | 1 | 0 | 0 | 0 | 0 |

The construction of an affinity metric from binary vectors consists essentially in measuring to what extent vectors match. These can be defined based on the following auxiliary parameters:

$$\psi_{11} = \sum_{k=1}^{l} \min(x_k, y_k) \qquad \psi_{10} = \sum_{k=1}^{l} x_k - \psi_{11}$$

$$\psi_{01} = \sum_{k=1}^{l} y_k - \psi_{11} \qquad \psi_{00} = l - (\psi_{01} + \psi_{10} + \psi_{11})$$

where x and y represent two binary vectors. Ψ_{11} counts the number of times 1 appears simultaneously in the corresponding entries of x and y; Ψ_{10} counts the number of times 1 appears in x and 0 in y for corresponding entries; Ψ_{01} counts the number of times 0 appears in x and 1 in y for corresponding entries; and Ψ_{00} counts the number of times 0 appears simultaneously in the corresponding entries of x and y. So Ψ_{11} and Ψ_{00} count the number of entries in which x and y agree, while Ψ_{10} and Ψ_{01} count the number of disagreements.

We propose three metrics to portray functional commonality based on the binary vector representation. The first metric is

$$A_2(X, Y) = \frac{\Psi_{11}}{l}$$

where X and Y represent the classes from which the binary vectors x and y are derived. $A_2(X, Y)$ assesses binary vector similarity in terms of 1-consensus relative to the length of the binary vectors.

The second metric is

$$A_3(X, Y) = \frac{\Psi_{11}}{\Psi_{11} + \Psi_{10} + \Psi_{01}}$$

With this metric the proportion of the 1-consensus is evaluated relative to the number of entries of the vectors excluding those that correspond to a 0-consensus; that is, the metric assesses affinity in terms of 1-consensus relative to disagreement. This means that $A_3(X, Y)$ is equivalent to $A_1(X, Y)$.

The third metric

$$A_4(X, Y) = \frac{\Psi_{11} \Psi_{00}}{\sqrt{(\Psi_{11} + \Psi_{10})(\Psi_{11} + \Psi_{01})(\Psi_{00} + \Psi_{10})(\Psi_{00} + \Psi_{01})}}$$

measures binary vector correlation but is not a metric similarity index as are $A_3(X, Y)$ and, consequently, $A_1(X, Y)$.

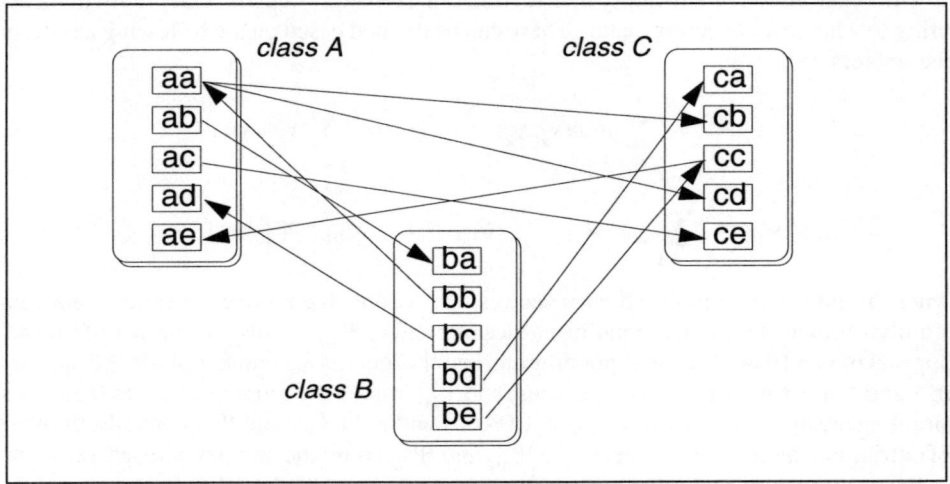

Figure 9.5   *A set of cooperating classes. The three classes cooperate by service exchange. Each slot represents the body of a method and the arrows represent the activation of a method from the body of another method.*

9.4.1.3   Class Acquaintances

The functionality of a class is not usually self-contained. Methods belonging to a class can invoke services from other classes. This perspective corresponds to a commonly accepted view of object-oriented systems as sets of collaborating objects.

We are interested in understanding patterns of collaboration between objects. However, collaboration has many aspects. We can focus, for instance, on the relationships between classes that can be observed by static analysis of the source code. Alternately, we may focus on dynamic acquaintances of classes measured by observing message sending patterns between objects of the classes.

Both perspectives are interesting and are, to a large extent, complementary. The former perspective usually reflects design decisions since "hard coded" relationships usually materialize links defined at the architectural level. Such links represent the required working environment for a class. But this perspective may fall short of providing an accurate picture if we are looking for working acquaintances between classes. In this case the latter perspective may be more helpful.

In practice, the collaboration patterns revealed by the two perspectives usually differ significantly. However, the analysis of the differences might offer useful insight about mismatch between the collaborations that have been foreseen by the designer and those that show up in specific execution contexts. We start with a metric intended to portray static class acquaintances. That is, acquaintances that can be determined without actually executing the methods of the class.

The Affinity Browser by Example

Figure 9.5 represents the analysis context for such a metric. Each class contains a set of methods and the methods activate methods belonging to other classes that, in turn, trigger other methods as well. So the execution of a class's method usually involves the execution of methods from many classes.

Let I_K^J denote the number of times class K invokes methods from class J, and let I_K denote the total number of invocations from class K to any other class. The following is a candidate metric to portray class acquaintances:

$$A_5(K, J) = \max\left(\frac{I_K^J}{I_K}, \frac{I_J^K}{I_J}\right)$$

which means that the acquaintance affinity between two classes is defined as the maximum of relative invocation frequency of both classes. We may notice, however, that many different functions can be used instead of max() to combine the two "one-sided" acquaintances. We can define a more general metric as follows:

$$A_5(K, J) = 1 - \log\left(\frac{\left(\lambda^{1-\frac{I_K^J}{I_K}} - 1\right)\left(\lambda^{1-\frac{I_J^K}{I_J}} - 1\right)}{\lambda - 1} + 1\right)$$

where $\lambda \in (0, 1) \cup (1, \infty)$ and $\log(x)$ has base λ. This metric is inspired from a function proposed by Frank [1] to define the union operation on fuzzy sets. The reader might want to refer to [28] for a detailed discussion about other functions that can be used in this context. This way of doing things may suggest an interpretation where I_K^J/I_K represents the affinity degree of an element J to affinity set K which depicts the unilateral affinity acquaintance between class K and the other classes.

9.4.1.4 Class Acquaintance Similarities

We may also be interested in class acquaintance similarity. In other words, we want to discover to what extent classes match in terms of the services they ask for from other classes. Let $s_{C,m}$ denote a service; that is, s is an association of a class name C and one of its methods represented by its method's signature m. Let f_K^s denote the frequency of invocation of service s from inside the methods of class K. We can associate to each class K a vector v_K with entries containing f_K^s. The dimension d of vector v_K is equal to the number of different services invoked by the classes of the system.

So, the collection of classes can be represented in the d-dimensional space of the services, where each class will appear as a point. The idea is that classes lying close together in this space ask for similar services. We may want to modify slightly the service weighting scheme to improve selectivity. Let i_s denote the number of classes from which service s is invoked, and let n denote the number of classes. We can define

$$L_s = \lceil \log_2 n \rceil - \lceil \log_2 i_s \rceil + 1.$$

A service weighting proportional to $f_K^s \cdot L_s$ will assign larger weights to services which are invoked with high frequency in individual classes, but that are only invoked by a few classes. This type of weighting scheme improves substantially both recall and precision when applied to document retrieval [32]. Finally, we can define a distance metric between two classes K and J as the Euclidean distance between the associated vectors v_K and v_J.

9.4.2 Creation and Destruction Relationships

In an object-oriented environment, objects are usually created and destroyed by other objects. Understanding creation and destruction relationships is important for many reasons. First, it provides essential information about which classes are managing the object population in the system and, in particular, which are the typical procreators of objects that provide specific kinds of services. Second, this understanding is crucial for debugging and, in particular, memory allocation related errors. As a matter of fact, the very nature of object-oriented systems as sets of cooperating agents raises the problem of object cleanup. Designers need to decide who is responsible for freeing the objects. It is often difficult to assign this responsibility to its creator, especially if the creator is not the consumer of the services. The non-destruction of stale objects may become a particularly important issue in the absence of automatic garbage collection.

Creation and destruction relationships can be analyzed either statically or dynamically. Similar to acquaintance relationships, dynamic and static analysis provide different perspectives on the creation and destruction relationship. Static analysis based on source code scanning essentially provides information about the structure of the creation and destruction process. We can learn, for instance, which classes can create and destroy instances of given classes.

Dynamic analysis provides another perspective on the relationship by showing which class instances are actually creating and destroying objects, and also how many objects are created and destroyed. However, the static perspective falls short of portraying an important aspect of software execution: execution phases. A typical software system or subsystem goes through a number of execution phases. It may start with an initialization phase, then alternate through several phases. Different phases become evident by analysis of both interclass acquaintances and creation and destruction relationships. Entering a new phase usually corresponds to a significant modification of interaction patterns and an intense activity of object destruction — for phase cleanup — and creation of new objects for the new execution phase.

The information about the creation relationship can be represented by a matrix like

$$C = \begin{bmatrix} C_{A,A} & C_{A,B} & C_{A,C} \\ C_{B,A} & C_{B,B} & C_{B,C} \\ C_{C,A} & C_{C,B} & C_{C,C} \end{bmatrix}$$

where $C_{X,Y}$ represents the number of times creation of an instance of class Y can be identified inside the source code specifying class X, if we are in the context of static analysis. In the context of dynamic analysis, $C_{X,Y}$ represents the number of times instances of class X create instances of class Y during a given time interval. In order to explore execution phases we can collect data for several time intervals that should reveal the changes in creation patterns. The destruction relationship can be represented by a matrix D that has a similar form to C where entry $D_{X,Y}$ represents the number of times instances of class X destroy instances of class Y during a given time interval.

We can derive a matrix

$$R = \begin{bmatrix} C_{A,A} - D_{A,A} & C_{A,B} - D_{A,B} & C_{A,C} - D_{A,C} \\ C_{B,A} - D_{B,A} & C_{B,B} - D_{B,B} & C_{B,C} - D_{B,C} \\ C_{C,A} - D_{C,A} & C_{C,B} - D_{C,B} & C_{C,C} - D_{C,C} \end{bmatrix}$$

which might represent an acceptable view of the balance between creation and destruction responsibilities. For instance, $R_{X,Y} < 0$ means that class X destroyed more instances of class Y than it created during the time interval under analysis. Many insightful metrics can be derived from the information contained in these matrices.

We convey creation relationships in such a way that classes that are frequently involved in creation (either by creating or by being created) have more affinity and thus cluster together in the representation. A candidate metric is:

$$A_6(X, Y) = \frac{\max(C_{X,Y}, C_{Y,X})}{\max(C)}$$

where $\max(C)$ denotes the maximum value in matrix C. $A_6(X, Y)$ fails to show which one of two classes displaying high affinity is responsible for creation. To obtain such information we may either define a pair of metrics to be used in exploration with synchronized views or create a metric that highlights asymmetry. Both approaches have already been discussed in the context of the formulation of previous metrics.

We provide another metric to convey the balance between creation and destruction. The idea is that instances of a class X that create more instances of another class Y than they destroy, display more affinity while a negative balance in the creation/destruction process reduces the affinity between X and Y.

$$A_7(X, Y) = \frac{\max(R_{X,Y} - \min(R), R_{Y,X} - \min(R))}{\max(R) - \min(R)}$$

9.4.3 Object Relationships

We discussed in the previous section metrics to portray class relationships. The information needed to apply those metrics relies either on static analysis of the class definitions, on dynamic analysis of execution activity, or on both. We may notice, in passing, that many of the metrics discussed could be used to portray object relationships as well. In this section we focus specifically on object relationships that are related to dynamic aspects of the system's execution and, therefore, require dynamic behaviour analysis. Understanding the dynamic behaviour of a set of objects that collaborate to perform a task can provide useful information for reuse and for class management. Dynamic behaviour analysis can be helpful:

- in giving useful hints about the usage a developer intended for a particular class;
- by showing the typical utilization of classes inside an application;
- to tune the performance of classes;
- in providing information for the assessment of class designs;
- in application debugging.

We now discuss candidate metrics intended to portray different aspects of the dynamic behaviour of objects defined in terms of object affinity. In order to perform tasks collectively, objects exchange messages. As a first goal we want to know which objects collaborate closely. Because we are interested in dynamic patterns of collaboration, the information needed to build the metrics is collected by monitoring message passing activity.

Let $O = \{O_1, O_2, ..., O_n\}$ denote the set of interacting objects during a given time interval. We may define an affinity metric $A_8(X, Y)$ between object $X \in O$ and object $Y \in O$ by:

$$A_8(X, Y) = \frac{\text{card}(\text{send}(X, Y)) + \text{card}(\text{send}(Y, X))}{\sum_i \text{card}(\text{send}(O_i))}$$

where send (X, Y) is a function that returns the set of messages sent by object X to object Y, and card (x) returns the cardinality of a set. So $\Sigma_i \text{card}(\text{send}(O_i))$ represents the total number of messages exchanged during the monitored time interval. With such a metric of affinity, objects that exchange messages frequently will have more affinity and will therefore cluster together in the affinity browser's visual representation.

9.4.3.1 Detecting Object Interaction Asymmetry

However, metric $A_8(X, Y)$ does not show asymmetric interaction patterns. Suppose, for example, that object X sends messages frequently to object Y while object Y seldom sends messages to object X. Measure $A_8(X, Y)$ will not reveal this fact. In order to expose asymmetry we define two metrics, $A_{9a}(X, Y)$ and $A_{9b}(X, Y)$, that are intended to be used in two synchronized views:

$$A_{9a}(X, Y) = \frac{\text{card}(\text{send}(\text{src}(X, Y), \text{dest}(X, Y)))}{\sum_i \text{card}(\text{send}(O_i))}$$

$$A_{9b}(X, Y) = \frac{\text{card}(\text{send}(\text{dest}(X, Y), \text{src}(X, Y)))}{\sum_i \text{card}(\text{send}(O_i))}$$

We introduce the notion of *source* and *destination* to cope with the asymmetry between the two metrics; the functions src() and dest() return respectively the *source* object and the *destination* object. The role of these functions is to enforce a rule so that an object that plays the source role for a given pair (X, Y) in the first metric plays the destination role for the same pair in the other metric. Additionally, the rule copes with pair symmetry so that $A_{9a}(X, Y) = A_{9a}(Y, X)$ and $A_{9b}(X, Y) = A_{9b}(Y, X)$. The rule works as follows: for an affinity context with n objects we generate the $(n(n-1))/2$ pairs that correspond to the upper right half of a matrix which is illustrated for $n = 4$:

$$\begin{bmatrix} (O_1, O_2) & (O_1, O_3) & (O_1, O_4) \\ & (O_2, O_3) & (O_2, O_4) \\ & & (O_3, O_4) \end{bmatrix}$$

The rule specifies that for each pair, the object that appears on the left-hand side plays the role of the source and the object on the right plays the role of the destination. Furthermore, for any such pair (X, Y) the roles for the symmetric pair (Y, X) are assigned to the same objects. For example, O_1 plays the role of the source and O_3 the role of the destination in both (O_1, O_3) and (O_3, O_1).

When metrics $A_{9a}(X, Y)$ and $A_{9b}(X, Y)$ are represented in synchronized views, the user can spot asymmetry by looking for pairs of objects that appear close in one view and farther apart in the other. These two metrics provide both global information about collaboration as well as information about collaboration asymmetry.

However, if we are mostly interested in detecting asymmetry, it might be more appropriate to emphasize pairwise interaction instead of global interaction affinity. To this end we may consider the replacement of metrics $A_{9a}(X, Y)$ and $A_{9b}(X, Y)$ by $A_{10a}(X, Y)$ and $A_{10b}(X, Y)$. Let

$$\Delta(X, Y) = \text{card}(\text{send}(\text{src}(X, Y), \text{dest}(X, Y)) \cup \text{send}(\text{dest}(X, Y), \text{src}(X, Y)))$$

and

$$A_{10a}(X, Y) = \frac{\text{card}(\text{send}(\text{src}(X, Y), \text{dest}(X, Y)))}{\Delta(X, Y)}$$

$$A_{10b}(X, Y) = \frac{\text{card}(\text{send}(\text{dest}(X, Y), \text{src}(X, Y)))}{\Delta(X, Y)}$$

It is also possible to synthesize information about symmetry of message passing in one metric, although the resulting display might be more difficult to interpret. $A_{11}(X, Y)$ is a candidate measure for such a view. This measure focuses on symmetry of message exchanges and, therefore, suppresses information about frequency of communication.

$$A_{11}(X, Y) = 1 - \frac{\text{abs}(A_{9a}(X, Y) - A_{9b}(X, Y))}{\text{abs}(A_{9a}(X, Y) + A_{9b}(X, Y))}$$

Interaction asymmetry is an important issue at the design level. For instance, Booch [4] identifies three roles for objects in terms of message passing activity:
- **Actor**: an object that operates upon other objects but that is never operated upon by other objects.
- **Server**: an object that never operates upon other objects; it is only operated upon by other objects.
- **Agent**: an object that can both operate upon other objects and be operated upon by other objects; an agent is usually created to do some work on behalf of an actor or another agent.

Such roles can be identified with metric $A_{11}(X, Y)$. The comparison of the roles assigned to objects during the design phase, with the effective role they play in given execution contexts, might be instrumental to assess to what extent reusable software components are used as intended by their designers.

9.5 Conclusion

This chapter dealt with the exploration of object relationships in the context of object-oriented environments. We addressed the important issue of understanding how objects are related because such understanding plays an important role in many key issues related to software engineering such as reuse, debugging and software maintenance. Early object-oriented environment designers have identified these issues and provided browsing tools to help users explore the environment.

We have proposed a new approach to the exploration of an object-oriented environment where object relationships are translated into affinity relations so that the object relationships can be graphically represented in terms of distance: objects that are strongly related appear closer in the representation. The approach has the advantage that many different relationships can be represented and explored with the same tool and with the same exploration paradigm. From the user's perspective, affinity is a very intuitive concept that has the advantage of being easily translated into a visual distance.

References

[1] Hans-Dieter Böcker, Jürgen Herczeg, "What Tracers are Made Of," *Proceedings of OOPSLA/ECOOP '90, ACM SIGPLAN Notices*, 1990, pp. 89–99.

[2] R. Bolt, "Spatial Data Management," DARPA Report, MIT, Architecture Machine Group, 1979.

[3] Bernd Brüegge, Tim Gottschalk, Bin Luo, "A Framework for Dynamic Program Analysers," *Proceedings of OOPSLA '93, ACM SIGPLAN Notices*, 1993, pp. 65–82.

[4] Grady Booch, *Object Oriented Design With Applications*, Benjamin/Cummings, 1991.

[5] Michael Caplinger, "Graphical Database Browsing," *Proceedings of ACM-SIGOIS, SIGOIS bulletin*, vol. 7, no. 2–3, Oct. 1986.

[6] Matthew Chalmers and Paul Chitson, "Bead: Explorations in Information Visualization," *Proceedings of SIGIR '92*, June 1992, pp. 330–337.

[7] William Donelson, "Spatial Management of Information," *Computer Graphics (Proceedings of SIGGRAPH '78)*, Aug. 1978, pp. 203–209.

[8] Furnas Fairchild, Poltrock, "Semnet:Three-dimensional Graphic Representation of Large Knowledge Bases," in *Cognitive Science and its Applications for Human–Computer Interaction*, ed. R. Guindon, Lawrence Erlbaum, Hillsdale, NJ, 1988.

[9] Steven Feiner, "Seeing the Forest for the Trees: Hierarchical Display of Hypertext Structures," *Proceedings of COIS '88*, Palo Alto, March 1988, pp. 205–212.

[10] C. Fields and N. Negroponte, "Using New Clues to Find Data," Third International Conference on Very Large Data Bases, Tokyo, Oct. 1977, pp. 156–158.

[11] David Gedye and Randy Katz, "Browsing the Chip Design Database," University of California at Berkeley, Computer Science Division, Oct. 1987.

[12] Adele Goldberg, *Smalltalk-80: The Interactive Programming Environment*, Addison-Wesley, Reading, Mass., 1984.

[13] I. Goldstein and D. Bobrow, "Browsing in a Programming Environment," *Proceedings of the 14th Hawaii International Conference on System Science*, January 1981.

[14] Charles Herot, "Spatial Management of Data," *ACM Transactions on Database Systems*, vol. 5, no. 4, Dec. 1980, pp. 493–513.

[15] William P. Jones, "On the Applied Use of Human Memory Models: The Memory Extender Personal Filing System," International Journal Man–Machine Studies, vol. 25, no. 2, 1986, pp. 191–228.

[16] George Klir, Tina Folger, *Fuzzy Sets, Uncertainty and Information*, Prentice Hall, Englewood Cliffs, NJ, 1988.

[17] M. Kleyn, P. Gingrich, "GraphTrace — Understanding Object-oriented Behaviour Systems Using Concurrently Animated Views," *Proceedings of OOPSLA '88, ACM SIGPLAN Notices*, 1988, pp. 191–205.

[18] Jeffrey T. LeBlanc, "N-Land: A Visualization Tool for N-Dimensional Data," Technical Report Computer Science Department, University of Worcester, May 1991.

[19] Bertrand Meyer, *Object-Oriented Software Construction*, Prentice Hall, 1988.

[20] Amihai Motro, "Browsing in a Loosely Structured Database," *Proceedings of ACM–SIGMOD 1984, International Conference on Management of Data*, 1984, pp. 197–207.

[21] Amihai Motro, "BAROQUE: A Browser for Relational Databases," vol. 4, no. 2, April 1986, pp. 164–181.

[22] Amihai Motro, "VAGUE: A User Interface to Relational Databases that Permits Vague Queries," *ACM Transactions on Office Information Systems*, vol. 6, no. 2, July 1988, pp. 187–214.

[23] Amihai Motro, Alessandro D'Atri, Laura Tarantino, "The Design of KIVIEW: An Object-Oriented Browser," *Proceedings of the Second International Conference on Expert Database Systems*, Virginia, 1988, pp. 17–31.

[24] P. O'Brien and D. Halbert and M. Kilian, "The Trellis Programming Environment," *Proceedings of OOPSLA '87, ACM SIGPLAN Notices*, Oct. 1987.

[25] Xavier Pintado, Eugene Fiume, "Grafields: Field-directed Dynamic Splines for Interactive Motion Control," *Computers & Graphics*, vol. 13, no. 1, Jan. 1989, pp. 77–82.

[26] Xavier Pintado, Dennis Tsichritzis, "An Affinity Browser," Technical Report, Centre Universitaire d'Informatique, University of Geneva, June 1988.

[27] Xavier Pintado, "Selection and Exploration in an Object-oriented Environment: The Affinity Browser," in *Object Management*, ed. D. Tsichritzis, Centre Universitaire d'Informatique, July 1990, pp. 79–88.

[28] Xavier Pintado, "Objects' Relationships," Ph.D. Thesis, Centre Universitaire d'Informatique, University of Geneva, Switzerland, 1994.

[29] Xavier Pintado, "Visualization in the Financial Markets," *VR '94, Proceedings of the Fourth Annual Conference on Virtual Reality*, Mecklermedia, London, 1994, pp. 80–84.

[30] Andy Podgursky, Lynn Pierce, "Retrieving Reusable Software by Sampling Behaviour," *ACM Transactions on Software Engineering and Methodology*, vol. 2, no. 3, July 1993, pp. 286–303.

[31] Kenneth Rubin, Adele Goldberg, "Object Behaviour Aanlysis," *Communications of the ACM*, vol. 35, no. 9, Sept. 1992.

[32] Gerard Salton, *Automatic Text Processing: The Transformation, Analysis, and Retrieval of Information by Computer*, Addison-Wesley, Reading, Mass. 1988.

[33] Michael Stonebraker and J. Kalash, "Timber: a Sophisticated Database Browser," *Proceedings of the 8th International Conference on Very Large Data Bases*, Sept. 1982, pp. 1–10.

[34] David Stotts and Richard Furuta, "Petri-Net-Based Hypertext: Document Structure with Browsing Semantics," *ACM Transactions on Information Systems*, vol. 7, no. 1, Jan. 1989.

PART V

Frameworks and Applications

Chapter 10
Visual Composition of Software Applications

Vicki de Mey

Abstract Open applications can be viewed as compositions of reusable and configurable components. We introduce visual composition as a way of constructing applications from plug-compatible software components. After presenting related work, we describe an object-oriented framework for visual composition that supports open system development through the notion of domain-specific *composition models*. We illustrate the use of the framework through the application of a prototype implementation to a number of very different domains. In each case, a specialized visual composition tool was realized by developing a domain-specific composition model. We conclude with some remarks and observations concerning component engineering and application composition in a context where visual composition is an essential part of the development process.

10.1 Introduction

We define *visual composition* as the interactive construction of running applications by the direct manipulation and interconnection of visually presented software components. The connections between components are governed by a set of plug-compatibility rules specified within a *composition model*.

Visual composition is a response to the trends in software development towards more component-oriented lifecycles described in chapter 1. With a large number of components supplied by component engineers, application development becomes an activity of composing components into running applications. Visual composition can be used to communicate reusable assets from component engineers to application developers, reusable designs to application developers, and open applications to end-users. A visual composition framework enables the construction of environments and tools to facilitate component-oriented software development.

In this chapter we present a framework for visual composition. The framework addresses four issues: (1) components, (2) composition models, (3) user interaction, and (4) component management. Components are made up of a *behaviour* and a *presentation*. The behaviour is responsible for the component's composition interface and the work the component was designed to do. The presentation is the visual display of the component. A component can have more than one presentation, and the presentations reflect the state of the component. A set of components can be grouped together to function as a single component through the *composite component* mechanism. Component composition is defined as communication between components through their composition interfaces. The framework defines the notions of *port* and *link* to handle the communication. A *composition model* is the set of rules for component composition in a particular application domain. Decoupling the rules for composition from components allows a variety of different software composition paradigms and increases the potential for reuse of a component.

Vista is a prototype implementation of the visual composition framework. A concrete implementation of a visual composition tool is obtained by a *component engineer* (chapter 1) by completing the framework with components, their presentations and the composition model governing their interconnection. Finally, the resulting tool can be used by an application developer to visually compose running applications, as shown in section 10.5.

In reference to software development environments, Ivar Jacobson made the following statement:

> In the long run, we shall see new development environments that place more emphasis on applications and less on technique. Developers will be application experts, not Unix or C++ experts. They will work with graphical objects presented in several dimensions, not simply text. The language of today may be handled as a machine language that is invisible to developers. [23].

These new development environments will have the potential to transform software development. End-users will play a larger role in putting applications together and new ways of creating applications will be necessary. Visual composition is one of these new ways.

10.2 Related Work

Visual composition is based on work done in many different fields from software lifecycles to graphical user interfaces and graphical object editors, visual programming, components and connectivity, and component integration. Since the latter two areas are the most relevant for this chapter, they will be discussed here.

Visual composition supports components and connecting components together to form running systems. Some exemplary systems based on these ideas are ConMan, Fabrik, Silicon Graphic's IRIS Explorer™, Apple's ATG Component Construction Kit and IBM's VisualAge™. ConMan [14] is a high-level visual language that allows users to build and modify graphics applications. To create an application the user interactively connects simple components using a directed dataflow metaphor. No concept of composite components exists. Fabrik [22] is a contemporary of ConMan. Fabrik is a visual programming environment that supplies a kit of computational and user interface components that can be wired together using a bidirectional dataflow metaphor. The environment can be used to build new components and applications. Composite components are supported through the gateway construct. IRIS Explorer is an application creation system and user environment that provides visualization and analysis functionality. It is based on a distributed, decentralized dataflow model. Its graphical user interface allows users to build custom applications by connecting modules together. Apple's ATG Component Construction Kit (CCK) [43] is a prototype component architecture and set of test components that allows end-users to plug components into a framework at run-time. The kit has four elements: (1) a component framework (the structure within which components are connected); (2) a component palette (source of components); (3) an inference engine for automatically connecting components; (4) a component inspector for display and modification of component information. Objects are the medium of communication between components in the CCK. VisualAge [20] is a product from IBM designed to build the client side of client–server applications, focusing on business applications and decision support systems. The tool is based on the "construction by parts" paradigm that is supported by a visual programming tool for creating applications non-procedurally. These systems are interesting but limited since some cater only to specific application domains or are based on one way of expressing the relationships between components.

A component can be seen as a separate tool, application or process. This brings up component integration issues that run very close to the issues of component interfaces and component interconnection. Visual composition needs component integration mechanisms to implement the connections between components. Integration issues can be viewed on two levels: coarse-grained and fine-grained. Coarse-grained integration concerns components that may be large objects that cooperate by exchanging messages, or tools that cooperate through shared files. Fine-grained integration concerns components that are smaller and usually need to communicate with each other more frequently. Harrison, Ossher and Kavianpour [17] have discussed this issue and proposed an approach called Object-Oriented Tool Integration Services (OOTIS). They believe that applications are moving more towards fine-grained integration, but that current systems, which are coarse-grained, must still be supported while this move takes place.

Many proposals have been made for specific solutions to coarse-grained integration. Some examples are: Unix facilities that provide a variety of different tools and tool integration mechanisms (character files, I/O redirection, pipes, shell programming); Hewlett Packard's Softbench environment [19]; and Sun's ToolTalk [26] for interapplication communication. Fine-grained integration solutions include efforts by the OMG (Object Request Broker), NeXT (Distributed Objects [36]), Microsoft (OLE [34]) and Apple (Apple events and the Apple event object model [1], and OpenDoc [2]). See also chapter 12 for a more thorough discussion of these commercial efforts, and chapter 3 for an example of an object-oriented framework to support interoperability.

10.3 A Framework for Visual Composition

The framework we present provides a simple and flexible core for visual composition. There are three pieces of information that are needed in order to use the framework: component behaviours, component presentations and rules for composition. This information is plugged into the framework to produce a visual composition tool for a specific purpose.

10.3.1 Component Definition

The framework defines a component as a *behaviour* together with one or more *presentations*. Such a "division of labour" has been seen in other frameworks including Smalltalk's MVC framework [13], Unidraw [48] and Andrew [38]. Table 10.1 shows the corresponding terms in the different frameworks. This division promotes reuse, because different presentations can be reused with the same or different behaviours.

Behaviour

The behaviour is responsible for the following:
- Communication with the presentation(s).
- The component's composition interface. The composition interface advertises the component's services and requests for services. The composition interface allows the component to be reused in different contexts. A component's context includes the components it is immediately connected to as well as the entire ensemble of components in which it finds itself embedded. The composition interface of a component consists of a set of *ports*, each of which has a name, a type and a polarity. Ports may be visually presented in a variety of ways, such as knobs, buttons, text fields, menus, etc., depending on the intended semantics.
- Executing whatever the component was designed to do. The behaviour reflects the inner part of the component. From the outside, two components can look like they have the same behaviour, but their internal implementations could be very different (e.g. implemented in different programming languages). A component can also behave differently depending on the other components it is connected to.

Visual composition	Behaviour	Presentation
MVC	Model	View, Controller
Unidraw	subject	view
Andrew	data object	view

Table 10.1 *Comparison of the behaviour/presentation division of labour.*

A Framework for Visual Composition

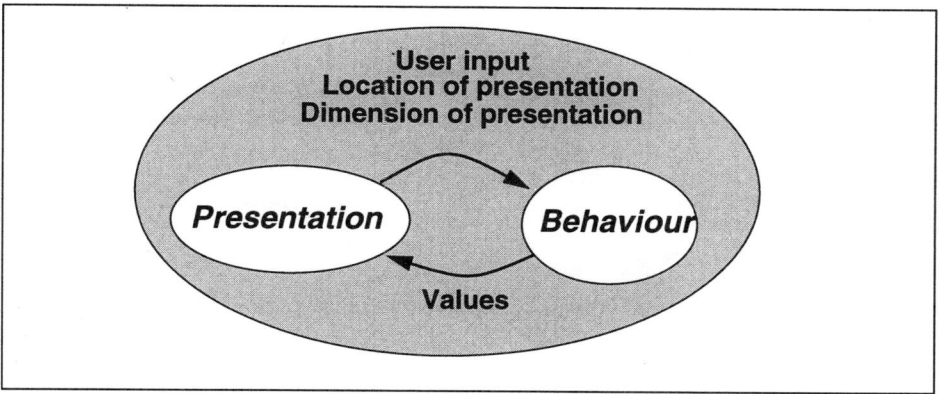

Figure 10.1 *Communication between the behaviour and presentation entities in the framework.*

Presentation

The presentation is responsible for the following:
- Communication with the behaviour.
- Visual display of the component. All components, whether inherently visual or not, have a visual presentation. A presentation can also process user input if it contains an interaction component such as a button or a text field.

Communication between the behaviour and presentation is pictured in figure 10.1. The presentation informs the behaviour of its location and dimensions so that this information can be passed on to other components that need it to display themselves. Also, input can be done through the presentation, and this information is communicated to the behaviour. The behaviour only informs the presentation of information that it might need to display on the screen.

Composite Components

Components can be created by programming or by composition. When a component is created by programming, only the behaviour and presentation need to be specified (or re-used if an appropriate behaviour or presentation already exists) and hooked into the framework. A composite component is a set of components linked together that is considered useful as a component in its own right. To define a composite component, one must add to the set of components (1) a composition interface (by specifying which ports of the set of components are to become ports of the composite component), and (2) a visual presentation (which can be composed of existing presentations). The behaviour of a composite component is simply the behaviour of the components it encapsulates. Figure 10.2 illustrates the idea of composite component. The framework supports composite components by defining *external_port* and *external_view* entities. A set of external_port entities represents the composite component's composition interface, and an external_view entity

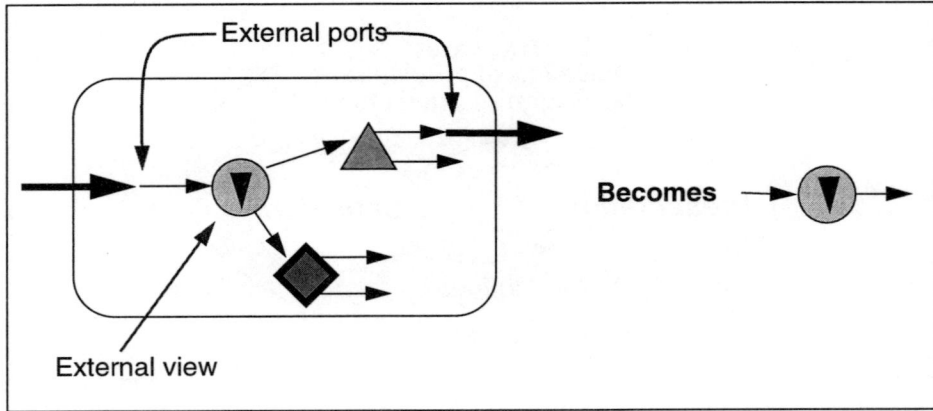

Figure 10.2 *Composite component.*

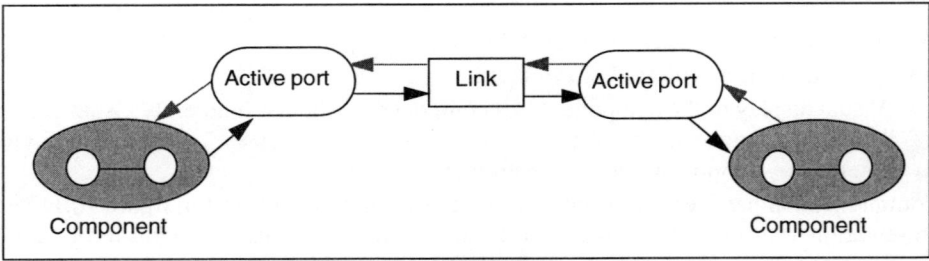

Figure 10.3 *Framework entities.*

is the presentation used for the composite component. Both external_port and external_view entities are created interactively when a composite component is being defined.

10.3.2 Component Composition

The way component composition is supported in the framework is through the creation of networks. The framework uses components for the nodes in the network and defines *active_port* and *link* entities for edges in the network. Not all ports in the composition interface of a component need to be used. An active_port is created only when a port in a component's composition interface is connected to a port in another component's composition interface. A link represents the connection from one active_port to another. Figure 10.3 illustrates the relationship between the elements of the framework. Communication between components can be either one-way (the dark arrows in figure 10.3) or bidirection-

A Framework for Visual Composition

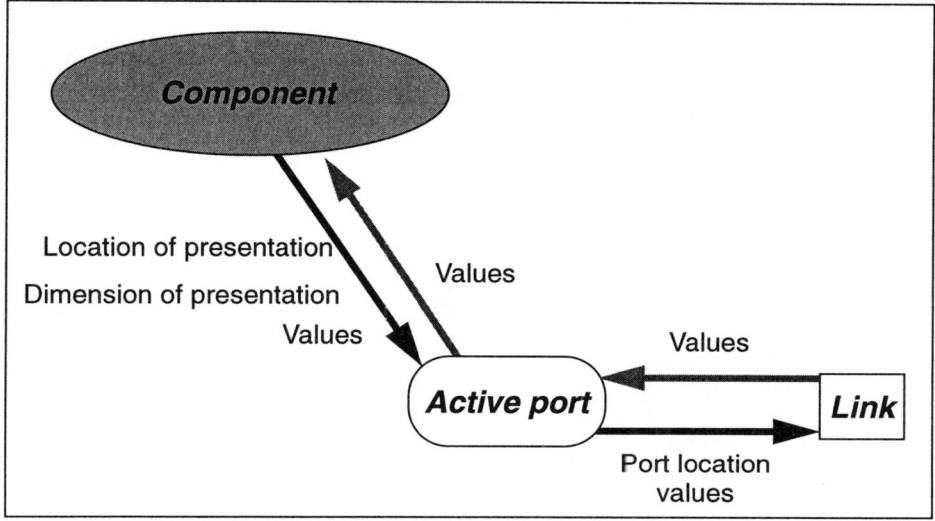

Figure 10.4 *Communication between a component, active_port and link.*

al (both the dark and the grey arrows in figure 10.3). The format of the information that passes from component to component is defined in the behaviour of the component. The format is not restricted by the framework. The display information is internal to the framework and should at least include the location and dimensions of the presentation so that the active_ports and links can be displayed correctly. Figure 10.4 summarizes the information that is communicated between the active_port and link entities of the framework.

As components are composed, networks, such as the one pictured in figure 10.5, are generated. The grey ovals in the figure are components, the black circles are ports, the clear circles are active_ports and the rectangles are links. These networks have certain characteristics:

- *Automatic network update*: Information must be automatically propagated through the network. Propagation occurs when a node indicates some change to the information on its outputs. This indicates the need for some type of constraint mechanism to specify the relations in the network that must always be satisfied. Information propagation could imply some change to the display that must be done automatically and immediately to support the requirement of direct manipulation. There must be the option for immediate propagation or batching for the display, since the update of a densely populated screen can be expensive and possibly postponed
- *Hierarchical decomposition*: The network must support nodes that are made up of other network structures.
- *Cyclic networks*: In visual composition, the relationships between components can create cycles in the network.

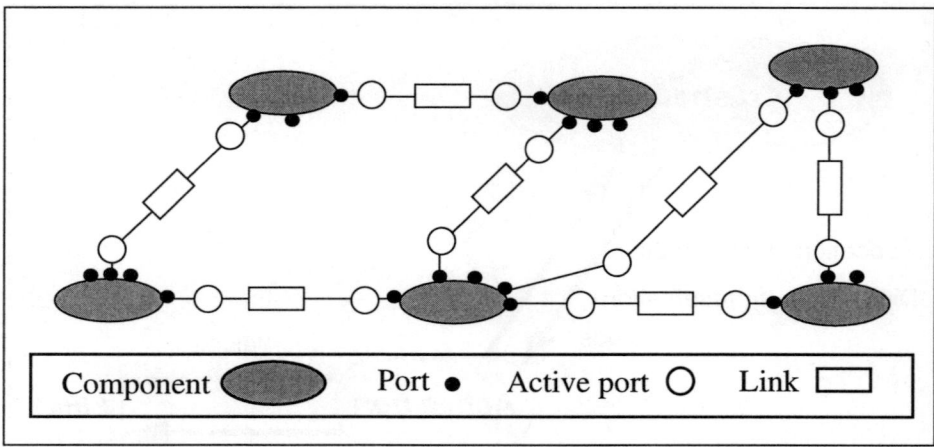

Figure 10.5 *Network of components.*

The division of labour among components, active_ports and links is flexible, but in general, a link is used to transport information between two active_ports, an input active_port controls whether information should be passed into a component, and an output active_port packages up information for leaving a component. Both active_ports and links can have an associated visual display.

Composition Model

The active_port and link framework entities do not impose rules on connections; they just enable connections. Whether or not a connection is valid is determined by a *composition model*. The composition model is the set of rules for component composition in a particular application domain. The rules determine compatibility between components, i.e. which component can be linked to which other component. The type of rules is open-ended and based on the component, the component's composition interface, and other application domain-specific information. Different from many other frameworks, the compatibility between components is not determined by the components. Decoupling composition models from components supports a variety of different software composition paradigms and increases the potential for reuse of a component, because a component can be reused without modification in different application domains by associating it with different composition models. A composition model is *active* when it is dynamically applied to a set of components to get them to cooperate in a specific application. The composition model can have some knowledge of what components it can be used with, but usually components do not have to be designed with particular composition models in mind.

A Framework for Visual Composition

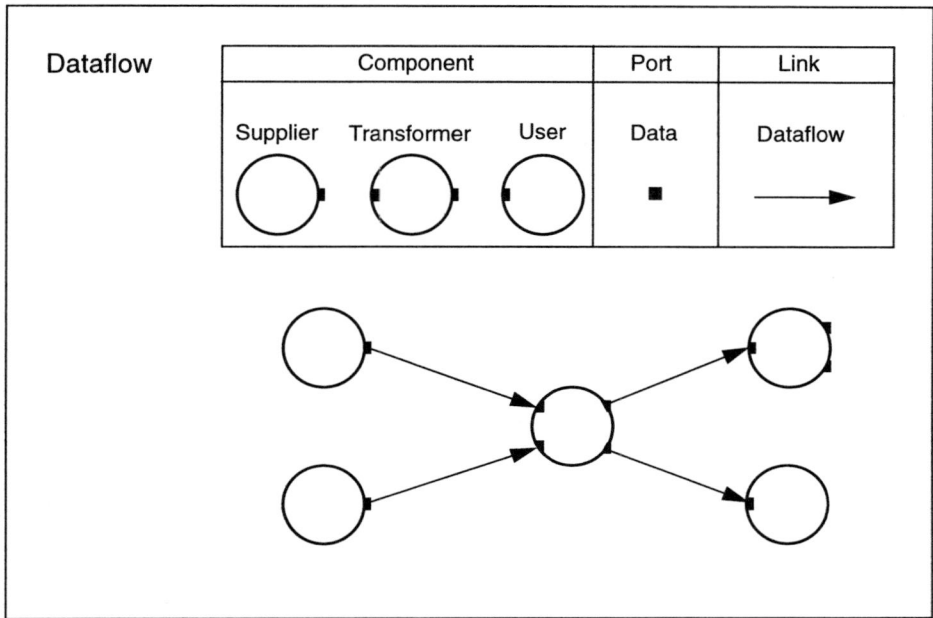

Figure 10.6 *Dataflow composition model and some connected components.*

Composition Model Examples

Three examples of composition models will be given: dataflow, two-dimensional graphic objects and class hierarchy diagrams. Dataflow composition is used for specifying flows of data in a network of components. Components have input and output ports through which dataflow. Each data value is associated with some component responsible for computing the value as a function of its inputs. The component makes the data value available at one or more of its output ports. Input and output ports can be joined by links. All ports have an associated type reflecting the type of the data that passes through the port. If a component has only output ports, then it is a supplier of data; if it has only input ports, then it is a user of data; and if it has both input and output ports, then it is a transformer of data. Links represent data flowing between components. Links are primarily responsible for enforcing valid dataflow networks. They allow ports to be connected only if they have compatible types and compatible directions (input to output and output to input). The dataflow components and composition model are pictured in figure 10.6

Another example is a composition model for two-dimensional graphic objects. This model is used to attach and keep two-dimensional graphics objects connected. A component (a graphic object) has ports that represent points on the object, i.e. ports are of type point. These ports are either input or output depending on the operation being carried out on the graphic object to which they belong. The points are the location of the object in two-

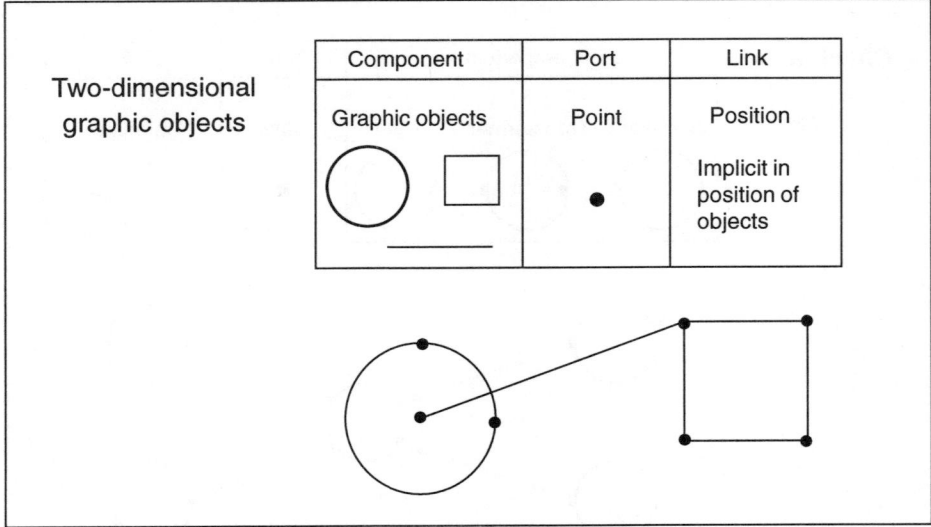

Figure 10.7 *Two-dimensional graphic composition model and some connected components.*

dimensional space. Links are created between components by placing one point on top of the other. Any point can be linked to any other point. When some point changes, as when a graphic object is moved, all other points linked to this point will be updated. This update guarantees the connectivity between graphic objects. The composition model for two-dimensional graphic objects is pictured in figure 10.7.

A third example is that of a class hierarchy diagram. Class hierarchy diagrams are used to show the class structure of an object-oriented application. There is one kind of component for this type of diagram, namely the class component. The class component can have ports of type subclass and superclass. Some class components will not have ports of type superclass; these are leaf classes in the class hierarchy. Some class components will not have subclass ports; these components are top-level classes in the class hierarchy. Links, which represent class relationships, are unidirectional and connect ports of type subclass to ports of type superclass. Links do not pass data from one class component to another; their role is to make relationships between classes so that when a class is asked about its superclasses and subclasses, it will be able to respond. The class hierarchy components and composition model are pictured in figure 10.8.

10.3.3 Interactive Environment

The interactive environment is responsible for ensuring that the framework entities are used correctly. The interactive environment supplies ways for the user to manipulate

A Framework for Visual Composition

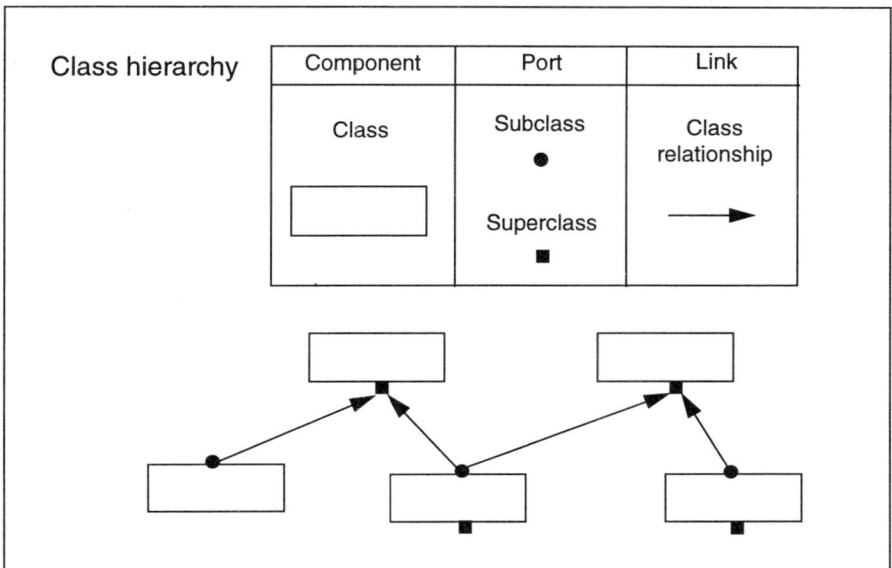

Figure 10.8 *Class hierarchy composition model and some connected components.*

components, ports and links. This is accomplished using various user interface metaphors depending on the implementation. The operations listed in table 10.2 make up a minimal set. The interactive environment is customizable so that operations can be added and/or removed.

The interactive environment supports direct manipulation [42]. Direct manipulation makes objects more concrete and thus helps people to grasp better the ideas and concepts being described. Users get immediate feedback to their actions and are informed when any of their actions cause a change in the system. Ideally, users always know what to expect from the system. Development becomes more of an exploratory activity where a "try it and see what happens" attitude is encouraged. Being able to see immediately what is going on in an application is important in the early stages of application development. At the same time, the interactive environment is as transparent as possible so that users do not have to do things that make no sense in their specific application domain.

The environment is visual — a mixture of text, graphics (two-dimensional and/or three-dimensional), and other media like video, sound and images — and therefore visibility control is very important. Visibility control is used to modify the presentations of components, ports and links. There are operations (see table 10.2) that allow a user to make elements invisible according to different criteria like, for instance, what group they are in, what component they are attached to, etc. An application developer using visual composition usually needs more objects visible than an end-user. The developer is working in more general terms, while the end-user is working in a specific domain. To accommodate this situation, visibility control can hide information that is not appropriate. The compos-

Components	Ports	Links
instantiation make a functional copy of the chosen component	**identification** name, type and polarity of port	**create** Manual creation relies on the user manually selecting the start port and target port for the link Automatic connection would attempt to automatically connect compatible ports when a component is placed in a composition composition model verifies link
determine location in space fixed into a particular location in space, fixed in relation to other components' locations, or left free to be moved		
copy state is also copied		
delete links referencing the deleted component are also deleted		**delete**
replace The links that referenced the original component are reconnected to the new component		
display different presentations		

Table 10.2 *Manipulations on components, ports and links.*

ite component capability can also be used to shield an end-user from unwanted or unnecessary detail.

Some of the more common characteristics of interactive environment must also be considered. It is necessary that some type of grouping mechanism be available, such as windows in the desktop metaphor. The environment supports the undo/redo functionality, because all users make mistakes. Skill levels, such as novice or expert, are ways of helping users learn to use a system. These levels usually assume that a novice is not familiar with the system and therefore needs a bit of "hand-holding." Expert users, on the other hand, could consider such hand-holding distracting. Skill levels can be implemented by allowing or disallowing certain actions on the objects being manipulated. Different presentations of a component can be used to reflect different skill levels. To further facilitate the usage of the environment, mode switches, such as those between building and running an application, are minimized. The literature [39] suggests that avoiding such mode switches is important for new users because it gives them the flexibility simultaneously to use and modify an application, and that typically there is almost no confusion about when input is directed to the tool and when it is directed to the application.

10.3.4 Component Management

The activities of storing, organizing and retrieving components are external to the framework, but the framework supplies a simple mechanism that records enough information about the network to a text file so that when the file is read, the network can be re-created. Composition models also need to be stored, organized and retrieved. The information stored in the composition model must be activated when a network is used and constantly accessible since it is consulted whenever a link is created and possibly whenever information flows through a link. Some notation, possibly textual, for the composition model is necessary. The framework supports "hooks" for more sophisticated tools, such as the software information base described in chapter 7, for these activities.

10.4 Vista — A Prototype Visual Composition Tool

Vista is a prototype visual composition tool based on the framework described above. The prototype is meant as a test-bed for the visual composition framework. Vista [29][37] was developed as part of ITHACA's application development environment. (See the preface and chapter 7 for more information about the ITHACA project.) Vista is a second generation prototype; some of the ideas of visual composition were demonstrated in VST, an earlier prototype based on a Unix composition model [45]. Vista is meant to be a simple and evolutionary prototype.

The layers of software supporting Vista are pictured in figure 10.10. The major parts of Vista are in the shaded region of the figure. The implementation of Vista conforms to the ITHACA software platform which includes C++, X Windows and OSF/Motif. Graph management for Vista is supplied by a set of class definitions and functions extracted from the Labyrinth System [27], a generic framework for developing graphical applications. In Vista, components and links are displayed on the screen using Motif widgets and the display capabilities of Labyrinth.

288   *Visual Composition of Software Applications*

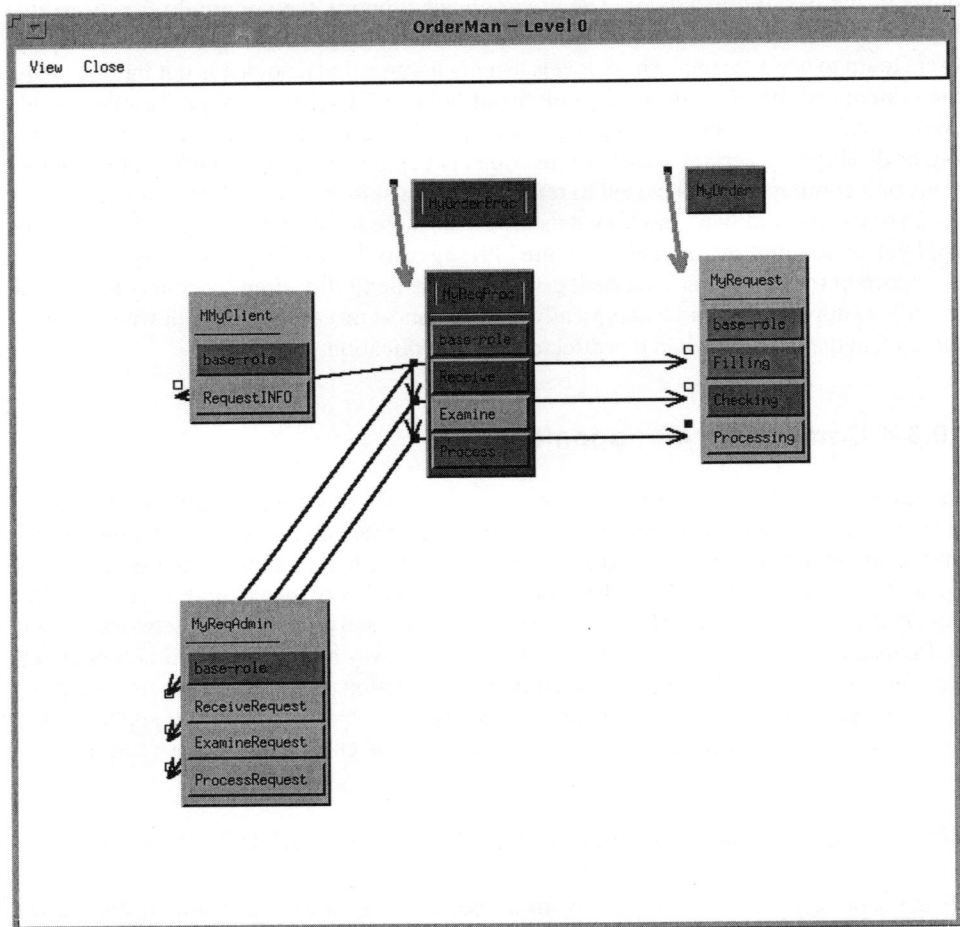

Figure 10.9 *RECAST example.*

Composition Model Manager

There are at least two ways to go about implementing the functionality of the composition model. One possibility is to implement a composition model manager as an oracle that oversees the correct functioning of the framework based on the active composition model.

The other possibility is to delegate responsibility for checking and maintaining compatibility rules to framework entities. If composition models are used to define global compatibility between components or global rules encompassing large groups of components, an oracle would probably be the best choice. The oracle can have an overview of sets of

Vista — A Prototype Visual Composition Tool

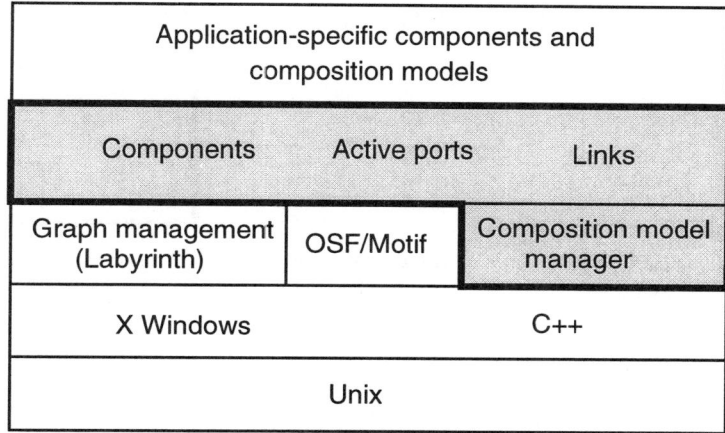

Figure 10.10 *Layers of software supporting Vista.*

networks on which to base global decisions. Some powerful graph management systems can also work on a global level in the network; thus the decision for a certain type of graph manager could influence the implementation of the composition model manager. In Vista, the composition model manager is an oracle implemented as a C++ class. A composition model is expressed in a textual notation that expresses port compatibility and is parsed by the composition model manager.

Components, Active_ports and Links

In Vista, components (behaviours and presentations), active_ports and links are implemented as C++ classes. Vista supplies default active_port and link classes. To implement the component behaviour and presentation, four classes are defined. The behaviour of a component is implemented in the *cmp_Node* class and subclasses of the abstract class *V_Base*. The presentation of a component is implemented in the *view_Node* class and subclasses of the abstract class *Framer*. The cmp_Node and view_Node classes are internal to Vista and maintain network connectivity. The V_Base and Framer classes are subclassed by the user of Vista. This division is advantageous because Vista is implemented in C++ and modifications to superclasses necessitate recompilation of subclasses. The division avoids much of this recompilation since the information added from outside the system does not directly impact the internal framework classes and vice versa.

Dividing up the responsibilities of components, active_ports and links is not always straightforward. For example, if two ports of different types are defined to be compatible by a particular composition model, and they are linked, where should the coercion between port types take place? The input active_port participating in the connection has a type and can coerce things that it receives into that type. The link participating in the connection knows it is connecting ports of compatible types and can coerce the type of the information from the output active_port to the type that the input active_port expects.

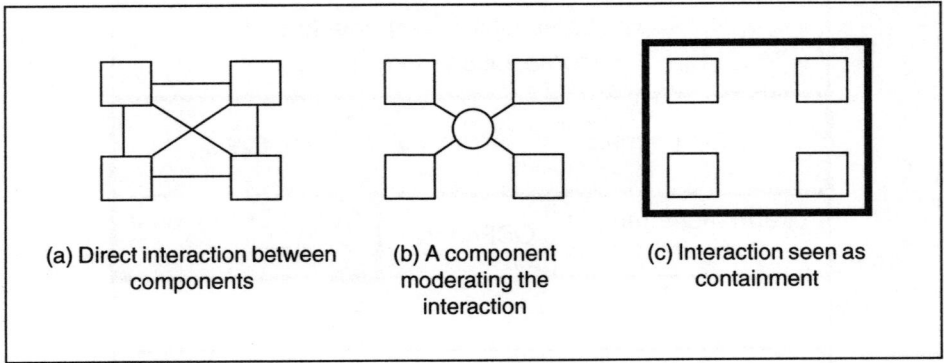

Figure 10.11 *Four-way component interaction.*

Responsibilities can be divided up in certain ways to ameliorate the user's experience. For example, a four-way interaction where all four components interact. The interaction can be a new component with the original four components linked to it by "interaction" links or all of the components can be linked together. These two options are pictured in figure 10.11. Figure 10.11(a) might not look hard to understand as it is pictured here, but the picture would become indecipherable if twenty components were interacting. Ports could accept more than one connection, but this does not reduce the number of links. Adding components to a system does not necessarily imply that the system becomes more complex. The number of components is not that important; it is how the components are presented that is important, as seen in figure 10.11(b) and 10.11(c). In figure 10.11(c) links are represented by the location of components (e.g. all components contained in another component interact) and not by lines connecting the components.

In Vista, active_ports and links can be used to implement any of the scenarios described above. But as classes are developed, the goal should be to keep active_ports and links simple, since too much hidden behaviour will make the system unpredictable and harder to understand.

Application-Specific Components and Composition Models

Components and composition models for specific domains are defined using the classes and functionality of the lower layers of software. For components, only the behaviour and presentation need to be defined as subclasses of abstract classes supplied by Vista. Composition models are expressed in the textual notation supported by Vista.

10.5 Sample Applications

Johnson and Russo [25] have stated that:

Sample Applications

a use of a framework validates it when the use does not require any changes to the framework, and helps improve the framework when it points out weaknesses in it.

Iteration is a major part of the validation cycle of a framework. The framework should get better (more reusable) as results are gathered from its usage. To this end, the visual composition framework was used in three sample applications. The sample applications came from actual ongoing projects and were not artificially devised as test cases for visual composition.

The first application was part of a project that addresses the creation of a framework and rapid prototyping environment for distributed multimedia applications [32] (see chapter 11). The visual composition framework was then used to implement a visual composition tool for multimedia applications.

The second application was part of a project that addresses the requirements collection and specification phase of software development. The project defines a methodology that functions as a formal basis for requirements specification and support tools. The visual composition framework was used to implement one of the support tools called RECAST.

The third application was part of a project that addresses workflow applications. The project defines a complete environment for designing and running coordination procedures. The need for some type of visual representation of coordination procedures was recognized by the participants in the project. The visual composition framework satisfied this need and was used to draw pictures of coordination procedures and generate the code that the procedures represented.

The scope of these sample applications varies considerably. The first deals with running applications and components represent actual executing modules. The other two are related to software specification, where components represent elements of the software specification model. We will describe the first and second sample applications here. More information about all three applications can be found in the author's thesis [30].

Sample Application 1: Multimedia Component Kit

Chapter 11 introduces the basic concepts of a multimedia framework and multimedia components. Based on this work, multimedia components and composition models were created for visual composition. The visual composition tool for multimedia applications is a rapid prototyping tool for experimenting with different combinations of multimedia components.

A multimedia application is implemented by large number of interconnected hardware and software components. Visual composition can be used to interactively plug components together — rather than permanently "hard-wiring" them — thus making applications more flexible and reconfigurable.

Various composition paradigms are appropriate to multimedia applications. Three example composition models follow:

1. *Dataflow composition* describes an application as a configuration of media components and the data (media streams) that flow between them.

2. *Activity composition* describes the behaviour of an application with respect to activities and events.

3. *Temporal composition* describes relationships between temporal sequences and is a special case of activity composition [31].

These three ways of viewing multimedia applications can be reflected in composition models that determine the types of components useful in the applications and how the components interact. The dataflow composition model has been implemented and will be discussed in detail here.

Viewed from a dataflow perspective, a typical multimedia application accepts user input and displays multimedia information related to the input. This type of application can be built from components that represent input devices and multimedia renderers. Some example multimedia components for dataflow composition are listed in table 10.3. The GeoBall and Navigator components are responsible for getting user input into the application. The GeoBall component represents an actual hardware device, pictured in the presentation of the component, that generates 4×4 geometric transformation matrices. This component can be considered a producer of information of type GeoTransSeq (sequences of 4×4 geometric transformation matrices). The Navigator component, a transformer component, is responsible for taking the information produced by the input device and transforming it into a type understandable by other components in the application. Here, the Navigator component produces information of type MoveSeq (sequences of Render requests dealing with movement of objects in the three-dimensional world).

GeoBall	Renderer	Modeler	Navigator	ActiveCube
out: GeoTransSeq	in: RenderSeq	in: MoveSeq in: RenderSeq out: RenderSeq	in: GeoTransSeq out: MoveSeq	out: RenderSeq

Table 10.3 *Components for dataflow composition.*

The Modeler component represents the content that will be displayed by the application. The Modeler gathers together all the information in the application that will contribute to the content and prepares the information for display. The Modeler can accept information from the Navigator component to incorporate user input into the display, as well as information from other components that generate content such as the ActiveCube component. The ActiveCube component represents a graphical cube object that can be displayed. The Modeler produces information of type RenderSeq (sequences of Render

Sample Applications

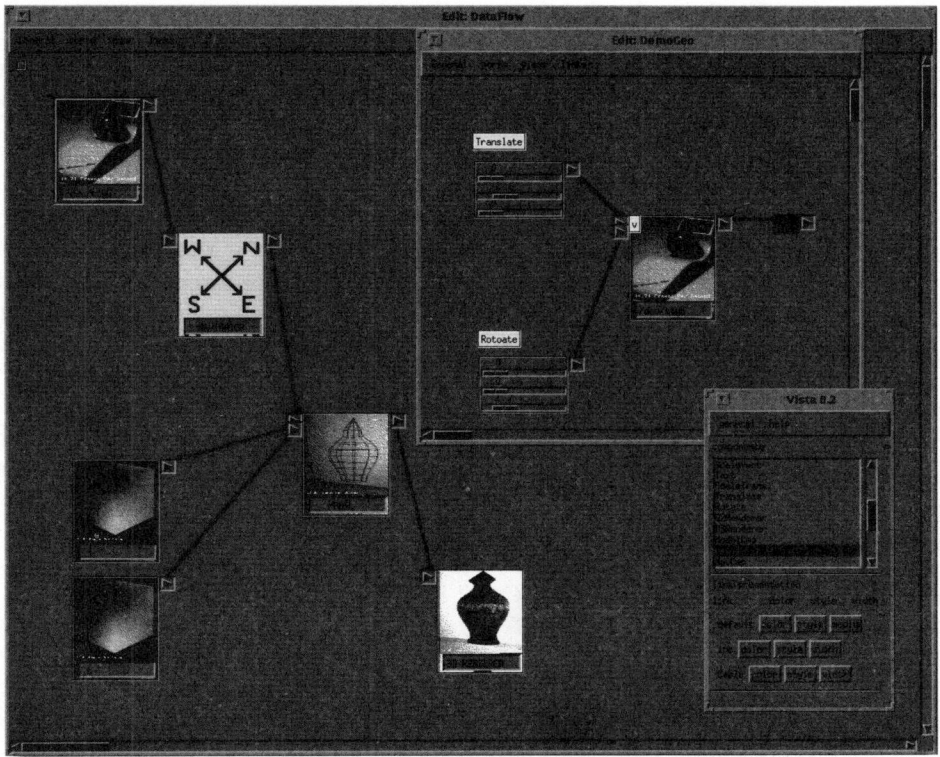

Figure 10.12 *Multimedia dataflow composition.*

requests) that represent the content in a format suitable for rendering. The Renderer component accepts information of type RenderSeq and is responsible for its display.

A simple composition model for dataflow can check to make sure that only ports of the same type are connected as a user interactively creates an application. This model ensures that the components making up the application are correctly connected but cannot ensure that the application is producing the desired result. More semantic information can be put into the composition model to produce a particular desired result. For example, a rule like "if a GeoBall component is in the application, then it must be connected to a Navigator component" would eliminate the need to explicitly connect them, and would guarantee the correct use of these two components.

Figure 10.12 shows a screen image of the tool displaying a simple dataflow of a multimedia application using the components described in the preceding paragraphs. The Geo-Ball component is implemented as a composite component. The internal view of the composite component is pictured in the upper right side of the figure. The composite component contains a geometry ball component and two sets of horizontal sliders. The sliders adjust the parameters of the device (x, y, z translation and x, y, z rotation sensitivity). These parameters can be changed interactively and thereby modify the behaviour of the input device as a user navigates through the museum. The input device is connected to a Navigator component, which connects to a Modeler component, which, in turn, is connected to a Renderer component. ActiveCube components, which move cube-shaped graphic objects given a velocity, are also connected into the Modeler component.

Sample Application 2: RECAST

The RECAST tool [3][4] in the ITHACA software development environment uses a composition-based approach to requirements specification and provides assisted inspection of available components by accessing the software information base (SIB). RECAST assumes that requirements are specified according to an object-oriented specification model, called the Functionality in the Objects with Roles Model (F-ORM), which is used for requirements representation. The model is based on the object-oriented paradigm extended with the concept of roles [8] to represent the different behaviours that an object can have during its lifetime. F-ORM is a textual definition language and RECAST is a tool that graphically manipulates F-ORM requirements. RECAST was built using the visual composition framework. F-ORM classes and class elements are represented by components and class relationships are represented by links. The class relationships are recorded in a composition model so that a user of RECAST is assured of using F-ORM correctly.

The composition concept of RECAST is reflected in a set of diagrams defined by the ITHACA object-oriented methodology [9]. The methodology defines five types of diagrams at the application design level: class diagram, cluster tree diagram, cluster cooperation diagram, state/transition diagram and IsA/PartOf diagrams. These five diagrams are used by the application designer when specifying requirements. The class diagram implemented in RECAST is described here.

The class diagram represents F-ORM classes and roles along with the dependencies between classes and roles. Classes have corresponding Class components in the framework. The presentation of the Class component contains at least the name of the class. Roles have corresponding Role components and are graphically displayed embedded in the Class component to which they belong. Class components can be in their *base* representation, where all the roles are visible, or in a *compact* representation, where only the class name is visible. Role components are connected by message links that represent either unidirectional or bidirectional message flows.

Colours are used extensively to distinguish different types of components and different types of links. Shading is used to signal if certain classes or roles are selected. For example, if a class or role is not selected, it is not shaded. If a class or role is darkly shaded, then it was selected by the user. If a class or role is lightly shaded, then it was selected by a possible design action. If a class or role is moderately shaded, then it was selected as a consequence of a design action.

The components for class diagrams are summarized in table 10.4. The behaviour of the Class component is responsible for changes in the F-ORM requirements specification. These changes are made by direct manipulation of the graphical representation of the

Sample Applications

class. Such changes include the addition of classes to the diagram, adding and deleting roles, and the transformation of a class into a set of classes. The behaviour is also responsible for the display of the class (base or compact) and the display of information about the class. The behaviour of the Role component is responsible for managing design actions of the role, the presentation of the role, access to the properties of the role, and access to the state/transition diagram for the role. The behaviour of the Cluster-reference component is responsible for mediating the connection between the active class diagram and the cluster the reference is representing.

Process class	Resource class	Role	Cluster-reference
[image: class box with name, base-role, role1, role2, role3]	*[image: class box with name, base-role, role1, role2, role3]*	*[image: role box]*	name level
in: message in: role out: message out: class in/out: class in/out: class in/out: message	all from process class plus: in/out: resclass in/out: resclass	in: message in: class in: stdiagram out: message out: role in/out: message	in: message out: message in/out: message in/out: class in/out: class in/out: resclass in/out: resclass

Table 10.4 *Class diagram components.*

Figure 10.13 shows the class diagram for the OrderManagementSystem cluster. This diagram is generated by using RECAST to transform a request-processing application into an order-processing application. Interacting with RECAST in the following way produces the OrderManagementSystem cluster:

1. The user starts a new application called OrderManagementSystem.
2. The user consults the SIB for the application domain and a generic application frame. In this case the application domain is sales and the generic application frame is request processing. The RequestProcessing class is chosen.
3. The RequestProcessing class is copied into the diagram generating a Class component called MyReqProc. The MyReqProc component has a set of associated roles, represented as Role components in the diagram, which are embedded inside the presentation of MyReqProc.

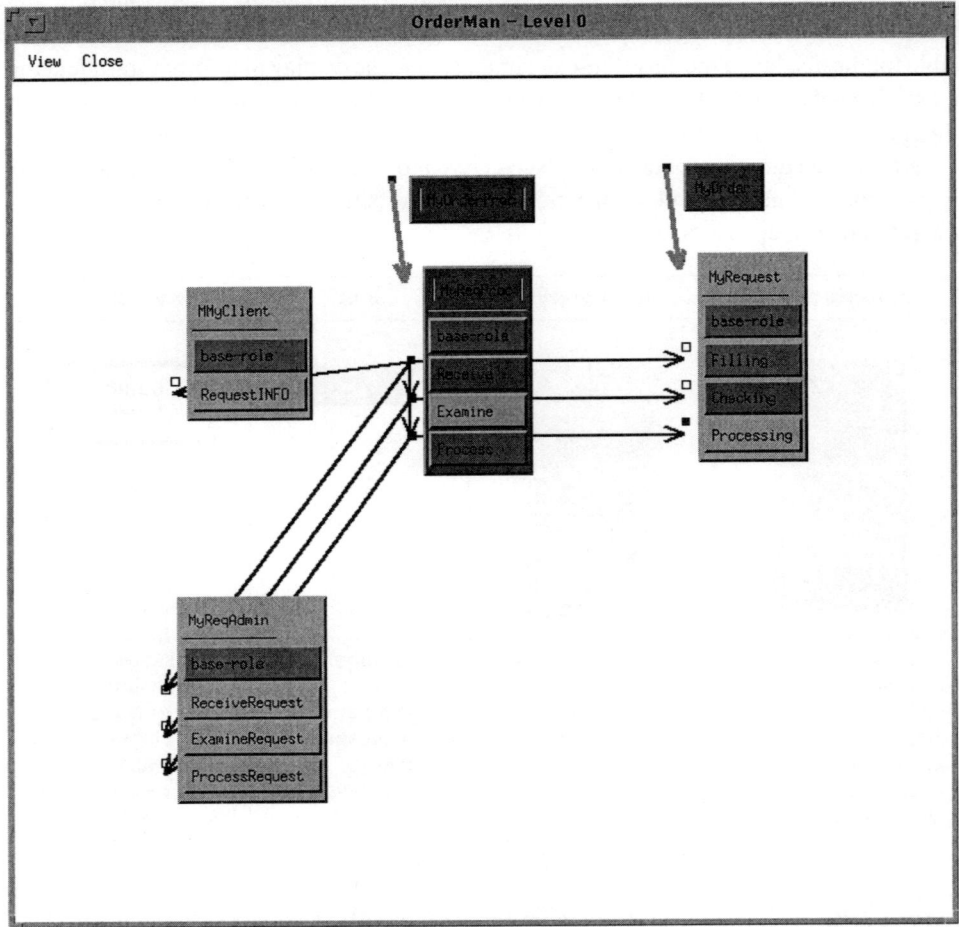

Figure 10.13 *RECAST example.*

4. The Receive Role component is selected. Because of the selection, RECAST consults its design suggestions and suggests adding a request manager agent and a client agent to the diagram. The client agent represents the source of the information for MyReqProc. The request manager agent represents the requested information of MyReqProc.

5. The suggestions are executed and the corresponding Class components are retrieved. For the client agent, MyClient class is retrieved. For the request manager agent, MyRequest and MyReqAdmin are retrieved. The message links, represented by thin black arrows, between all the Class components are displayed.

6. MyReqProc is specialized to MyOrderProc and MyRequest is specialized to MyOrder. Specialization is represented by thick grey arrows.

The sample applications demonstrate that the visual composition framework makes the process of building graphical, component-based applications easier by supplying much of the infrastructure such applications require.

10.6 Discussion

As a result of the work done on the visual composition framework, the prototype implementation of a visual composition tool and the sample applications, certain suggestions concerning component definition, composition and visualization can be made.

10.6.1 Component Definition

The choice of components for a particular application is still somewhat *ad hoc*, and results from other fields, such as the reverse engineering of applications, could supply useful information for component design. Work by, among others, Johnson [24] [11] on framework design has highlighted some key strategies such as finding common abstractions, decomposing problems into standard components, parameterizing and finding common patterns of interaction. With this work in mind and the experience from the sample applications described in the previous section, we present the following list of guidelines for designing reusable components:

- If a concept is used, or looks like it could be used, in a number of different places or application domains, this concept should probably be a component.
  If the same concept were included explicitly in every component, there would be the same functionality spread throughout the component set, proliferating redundant information and negating efforts of encapsulation and reuse.
  Parameterization can be used to generalize concepts that might look different at first glance but, with further investigation, they could really be the same concept with different values for a few different parameters.
  User interface components are a good example since they represent concepts that are reused in many applications. The Modeler component in the multimedia component kit is also a good example. If the Modeler component had not been separate from the 3DRenderer component, the same model information would not be able to drive two different renderers, say a three-dimensional and a two-dimensional renderer, at the same time.
- If a component requires an undetermined or variable number of resources, these resources should probably be components.
  Since this type of information can be quite variable, it seems natural to define a set of lower-level primitive components and compose them into different configurations.

An example of this is found in RECAST for the implementation of the class and role components. Since a class can have a variable number of roles, and roles can be dynamically added or removed, it is much easier to make classes and roles different components that share the relationships roleOf and class than to include the role as part of the class.

- Composite components should contain a small number of components and take advantage of hierarchical decomposition.
  This allows concepts to be organized more effectively and reduces the amount of screen clutter.
- The number of components should be small but extensible.
  A small set of components helps people remember what components they have to work with, but the set must be extensible so that when valuable new primitives are discovered they do not have to be simulated with the existing components.
- Components should strike a balance between concreteness and abstraction.
  From their experience with the world around them, people are more used to thinking concretely rather than abstractly. Visual composition uses a set of components, which are abstractions, for application construction. A balance between the two must be made. Components cannot require the user to fill in every detail — if they had to do that, then visual composition would be worthless. But components cannot conceal all the details since the user would never figure out what to do with them.
- Big components can be reusable.
  It is claimed that the bigger a component gets, the harder it is to reuse [5]. Here, "bigger" means more complex *and* more specific. A component being more specific does make it harder to reuse, but being complex does not have to cause problems. As long as the composition interface of a component correctly reflects its behaviour, more complex components can be reused just as well as less complex components.

10.6.2 Composition

Choosing an effective set of rules for composition is not easy. Visual composition delegates this decision to the users, on the basis that they know best how components should communicate in their particular application. More effort is needed to determine common sets of rules that are often observed in applications as well as domain-specific rules. Efforts such as the Law of Demeter [28], contracts [18], law-governed systems [35] and design by contract [33] all contribute to this area.

Alternative ways for expressing composition models are needed. The composition model was implemented as a small textual language (essentially just listing the port types and their compatibilities) in Vista. It could be useful to use visual composition to describe composition models. Certain rules, like no cycles allowed between components, could be illustrated by diagrams like the ones pictured in figure 10.14. If a component set contains a huge number of components, and a composition model has a huge number of rules, both

Discussion

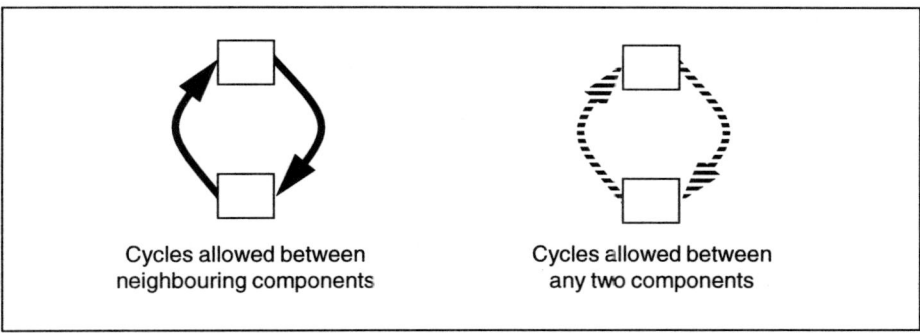

Figure 10.14 *Example visualizations of some composition model rules.*

the textual and graphical representation of the model could get awkward, and another strategy might become necessary.

10.6.3 Visualization

The visual aspect of visual composition is one of its most important features. Being able to see the pieces that make up applications and manipulate these pieces directly contributes greatly to the understanding of an application. Seeing the impact of certain design choices is very advantageous. But, as with all visual communication, a suitable presentation must be chosen otherwise the effectiveness and quality of the visual expression will be brought into question. What is suitable can vary from person to person, so flexibility is important, but people still have to understand each other. Any enhancements to the visual presentation must give a user a more comfortable, informative and familiar environment in which to work.

Visualization is the visual representation of information using, for example, two-dimensional/three-dimensional computer graphics. Solutions and problems can often be easier and faster to recognize visually than having to sort through program text. Brooks does not favour visualizing software, saying: "In spite of progress in restricting and simplifying the structures of software, they remain inherently unvisualizable, and thus *do not permit the mind to use some of its most powerful conceptual tools*" [6] (emphasis added). Despite Brooks's pessimistic view, a person's visual capacity is such a powerful conceptual tool that it must be explored as a possible aid in dealing with complex systems. It is possible that not every level of software is visualizable, but this should not limit attempts to try to profit from visualization where appropriate. Scientific visualization has "demonstrated previously unknown flaws in numerical simulations and made possible new knowledge and insight" [41]. Harel [15] takes a more optimistic view about the possibilities of visualization. Like Brooks, he agrees that the "traditional" diagrams, such as flow-charts, are not what is needed for modeling systems. But a lot of the conceptual constructs underlying software systems can be captured naturally by notions from set-theory and topology that have natural spatial/graphical representations. Harel calls these representations *visual formalisms* [16] and they all have rigorous mathematical semantics. Concepts such as containment, connectedness, overlap and adjacency as well as shape, size and colour are used to depict a system. Combining these techniques can trigger many useful mental images of what is going on in a system.

In Vista, only two-dimensional presentations have been used, and it would be interesting to see if a third dimension could enhance the effectiveness of the tool. Situations that currently use up too much screen space could be more effectively treated in three dimensions. Examples of this type of work exist [7][40][46]. Different conclusions can be drawn if the application domain is inherently non-graphic or inherently graphic. Animation has also been used to help understand systems [10][12][44] and would enhance visual composition. For example, a "data map" that shows where data is, how it is used and how it moves around the application could give a global picture of data usage. Data could be tagged and followed through the executing application.

10.7 Conclusion

The landscape of software is changing from monolithic closed applications to open applications composed of reusable components. As the landscape changes, end-users become application developers and application developers become component engineers. To support this new landscape, the software industry needs to promote the idea of investment in components. Among other things, this means developing repositories of components and tools for developing applications from components. Visual composition can lead to new tools and environments which would contribute to the fulfilment of our duty, as Harel puts it, "to forge ahead to turn system modeling into a predominately visual and graphical process."

Acknowledgements

The work described in this chapter has benefited from the efforts of many past and present members of the Object Systems Group. The prototype visual composition tool described here includes efforts by Betty Junod, Oscar Nierstrasz, Serge Renfer, Marc Stadelmann and Ino Simitsek. The precursor to Vista — VST — was implemented by Jan Vitek and Marc Stadelmann, with contributions from Gerti Kappel. The work on the multimedia framework includes efforts by Christian Breiteneder, Laurent Dami, Simon Gibbs, Michael Papathomas and Dennis Tsichritzis.

Much of this work was done in the context of the ITHACA project. Roberto Bellinzona of Politecnico di Milano worked on the RECAST sample application and Hayat Issad of IFATEC worked on the component set of the workflow sample application.

References

[1] Apple Computer, Inc., *Inside Macintosh: Interapplication Communication*, Addison-Wesley, Reading, Mass.

[2] Jeff Alger, "OpenDoc vs. OLE," *MacTech Magazine*, vol. 10, no. 8, Aug. 1994, pp. 58–70.

[3] Roberto Bellinzona and Mariagrazia Fugini, "RECAST Prototype Description," ITHACA.POLIMI.91.E.2.8.#1, Politecnico di Milano, Nov. 28, 1991.

[4] Roberto Bellinzona, Mariagrazia Fugini and Giampo Bracchi, "Scripting Reusable Requirements Through RECAST," ITHACA.POLIMI.92.E.2.9.#1, Politecnico di Milano, July, 1992.

[5] Ted J. Biggerstaff and C. Richter, "Reusability Framework, Assessment and Directions," *IEEE Software*, March 1987, pp. 41–49.

[6] Fred P. Brooks, "No Silver Bullet," *IEEE Computer*, April 1987, pp. 10–19.

[7] Stuart Card, G. Robertson and J. Mackinlay, "The Information Visualizer: An Information Workspace," *CHI '91 Conference Proceedings*, New Orleans.

[8] Valeria De Antonellis, Barbara Pernici and P. Samarati, "F-ORM METHOD: A F-ORM Methodology for Reusing Specifications," *IFIP WG 8.4 Working Conference on Object-Oriented Aspects in Information Systems*, Quebec, Oct. 1991.

[9] Valeria De Antonellis and Barbara Pernici, "ITHACA Object-Oriented Methodology Manual — Introduction and Application Developer Manual (IOOM/AD)," ITHACA.POLIMI.UDUN-IV.91.E.8.1, Oct., 1991.

[10] Wim De Pauw, Richard Helm, Doug Kimelman and John Vlissides, "Visualizing the Behavior of Object-Oriented Systems," in *Proceedings OOPSLA '93, ACM SIGPLAN Notices*, vol. 28, no. 10, Oct. 1993, pp. 326–337.

[11] Erich Gamma, Richard Helm, John Vlissides and Ralph E. Johnson, "Design Patterns: Abstraction and Reuse of Object-Oriented Design," in *Proceedings ECOOP '93*, ed. O. Nierstrasz, *Lecture Notes in Computer Science*, vol. 707, Springer-Verlag, Kaiserslautern, Germany, July 1993, pp. 406–431.

[12] Steven C. Glassman, "A Turbo Environment for Producing Algorithm Animations," in *Proceedings IEEE Symposium on Visual Languages*, Aug. 1993, pp. 32–36.

[13] Adele Goldberg, "Information Models, Views and Controllers," *Dr. Dobb's Journal*, July, 1990.

[14] Paul E. Haeberli, "ConMan: A Visual Programming Language for Interactive Graphics," *ACM Computer Graphics*, vol. 22, no. 4, Aug. 1988, pp. 103–111.

[15] David Harel, "Biting the Silver Bullet," *IEEE Computer*, vol. 25 no. 1, Jan., 1992, pp.8–20.

[16] David Harel, "On Visual Formalisms," *Communications of the ACM*, vol. 31, no. 5, May 1988, pp. 514–530.

[17] William Harrison, Harold Ossher and Mansour Kavianpour, "Integrating Coarse-Grained and Fine-Grained Tool Integration," *Proceedings CASE '92*, July 1992.

[18] Richard Helm, Ian Holland and Dipayan Gangopadhyay, "Contracts: Specifying Behavioural Compositions in Object-Oriented Systems," *Proceedings OOPSLA/ECOOP '90, ACM SIGPLAN Notices*, vol. 25, no. 10, Oct. 1990, pp. 169–180.

[19] *HP Journal*, vol. 41, no. 3, June 1990 (HP SoftBench).

[20] IBM, VisualAge documentation and demo diskette.

[21] ITHACA Tecnical Annex, Sept. 1988.

[22] Dan Ingalls, "Fabrik: A Visual Programming Environment," *ACM SIGPLAN Notices*, vol. 23, no. 11, Nov. 1988, pp. 176–190.

[23] Ivar Jacobson, "Is Object Technology Software's Industrial Platform?" *IEEE Software*, vol. 10, no. 1, Jan. 1993, pp. 24–30.

[24] Ralph E. Johnson, "How to Design Frameworks," OOPSLA '93 tutorial notes.

[25] Ralph E. Johnson and Vincent F. Russo, "Reusing Object-Oriented Designs," University of Illinois, TR UIUCDCS 91-1696.

[26] A. Julienne and L. Russell, "Why You Need ToolTalk," *SunExpert Magazine*, vol. 4, no. 3, March 1993, pp. 51–58.

[27] Manolis Katevenis, T. Sorilos and P. Kalogerakis, "Laby Programmer's Manual (version 3.0)," ITHACA report FORTH.92.E3.3.#1, Foundation of Research and Technology — Hellas, Iraklion, Crete, Jan. 1992.

[28] Karl Lieberherr and Ian Holland, "Assuring Good Style for Object-Oriented Programs," *IEEE Software*, Sept. 89, pp. 38–48.

[29] Vicki de Mey, Betty Junod, Serge Renfer, Marc Stadelmann and Ino Simitsek, "The Implementation of Vista — A Visual Scripting Tool," in *Object Composition*, ed. D. Tsichritzis, Centre Universitaire d'Informatique, University of Geneva, June 1991, pp. 31–56.

[30] Vicki de Mey, "Visual Composition of Software Applications," Ph.D. thesis no. 2660, University of Geneva, 1994.

[31] Vicki de Mey, Christian Breiteneder, Laurent Dami, Simon Gibbs and Dennis Tsichritzis, "Visual Composition and Multimedia," *Proceedings Eurographics '92*.

[32] Vicki de Mey and Simon Gibbs, "A Multimedia Component Kit," *Proceedings ACM Multimedia '93*.

[33] Bertrand Meyer, "Applying 'Design by Contract'," *IEEE Computer*, Oct. 1992, pp. 40–51.

[34] Microsoft, Object Linking and Embedding Programmer's Reference (pre-release), version 2, 1992.

[35] Naftaly H. Minsky and David Rozenshtein, " A Law-Based Approach to Object-Oriented Programming," *Proceedings OOPSLA '87* , Oct. 1987, pp. 482–493.

[36] NeXT, Distributed Objects, release 3.1, 1993.

[37] Oscar Nierstrasz, Dennis Tsichritzis, Vicki de Mey and Marc Stadelmann, "Objects + Scripts = Applications," *Proceedings, Esprit 1991 Conference*, Kluwer, Dordrecht, 1991, pp. 534–552.

[38] Andrew J. Palay, "Towards an 'Operating System' for User Interface Components," in *Multimedia Interface Design*, ed. M. M. Blattner and R. B. Dannenberg, Frontier Series, ACM Press, 1992, pp. 339–355.

[39] Randy Pausch, Nathaniel R. Young and Robert DeLine, "SUIT: The Pascal of User Interface Toolkits," *Proceedings of the Fourth Annual Symposium on User Interface Software and Technology*, Nov. 1991, pp. 117–125.

[40] Steven P. Reiss, "A Framework for Abstract 3D Visualization," in *Proceedings IEEE Symposium on Visual Languages*, Aug. 1993, pp. 108–115.

[41] Lawrence J. Rosenblum and Gregory M. Nielson, "Guest Editors' Introduction: Visualization Comes of Age," *IEEE Computer Graphics and Applications*, vol. 11, no. 3, May 1991, pp. 15–17.

[42] Ben Shneiderman, "Direct Manipulation: A Step Beyond Programming Languages," *IEEE Computer*, vol. 16, no. 8, Aug. 1983, pp. 57–69.

[43] David C. Smith and Joshua Susser, "A Component Architecture for Personal Computer Software," in *Languages for Developing User Interfaces*, ed. B. Myers, Jones & Bartlett, 1992, pp. 31–56.

[44] Randall B. Smith, "Experiences with the Alternate Reality Kit: An Example of the Tension Between Literalism and Magic," *IEEE Computer Graphics and Applications*, Sept. 1987, pp. 42–50.

[45] Marc Stadelmann, Gerti Kappel and Jan Vitek, "VST: A Scripting Tool Based on the UNIX Shell," in *Object Management*, ed. D. Tsichritzis, Centre Universitaire d'Informatique, University of Geneva, July 1990, pp. 333–344.

[46] John T. Stasko and Joseph F. Wehrli, "Three-Dimensional Computation Visualization," in *Proceedings IEEE Symposium on Visual Languages*, Aug. 1993, pp. 100–107.

[47] Dennis Tsichritzis and Simon Gibbs, "Virtual Museums and Virtual Realities" *Proceedings International Conference on Hypermedia & Interactivity in Museums, Archives and Museum Informatics,* Technical Report no. 14, Pittsburgh, Oct. 14–16, 1991, pp. 17–25.

[48] John Vlissides, "Generalized Graphical Object Editing," Technical Report CSL-TR-90-427, Stanford University June 1990.

Chapter 11
Multimedia Component Frameworks

Simon Gibbs

Abstract This chapter looks at the use of object-oriented technology, in particular class frameworks, in the domain of multimedia programming. After introducing digital media and multimedia programming, the central notion of multimedia frameworks is examined; an example of a multimedia framework and an application that uses the framework are presented. The example application demonstrates how object-oriented multimedia programming helps to insulate application developers from "volatility" in multimedia processing capabilities — this volatility and related uncertainty is currently one of the key factors hindering multimedia application development.

11.1 Digital Media and Multimedia

In discussing object-oriented multimedia, a convenient starting point is the notion of *media artefacts*. Here the term "media" is used in the sense of materials and forms of expression. This includes both *natural media*, such as inks and paints, and *digital media* made possible by computer technology. The latter either mimic natural media, as is the case with drawing and paint programs, or have no natural counterparts. Those things produced by working in or with a particular medium are what we call media artefacts.

The distinction between natural and digital media also applies to artefacts. Natural artefacts are those produced using natural media. Among natural artefacts are paintings, prints, sculptures, photographs, musical recordings, and video and film clips. Digital artefacts include both the artefacts of digital media, such as an image produced by a paint program, and the digitized artefacts of natural media, for instance an image produced by scanning a photograph.

Until fairly recently, artists and designers primarily worked with natural media and so produced what we have just described as natural artefacts (it should be noted, though, that we are including such technologies as film and video as "natural" media). But the tools of the trade are changing, and now, as a result of the increasing capabilities of the computer, high-quality digital artefacts are becoming easier, and less expensive, to produce. There are many advantages to digital, as opposed to natural, artefacts — digital artefacts can be easily modified, copied, stored or retrieved. They can be sent over communications networks and can be made interactive. Equally intriguing is the ease with which digital artefacts are combined. Because, ultimately, digital artefacts simply reduce to bits and bytes, there are no physical restrictions on combining artefacts of different digital media. Digital video can be placed in text, or, vice versa, text can be placed in video; similarly audio and graphics can be combined, speech and text can be combined, and so on.

The notion of media artefacts leads to a natural definition for *multimedia*. We consider multimedia to be broadly concerned with the creation, composition, presentation, recording, editing and, in general, manipulation, of artefacts from diverse media. Since multimedia is so free in style, an immense variety of techniques, and combinations of techniques, are available to the artist. This is reflected in the wealth of media manipulation, composition and transformational capabilities packaged in multimedia authoring tools.

11.2 Multimedia Systems and Multimedia Programming

A complex multimedia production, whether a video game, a multimedia encyclopaedia or a "location-based entertainment environment," often requires the concerted effort of large teams of people. Like film and video production, multimedia production calls upon the talents of artists, actors, musicians, script writers, editors and directors. These people, responsible for "content design" to use current terminology, create raw material and prepare it for presentation and interaction. In doing so they rely on multimedia authoring environments to edit and compose digital media.

The authoring environments used for multimedia production are examples of *multimedia systems* [9]. Some other examples are:

- *multimedia database systems* — used to store and retrieve, or better, to "play" and "record" digital media;
- *hypermedia systems* — used to navigate through interconnected multimedia material;
- *video-on-demand systems* — used to deliver interactive video services over widearea networks.

The design and implementation of the above systems, and other systems dealing with digital media, forms the domain of *multimedia programming*.

Multimedia programming is based on the manipulation of media artefacts through software. One of the most important consequences arising from the digitization of media is that artefacts are released from the confines of studios and museums and can be brought into the realm of software. For instance, the ordinary spreadsheet or wordprocessor no longer need content itself with simple text and graphics, but can embellish its appearance with high-resolution colour images and video sequences. (Although the example is intended somewhat facetiously, we should keep in mind that digital media offer many opportunities for abuse. Just as the inclusion of multiple fonts in document processing systems led to many "formatting excesses," so the ready availability of digital media can lead to their gratuitous use.)

With the appearance of media artefacts in software applications, programmers are faced with new issues and new problems. Although recent work in data encoding standards, operating system design and network design has identified a number of possible services for supporting multimedia applications, the application programmer must still be aware of the capabilities and limitations of these services. Issues influencing application design include:

- *Media composition* — digital media can be easily combined and merged. Among the composition mechanisms found in practice are: *spatial composition* (the document metaphor) which deals with the spatial layout of media elements; *temporal composition* (the movie metaphor) considers the relative positioning of media elements along a temporal dimension; *procedural composition* (the script metaphor) describes actions to be performed on media elements and how media elements react to events; and *semantic composition* (the web metaphor) establishes links between related media elements.

- *Media synchronisation* — media processing and presentation activities often have synchronisation constraints [10][13]. A familiar example is the simultaneous playback of audio and video material where the audio must be "lip synched" with the video. In general, synchronisation cannot be solved solely by the network or operating system and, at the very least, application developers must be aware of the synchronisation requirements of their applications and be capable of specifying these requirements to the operating system and network.

- *User-interfaces* — multimedia enriches the user-interface but complicates implementation since a greater number of design choices are available. For example, questions of "look-and-feel" and interface aesthetics must now take into account audio, video and other digital media, instead of just text and graphics. Multimodal interaction [2], where several "channels" can be used for information presentation, is another challenge in the design of multimedia user-interfaces.

- *Compression schemes* — many techniques are currently used, some standard and some proprietary, for the compression of digital audio and video data streams. Application developers need to be aware of the various performance and quality trade-offs among the numerous compression schemes.

- *Database services* — application programming interfaces (APIs) for multimedia databases are likely to differ considerably from the APIs of both traditional databases and the more recent object-oriented databases. For example, it has been argued that multimedia databases require asynchronous, multithreaded APIs [6] as opposed to the more common synchronous and single-threaded APIs (where the application

sends the database a request and then waits for the reply). The introduction of concurrency and asynchrony has a major impact on application architecture.
- *Operating system and network services* — recent work on operating system support for multimedia — see Tokuda [14] for an overview — proposes a number of new services such as real-time scheduling and stream operations for time-based media. Similarly, research on "multimedia networks" (e.g. [4], [12]) introduces new services such as multicasting and "quality of service" (QoS) guarantees. Developers must consider these new services and their impact on application architecture.
- *Platform heterogeneity* — cross-platform development, and the ability to easily port an application from one platform to another, are important for the commercial success of multimedia applications. It is also desirable that multimedia applications adapt to performance differences on a given platform (such as different processor speeds, device access times and display capabilities).

In summary, a rich set of data representation, user interface, application architecture, performance and portability issues face the developers of multimedia systems. What we seek from environments for multimedia programming are high-level software abstractions that help developers explore this wide design space.

11.3 Multimedia Frameworks

In identifying abstractions for multimedia programming one should consider the prevailing programming paradigms such as functional programming, rule-based programming and object-oriented programming. While discussion of this topic is beyond the scope of this chapter, our position is that each of these paradigms has something to offer to multimedia, but that object-oriented programming, because of its support for encapsulation and software extension, is perhaps the most natural.

The apparent affinity between multimedia and object-oriented programming is clearly evident if one looks at the short history of programming environments for multimedia applications. From the earliest multimedia toolkits, such as Muse [8] and Andrew [3], to recent commercial multimedia development environments (e.g. Apple [1], Microsoft [11]) one can see the influence of the object-oriented paradigm. Often these environments and toolkits, in addition to structuring interfaces into classes and class hierarchies, have the more ambitious goal of building class frameworks for multimedia programming.

Perhaps the main benefits of object-oriented technology to multimedia programming are its mechanisms for extending software environments. Many of the issues listed in the previous section (media composition techniques, compression schemes, etc.) are, at their core, questions of how best to cope with the uncertainties of evolving environments. Frameworks, or hierarchies of extensible and interworking classes, offer developers a way of coping with evolution (see chapter 1). In the case of multimedia programming, several "evolutionary processes" are of concern, in particular:

- *Platform evolution* — the hardware platforms for multimedia applications are rapidly evolving. Capabilities that were once considered exotic, such as video compression and digital signal processing, are now found on the desktop (and soon the "set top").
- *Performance evolution* — many of the operations of interest to multimedia programming have real-time constraints, consider audio or video playback as examples. Such temporal dependencies make multimedia applications particularly sensitive to platform performance. It may be necessary, for instance, to adapt to less than optimal processing capacity by reducing presentation "quality" (e.g. lowering frame rates or sample sizes).
- *Format evolution* — new data representations for image, audio, video and other media types are likely to appear as a result of on-going standardization activities and research in data compression and media composition.

Developers want to create applications that can adapt to and take advantage of changes in platform functionality, increases in platform performance and new data representations. Of course it is impossible to write applications that can fully anticipate future developments in multimedia technology, but frameworks at least offer a mechanism for incorporating these changes into the programming environment.

11.4 A Multimedia Framework Example — Components

We now look at a particular multimedia framework — one that provides explicit support for component-oriented software development. This framework is described more fully elsewhere [5]. In essence it consists of four main class hierarchies: media classes, transform classes, format classes and component[*] classes (see figure 11.1):

- *Media classes* correspond to audio, video and the other media types. Instances of these classes are particular media values — what were called media artefacts earlier in the chapter.
- *Transform classes* represent media operations in a flexible and extensible manner. For example, many image editing programs provide a large number of filter operations with which to transform images. These operations could be represented by methods of an image class; however, this makes the image class overly complicated and adding new filter operations would require modifying this class. These problems are avoided by using separate transform classes to represent filter operations.
- *Format classes* encapsulate information about external representations of media values. Format classes can be defined for both file formats (such as GIF and TIFF, two

---

[*] The term "component" appears throughout this book, here the term is used in the specific sense of a software interface encapsulating software and/or hardware processes that produce, consume or transform media streams. Some examples are video codecs and audio players.

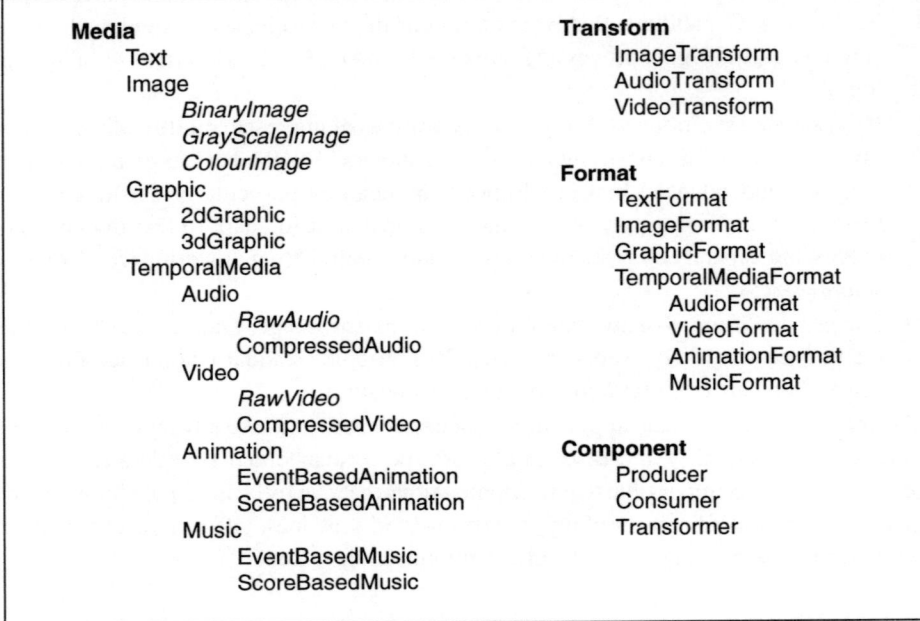

Figure 11.1 *Four class hierarchies of a multimedia framework: the Media, Format, Transform and Component classes and examples of their immediate subclasses. The classes shown are abstract (with the exception of those in italics) — concrete classes appear deeper in the hierarchies.*

image file formats) and for "stream" formats (for instance, CCIR 601 4:2:2, a stream format for uncompressed digital video).

- *Component classes* represent hardware and software resources that produce, consume and transform media streams. For instance, a CD-DA player is a component that produces a digital audio stream (specifically, stereo 16 bit PCM samples at 44.1 kHz).

Components are central to the framework for two reasons. First, the framework is adapted to a particular platform by implementing component classes that encapsulate the media processing services found on the platform. Second, applications are constructed by instantiating and connecting components. The remainder of this section looks at components in more detail.

11.4.1 Producers, Consumers and Transformers

The structure of a component is depicted graphically in figure 11.2. Of central importance are the *ports* through which media streams enter and leave. Components can be divided

A Multimedia Framework Example — Components

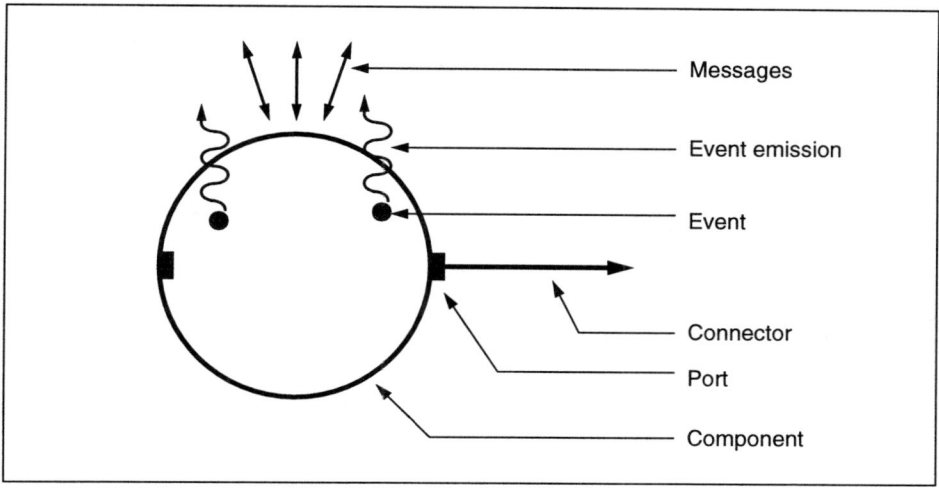

Figure 11.2 *Structure of a component. Three interfaces are available to the programmer: a synchronous interface based on message passing, an asynchronous interface based on events, and an isochronous interface based on streams. Streams enter and leave components through their ports and flow over the connectors joining components.*

into three broad categories based on the directionality of their ports: *producers* have only output ports, *consumers* have only input ports, and *transformers* have both input and output ports.

11.4.2 Component Interfaces

Components communicate with other components, and with other objects, via three interfaces:

- *Synchronous interface* — components, since they are objects, have a method interface describing messages that can be sent to the component and the associated replies. This interface is intended to allow external control over the component. For example, methods might include starting and stopping the component and querying or modifying operational parameters.
- *Asynchronous interface* — components emit events that can be caught by other objects (including other components, although building in dependencies between components is not recommended). As an example of event generation, a video player component might emit a "frame completed" event each time it produces a new frame on its output port. Generally the asynchronous interface is intended for monitoring and coordinating component behaviour.

- *Isochronous interface* — finally the input and output ports provide a third form of interface. Streams of media data (such as audio samples, video frames or animation events) enter and leave through ports. If congestion (or starvation) is to be avoided, connected components must operate at the same rate — in other words, connected components are *isochronous*.

11.4.3 Plug Compatibility

Several conditions must be satisfied before a pair of ports can be connected. In particular:
- One port must be an output port, the other an input port.
- The ports must be *plug compatible*.
- Creating the connection cannot exceed either port's *fan-limit* (the number of simultaneous incoming or outgoing connections a port may accept).
- The ports must accept the same form of connector. Generally connectors come in a variety of "forms" such as shared memory connectors, network connectors and connectors using a hardware bus.

Plug compatibility is related to type compatibility. Each port is associated with a set of stream format classes; these are the *supported types* of the port. When a port is to be connected, a specific member of this set is specified and is called the *activated type* of the port. An input and output port are then said to be plug compatible when the activated type of the output port is either identical to or a subtype of the activated type of the input port.

Plug compatibility rules out such errors as connecting a video output to an audio input. Of more interest though, are the situations involving subtyping. It is best to think of a port type as specifying the form of elements in the stream that flows through the port. Note that streams need not be homogeneous, one could have a stream containing both "circular" elements and "square" elements. Plug compatibility then says that an output port producing, for instance, only "circular" elements, can be connected to an input port that accepts streams containing both "circular" and "square" elements. In practice this means that we can connect a source to a sink provided the "vocabulary" of the source is included in that of the sink.

11.4.4 Component Networks

Groups of connected components are called *component networks*. A component network resembles a dataflow machine — streams of media data flow from producers, through transformers, and finally to consumer components. Applications are responsible for building component networks — in other words, applications build the virtual machine on which they run. This involves:

Video Widgets — A Programming Example

- *Instantiation* — the instantiation of a component results in resources being allocated for its operation. Resources include such things as memory, bus and network bandwidth, processor cycles, and hardware devices.
- *Initialization* — after creating a component object it must be initialized, i.e. operational parameters such as "speed" or "volume" must be set. The component's method interface is used for this purpose.
- *Connection* — after instantiating and initializing components, they can then be connected. Depending on the application, all connections may be made statically when the application begins (e.g. a two-party desktop conferencing application) or dynamically as the application runs (e.g. a multi-party desktop conferencing application where users have the ability to enter and leave conferences as they are running). An example of a tool that can be adapted to allow the visual configuration of media processing components is described in chapter 10.
- *Synchronisation* — components are subject to real-time constraints. In particular, media values enter and leave their ports at specific rates. If for some reason components are no longer able to process streams at the proper rates, then synchronisation errors start to appear (such as video lagging behind audio). When a component network falls "out-of-sync" it may be necessary for the application to specify corrective action (such as shutting down components, reducing quality, or acquiring more resources).
- *Event-handling* — during operation, components generate a variety of events. Applications can register interest in events and must then provide appropriate event handlers.

11.4.5 Media Processing Platforms and Component Kits

Finally, two important notions related to components are *media processing platforms* and *component kits*. A media processing platform is simply a set of hardware and software resources. Some examples would be a CD-i player, a MIDI network, a PC with a sound board, a video editing suite, a digital signal processor, and a network of "multimedia workstations" (workstations with audio and video capabilities).

Given a media processing platform, a component kit is the set of components offered by the platform. Clearly applications can only use available components. However, it should be possible for applications to adapt themselves, at least to some extent, to different platforms and different component kits. For instance, consider an application that plays multiple audio, video and MIDI tracks. If the application finds itself on a platform with no MIDI components, it might select simply to ignore any MIDI tracks during playback.

11.5 Video Widgets — A Programming Example

The preceding section contained a short overview of a proposal for an object-oriented framework for multimedia programming. To give a better idea of how such frameworks

Figure 11.3 *A video widget and application windows.*

can be used, and how they can help shield applications from changes in platform architecture, we will look at a programming example based on an existing prototype.

The programming example we have chosen is the implementation of "video widgets" [7]. Video widgets, like graphics widgets (menus, buttons, icons and so on) are user-interface elements encapsulating both visual and behavioural information. Video widgets are rendered (i.e. displayed) by compositing video sequences (stored either in analog or digital form) over application graphics.

An example of a video widget is shown in figure 11.3. This widget is the basis of a simple "video assistant" for explaining and demonstrating the use of buttons belonging to some application. Such a video widget could be of use in multimedia kiosks or other situations where users may not be familiar with the operation of the application.

The implementation of video widgets involves components for playing, mixing and displaying video — these are producers, transformers and consumers respectively. The instantiation and connection of these components is performed by a class called VideoWidget, this class also provides application programmers methods for controlling widget behaviour. A partial class definition for VideoWidget is as follows:

```
class VideoWidget {
private:
    VideoPlayer*     player;      // a Component object (a Producer)
    VideoMixer*      mixer;       // a Component object (a Transformer)
    WindowServer*    wserver;     // a Component object (a Producer)
    Display*         display;     // a Component object (a Consumer)
    ActionTable*     atab;        // identifies widget actions
```

Video Widgets — A Programming Example

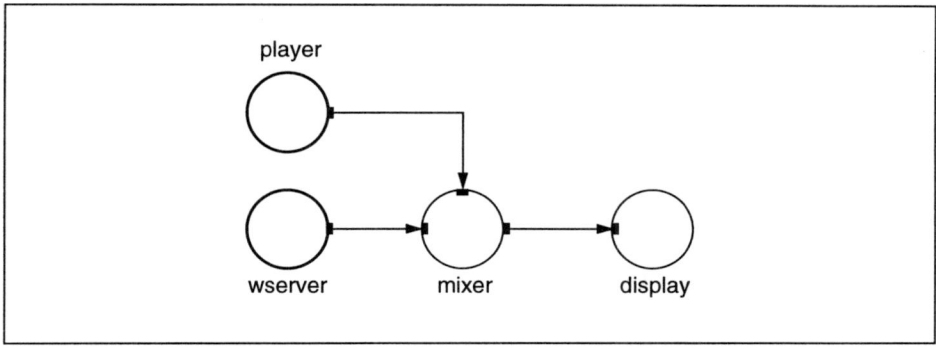

Figure 11.4 *A component network for a video widget.*

```
public:
            // create a video widget
            VideoWidget(WindowServer* w, Display* d,
                Video* v, ActionTable* a, ChromaKey k);

            // have widget perform some action
            // this may generate events that can be
            // caught by the application
    void    Perform(ActionId aid, float speed, bool blockFlag);
};
```

The VideoWidget class includes instance variables that refer to the component objects used to build the "virtual machine" (i.e. component network) on which a video widget runs. The classes of these components are:

- VideoPlayer — an abstract class for components that playback video values (either analog or digital). Some specializations could include: VideoTapePlayer, VideoDiscPlayer, MpegPlayer and JpegPlayer. Methods declared by VideoPlayer (and implemented by the subclasses) include Load, Cue, Play and Pause.
- VideoMixer — a class for components that mix video using techniques such as chroma-keying. Methods include SetChromaKey, EnableKeying, BypassKeying.
- WindowServer — a class used to encapsulate window server functionality. A window server is represented by a producer component with a video-valued output port.
- Display — a class used for display devices. A particular display is represented by a consumer component with a video-valued input port.

Using the framework's notion of components and connections, a typical graphics application would consist of a WindowServer component connected to a Display component. Video widgets can then be implemented by "splicing" a video mixer and a video player into this connection. The resulting component network is shown in figure 11.4.

Configuration of the component network takes place in the constructor for VideoWidget. An outline of this method is:

```
VideoWidget::VideoWidget(WindowServer* w, Display* d,
                        Video* v, ActionTable* a, ChromaKey k)
{
    player = new VideoPlayer(v->Format( ));
    mixer = new VideoMixer;
    wserver = w;
    display = d;
    atab = a;

    // connect player and wserver outputs to mixer inputs
    // connect mixer output to display input

    // initialize components
    player->Load(v);
    mixer->SetChromaKey(k);
    mixer->EnableKeying( );
}
```

In addition to making component connections, the constructor loads a video value onto the video player and configures the mixer for chroma-keying. The constructor also takes an ActionTable argument; this is a data structure identifying offsets within the video value for particular "actions" that can be performed by the widget. A particular action is played back by using the Perform method:

```
VideoWidget::Perform(ActionId aid, float speed, bool blockFlag)
{
    player->Cue(atab[aid]);              // cue at start frame of action aid
    player->Play(speed, blockFlag);      // start playing, this method blocks
                                         // if blockFlag is TRUE
}
```

The VideoWidget class can be expanded in many ways to include such things as audio capabilities, multi-layer mixing and video effects (e.g. fading in or out a video widget). However, our purpose here is not really to discuss the use of video widgets or their design requirements, but rather to provide a non-trivial example of how component networks are mapped to media processing platforms.

Two possible, but radically different, platforms for video widgets are shown in figures 11.5 and 11.6. The first is based on analog video and external devices for mixing and switching. The second assumes a fast internal bus and hardware components for processing high data rate uncompressed digital video.

The important point of this example is that the differences between the platforms need not be visible to the user of video widgets. More specifically, it is possible to have a single implementation of the VideoWidget class for both platforms. The code for methods such as Perform remains the same; what changes between platforms are the implementations of the components used by VideoWidget. However, as long as implementations of VideoMixer, VideoPlayer, etc., provide the same interfaces, there is no reason to change the VideoWidget class.

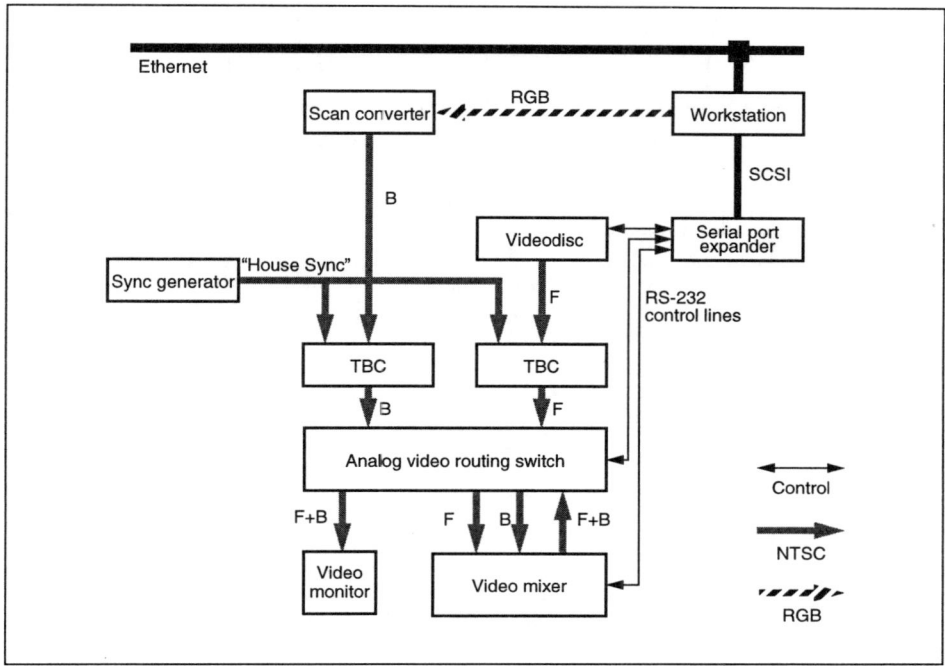

Figure 11.5 *An analog video platform for "video widgets". The two video signals F (front) and B (back) come from the video widget and the application respectively. The central part of this layout is an analog video routing switch allowing video equipment to be connected under computer control. The TBCs (time-base correctors) synchronize video signals against some reference signal (coming here from a sync generator) and are needed when video signals are mixed.*

11.6 Summary

Multimedia raises a host of new design issues for application developers. Questions of media composition, media synchronisation, data formats, user interfaces and database interfaces must be re-examined in the light of the capabilities of multimedia platforms. To take one example, advances in video compression techniques now make it possible to construct "video servers." These digital video storage and delivery systems are the basis of the new family of video-on-demand services and lead us to question the nature of the interface between applications and database systems.

One of the more severe practical difficulties facing developers of multimedia applications is the lack of stable target platforms. What can be called "platform volatility" results from the rapid pace of additions to the functionality of multimedia hardware, improve-

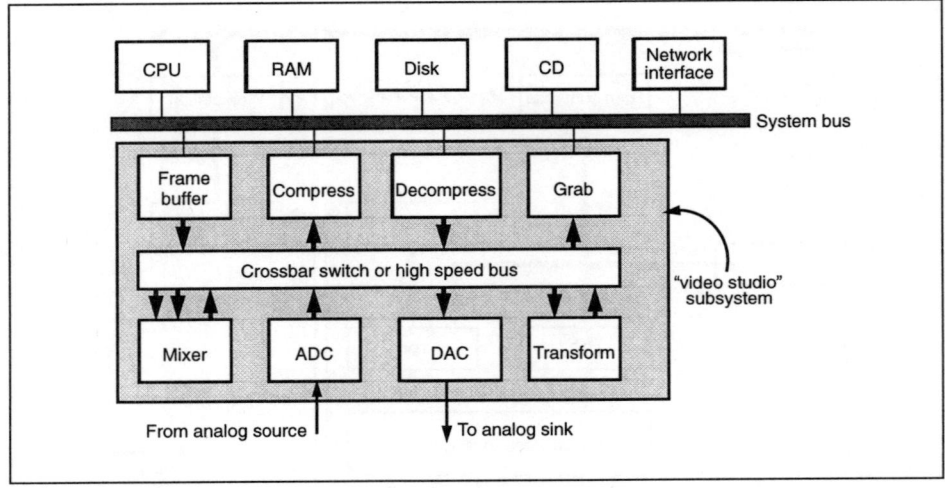

Figure 11.6 *A digital video platform for "video widgets". Heavy lines indicate high data rate streams. The analog-to-digital converter (ADC) and digital-to-analog converter (DAC) connect the "video studio subsystem" to external analog sources (e.g. video cameras) and sinks (e.g. monitors).*

ments in performance and quality characteristics, and the introduction of new media formats. In order to simplify cross-platform development, multimedia programming environments must address the issue of platform volatility. This chapter has argued, through a concrete example, that object-oriented programming, class frameworks and component-based software allow us to cope with platform evolution — that constructing applications from connectable and "swappable" components helps protect developers from even radical changes in target platforms.

References

[1] Apple Computer Inc., *QuickTime 1.5 Developer's Kit*, 1992.
[2] Meera Blattner and Roger Dannenberg (eds.), *Multimedia Interface Design*, ACM Press, Reading, Mass., 1992.
[3] Nathaniel Borenstein, *Multimedia Applications Development with the Andrew Toolkit*, Prentice Hall, Englewood Cliffs, NJ, 1990.
[4] Dominico Ferrari, Anindo Banerjea and Hui Zhang, "Network Support for Multimedia: A Discussion of the Tenet Approach," Technical Report TR-92-072, International Computer Science Institute, University of California at Berkeley, 1992.
[5] Simon Gibbs and Dennis Tsichritzis, *Multimedia Programming: Objects, Environments and Frameworks*, Addison-Wesley / ACM Press, Wokingham, England, 1994.

[6] Simon Gibbs, Christian Breiteneder and Dennis Tsichritzis, "Audio/Video Databases: An Object-Oriented Approach," in *Proceedings IEEE Data Engineering Conference*, Vienna, 1993, pp. 381–390.

[7] Simon Gibbs, Christian Breiteneder, Vicki de Mey and Michael Papathomas, "Video Widgets and Video Actors," in *Symposium on User Interface Software and Technology* (UIST '93), 1993, pp. 179–185.

[8] Matthew Hodges, Russel Sasnett and Mark Ackerman, "A Construction Set for Multimedia Applications," *IEEE Software*, vol. 6, no. 1, 1989, pp. 37–43.

[9] John Koegel Buford (ed.), *Multimedia Systems*, Addison-Wesley, Reading, Mass., 1994.

[10] Thomas D.C. Little *et al.*, "Multimedia Synchronization, *IEEE Data Engineering Bulletin*, vol. 14, no. 3, 1991, pp. 26–35.

[11] Microsoft Corporation, *Microsoft Windows Multimedia Programmer's Reference*, Microsoft Press, 1991.

[12] Doug Shepherd and Michale Salmony, "Extending OSI to Support Synchronization Required by Multimedia Applications," *Computer Communications*, vol. 13, no. 7, 1990, pp. 399–406.

[13] Ralf Steinmetz, "Synchronization Properties in Multimedia Systems," *IEEE Journal on Selected Areas in Communications*, vol. 8, no. 3, 1990, pp. 401–412.

[14] Hideyuki Tokuda, "Operating System Support for Continuous Media Applications," in *Multimedia Systems*, ed. John Koegel Buford, Addison-Wesley, Reading, Mass., 1994, pp. 201–220.

Chapter 12

Gluons and the Cooperation between Software Components

Xavier Pintado

Abstract A major problem in software engineering is how to specify the patterns of interaction among software components so that they can be assembled to perform tasks in a cooperative way. Such cooperative assembly requires that components obey rules ensuring their interaction compatibility. The choice of a specific approach to specifying rules depends on various criteria such as the kind of target environment, the nature of the software components or the kind of programming language. This chapter reviews major efforts to develop and promote standards that address this issue. We present our own approach to the construction of a development framework for software applications that make use of real-time financial information. For this domain, the two main requirements are (1) to facilitate the integration of new components into an existing system, and (2) to allow for the run-time composition of software components. The goal of the development framework is to provide dynamic interconnection capabilities. The basic idea is to standardize and reuse interaction protocols that are encapsulated inside special objects called *gluons*. These objects mediate the cooperation of software components. We discuss the advantages of the approach, and provide examples of how gluons are used in the financial framework.

12.1 Introduction

The advent of object-oriented techniques has brought many benefits to the field of software engineering. One notable benefit is that objects provide a higher degree of autonomy than obtained with the traditional separation of software into functions and data structures. This autonomy promotes component-oriented software construction, since autonomous objects can be reused in many different context with reasonable integration efforts. Component reuse can reduce development time and costs, and can lead to improved reliability, since reusable components will become thoroughly tested as a consequence of reuse.

Although component-oriented software is fairly promising in terms of its reuse potential some major problems remain to be solved. Among these, a salient problem is the definition of the patterns of cooperation between software components, to which considerable effort has already been devoted. We may notice, for instance, that a class interface condenses assumptions about the objects that can be instantiated from it, but not assumptions about the interactions that those objects may have with other objects.

We may better capture the essence of the problem by observing that virtually any kind of cooperation requires agreement between the cooperating entities [29]. Cooperation agreements can take many forms, however. They can be specified, for instance, by a "law" to which all the cooperating entities obey. But cooperation can also rely on bilateral agreements each defining the cooperation between pairs of entities.

In the context of component-oriented software design, the goal is to make software components cooperate through reliable and flexible mechanisms that appropriately support and enforce convenient interaction patterns. In this context, the interaction "law" or cooperation agreement is usually captured by the notion of an object-oriented development framework [9] [10]. An object-oriented framework is a collection of classes that are designed to work together. A framework is intended to provide a development environment that promotes reuse and reduces development effort by providing a comprehensive set of classes and development rules. Frameworks come in many different flavours: they can, for example, target a narrow application domain such as the development of device drivers (e.g. NeXTStep Driver Kit [19]), or they can address the requirements of a generic development environment (e.g. Visual C++ framework [4]) comprising multiple sets of classes and development rules.

The distinguishing characteristic of a framework is the design philosophy that pervades all aspects of the framework such as the definition of foundation classes, the rules for the design of new classes and the tools that support the development process. By applying a consistent design philosophy to all the aspects of the framework, designers attempt to provide the user with a uniform development model that reduces the learning effort and defines a generic architecture for applications developed with the framework.

In this chapter we develop a framework for the development of financial applications. The framework is intended for the development of applications that involve the retrieval of real-time financial data sources. The typical target environment for the framework is rapidly evolving, in the sense that the behaviour of the objects and the way they are related evolves at a fast pace to reflect the real world of finance. The framework focuses on run-time connection of software components and on capabilities that support the incremental development of applications. Figure 12.1 shows a typical display of an application developed with the financial framework.

The distinguishing feature of the framework is the introduction of a special family of objects, called *gluons*, which are responsible for the cooperation among software compo-

Introduction

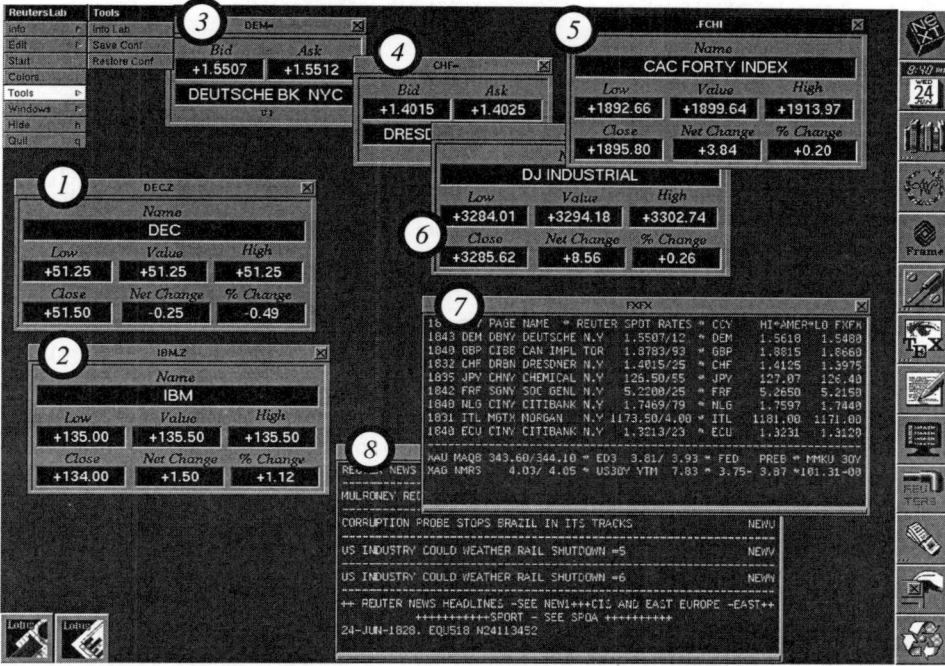

Figure 12.1 *Display presenting some of the visualization tools available for the display of real-time information. Windows 1 and 2 display real-time information about DEC and IBM stocks in the Zurich stock exchange. Windows 3 and 4 provide transaction information about foreign exchange rates. Window 5 and 6 display index values (French Cac 40 and Dow Jones Industrial). Finally, window 7 displays information in page format, and window 8 offers news highlights.*

nents. Although gluons essentially encapsulate communication protocols, they play a prominent role at the design level by promoting a protocol-centered design.

This chapter is organized as follows: the next section provides an overview of how different frameworks address the issue of object cooperation and the patterns of cooperation that they promote. We focus on standardization proposals promoted by major software houses since they will most likely have a significant impact on the future architecture of software applications. Section 12.3 discusses the requirements for the financial framework. Such requirements cannot be easily satisfied with the previously described approaches and we therefore introduce a new protocol-centered approach. Section 12.4 discusses gluons as special components that enable a protocol-centered approach. Section 12.5 presents the financial framework, focusing on the illustration of commonly used gluons. We conclude with a summary of the advantages of protocol-centered frameworks.

12.2 An Overview of Cooperation Patterns

The development of mechanisms that support communication between software components is hardly a new problem. A significant effort has been devoted in the past, for instance, to interapplication communication. A typical mechanism is the remote procedure call (RPC), which allows an application to invoke routines belonging to another application. RPC is the kind of cooperation mechanism one expects in software environments where the principal entities are functions and data structures. In a word of objects, however, we might expect to have remote message capabilities since the message is the inter-object communication mechanism.

To the best of our knowledge the first commercially available implementation of remote messages came bundled with NeXTStep AppKit framework[19]. However, remote messaging only provides a communication layer. For software components to cooperate in a dependable and flexible way we need to define the laws of cooperation. In what follows we provide an overview of various standardization efforts that address, in a broad sense, the problem of defining laws of cooperation in the context of software development frameworks.

12.2.1 Object Management Group

The Object Management Group (OMG) promotes a standard to support the interaction of software components within a framework called the Object Management Architecture (OMA). One of the main goals of OMA is to achieve object distribution transparency, which means that the interaction between a client component and a server component through the server's interface should be independent of its physical location, access path, and should be relocation invariant. This standard relies on a common object model, the OMG Object Model which is used by all OMG-compliant technologies.

12.2.1.1 The OMG Object Model

The OMG Object Model defines a way to specify externally visible characteristics of objects in an implementation-independent way. The visible characteristics of an object are described as a collection of operation signatures called the object's interface. The OMG Object Model definition of an operation signature extends in interesting ways the typical definition of a method's signature in order to make it more convenient for distributed computing environments. The optional **oneway** keyword specifies an exactly-once operation semantics if the operation successfully returns results or a at-most-once semantics if an exception is returned. Each parameter is flagged with one of the three qualifiers — **in**, **out** or **inout** — to specify the write access to the parameter of the client, the server or both. An exception is an indication that the request was not performed successfully. The **raises** keyword introduces the list of possible exceptions that can be raised by the operation. Finally, the **context** keyword allows for the specification of additional information that may affect the performance of the operation. These extensions address issues related to distributed

```
[oneway] <return_type> <operation>(in|out|inout param1, ..., in|out|inout paramK)
    [raises (except1, ..., exceptL)]
    [context (name1, ..., nameM)]
```

Figure 12.2 *The OMG Object Model operation signature.*

environments such as unreliable communications, and the need for appropriate mechanisms for exception handling.

12.2.1.2 Object Request Broker

The communication between objects is mediated by an Object Request Broker (ORB). The ORB is responsible for finding the object implementation for the requested operation, to perform any preprocessing needed to perform an operation, and to communicate any data associated with the operation. The functionality of object request brokers is defined in the Common Object Request Broker Architecture (CORBA)[21]. In order to ensure language independence, CORBA defines a Interface Definition Language (IDL) that obeys the same lexical rules as C++, although additional keywords are introduced essentially to support distributed environments. However, IDL differs from C++ in that it is only a declarative language. In order for object implementations to communicate with the ORB they need to implement a Basic Object Adaptor (BOA) which deals with such aspects as interface registration, implementation activation, and authentication and access control. An important component of the ORB is the interface repository which provides access to a collection of object interfaces specified in IDL.

To summarize, the OMG provides a standard for the communication of objects in distributed environments. The standard focuses on interoperability of heterogeneous systems, where interoperability is achieved through a request broker that defines standard interface rules which the interacting agents need to obey.

12.2.2 Microsoft DDE and OLE

Microsoft provides two main standards for interapplication cooperation: DDE (Dynamic Data Exchange) and OLE (Object Linking and Embedding). DDE is much simpler than OLE since it addresses essentially the exchange of data between applications that run on the same computer. On the other hand, OLE is an ambitious standard that encompasses many aspects related to the structures of software components.

12.2.2.1 Dynamic Data Exchange

DDE focuses on data exchange between applications based on a client–server model. In DDE parlance, a client is any application that initiates a DDE connection. Usually a client requests data after establishing a connection with a server. The connection establishes a

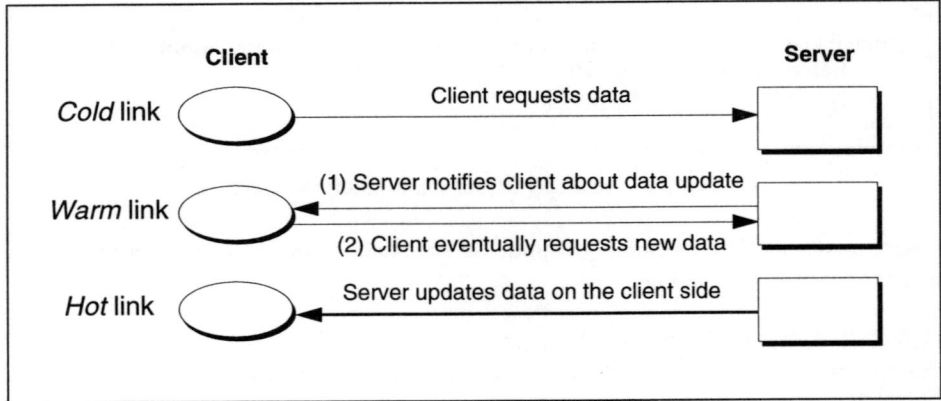

Figure 12.3 *DDE involves three types of links between clients and servers. The variety of links reflects the different requirements of applications on how to maintain client's data consistent with the corresponding server's data.*

link that according to the way the link deals with data updates on the server side can be one of three types: *cold*, *warm* and *hot*. These three links are illustrated in figure 12.3. With *cold* links the server plays a passive role: it takes no action whenever data is updated. The client is, therefore, responsible for implementing the update policy by issuing data requests when appropriate. With *warm* links the responsibility for data update is shared between the client and the server: the server notifies the client upon a data update but the data request to perform the update on the client's side is initiated by the client. Finally, with *hot* links the server is responsible for the whole update process on the client's side.

The three types of links allow for the implementation of data consistency policies between the client and the server that appropriately reflect the requirements of the client application. The actions on both the client and the server side are carried out through callback functions.

The data organization at the server end follows a three-level hierarchy that recognizes three entity types: services, topics and items, as illustrated in figure 12.4. Typically, a topic corresponds to a document (e.g. an open document in a wordprocessor server) but it can also represent a relation in a relational database since the DDE standard does not specify what a topic should be. Items are the smallest entities that can be addressed through DDE. Items can be of any type and format recognized by the Windows clipboard. In order for a client to request data from a server it needs to know the name of the service provided by the server, the name of the topic and the name of the item it is looking for. A client can connect to multiple servers and a server can be linked to multiple clients. Although DDE is essentially a mechanism for data exchange among applications it also provides limited capabilities that allow a client to execute commands on the server side. These capabilities can be used to implement cooperation mechanisms that are, to some extent, similar to remote messaging in other environments.

An Overview of Cooperation Patterns

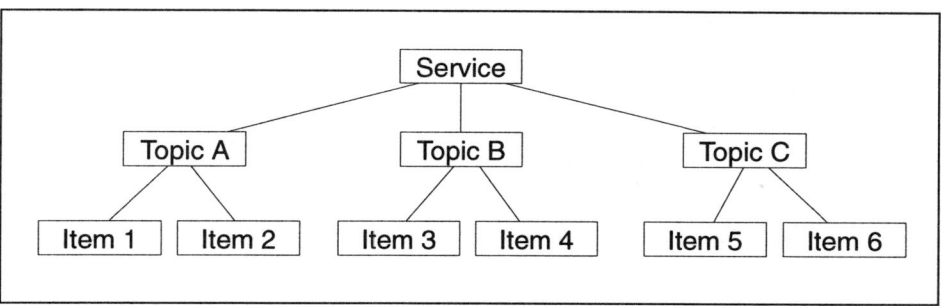

Figure 12.4 *DDE hierarchy showing the service provided by a server and how it is hierarchically organized in topics and items.*

12.2.2.2 OLE 2.0

OLE is another standard defined by Microsoft that enables the cooperation of applications. In its current 2.0 version [17][18] it shares many similarities with OpenDoc that we will describe in section 12.2.4.2. For instance, both standards comprise a set of cooperation protocols and a definition for compliant structured documents. OLE 2.0 is relatively hard to summarize briefly. In fact OLE 2.0 is much more than a application cooperation standard; it is the foundation for a Microsoft strategy to make MS-Windows migrate to object-oriented technology. As such, OLE 2.0 comprises a set of apparently loosely related standard definitions, models and implementations which provide, as a whole, a coordinated platform for future object-technology. OLE 2.0 provides standard definitions and implementation support for compound documents, drag-and-drop operations, name services, linking and embedding of documents, and application interaction automation.

The unifying concept underlying the OLE 2.0 platform is the Component Object Model (COM). All the other pieces of OLE 2.0 either rely on the COM definitions or use COM objects, usually called Windows objects [17]. Windows objects differ slightly from the objects proposed by commonly used programming languages such as C++ or Eiffel. A Windows object is fully defined by its set of *interfaces*. An *interface* is a collection of function pointers and there is no such notion as references to Windows objects. When we obtain a reference to an object it is in fact a reference to one of its *interfaces*. Another interesting aspect of Windows objects is that there is no inheritance mechanism, but because Windows objects provide multiple *interfaces,* it is easy to encapsulate Windows objects with programming languages that offer either single or multiple inheritance. The COM presents Windows objects essentially as collections of functions [7][17] (i.e. *interfaces*), which can be fairly confusing for readers acquainted with object-oriented concepts. The main reason, we believe, is that the OLE 2.0 is to be implemented with many different programming languages, such as BASIC, C, C++, which may or may not endorse object-oriented techniques. With different programming languages the binding between the object's data and the object's methods may be implemented in different ways that are not specified in OLE. Microsoft offers an OLE 2.0 software development kit for C++ environments.

A key feature of OLE 2.0 is the definition of structured documents. Structured documents contain *storages* and *streams* that are organized in a similar way to traditional file systems: *streams* are analogous to files while *storages* act as directories. So, *storages* contain either *streams* or *storages*. Storages and streams provide support for structured or composite documents that are organized in a hierarchical structure. OLE 2.0 provides a standard definition for the document's structure and also a set of functions that support the standard operations on structured documents.

The best-known features of OLE 2.0 are probably embedding and linking. A typical compound document (e.g. a text with graphics, sound, data in spreadsheet format, etc.) contains data objects that have been created by different applications. The owner of the compound document, say a wordprocessor, may know how to display most of these items but cannot deal with the full complexity of retrieving and modifying them. An OLE *container* is any application that can incorporate OLE objects. *Containers* usually display the OLE objects and accept commands for them. However, *containers* are not intended to process the objects. Objects retain an association with *server* applications that are responsible for servicing the requests addressed to the objects. The idea here is that clients do not need to be aware of the internals of the objects they contain. The object (data) together with its associate server corresponds to the usual notion of object in object-oriented terminology which encapsulates both data and operations on the data. *Servers* accept commands, called *verbs*, that correspond to actions that can be applied to the objects. An interface is the set of operations that can be applied to an object via its server.

OLE 2.0 offers two ways to integrate an object into a compound document: *linking* and *embedding*. Embedding is most frequently used. The *container* application owns and stores each embedded object, but the server retrieves the object. The server plays an anonymous role by processing the object on behalf of the container application. Conversely, an object can be linked into a document. A linked document belongs to a given document (and is stored in the document's file) but it is referenced in another document. In this way several *containers* can share a single linked object.

Additionally, OLE 2.0 provides a standard for data transfer called Uniform Data Transfer (UDT) and a standard for scripting called Automation. Automation allows objects associated with one application to be directed from another application, or to perform operations on a set of objects under the control of a macro language [18].

To summarize the OLE 2.0 standard suite we may say that the Component Object Model standardizes how an object and an object's client communicate; compound documents standardize document structure and storage; Uniform Data Transfer standardizes data exchange capabilities and Automation provides a support for remote control of applications.

It should be noted that with OLE version 2.0 the interapplication cooperation primitives are restricted to the scope of the same machine. However, these mechanisms could easily be extended to provide the same capabilities across networks and serve, therefore, as a foundation for distributed computing.

An Overview of Cooperation Patterns

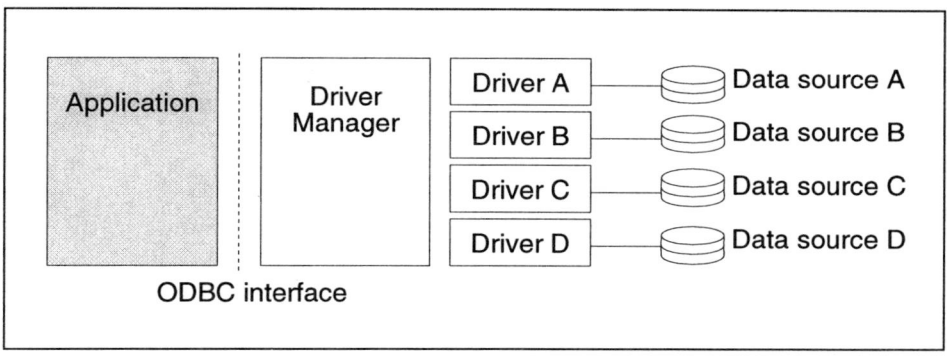

Figure 12.5 *ODBC 2.0 application architecture.*

12.2.3 ODBC 2.0

Although the Open Database Connectivity standard from Microsoft is more a standard for the interconnection of applications and databases, it is worth mentioning here for two reasons. First, it represents a much-needed standardization effort to isolate applications from the access to specific databases. Second, databases will be, at least in the near future, one of the most prominent reusable software components since they are responsible for object persistence.

The architecture of an ODBC 2.0 application is represented in figure 12.5. From the view point of the application, the access to the various data sources is transparent through the ODBC interface. The ODBC 2.0 standard interface provides the following:

- a standard way to connect to databases;
- a set of function calls that allows an application to connect to one or many databases, execute SQL statements, and retrieve the results;
- a standard representation for data types.

The Driver Manager loads drivers on behalf of the application, while the Drivers implement ODBC function calls and submit, when appropriate, requests to the associated data source. The Drivers are responsible for adapting to the specific syntax of the associated DBMS. ODBC 2.0 does not rely on object-oriented principles and is fairly low level in the sense that it provides a vendor-independent mechanism to execute SQL statements on host databases.

12.2.4 Apple's Interapplication Communication Architecture and OpenDoc

Like Microsoft, Apple devoted significant efforts to the definition and implementation of standard mechanism for the cooperation of applications. Also like Microsoft, Apple has a

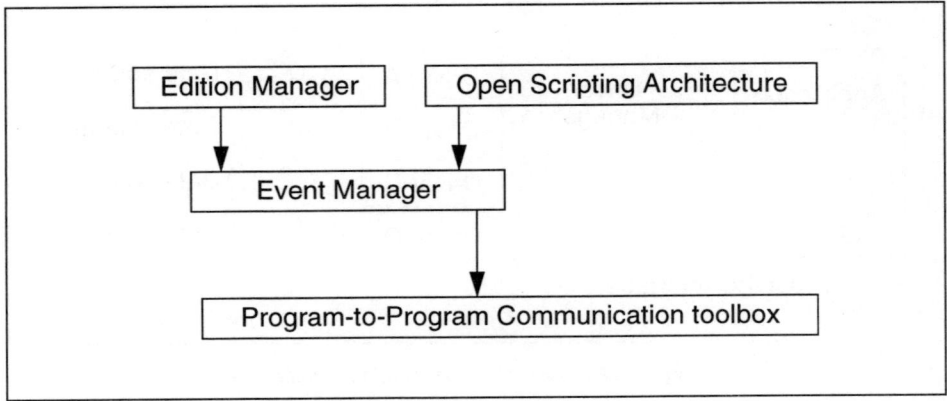

Figure 12.6 *The layers of the Interapplication Communication Architecture.*

large developer base and a large software base that did not already fully adopt object-oriented tools. The consequence is that the migration towards an object-oriented platform started by the introduction of object-oriented concepts such as message passing into development environments that are not object-oriented.

12.2.4.1 Interapplication Communication Architecture

This migration was the driving force for the development of the Interapplication Communication architecture (ICA), which provides a standard mechanism for communication among Macintosh applications[1]. More specifically the goal is to allow applications to:

- exchange data through copy-and-paste operations;
- read and write data blocks from and to other applications;
- send and respond to Apple events;
- be controlled through scripts.

A significant effort has been devoted by Apple to define a common vocabulary of high-level messages, called Apple events, that are published in the Apple Event Registry: Standard Suites. To the best of our knowledge, this has been the only effort to date to standardize the messages that applications may respond to.

- Applications typically use Apple events to request services from other applications or to provide services in response to other applications requests. A *client application* is an application that sends an Apple event to request a service, while the application that provides the service is the *server application*. The client and server applications can reside on the same machine, or on different machines connected to the same network.

The ICA comprises the following:

- The *Edition Manager*, which provides support for copy-and-paste operations among applications and updating information automatically when data in the source document changes.
- The *Open Scripting Architecture*, which defines the standard mechanisms that allow for the external control of single or multiple applications. OSA is comparable, to some extent, to Automation in OLE 2.0. OSA is not tied to any specific scripting language. Each scripting language has a corresponding scripting component that translates the scripts into events.
- The *Event Manager*, which provides the support that allows applications to send and receive events. The Event Manager standard defines the architecture and the pieces of Apple messaging backplane.
- The *Program-to-Program Communication toolbox*, which provides low-level support that allows applications to exchange blocks of data in an efficient way. The Edition Manager and the Open Scripting Architecture provide the user level support. They both rely on the Event Manager to exchange data and messages across applications. The Event Manager, in turn, relies on the Program-to-Program Communication toolbox to transport data. Figure 12.6 illustrates how the different parts of the ICA are related.

12.2.4.2 OpenDoc

As opposed to OLE, the ICA only deals with the problem of application interaction and does not define a standard for documents. Apple, together with other companies such as Novell and IBM, is proposing another standard, OpenDoc, that is quite similar in scope to OLE 2.0. It defines both standards for application interaction mechanisms and for structured documents. In reality, OpenDoc integrates three other standards: (1) System Object Model (SOM), which originated as a CORBA compliant IBM standard for interapplication message exchange; (2) BENTO, which standardizes the format of structured documents and (3) the Open Scripting Architecture that we already mentioned as part of Apple's ICA.

BENTO defines the standard elements for structuring documents in OpenDoc. BENTO documents are stored in containers which are collections of objects. BENTO objects are organized as schematized in figure 12.7. An object has a persistent ID which is unique within its container. Objects contain a set of properties, which in turn contain values of some type. The values are where data is actually stored and their types describe the corresponding formats.

The ideas underlying OpenDoc are quite similar to those on which OLE 2.0 is based: composite documents may contain heterogeneous objects that are managed and manipulated using a variety of specialized software components. With OLE 2.0 the specialized components are heavyweight applications such as wordprocessors and spreadsheets. On the other hand, OpenDoc targets components that are more fine-grained. The goal is to make the concept of application vanish, giving place to a document-centered approach that promotes the document as the main user concept. Each part of a document retains an association with a specialized component that knows how to retrieve it. Naturally, the in-

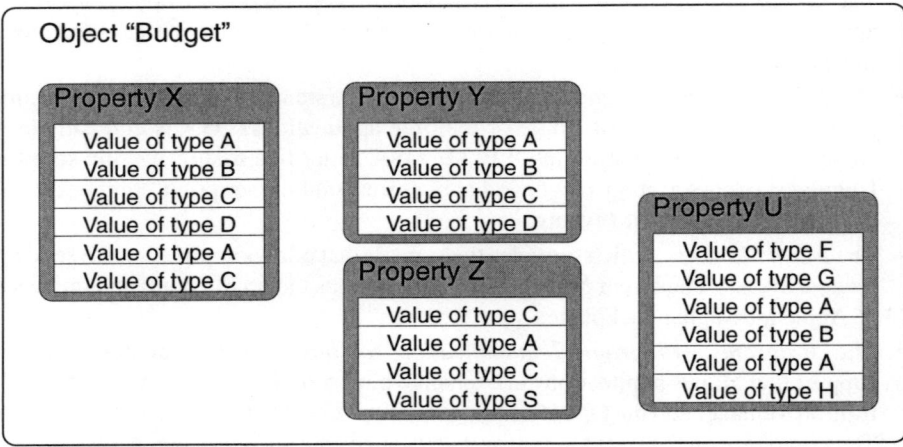

Figure 12.7 *A Bento object contains a collection of properties and properties contain values which are the placeholders where data is actually stored.*

vocation of the retrieving component is transparent to the user, who can easily increase the variety of the parts that can be incorporated into composite documents by purchasing new specialized software components.

12.2.5 Discussion

The considerable effort that has been devoted to designing, implementing and promoting the adoption of these cooperation standards suggests the critical role that such standards may play in future software technology. We may notice, however, that the various standards differ considerably in scope.

For example, OMG standards focus on interoperability among heterogeneous subsystems and they essentially provide mechanisms that allow software components to request services from other software components. Software components need to provide a standard layer that adapts them to the request broker in much the same way that ODBC 2.0 applications need drivers to adapt data sources to the ODBC 2.0 interface. Conversely, OLE 2.0 and OpenDoc each provide a complete integration platform-centered on a standard definition of composite document. The document-centered approach that underlies both standards seems appropriate for office information systems where the composite document seems to be indeed the fundamental user abstraction.

However, there exist many software application domains that do not revolve around the notion of document. For example, in real-time software and communications software, the notion of document does not play an important role. We may also notice that these standards do not promote interaction at the software component level, but rather at the application level, even though OpenDoc encourages document retrieval through a set of small and specialized retrieval units while OLE 2.0 promotes communication among full-fledged applications such as wordprocessors, spreadsheets, etc.

The ICA from Apple (in particular, the Apple events suite) takes a rather different approach, focusing on the standardization of operations. The goal is to promote a standard vocabulary for services so that applications that provide similar services (e.g. spreadsheets) can be replaced by one another.

Another observation is that any of the standards discussed requires mechanisms that are specific to object-oriented languages such as inheritance and encapsulation. In fact, they are being used as a vehicle for the migration towards object-oriented environments by introducing object-oriented concepts expressed in non-object-oriented languages. This is probably the reason why these standards focus mainly on interaction between applications; the same interaction rules do not usually apply to interaction of software components occupying the same address space.

12.3 Requirements for a Financial Framework

The application cooperation standards we have discussed address the needs of a generic software environment and reflect many other constraints not all related to software engineering, such as market constraints and applicability of standards to old development environments. Our financial framework targets applications that retrieve real-time and historical data from financial information sources. Typically, these applications display data such as the price of securities, interest rates and currency exchange rates, and allow users to explore real-time and financial historical information. These applications present to the professional user a window into financial activities which provides access to the distributed world-wide financial market.

Financial markets are characterized by rapidly evolving, complex relationships among the wide variety of financial instruments. Market relationships that hold among financial instruments are continuously evolving, and professional investors are constantly tracking that evolution in order to detect new investment opportunities. Decision support systems (DSSs) play an important role in supporting the user while finding such investment opportunities. The user needs to combine financial instruments, test the combination with various economic scenarios, look at the present cost of the combination, refine the choice of instruments, re-evaluate them, and eventually make an investment decision. In order to provide the appropriate support the DSS should allow the dynamic combination of financial instruments so that any instrument can be combined with any other instrument. This asks for a DSS architecture that facilitates the run-time interaction of software components. Furthermore, new financial instruments are frequently added so the DSS should be easily extendable with operational models for new instruments. To summarize, the architecture needs to provide capabilities for the dynamic connection of software components and facilitate the integration of new software components.

12.3.1 Towards a Protocol-Centered Framework

As we already mentioned, the goal of a framework is to provide a set of classes that are designed to work together. This operational compatibility can be achieved in many ways. The Object Management Group focuses on compatibility mediated by an object request broker. They impose no restriction on the software components themselves. Their main concern is to provide interoperability in heterogeneous environments. OLE 2.0 and OpenDoc emphasize the compound document as the main shared entity. Their main concern is to provide the most flexible environment for document retrieval. Apple's ICA approach, on the other hand, attempts to standardize common operations by defining a standard operations vocabulary and its associated semantics. ICA pursues two main goals. The first goal is to make the access to core standards functionality, such as common spreadsheet operations, database access and wordprocessor tasks, application independent. The second goal is to offer powerful scripting capabilities to automate tasks and to compose applications together.

The goal of the financial framework is to provide support for dynamic control of the interaction between software components. To achieve such a goal we need to provide a mechanism that allows for dynamic interconnection of software components.

12.3.2 Standardizing a Service's Vocabulary

During the early stages of the framework's design we considered a number of alternative intercomponent interaction principles. The goal was to find a mechanism that could provide the highest degree of dynamic interconnection for the kind of applications we are targeting with the financial framework. We tried, for instance, to standardize a set of core services so that each service is associated to a unique name called a verb, much in the same way as the Apple events suite standardizes the operations vocabulary of common services provided by wordprocessors, spreadsheets, databases, etc.

12.3.2.1 The Advantages
The intuition behind this approach is that we can identify among the services provided by the various software components of a framework many services that, although not identical, have comparable semantics. For example, most components in our environment provide services such as *evaluate*, *print*, and *notify*. We attempted to identify within the scope of the financial framework the principal groups of services and we ended up with the list shown in table 12.1. Software components may provide other services as well. These services belong either to more specialized groups, such as a group that is related to real-time services, or they do not belong to any group since they are too specific to a particular class of components.

A major advantage of this approach is simplicity. A service request can be performed by sending a message, a mechanism that every object-oriented environment offers. The advantage of standardizing a vocabulary for services is perhaps more compelling for

Service group name	Description
Common services	Services that are usually provided by most components such as: *print, show-services, identify-error,* and *store*
Messaging and notification	Services related to messaging and event notification such as: *call-back, notify, add-to-broadcast-list, message, forward-message*
Computational	Services related to computational servers: *evaluate, iterate, perform-aggregation, set-value, get-value*
Display	Services related to visual operations such as: *display, undisplay, front, drag-and-drop*
Object management	Services related to software component management such as: *create, replicate, destroy, add-object, instance-of-class, component-id*

Table 12.1

many reasons. First, reusing components is made easier since services with similar or close semantics bear the same name on all the software components, thus simplifying the name space. Second, dynamic interconnection of software components is improved because if a component provides a service conforming to a standard protocol, such as a print service, then that service can be invoked by any client understanding the same protocol. Third, interchangeability of software components is increased since two software components that provide similar functionality will most probably show a fair degree of commonality in their interfaces.

12.3.2.2 The Shortcomings

We noticed, however, that this approach is not the best in terms of dynamic interconnection. The main reason is that, in general, the interaction between two or more components involves more operations than simply sending a message. Although we can compose software components by specifying the appropriate sequences of messages to be exchanged between the components, a collection of sequences of messages is not the appropriate way to specify components' interactions. All but the simplest interactions involve a state, and the set of permissible messages that can be exchanged between interacting components, at a given point in time, usually depends on the present state of the interaction. Real-time financial environments provide many illustrations. Consider, for example, a software component, called the server, that offers real-time data updating services to other components. A component may register to be notified for data updates. Registering starts an interaction that ends, hopefully, when the client component requests the server to stop notification. Such interaction may comprise many data updates, error messages, notification of temporary interruption of real-time services, with subsequent service resumption, etc. Another example is a database transaction. A server may execute a database transaction on a client component's behalf. The transaction may involve many different oper-

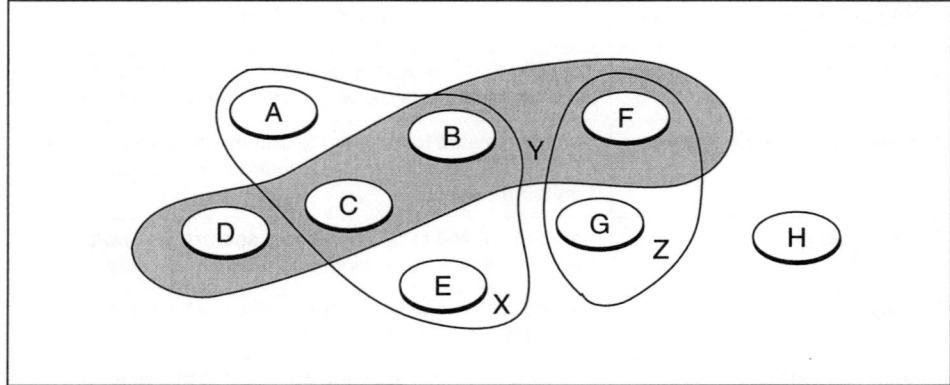

Figure 12.8 *Protocols define compatibility classes inside which members are able to interact. Protocol X allows interaction between objects A, B, C and D, while protocol Y defines an interaction pattern between D, C, B and F. Object H cannot interact with other objects since it does not adhere to any specified protocol.*

ations that individually succeed or fail. The transaction succeeds if all its operations succeed, otherwise the transaction fails. The interaction between the client and the server depends on the state of the transaction, which can be defined as the logical "and" of the individual operation results. Whenever, the state condition switches to fail, the already executed operations need to be unrolled before terminating the transaction.

The two examples illustrate the need for a higher-level mechanism to specify components' interactions that allows for interaction states and state-dependent actions. We call such a mechanism a component's interaction protocol. These observations lay the foundations that lead us from message-based frameworks to protocol-centered frameworks which focus on protocols as the main components interaction mechanisms.

12.3.3 Component Interaction Protocols

Software component protocols share many similarities with computer communication protocols. Both specify object interaction patterns. As such they fulfil two important functions. First, they provide a mechanism or a formalism to specify the rules of interaction between objects. Second, protocols define compatibility classes in the sense that entities that obey the same protocol display an interaction compatibility as illustrated in figure 12.8

12.3.3.1 Requirements for Interaction Protocols

Software component interaction protocols should support a number of important features. First, they should be appropriate to specify various aspects of component interactions such as synchronization, negotiation and data exchange. Second, they should play the role

Requirements for a Financial Framework

of "contracts" or "interaction agreements" that represent the necessary and sufficient conditions for a software component to interact with other software components that comply with the same "agreement". Helm *et al.* [12] focus on this important aspect of interactions. Third, the interaction specifications should be multilateral agreements rather than bilateral interaction agreements between two software components.

Another desirable property of component interaction protocols is that their implementations reside as much as possible outside the components since as an agreement, a protocol does not belong to any component. We may observe, looking at programs written in an object-oriented language, that a significant fraction of a component's code is devoted to the communication of the component with other software components. Most of the communication functionality is inside the component. This has two main objectionable consequences. First, components tend to become "hard-wired" to their environments, which has the undesirable side effect of reducing their reuse potential within other environments. Second, the intermix of code responsible for interaction with the code that is proper to the component reduces readability and maintainability. Naturally, it might be impossible and perhaps undesirable to strip all the interaction code out of a component. The goal is to leave inside the component only the sufficient interaction functionality that can be used by many different protocols. For example, we will keep inside the component methods to export values, methods to notify events, and methods to send generic messages since they do not implement any interaction among specific components and represent the hooks necessary to build protocols.

12.3.3.2 Roles and Interplay Relations

We will be more precise now about what we mean by a protocol. A protocol specifies the interaction between software components. A *protocol* $P = (R, I, F)$ consists of a set of *roles*, R, an *interplay relation*, I, and a *finite state automaton*, F.

P defines a set of roles:

$$R = \{R_1, R_2, ..., R_r\}$$

Each component that is P-compliant plays one or more roles. A typical example of roles are the client and server roles in a client–server protocol, where components can play either the client's role, the server's role, or both depending on the specific responsibility assigned to the components. In general, the number of roles defined by a protocol is small.

A protocol also defines an *interplay* relation that specifies the interaction compatibilities allowed by protocol P. The interplay relation is defined by a set:

$$I = \{I_1, I_2, ..., I_i\}, \text{ where } I_k \subseteq R, I_k \neq \emptyset, 1 \leq k \leq i$$

Moreover, if $R = \{r\}$, then $I = \{I_1\} = \{\{r, r\}\}$. In words, it is always assumed for a one-role protocol that all the software components obeying P are compatible in the sense that they are able to interact under P. Referring to the previous example, $I = \{\{\text{server,client}\}\}$ specifies that the protocol allows for the interaction between objects that play a server's role and objects that play a client's role. To specify that the protocol also allows for the interaction between objects that play the role of servers, the interplay relation should be specified as:

$$I = \{ \{server, client\}, \{server, server'\} \}$$

Each object of the environment O_i eventually conforms to roles of one or many protocols. Let $roles(O_i)$ denote a function that returns the set of all roles component O_i conforms to. A protocol P together with an element (i.e. a set of roles) $I_k = \{x_s, ..., x_t\}$, $x \in R$ of its interplay relation defines a domain of interaction compatibility $D = (P, I_k)$. Domains of interaction compatibility play an important role in our framework since they define which are the components that can potentially interact. The compatibility defined by a domain of interaction extends not only to the components that exist at the time the protocol is defined and implemented, but also to all future components that obey the same protocol and are compatible through an interplay relation.

Finally, each protocol is associated with a finite state automaton that specifies valid sequences of interactions between participants in the protocol. (See chapter 4 for a formal treatment of two-party protocols based on finite state processes.) In the following section we will see examples of how the state of a protocol can be specified, and how it controls the interactions between components.

12.4 Gluons

Gluons encapsulate and implement interaction protocols by instantiating an interplay relation for a given protocol. The principle idea underlying gluons is to standardize and encapsulate protocols, rather than just standardizing service names, since interaction protocols should represent one of the primary resources to be reused. Gluons support a protocol-centered reuse strategy. By embedding interaction protocols inside gluons we can use them as agents to implement many different interaction strategies.

Applications that we developed with the financial framework show that with this approach we can achieve the following:

- *A high degree of dynamic interconnection* — The reuse of interaction protocols provides significantly more flexibility to express interaction patterns than the reuse of a naming convention. In particular, we typically need a small set of interaction protocols to express interactions that would require a large quantity of standard service names to achieve the same result. For example, all interactions between two software components that involve a service request followed by an agreement on the data types to be exchanged, and ending with a notification of both components about the result of the operation, can be expressed with just one protocol. Service name standardization would require standard names for each possible service request, and would probably ask for additional code to build the sequence of messages needed to perform the interaction. This point will be better illustrated later with examples of gluons from the financial framework.

- *Easy integration of new software components into an environment* — This stems from the fact that the unique interoperability constraint is that the new component reuses existing interaction protocols that can be instantiated through gluons.

12.4.1 Gluons and Software Design

We already mentioned that in a protocol-centered framework the primary reuse resource is the protocol. The adoption of a protocol-centered approach has a significant impact in software design. While methods such as CRC [5] promote an iterative design procedure that emphasizes identification of the responsibilities and collaboration for each component, in a protocol-centered framework the design team attempts to identify the typical interaction protocols for the specific environment prior to any other design decisions. Once the choice of the basic interaction protocols has been made, we then proceed with the identification of the components' responsibilities and the collaborations needed to fulfil such responsibilities.

At first, we seem to be adding just another layer (i.e. the definition of the reusable interaction protocols) to the design process. However, experience shows that, at least in the case of the financial framework, the addition of such a layer simplifies significantly the whole design process provided the reusable protocols are properly defined. Our first design defined only eight protocols that allowed us to express most of the interactions in a simple system. The reusable interaction protocols represent the "glue" that allow for the connection of software components.

12.4.2 Anatomy of a Gluon

In terms of its internal structure, a gluon is a software component that handles a finite state automaton with output to control the execution of a protocol's interplay relation. It contains a start state and any number of intermediate states. A gluon can provide many end states (i.e. accepting states in finite automation parlance) but for simplicity it is better to have a unique end state. Figure 12.9 shows the symbols that can appear in a gluon's finite state automaton. States and state transitions are the common constituents that can be found in any finite state automaton [8]. A participant's role stores a reference to a software component that is compatible with the role defined by the interplay relation, while a message selector container stores an arbitrary message selector.

A state transition triggers the execution of an action which is composed of operations. A state transition is fired whenever the gluon receives a message.

There are three types of operations that compose an action: *messages sends*, *object assignments* and *message selector assignments*. A message send is what its name implies: the gluon sends a message to a software component requesting a service. Object assignments allows a gluon to keep a reference to software components. Message selector assignments are similar to object assignment operations, the difference lies in the fact that

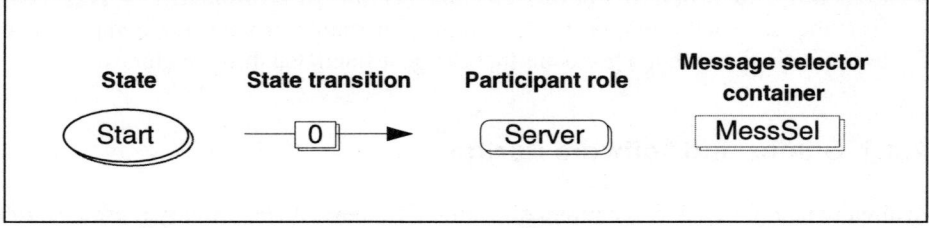

Figure 12.9 *Symbols for the gluon's finite state automaton.*

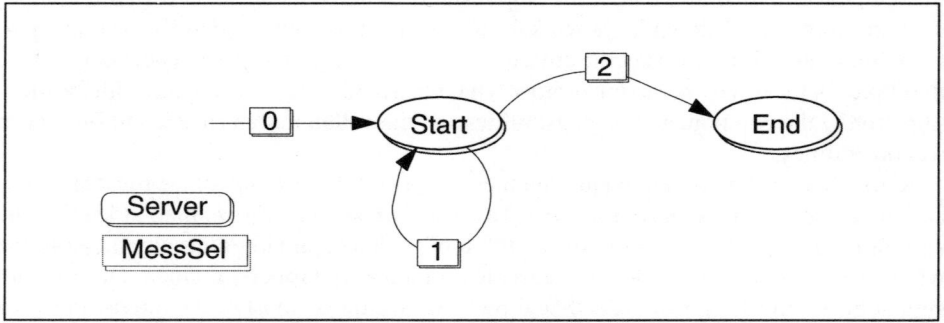

Figure 12.10 *The SimpleGluon finite state automaton. SimpleGluons forward messages to an attached software component called the Server.*

the gluon keeps a reference to a message selector instead of a reference to a software component. These are the only allowable operations in a gluon's action. Furthermore, the only assignments allowed are those that involve either a participant's role or a message selector container in the left side of the assignment.

Figure 12.10 shows the finite automaton embedded inside the simplest gluon provided by the financial framework. The SimpleGluon contains two states, Start and End, and three transitions. The diagram also shows a participant, the Server and a message selector MessSel that can store an arbitrary message selector. State transition triggers and the actions associated with state transitions are shown in table 12.2.

The SimpleGluon handles an asymmetric interaction protocol between a server and a client. The protocol handles message forwarding. The asymmetry stems from the fact that a gluon is associated with a unique server component while the client can be any component that can send a message to the gluon. The association between the server and the gluon is requested by the server component by sending message registerServer to the gluon (refer to table 12.2). This message triggers state transition 0 which initiates the gluon's protocol. Any component can now send messages to the gluon and these messages are forwarded to the server with transition 1. Finally, the gluon can be disconnected from the server by sending it the message exit. SimpleGluons are used in the financial framework

Protocol transitions			Event / action
State	Transition	State	
	0	Start	Source: registerServer{server}
			Server := server
Start	1	Start	<any_obj>: <message>
			MessSel := <message> <message> →Server
Start	2	End	<any_obj>: exit
			gluonDisconnecting{self} → Server Server := none

Table 12.2 *Protocol transition table for the SimpleGluon.*

for two main purposes. The first purpose is to isolate services from service providers. By assigning different components to the server's role, the clients can be granted services from different components. The SimpleGluon plays here the role of a proxy. The second typical usage of SimpleGluons requires a slightly modified gluon with multicasting capabilities. The modified version accepts the registration of multiple servers so that the messages sent by the clients are forwarded to all the servers.

12.5 Gluons and the Financial Framework

Gluons are the architectural elements of the financial framework that are responsible for the way in which other components are composed. The financial framework offers other components as well. One such component, the RealTimeRecord acts as a container for real-time information. This component plays a central role in the distribution of real-time information. The RealTimeRecord plays usually the role of a server to clients request update notifications. The structure of RealTimeRecords is illustrated in figure 12.11. Each entry of the record is a pair *(key, obj_ref)*, where the key allows for the lookup of an object by name.

Most of the components in an application act as data sinks, data sources or both. They are connected through notifications chains so that updates are readily broadcast down the chain. Pure data sources are those components that are either connected to external data source such as those provided by Reuters, or are associated to files providing streams of data. Components that act both as data sinks and data sources are data transformers. They usually get information from data sources, transform it and redistribute it to client components. Pure sink components usually correspond either to display components or to com-

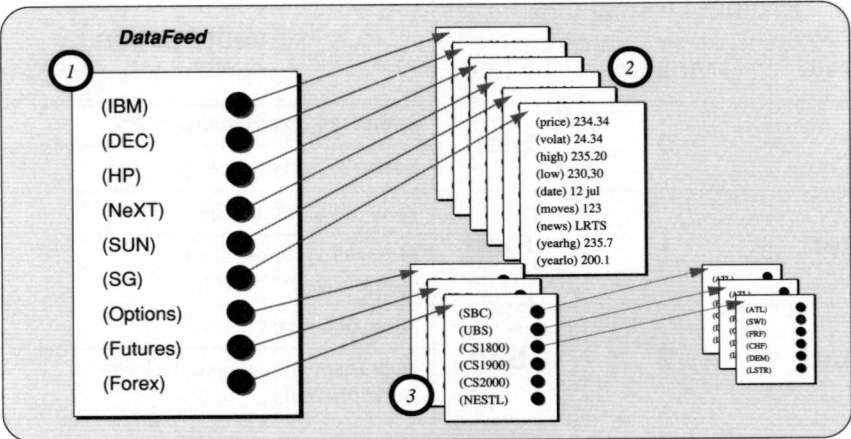

Figure 12.11 *Structure of the RealTimeRecord component. The data is contained in dictionaries. Dictionary 1, for instance, contains references to all the information updated in real time by a data source. The other dictionaries contain either values (2) or references to other objects (3).*

ponents that write to files. So an application can be seen as a set of components connected by a notification web.

The rest of this section illustrates the financial framework by providing two examples of gluons that play an essential role in the framework: the dragging gluon and the real-time data notification gluon.

12.5.1 The Dragging Gluon

The dragging gluon implements the common dragging mechanism we are acquainted with from most windowing systems (see figure 12.12). A drag operation is an operation initiated by a component, the dragging source, that attempts to find a partner component to cooperate with. The choice of the partner, the destination component, is performed by the user with the visual assistance of the windowing system. Both the dragging source and the dragging destination need to be associated with a visual representation since dragging is a visual operation. Figure 12.13 illustrates the finite state automaton associated with the dragging gluon, while table 12.3 shows the events that fire each state transition and the associated actions.

To simplify the understanding of how the dragging gluon works it is useful to consult simultaneously figure 12.13, which shows the state transitions, and table 12.3, which exhibits the events that trigger a state transition together with the actions executed during the transition. The three boxes in the lower left corner of figure 12.13 represent the roles of the components that participate in the dragging process.

Gluons and the Financial Framework 343

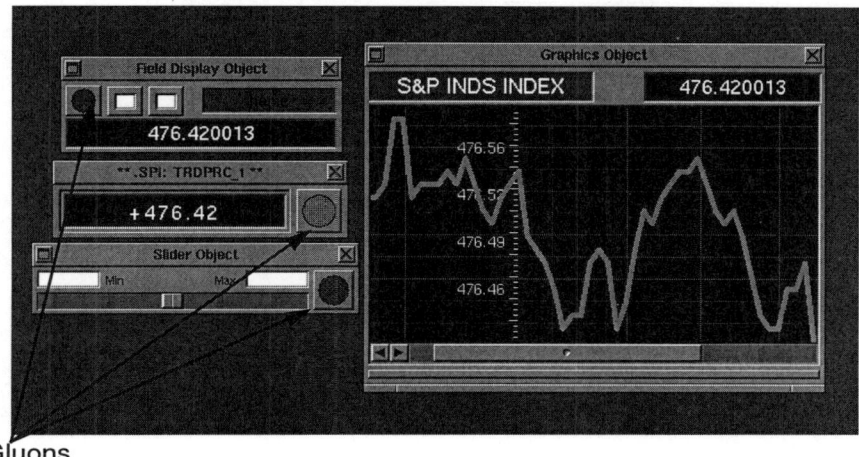

Figure 12.12 *User interfaces of some software components available. The gluons that allow for the connection of the components are indicated by arrows. To connect the components the user drags the circle from one gluon to another.*

The server is the component that initiates the interaction by sending the message start-Dragging to the gluon with its object identifier as parameter (see table 12.3, transition 0). Upon receipt of this message the gluon enters state Start followed by the execution of an action that makes the gluon send the message startDragging to the component that plays the WindowManager role, and assigns object identifiers to the destination and the source roles. The destination is assigned the void object identifier since at this stage the object that will play the destination role is not yet determined. The WindowManager responds to the first the message by sending back to the gluon the dragCandidateEntered message. The reception of this message triggers state transition 1 on the gluon. The candidate object identifier that is sent as parameter corresponds to the source component since at the beginning of the drag operation the mouse is over the visual representation of that component. Consequently, the first component that is assigned the destination role is always the same component as the one that plays the source role. Later, the assignment will change as the user drags the mouse out of the source visual representation to enter another visual representation (i.e. icon) that is associated to a software component that accepts dragging. In the process of finding the appropriate destination component, the user may move the mouse in and out of visual representations that accept dragging. This process corresponds to alternations between state IN and state OUT.

If the user releases the mouse button when the gluon is in state OUT, then the dragging operation stops with no side effects since the mouse has been released outside a visual representation that accepts dragging. Conversely, if the mouse is released when the gluon is

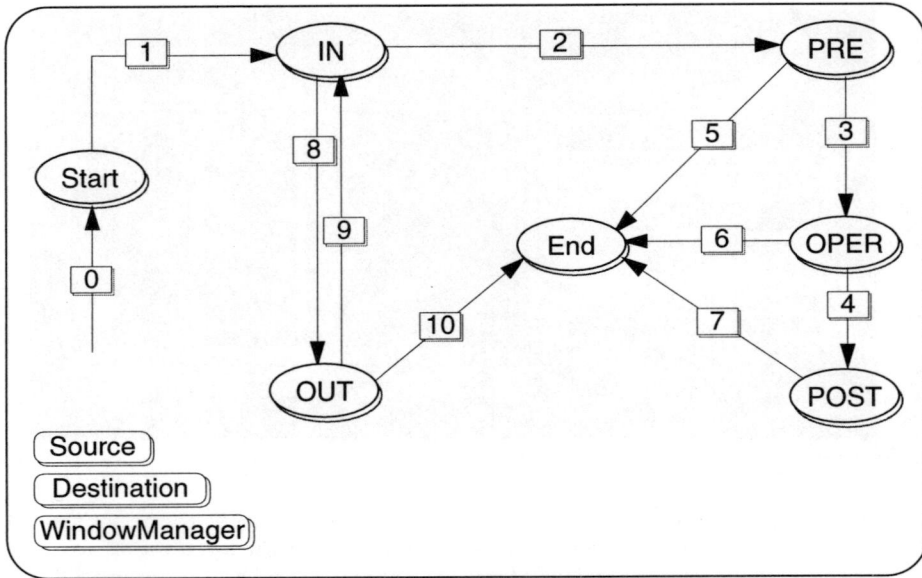

Figure 12.13 *Finite automata for the dragging protocol. The ellipses represent the states while the the arrows represent state transitions. The three boxes at the lower left corner represent the roles of the components that participate in the interaction.*

in the IN state, the gluon undergoes state transition 2 which puts the gluon in state PRE. This state corresponds to a pre-operation that is usually a negotiation between the source and destination components to agree on an operation to be performed. If both agree, the gluon transits to state OPER, which corresponds to execution of the agreed operation between the source and the destination. If no agreement is reached, then the dragging operation will end through transition 5. State POST allows for post-operation cleanup before the interaction ends.

We may notice that state IN and state OUT correspond to the visual process of establishing a relationship between two software components: the source and the destination. Likewise, states PRE, OPER and POST manage the negotiation and execution of an operation between two components.

The dragging gluon illustrates the generality and usefulness of an interaction protocol specified as a finite state automaton. Such generic protocols are intended to be refined. Typically, when the source component negotiates an operation with the destination component, they agree on another gluon to which both are compatible. This gluon manages the execution of an operation, or in other terms it mediates the delivery of a service. In the implementation of a visual workbench for the retrieval of real-time financial information, called ReutersLab [25], which has been implemented with the financial framework we extensively use the dragging protocol together with another protocol that negotiates the type

Protocol transitions			Event / action
State	Transition	State	
	0	Start	Source: startDragging{Source}
			startDragging{source} → WindowManager *Source := source* *Destination := none*
Start	1	In	WindowManager: dragCandidateEntered{candidate}
			Destination := candidate dragEnter{Source} → Destination
In	2	Pre	WindowManager: endDragging
			preOperation{Source} → Destination
Pre	3	Oper	Destination: ACK{destination} | Source: ACK{source}
			operation{source} → Destination
Oper	4	Post	Destination: ACK{destination} | Source: ACK{source}
			postOperation{Source} → Destination
Pre	5	End	Destination: NACK{destination}
			slideDragViewBack → WindowManager
Oper	6	End	Destination: NACK{destination}
			slideDragViewBack → WindowManager
Post	7	End	Destination: ACK{destination}
			operationComplete{Destination} → Source
In	8	Out	WindowManager:dragCandidateExit{candidate}
			dragExited → Destination *Destination := none*
Out	9	In	WindowManager: dragCandidateEntered{candidate}
			Destination := candidate dragEnter{Source} → Destination
Out	10	End	WindowManager: endDragging
			dragAborted → Source slideDragViewBack → WindowManager *Source := none*

Table 12.3 *Dragging gluon protocol transition table.*

of data to be exchanged between the source and destination components. Once the components agree on a data type, they interact under the control of another type of gluon that establishes a real-time update notification between the components. The real-time notification gluon is discussed next.

12.5.2 Real-time Data Notification Gluon

Since the financial framework is intended to support the access to information sources that are updated in real time, the framework provides a gluon that supports notification between data sources and client components so that after data updates on the source side the client can be updated to reflect the information change. In a typical situation the client component registers with the source to request update notification. The request creates a link between the source and the client.

In order to provide for flexible notification, the framework allows for three types of notification links — cold, warm and hot — which correspond to the three type of links provided by Microsoft DDE depicted in figure 12.3. The reason for providing three types of notification links stems from the fact that different components have different data update requirements. For example, a client software component that handles a visual display of real-time data usually needs to be updated as soon as the information changes on the source side since the user is expecting the fastest update possible. These requirements correspond to a hot link between the client and the source. Other components expect change notifications but they only need actually to update the values in a few cases. These correspond to the typical requirements for a warm link where the source is in charge of notifying the client while the client is responsible for eventually issuing an update request to the source. The least demanding kind of link is the cold link in which the client is responsible for requesting updates to the source at its own pace with no notification from the source. A typical usage of cold links is portfolio evaluations that require access to market data only when the portfolio is evaluated with no need for further updates.

Figure 12.14 represents the finite automaton embedded in a real-time data notification gluon. The protocol defines three roles: the source, the client and the data. The role of the source and client components has been discussed above, while the component that assumes the data role acts as an information container that is exchanged between the source and the client. The states COLD, HOT and WARM, correspond to three types of links available. When the link is established between the source and the client, the gluon enters the COLD state and waits for a message from the client requesting an update. Upon reception of the client's request the gluon enters state CUP in which it waits until an update message issued by the source puts the gluon back in state COLD through transition 3. A gluon can be requested to switch from one type of link to another provided it is in any one of the three states, COLD, HOT or WARM, so that the update mechanism can be changed at any point in time to adapt to evolving requirements on the client's side. We may notice that state WARM has a self-looping state transition (i.e. number 11), which is fired when the source notifies the client for an update, and two transitions (i.e. transitions 9 and 10) with an intermediary

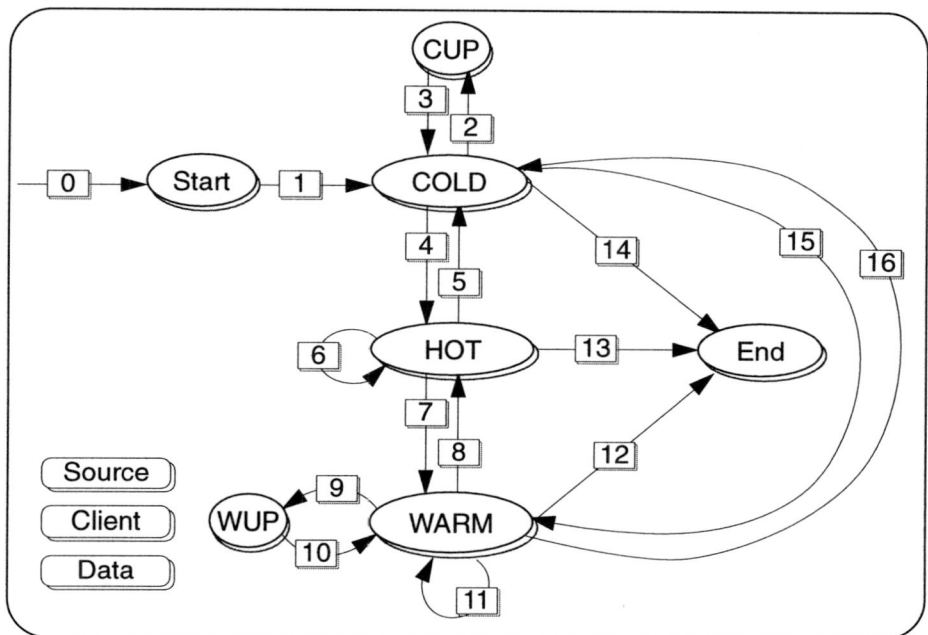

Figure 12.14 *Finite automata for a real-time data notification protocol.*

state WUP which handles the update request from the client component. As expected, the actions associated with transitions 9 and 10 are similar to actions associated with transitions 2 and 3 since they perform the same task.

12.6 Conclusion

We have addressed in this chapter the problem of defining patterns of interaction among software components. We adopt the point of view of component-oriented software design and development which promotes an approach to software construction based on the connection of software components.

We provide a survey of previous efforts that address similar problems. The focus is on work from large software houses since they represent significant efforts to standardize and promote approaches that may have a considerable impact, in the near future, on software design and development. The survey suggest that the sizeable differences that can be observed between such approaches reflect differences in design goals and differences in the requirements of the target environments.

Our development framework targets financial applications that retrieve real-time data and require support that allows for fast reconfiguration of the patterns of interaction among the software components as well as mechanisms that facilitate the introduction of new software components. These requirements can be equated to support for dynamic interconnection of software components. Unfortunately none of the approaches surveyed achieves the desired level of dynamic interconnection capabilities.

We propose a new approach which focuses on the reuse of component interaction protocols. We call a framework based on such principle a protocol-centered framework. Our experience with a financial framework shows that we can achieve a fairly high degree of dynamic interconnection with a small number of reusable protocols (typically less than twenty). However, the applications that we developed have a scope that is too narrow to allow us to infer that the approach is of wide applicability.

References

[1] Apple Computer Inc., *Inside Macintosh: Interapplication Communication*, 1993.
[2] Constantin Arapis, "Specifying Object Interactions," in *Object Composition*, ed. D. Tsichritzis, Centre Universitaire d'Informatique, June 1991.
[3] Constantin Arapis, "Dynamic Evolution of Object Behavior and Object Cooperation," Ph.D. thesis no. 2529, Centre Universitaire d'Informatique, University of Geneva, Switzerland,1992.
[4] Nabajyoti Barkakati, Peter D. Hipson, *Visual C++ Developer's Guide*, Sams, Carmel, 1993.
[5] Kent Beck and Ward Cunningham, "A Laboratory for Teaching Object-Oriented Thinking," *Proceedings of OOPSLA '89, ACM SIGPLAN Notices*, vol. 24, no. 10, Oct. 1989, pp. 1–6.
[6] Ted J. Biggerstaff and Alan J. Perlis, *Software Reusability, Volume I, Concepts and Models*, Frontier Series, ACM Press, 1989.
[7] Kraig Brockschmidt, *Inside OLE 2 : The Fast Track to Buiding Powerful Object-Oriented Applications*, Microsoft Press, Redmond, Wash., 1993.
[8] Daniel I. A. Cohen, *Introduction to Computer Theory*, John Wiley, 1986.
[9] L. Peter Deutsch, "Design Reuse and Frameworks in the Smalltalk-80 System," in *Software Reusability*, ed. T.J. Biggerstaff and A.J. Perlis, ACM Press, 1989, pp. 57–71.
[10] Erich Gamma, Andre Weinand and Rudolf Marty, "Integration of a Programming Environment into ET++," *Proceedings of ECOOP '89*, British Computer Society Workshop Series, Cambridge University Press, Cambridge, 1989.
[11] Simon Gibbs, Dennis Tsichritzis, Eduardo Casais, Oscar Nierstrasz and Xavier Pintado, "Class Management for Software Communities," *Communications of the ACM*, vol. 33, no. 9, Sept. 1990, pp. 90–103.
[12] Richard Helm, Ian Holland and Dipayan Gangopadhyay, "Contracts: Specifying Behavioral Compositions in Object-Oriented Systems," *ACM SIGPLAN Notices*, vol. 25, no. 10, Oct. 1990, pp.169–180.
[13] Dan Ingalls, "Fabrik: A Visual Programming Environment," *Proceedings of OOPSLA '88, ACM SIGPLAN Notices*, vol. 23, no. 11, Nov. 1988, pp. 176–190.
[14] Ralph E. Johnson and Brian Foote, "Designing Reusable Classes," *Journal of Object-Oriented Programming*, vol. 1, no. 2, 1988, pp. 22–35.
[15] Chris Laffra, "Procol, a Concurrent Object Language with Protocols, Delegation, Persistence, and Constraints," Ph.D. Thesis, Amsterdam, 1992.
[16] Michael Mahoney, "Interface Builder and Object-Oriented Design in the NeXTstep Environment," Tutorial Notes of CHI '91, available through anonymous ftp at nova.cc.purdue.edu.

[17] Microsoft Press, *OLE 2 Programmer's Reference: Working with Windows Objects*, Vol. 1, Redmond, Wash., 1994.

[18] Microsoft Press, *OLE 2 Programmer's Reference: Creating Programmable Applications with Ole Automation*, Vol. 2, Redmond, Wash., 1994.

[19] NeXT Computer Inc., *NextStep Concepts Manual*, 1990.

[20] Oscar Nierstrasz, Dennis Tsichritzis, Vicki de Mey and Marc Stadelmann, "Objects + Scripts = Applications," in *Object Composition*, ed. D. Tsichritzis, Centre Universitaire d'Informatique, June 1991, pp. 11–30.

[21] Object Management Group, *Common Object Request Broker: Architecture and Specification*, 1991.

[22] Object Management Group, *Object Management Architecture Guide*, 1992.

[23] Object Management Group (OMG), *The Common Object Request Broker: Architecture and Specification, Object Management Group and X Open*, OMG document 91.12.1, revision 1.1, 1992.

[24] Xavier Pintado, Dennis Tsichritzis, "Gluons: Connecting Software Components," in *Object Composition*, ed. D. Tsichritzis, Centre Universitaire d'Informatique, 1991, pp. 73–84.

[25] Xavier Pintado, Betty Junod, "Gluons: A Support for Software Component Cooperation," in *Object Frameworks*, ed. D. Tsichritzis, Centre Universitaire d'Informatique, 1992, pp. 311–330.

[26] Xavier Pintado, "Gluons: a Support for Software Component Cooperation," in *Proceedings of ISOTAS '93, International Symposium on Object Technologies for Advanced Software*, ed. S. Nishio and A. Yonezawa, Kanazawa, Japan, November 1993, Springer-Verlag, pp. 43–54.

[27] Xavier Pintado, "Fuzzy Relationships and Affinity Links," in *Object Composition*, ed. D. Tsichritzis, Centre Universitaire d'Informatique, 1991.

[28] Rajendra Raj, Henry Levy, "A Compositional Model for Software Reuse," *Proceedings of ECOOP '89*, British Computer Society Workshop Series, Cambridge University Press, Cambridge, 1989, pp. 3–24.

[29] Jeffrey S. Rosenschein and Gilad Zlotkin, *Rules of encounter: Designing Conventions for Automated Negotiation Among Computers*, MIT Press, Cambridge, Mass., 1994.

[30] Al Williams, *OLE 2.0 and DDE Distilled: A Programmer's Crash Course*, Addison-Wesley, Reading, Mass., 1994.

Index

ABCL/1 35, 38–42, 51, 52
ABCL/AP100 58
ABCL/R 40, 41, 43
Abramsky, Samson 168
abstract class 47
    abstract superclass 220
abstract state 59, 108, 109, 118
abstraction 13, 187
ACT++ 34, 36, 41, 42, 56, 118
ACTALK 41, 43
activated type 312
activation condition 42
active object 18, 43, 100, 187
ActiveCube component 292
activity composition 292
actor-based languages 43
ActorSpace 37, 38
Ada 34, 35, 41, 42
adaption function 85
administrator 45, 49, 50–54, 61
affinity 182
    browser xvi, 245, 252
        example 259
    engine 257
    neighbourhood 254
agents 9, 11
aggregation 181
Aït-Kaci, Hassan 156, 172
α substitution 156
α-Trellis 250
Andrew 278, 308
Apple 277, 329–331, 334
    ATG Component Construction Kit 276, 277

application development 21, 180
application engineer 180
application frame 180
    see also GAF, SAF
application programming interface 307
approximation ordering 169
Arcadia 72
Argus 34, 76
association 183
asynchronous
    communication 133
    interface 311
asynchronous interface 311
atomicity 32
attribute redefinition 203
attribution 180
AVANCE 215, 217

backtracking 252
backward scope restriction 239
Basic 327
Basic Object Adaptor 325
BEAD 250
become primitive 36
BEE++ 249
behaviour 19, 276, 278
BENTO 331
Bergmans, Lodewijk 59
Beta 58
bind reduction 158
blackboard 10, 11
Bloom, Bard 170
BOA 325
Böcker, Hans-Dieter 249

Booch, Grady 123
bottom element 168
Boudol, Gérard 168, 170, 171
bounded buffer 108, 109
Brinksma, Ed 99, 100, 107
broadcast primitive 37
browser
    message-set 249
    see also affinity browser
    see also Smalltalk browser
browsing 178, 182, 183, 247
    semantics 250
    spatial 250
    tool 247
Brüegge, Bernd 249
built-in proxy 52, 62
Bull, S.A. xv

C 15, 74
C++ xvi, 15, 47, 70, 74, 79, 91, 167, 179, 187, 188, 196, 216, 219, 225, 276, 287, 325, 327
CAD/CAM 217
CAML-Light 15
category 249
CBox 38, 51
CCS 19, 100
Ceiffel 56
Cell 75, 82
    framework 71, 74, 91
change avoidance 203, 230
channels 100
CHOCS 19
Church encoding of Booleans 154
Church, Alonzo xi
class
    evolution 202, 216
    refactoring 221
    relationship 259
    renaming 203, 210, 231
    reorganization 218–230
    surgery 202
    tailoring 202, 203, 230
    evaluation 205
    versioning 202
classification 181
CLOS 13, 225, 233, 235
close reduction 158
CLU 34
cobegin 35
Colibri 193, 195, 196
COM 327
combination and alternation 171
Common Object Request Broker Architecture, see CORBA
communicating processes 125
comp.object newsgroup 7
compatibility 11, 18, 153, 167, 205
    class 336
    ordering 169
component 18, 20, 309
    class 310
    classification 177–200
    constraints universalization 149
    definition 297
    engineer xiv, 23, 275, 276
    engineering 20–23
    framework 4, 22, 277
    initialization 313
    inspector 277
    instantiation 313
    interface 311
    management 287
    network 312–313
    palette 277
    synchronisation 313
    visual composition 280
Component Object Model 327
component-oriented
    development 4
    lifecycle 14
composition
    activity 292
    dataflow 283, 291
    framework 275
    functional 10

Index

higher-order 10
media 307
model 275, 276, 282
   manager 288
procedural 307
run-time 321
semantic 307
spatial 307
temporal 292, 307
Unix composition model 287
visual, *see* visual composition
compression scheme 307
concurrency 5, 8, 9, 14, 18, 25, 31–68, 100, 115, 119
   see also internal concurrency
Concurrent C 42
concurrent object 35
concurrent rewriting 56
ConcurrentSmalltalk 38, 51
condition variable 59
conformance 99, 100, 107, 108, 218
congestion 312
ConMan 276, 277
connection 275, 280, 282, 286, 289, 295, 312–316
   dynamic 335, 338
connector 311, 312
consumer 311
container 108, 328
contracts 16, 17, 100, 298, 337
conversion 203
CooL 79, 82, 85–86, 187, 193, 195
CORBA 72–76, 91, 325, 331
correspondence 181
   property 144
CSP 38, 40, 107
Curry type scheme 17
Curry-Howard isomorphism 172
currying 154, 163
Cusack, Elspeth 107

database service 307
dataflow 276, 283, 312
analysis 211
composition 283, 291
Datamont, S.p.A. xv
DDE 325, 346
de Bruijn
   calculus 158
   indices 153, 155, 156
de Bruijn, N. 156, 159, 162
deadlock 102, 116
decision support systems 333
delegated call 54
delegation 11, 38, 39
denotational semantics 17
dependency 187
dependent type 118
derivation graph 215
derived classification 191
design by contract 298
   see also contracts
design description 179
destination pattern 37
detach primitive 35
Dezani-Ciancaglini, Mariangiola 19
direct manipulation 285
distinct name invariant 207
distinct origin invariant 207
Distributed Objects 277
divergence 168
domain knowledge 23
dragging gluon 342
   see also gluons
DRAGOON 56–59, 60
dynamic analysis 266
Dynamic Data Exchange 325
dynamic interconnection 335, 338
dynamic linking 13

Eiffel 16, 47, 178, 201, 203, 327
   Ceiffel 56
   library 227, 229
Eiffel // 34, 38, 41, 42, 56
Emerald 34, 41, 54
enabled set 34

encapsulation 8, 178, 201, 225, 247, 297, 308, 333
    and concurrency 9
    blackboard 11
    violation of 8, 46
ENCORE 238
Engberg, Uffe 19
equivalent type 78
erroneous term 169
ESPRIT xi, xv, 79, 177, 178
event distribution mechanism 258
event-handling 313
evolution
    class 202, 216
    format 309
    framework 24
    platform 309
    schema evolution taxonomy 209
expert services team 24
explicit acceptance 42
extensibility 11, 48, 154, 165, 258
extension 99, 100, 107

Fabrik 276, 277
faceted classification 186
factorization 218
    algorithm 227
    class refactoring 221
    incremental 230
failures 106
    equivalence 107
F-bounded quantification 118
features 172
filtering 236
    mechanisms 237
financial framework 321
finite state
    automata 108, 111, 123, 124, 337, 338, 339, 344
    process 119, 338
    protocol 108, 109
    transition system 111

first class representation of requests and replies 39
Fisher, Kathleen 16
fixed-point
    induction 172
    operation 163
F-ORM 294
format class 309
format evolution 309
Forsythe 172
FORTH xv
forward scope restriction 239
Foundation of Research and Technology, Hellas xv
framework xiii, 4, 69, 99, 201, 291, 322
    Cell, *see* Cell framework
    component, *see* component framework
    design 24
    evolution 24
    financial 321
    multimedia, *see* multimedia framework
    NeXTStep AppKit 324
    protocol-centered, *see* protocol-centered framework
    visual composition 275
Freeman, Peter 178, 186
Frølund, Svend 56, 59–61
full inheritance invariant 207
functional commonality 260
functional composition 10
functionality phase 77
future variable 38, 39, 51
fuzzy querying 247

GAF 21, 23, 180
Garrigue, Jacques 156, 173
GemStone 207, 235
generalization 181
Generic Application Frame, *see* GAF
genericity 46, 57, 182
GeoBall component 292

Index 355

Gingrich, P. 271
global reorganization 226
global time 136
gluons xvi, 100, 321–349
Goguen, Joseph A. 17
Gottschalk, Tim 249
Guide 36, 41, 42, 47, 56–61

Haskell 16
Hennessy, Matthew 119
Hennessy–Milner logic 119
Herczeg, Jürgen 249
heterogeneous object model 34, 49
Hewlett Packard 277
higher-order
    composition xiv, 10
    process calculus 19
homogeneous object model 34, 49, 62
Hybrid xiv, 34, 35, 40, 41, 54, 77, 79, 82, 85–86
hypermedia systems 306
hypertext 184, 250

IAL 74, 81, 85–87
IBM 276, 277, 331
    repository 178, 180
ICA 333, 334
IDL 72, 76, 325
imitation 218
implementation description 179
incremental reorganization algorithm 220
inheritance 7, 8, 13, 201, 245, 260
    and synchronisation 47
    anomaly 56
    in Beta 58
    code sharing 205
    concurrency 5, 33, 46
    consistency 216
    dependencies 202
    in DRAGOON 57
    graph invariant 207
    hierarchy 178, 207
    interface 8, 9, 13

invariant 207
mixins 13
multiple, strict 179, 181, 188
request/reply scheduling 61
restructuring 225
reuse potential 47
strict 181
and subtyping 8, 47, 172
and synchronisation 43, 46, 47, 55, 63
versioning 216
Windows 327
initials 106
inner mechanism 58
inspector 249
interaction
    compatibility 321
    pattern 248, 322
    protocol 257, 321, 336, 337
Interapplication Communication Architecture, *see* ICA
interconnection, *see* connection
interface
    adaption 76, 87
    adaption language, see IAL
    bridging 74
    definition language, *see* IDL
    phase 78
    re-declaration 205
interference of features 32
internal concurrency 44, 46
Internet 7
inter-object 81, 83, 87–90
interoperability 69–95, 332
    object-oriented 71, 73
    procedure-oriented 71
    specification level 72, 79
intersection type 103, 118, 172
intra-object concurrency 59
IRIS 215, 217
    Explorer 276, 277
islands 11
isochronous interface 311, 312

ITHACA xi, xv–xvii, 20, 79, 177, 178, 180, 193, 287, 294, 301
    object-oriented methodology 294
    software development environment 294
    software platform 287

Kafura, Dennis G. 56
KAROS 76
Kleyn, M. 250
Knos xiv
Krueger, Charles W. 178

Labyrinth System 287
λ calculus 19, 154
    label-selective 156
λN calculus 153–174
Lamping, John 156
Lassie 178
lattice structure 170
Law of Demeter 221, 222, 225, 298
law-governed systems 298
lazy data structure 163
Lee, Kueng Hae 56
Leroy, Xavier 16
Lieberherr, Karl 221
lifecycle 134, 198
    component-oriented 14
    ITHACA 180
    object 134, 136, 146
    software 6, 198
    software development 177
lifting operation 158
link 276
Liskov, Barbara 116
LISP 166
local time 136
locality 251
LOTOS 100
Luo, Bin 249

Macintosh 330
Manna, Zohar 150

marked object 253
Matsuoka, Satoshi 56, 59, 60, 61
ME database system 251
media
    artefacts 305
    class 309
    composition 307
    synchronization 307
Meseguer, José 56
message-set browser 249
meta-class 188
meta-object 42
method set 60
metrics 245
    binary vector 261
    reuse 24
Meyer, Bertrand 16
Microsoft 277, 325, 327, 329, 346
MIDI 313
migration 73, 78, 85
Milner, Robin 19, 100, 119
Mitchell, John C. 16
mixin 4, 8, 13, 60
ML 16
    ML-like type system 16
    SML 16
modal process logic 119
mode switch 287
modeler component 292
module 14, 16, 69
    interconnection language 17
monitor 34, 35, 41, 53
Mosses, Peter D. 17
Motro, Amihai 248
MS-Windows 327
multimedia xvi, 185
    application 291
    component kit 291
    database 248
    database system 306
    framework xvi, 291, 305, 309
    programming 305
multimodal interaction 307

Index

multi-threaded object 53
Muse 308
mutual exclusion 44, 46, 49
MVC 278
MVS 180

navigation 245
navigator component 292
nested monitor call 53
NeXT 277
NeXTStep 13
    AppKit framework 324
    Driver Kit 322
nib file 13
Nielsen, M. 19
NIMBLE 71, 75
Nixdorf Informationssysteme xv
N-Land 250
non-determinism 107, 109
non-uniform service availability 99
normal-order reduction 160
Novell 331
NP-complete 227
ν calculus 19

O2 206, 207, 235
object calculus 19, 118
object invocation graph 250
Object Linking and Embedding, see OLE
Object Management Architecture 324
Object Management Group, see OMG
object mapping 76, 81, 87
object model 18
    COM 327
    heterogeneous 34
    homogeneous, see homogeneous object model
    OMG 324
    SOM 331
    temporal specification 124
Object Request Broker, see ORB
Object Systems Group xiii, xiv
Objective-C 167, 178, 205

object-oriented interoperability, see interoperability
Object-Oriented Tool Integration Services 277
Obliq 13
observational equivalence 172
ODBC 329, 332
offers 114
ogre 168
OLE 277, 325, 327, 332–334
OMA 324
OMG 72, 74, 277, 324
    Object Model 324
one-way message passing 38, 50, 53, 62
Open Database Connectivity, see ODBC
Open Scripting Architecture 331
open systems 3
OpenDoc 277, 327, 331–334
OpenStep 15
operation term 187
ORB 72, 277, 325
ORION 207, 208, 217, 239
Orwell 217
OSA 331
OSF/Motif 287
OTGen 206, 207, 234

PAL 51
parallel functions 170, 171
parallelism 32, 53
parameter phase 78
part-of relation 123, 220, 245
Pascal 16
path expressions 41, 42
PCTE+ OMS 180
performance evolution 309
Perl 15
persistence 12, 32
Petri net 125, 250
π-calculus 11, 19, 172
    polyadic 100
platform evolution 309
Plotkin, Gordon 170

plug compatibility xiv, xvi, 18, 154, 275, 312
plugs 6
PO 56–61
point-to-point navigation 249, 252
Polylith 71, 73
polymorphism 48, 100, 163, 205
    bounded 118
POOL-I 47
POOL-T 34, 35, 40–42
port 276, 278, 310
posing 205
powerdomains 170
pre- and post-conditions 203
presentation
    of component 276, 279
Prieto-Diaz, Ruben 178, 186
principle of substitutability 99, 100, 101
procedural composition 307
procedure-oriented interoperability, *see* interoperability
PROCOL 37, 38, 40–42, 56, 59
producer 311
propositional logic 126
propositional temporal logic, *see* PTL
protected method 216
protocol
    client/server 19
    conformance 99, 105, 335
    dragging 344
    errors 102
    generic 344
    implementation 338
    initialization 100
    interaction 7, 257, 321, 336, 337
    non-determinism 106
    protocol-centered framework 323, 334
    request/reply 38, 62
    RPC 62
    service provider 114
    specification 108, 337
prototypes 11

proximity 250
proximity-based navigation 246, 253, 255
proxy 38, 50, 61, 62, 81
PTL 126
    semantics 129
    syntax 127
public component constraints
    universalization 148

quasi-concurrent object 34, 54
querying 183, 247

Ranghanathan, Sarada 186
reader/writer
    property 47
    scheduling policy 58
real-time
    data notification gluon 346
    financial data 321, 333
    multimedia constraint 313
    multimedia scheduling 308
REBOOT 178, 186
RECAST 21, 291, 294, 298
records
    encoding of 165
re-engineering 23, 182
reference consistency invariant 207
reflective computation 42
regular
    expression 110
    language 110
    process 108
    type 99, 108, 151
relationship
    dynamically evolving 248
    evolving 246
relative failure 107
remote delay 54
renderer component 293
reorganization
    class library 201, 202
    global 226
    incremental algorithm 220

reply scheduling 36, 44, 46, 51
repository
    IBM 178, 180
representation invariant 207
request channel 103
request satisfiability 114
request scheduling 36, 44, 46
request substitutability 100, 106, 107
    multiple state 111
requirements description 179
reuse 70, 245
    metrics 24
Reuters 341
ReutersLab 344
roles 337
Rosette 34, 36
RPC 38, 39, 49–52, 55, 62, 71, 324
run-time composition 321

SAF 21, 180
Sangiorgi, Davide 19
satisfiability
    algorithm 144
    graph 130
    of PTL 130
scalability 13
Scheduling Predicates 56
schema evolution taxonomy 209
schema invariant 206, 208
scientific visualization 299
SDMS 250
Selection Tool 183
Self 15
self 48, 61
semantic composition 307
semantic domain 101
semantics 17, 153
    browsing 250
    concurrency 118, 172
    intersection types 104
    lazy operational 168
    of functions 155
    PTL 129

semaphore 34, 58
SemNet 250
send primitive 37
send/receive/reply 40
separate method argument 42
sequential objects 62
service type 100
set-at-a-time navigation 251
SIB xv, 178, 179, 287, 294
Siemens-Nixdorf xv, 193
similarity link 182
Sina 35, 41, 55, 56, 59–61
Singh, Vineet 56
SINIX 187
SLI 72, 73, 75
Smalltalk 15, 34, 35, 40, 41, 43, 47, 48,
    58, 70, 77, 166, 167, 178, 201,
    212, 225, 248
    browser 247, 248, 252
    class hierarchy 229
    environment 247
Smith, Scott 168, 172
SML 16
Softbench 277
software
    community 178
    component 5
    cookbook 23
    junkyard 22
    lifecycle, *see* lifecycle
    oscilloscope 249
    reuse 7, 31, 32, 202
Software Information Base, *see* SIB
SOM 331
spatial
    browsing 250
    composition 307
    data management system 250
    referencing 250
specialization 181
Specific Application Frame, *see* SAF
specification level interoperability, *see*
    interoperability

SPN 56
SQL 248
SR 35, 41, 42, 55
starvation 312
state predicate 42, 59, 61
static analysis 177, 266
storage 328
stream 311, 328
strongly distributed environment 77
strongly distributed object-based system 74
structured programming xiii
substitutability 100, 105
    see also request substitutability
substitution operation 158
subtyping 8, 101, 110, 153
super 48, 58
synchronisation constraint 46
Synchronising Actions 56, 59, 61
synchronized view 253
synchronizers 42, 56
synchronous interface 311
System Object Model 331

TAO xv
Tècnics en Automatitzaciò d'Oficines xv
Telescript 13
Telos 180
temporal
    composition 292, 307
    logic 119, 123
    scripting language xv
Temporal Specification Object Model 124
Tomlinson, Chris 56
ToolTalk 277
traces 106
transaction 76
transform class 309
transformer 311
translucency 257
transposed file 231
Trellis 249

α-Trellis 250
Owl 34, 40, 41, 54
TSOM 124
type
    compatibility 312
        invariant 207
    inference 118
    matching 80
    translation 79
    variable invariant 207
type translation 79

unconditional acceptance 41
Unidraw 278
unified system of parameterization 156
Unifying Type Model 72
Universal Decimal Classification 186
universalization 136
Unix 179, 187, 189, 195, 197
    composition model 287
UTM 72

verification
    composite objects 145
    correspondence property 149
    elementary objects 144
version
    compatibility 236
    identification 215
video
    assistant 314
    on demand 306
    widgets 313
Vista 287–297
visual
    composition xvi, 275
        framework 275
        tool 275
    configuration 313
    formalism 300
    representation 246
    scripting tool xv
Visual C++ 322

VisualAge 276, 277
VisualBasic 7
visualisation xvi
VLSI Design 217
VST xvi, xvii, 287

wait filter 59, 60
Wegner, Peter 8, 34, 47, 99–101
Wing, Jeannette 116
Wolper, Pierre 150
worker 45, 49, 51, 52, 54, 61
workflow application 291
World Wide Web xvii

X Windows 287

Zdonik, Stanley 47, 99–101